AFRICAN AMERICAN POETS

AFRICAN AMERICAN POETS

LIVES, WORKS, AND SOURCES

JOYCE PETTIS

GREENWOOD PRESS
Westport, Connecticut • London

Library of Congress Cataloging-in-Publication Data

Pettis, Joyce Owens.
    African American poets : lives, works, and sources / Joyce Pettis.
        p.   cm.
    Includes bibliographical references and index.
    ISBN 0–313–31117–X (alk. paper)
        1. American poetry—African American authors—Bio-bibliography—Dictionaries.   2.
American poetry—African American authors—Dictionaries.   3. African American
poets—Biography—Dictionaries.   4. African Americans in literature—Dictionaries.   I.
Title.
PS153.N5P48   2002
811.009'896073'03—dc21   2001050105
    [B]

British Library Cataloguing in Publication Data is available.

Library of Congress Catalog Card Number: 2001050105
ISBN: 0–313–31117–X

First published in 2002

Greenwood Press, 88 Post Road West, Westport, CT 06881
An imprint of Greenwood Publishing Group, Inc.
www.greenwood.com

Printed in the United States of America

The paper used in this book complies with the
Permanent Paper Standard issued by the National
Information Standards Organization (Z39.48–1984).

10 9 8 7 6 5 4 3 2 1

Every reasonable effort has been made to trace the owners of copyright materials in this
book, but in some instances this has proven impossible. The author and publisher will be
glad to receive information leading to more complete acknowledgments in subsequent
printings of the book and in the meantime extend their apologies for any omissions.

CONTENTS

Introduction	ix
Ai (1947–)	1
Maya Angelou (1928–)	9
Amiri Baraka (1934–)	18
Arna Bontemps (1902–1973)	26
Gwendolyn Brooks (1917–2000)	32
Sterling Brown (1901–1989)	41
Lucille Clifton (1936–)	49
Wanda Coleman (1946–)	60
Jayne Cortez (1936–)	66
Countee Cullen (1903–1946)	73
Toi Derricotte (1941–)	81
Rita Dove (1952–)	89
Paul Laurence Dunbar (1872–1906)	99
Cornelius Eady (1954–)	107
Mari Evans (n.d.–)	114
Nikki Giovanni (1943–)	121
Jupiter Hammon (1711–1806)	131

Frances Ellen Watkins Harper (1824–1911)   134

Michael S. Harper (1938–   )   141

Robert Hayden (1913–1980)   149

George Moses Horton (1797?–1883?)   157

Langston Hughes (1902–1968)   162

Georgia Douglas Johnson (1886–1966)   171

James Weldon Johnson (1871–1938)   177

June Jordan (1936–   )   185

Etheridge Knight (1931–1991)   193

Yusef Komunyakaa (1947–   )   201

Audre Lorde (1934–1992)   209

Nathaniel Mackey (1947–   )   217

Haki Madhubuti (1942–   )   225

Colleen J. McElroy (1936–   )   232

Claude McKay (1889–1948)   239

E. Ethelbert Miller (1950–   )   247

Thylias Moss (1954–   )   255

Marilyn Nelson (1946–   )   262

Dudley Randall (1914–   )   270

Ishmael Reed (1938–   )   277

Carolyn Rodgers (1945–   )   285

Sonia Sanchez (1934–   )   291

Melvin B. Tolson (1900–1966)   300

Jean Toomer (1894–1967)   307

Quincy Troupe (1943–   )   314

Margaret Abigail Walker (1915–1998)   322

Phillis Wheatley (1753–1784)   329

Jay Wright (1935–)   336

Al Young (1939–)   344

Selected Anthologies   351

Index   353

INTRODUCTION

According to poet Haki Madhubuti, "Poems bind people to language, link generations" and bring cultures together (*Earthquakes and Sun Rise Missions*, p. 14). The rich tradition of African American poetry dating from the eighteenth century bears out Madhubuti's observation. At one time or another, poetry has bent itself to the multiple needs of its composer, reader, or listener. Since its appearance in the literate tradition of American letters, African American poetry has also reflected the current styles and literary preoccupations, as the work of Phillis Wheatley illustrated in the eighteenth century when she embraced the European poetic tradition of shaping language to expectations of decorum and beauty. Twentieth-century poets Gwendolyn Brooks, Robert Hayden, and Melvin Tolson also distinguished themselves by subduing all the traditional forms that were considered a measure of poetic art.

But from its infancy ignited by particular historical and social circumstances, African American poetry also has been shaped by the writer's motivation to raise a distinctive voice. This tradition, reflected in the religious passion of both Jupiter Hammon and Wheatley's work, has consistently infused the centuries of poetry by writers of African descent in the United States. During different historical periods, in fact, the inclination to weight poetry with propaganda and political messages and to either exclude or minimize its aesthetic function has resulted in heated exchanges about the role of poetry and the definition of art in the black community. These were heady issues fought in formal and informal venues during the Harlem Renaissance of the 1920s and again during the Black Arts Movement of the 1960s.

While the claim that African American poetry has been a politically active art form denies refuting, the assertion is also valid that it is an individualistic art. The tradition of exploring the relationship of African Americans to their nation and their communities is well balanced by poetry's facility as an introspective mode of art. While eighteenth- and nineteenth-century black poets were sparse in this personal application, twentieth- and twenty-first-century poets have found it extremely useful. When thus employed for interior exploration, however, the personal issues become models and modes for reaching outside of the self to communicate to others that their experiences participate in a large and intricate frame. For example, one of Countee Cullen's significant issues is couched in the formality of the sonnet "Yet Do I Marvel," where he exposes his personal conflict over the relationship between reading his race and reading his poetry. The different, broader question, What is the relationship between my art and the education of the black community? animates the poems of several 1960s poets, including Madhubuti, Amiri Baraka, and Sonia Sanchez, who no longer experienced Cullen's dilemma. But poetry is the primary artistic mode through which they demonstrated answers to this question in work that spanned the decade.

African American poetry also operates on an intimate level when it is the mode for exploring other kinds of personal issues. Since the growth in artistic freedom of the 1960s, poetry has increasingly become the genre for subjects that were once relegated to memoir, autobiography, or the parlor. For example, Toi Derricotte explores psychic family violence and writes a book-length poem on childbirth. In most of these poems, the personal is angled so that it projects the subject onto a broad canvas. Similarly, Wanda Coleman examines issues of gender, race, and class that define and affect her personally, but the personal is inseparable from these issues as they impinge on the lives of most African Americans, particularly women. Examining familial conflict or stress in a single poem or entire volume is a consistent feature of black poetry. Rita Dove, for example, writes about the lives of her grandparents in *Thomas and Beulah*, an award-winning volume. Both Robert Hayden and Cornelius Eady focus on their fathers' relationship to the family. Eady's *You Don't Miss Your Water* and sections of *The Autobiography of a Jukebox* illustrate this exploration. Hayden's "Those Winter Sundays" captures an adult's perspective on a difficult childhood. Lucille Clifton, Marilyn Nelson, and Colleen McElroy also choose family as a recurring subject in their poems. These writers, along with many others, use poetry to examine ancestral forces that help us see who we are. Often, however, the seeing remains stubbornly obscure.

Among the many persistent subjects that have traditionally informed

African American poetry, music is arguably its most visible. Since the 1920s when Langston Hughes pioneered the integration of blues and jazz rhythms with lyrics in his poems, music has been as indispensable to the art as sunlight to a plant that produces flowers. Music, generally, becomes a metaphor for life experiences; specifically identified songs may be the structure and backbone of a poem; or musicians and their instrument can be the poem's focus. Sacred music, jazz and blues rhythms, and the mood, structure, and lyrics of blues are staples in the work of numerous poets. The musical heritage of West Africa as well as the musical origins of poetry perhaps explain this interdependent relationship in the work of black poets. Titles of songs, musicians, apparent and elusive references, too, pepper the poems of black writers. The prevalence of music in poetry has, in fact, inspired anthologies of jazz and soul poetry as well as critical studies. The black poet who does not reference music in some manner is rare indeed. Among those who aggressively and lovingly incorporate music as an integral and indispensable feature of their art are Langston Hughes, Michael Harper, Etheridge Knight, Wanda Coleman, Yusef Komunyakaa, Sonia Sanchez, Al Young, Amiri Baraka, Quincy Troupe, Cornelius Eady, Maya Angelou, Nikki Giovanni, Jayne Cortez, and many more.

The flexibility of poetry—its structure, its accommodation of infinite subjects, its rhythms, meter, and language—is the continuum that assures its vitality and survival. The poets in this volume repeatedly illustrate their astoundingly creative and original ability to fashion poems that seem perfect for the function that the poem is understood to have. And part of the marriage of function, form, and perception depends on the configuration of the poem on the page. In interviews and essays where poets discuss or write about the crafting of their work, they often talk about their conceptualizations and what they require of a particular poem. "The ear and page coexist," Nathaniel Mackey has said (*Callaloo* 23.2 (2000), p. 713), and this statement resonates through the work of most successful poets. The flexibility of the poem is thus linked to the numerous techniques that a skilled poet has at hand and employs in the service of his or her unique vision. The range of flexibility of the poets discussed here and the potentials of the art form are infinite. Structurally, contemporary poets are not enslaved by formulaic requirements. Thus the work as printed on the page may either satisfy some general notion that identifies it as poetry or puzzle the reader a little (or largely) because the writer's form is unconventional. Mari Evans has said that her primary goal is to command the reader's attention. Thus for her, "[T]he poem is structure and style as well as theme and content; I require something of my poems visually as well as rhetorically. I work hard at how the poem 'looks' as at crafting; indeed for me the two are synonymous" (*Black Women Writers*, p. 168).

Interestingly, Evans' generation of poets in the 1960s was accused of writing polemical and artless poetry, and it is the flexibility, the anticonventional use of language form, and structure that elicited the charges. Some poetry of the Black Arts Movement (also known as Black Aesthetics), in its departure from traditional Western aesthetics, flaunted an energetic language and called for revolution. Perhaps some work was what it was accused of being in its haste to identify with the conflicting prescriptions of art in that era and to unify with the black community. However, like the force of the Harlem Renaissance, the poetry of the 1960s and 1970s has created a resounding impact that continues to influence the poetry of a new millennium. Derrick Gilbert's anthology *Catch the Fire: A Cross-Generation Anthology*, whose title comes from Sonia Sanchez, whose career began in the 1960s, is testament to the influential work and continuing presence of poets of that decade. Many of the poets whose careers began in the 1960s have continued with their art by continuing to publish and to teach in university writing programs. They are models for a developing generation of writers.

Language is the other component of poetry. Its flexibility is challenged only by the limitations of the poet using it. Symbols and images can be allusive and problematic in the hands of poets such as Nathaniel Mackey and Jay Wright. But in the work of Lucille Clifton, E. Ethelbert Miller, or Cornelius Eady we read the words of everyday discourse shaped and crafted to explore family, revisit history, or reveal special moments. In the language of Margaret Walker and Sterling Brown, folk portraits emerge. Poets can enhance existing words or create them as illustrated in Robert Hayden's "a-murbling" in the line "fear starts a-murbling" in "Runagate, Runagate." Breath-stopping imagery and profound symbol can knock up against brash, unveiled violence as in the dramatic monologues that Ai writes. Given the variety and creativeness of African American poetry, it is an art form whose ability to prosper amid a developing generation of writers is unbounded.

This volume selectively offers an introduction to poets across the spectrum of the African American poetic tradition. It presents representative writers whose works constitute significant contributions to an ever-evolving and dynamic artistic tradition. Alongside the established nineteenth-century poets, one finds many contemporary poets as well. Organized alphabetically, the entry on each poet offers biographical information, places the poet in his or her historical time and literary context and provides an overview of the poet's major themes and concerns. In addition, each entry provides a selected listing of the author's published work, organized chronologically by publication date, with emphasis on poetry in cases where the writer publishes across genres. Finally, each entry concludes with a selected list of references for further study.

Aɪ
(1947–   )

Ai
Credit: W.W. Norton
Photo credit: Heather Conley

Profiting from the momentum of the 1960s Black Arts Movement and the increased numbers of women writers being published, the 1970s have been identified by some as a second literary renaissance. Ai's distinctive poetry began appearing during this decade, although her work defies most comparisons with the women poets whose work helped set the directions of black poetry in the 1960s. Perhaps the most compelling distinction in Ai's poetry is her exclusive use of a singular voice: She writes dramatic monologues. She explains that decision as a "happy accident" based on the advice of her first poetry teacher, Richard Shelton, who convinced her that the first-person voice was the strongest voice in writing. This form and Ai's aggressive manner of unveiling her subjects result in poems that are starkly original.

Born in Tuscon, Arizona, the poet was christened Florence Anthony. She was born to a woman whose ancestry was African American, Choctaw, and Irish and to a man of Japanese ancestry. In an article in *Ms.* magazine in 1974, Ai identified her multiethnic composition as one-half Japanese, one-eighth Choctaw, one-fourth black, and one-sixteenth Irish. When she was twenty-six years old the facts about her biological father and his heritage were revealed to her. She also learned that her birth resulted from an extramarital affair. She took the name Ai, which means "love" in Japanese, in deference to her Japanese ethnic heritage. Ai embraces all the components of her racial identity.

Ai attended an integrated Catholic school until she was in the seventh grade and says she was a "Mexican Catholic." She lived at various times in Texas with her ethnically mixed great-grandparents but also spent time in Los Angeles when she was twelve and in San Fransciso as well. The childhood memories in San Francisco were not so positive. Ai recalled her stepfather having to be very creative just to provide food for her and her sister. For undergraduate study, Ai attended the University of Arizona in Tempe, where she majored in Oriental studies, and graduated with a B.A. degree in 1969. She earned the M.F.A. in creative writing from the University of California at Irvine in 1971. She has taught in Massachusetts, New York, Tempe, and presently is on the faculty at the University of Oklahoma. She is married to poet Lawrence Kearney.

Ai's poetry has been recognized through several awards. *Killing Floor* was the 1978 Lamont Poetry Selection of the American Academy of Poets, and *Vice* won the 1999 National Book Award. Ai has also received the Henry Blakely II Award for excellence in writing given by Gwendolyn Brooks. Additionally, Ai has been granted Guggenheim and the National Endowment for the Arts fellowships.

To have won awards and fellowships for writing dramatic monologues in six volumes of poetry extending from 1973 to 1999, when *Vice: New and Selected Poems* appeared, would suggest that Ai's artistry with this form is superior. That may well be true. She has expanded the parameters of the dramatic monologue by effectively manipulating all its inherent advantages: the expectation that a monologue will tell a compelling, dramatic story; its infinite capacity for expressive voice; and the intimacy readily achievable between reader and speaker because the poem's personna narrates his or her own story. Ai's manipulation of the latter quality, paradoxically, is minimal. Whether the speaker is a boy who murders, the builder of the atomic bomb, or an unidentified midwife, the qualities of the voice—such as diction and language style—remain essentially unaltered from poem to poem. The speakers deliver their stories in the same dispassionate tone. Rather than creating monotony in Ai's work, however, the narrator's consistent and dispassionate delivery channels the reader's attention to the details of the experience. Moreover, because the experiences almost without exception are horrendous, graphically detailed, and morally uncondemned within the poem, the reader's discomfort or uneasiness has no ally. The narrator's point of view within the parameters of the poem is absolute.

The voices in Ai's dramatic monologues, particularly in the early volumes, are the marginalized, the poor, the socially disenfranchised, and the physically or psychologically mutilated. These people harbor no illusions about the realities or expectations of their lives. They unflinchingly accept pain, and they dish it out, too. They depersonalize each other, even in personal relationships, and refer to intimates merely as "husband" or "my woman." Remorse and regret are not companions to violence and death, and love or obligation does not bind these people. Even copulation is a kind of embattlement and is always void of romantic idealism and emotion. In her more recent volumes, however, Ai ventures out to include the voices of national or internationally known figures as well as the voices of lesser-known figures associated with events of notoriety. Because their monologues engage known facts alongside Ai's creative invention, she subtitles the monologue a "fiction." Figures such as J. Edgar Hoover, William Jefferson Clinton, and Jack Ruby are among these speakers.

In addition to these highly recognizable speakers, Ai's subjects are ordinary men, women, and children depicted in various kinds of destructive relationships including child abuse, homocide, patricide, infanticide, and prostitution. Some kind of violence in the monologues is consistent—suicide, murder, rape, or whipping—but it is offered matter-of-factly, as the rule rather than the exception. Violence can be perpetrated against the spirit as well as the body, or it can provide a background for the speaker and the situation of the monologue. Age and gender are inconsequential in the violence that sustains Ai's work, as are her settings. The settings vary from the midwestern plains and Mexico, where she writes about Native Americans and Hispanics, to sites in Europe and South America, where she also writes about the dispossessed, soldiers, and the Jewish. Like race and ethnicity, setting is secondary to the story being told and to the magnetism that emanates from the speaker. The setting is more important for the context it suggests than for any specificity of geography.

The emphasis on violence, death, and harsh life experience in Ai's work has been controversial, evoking both condemnation and praise. Some reviewers see only unrewarding monotony in Ai's consistent explorations of violence. However, others argue that readers have to look beyond the intense violence to discover the human longing for divinity and transcendence.

The poems appearing in Ai's first two published volumes of the 1970s, *Cruelty* and *Killing Floor*, are fairly short pieces. *Cruelty*, originally titled *Wheel in a Ditch*, was written between March and July 1972 when the poet was twenty-four. *Killing Floor*, with its stark images, is considered a more mature work. In *Sin* (1986) Ai includes longer poems, and a thematic focus on acquiring and dispensing power. Some of the poems with women narrators question the ways women relinquish their power to men. In "The Mother's Tale," for example, a Peruvian mother, with her son's wedding day as backdrop, reflects on her lost youth and innocence. But instead of empathizing with her new daughter-in-law, the mother acknowledges her son's masculine power as she advises him to beat his wife because of Eve's sin. Although the volume's focus is on men, masculinity, and power, the women speakers emerge as collaborators in their own lack of power and in their own victimization.

Many of the voices in *Sin* and *Greed* belong to public figures in extraordinary historical times such as John F. Kennedy and his brother Bobby Kennedy; J. Robert Oppenheimer, the creator of the atomic bomb; Senator Joseph McCarthy, an anticommunist crusader during the 1950s; the man accused and convicted in the Atlanta child murders who is unnamed in the poem; and the voices of participants in historical calamities such as the Vietnam conflict. Since the poet's intention is not a simple inscription of history into a poetic form, the "fiction" provides Ai the latitude to scrutinize motivation, to question guilt and blame, or to look into the recesses of power. In some cases, the poem critiques the culture that produced and sustained the speaker. In "The Testimony of Robert Oppenheimer," for example, after the physicist praises the bomb as proof of modern knowledge, he admits and tries to rationalize his guilt. He was motivated "by a ferocious need to know." Through Oppenheimer's perspective, the poem also questions the view of history as progressive and critiques the emphasis of scientific inquiry on increasing knowledge as an indication of spiritual decay. Unlike the Oppenheimer poem, "Hoover, Edgar J" projects the image of Hoover as a monster and an egotist to explore his obsession with power. The poem evokes Jack Kennedy, Martin Luther King, Malcolm X, and Lyndon B. Johnson as the high-profile figures that Hoover could unseat. Hoover's voice reveals him as an unstable egotist who believes his "strength is truth." Yet he alludes to himself as "Frankenstein," who feeds off "the weakness of others." Through gross, descriptive language Hoover paints a self-portrait of an empty man whose motivation is to "get some dirt" on any public figure to ensure that "J. Edgar Hoover rules."

The poems of abuse perpetrated by priests are among Ai's most provocative explorations of power and the personal responsibility for one's own actions. In "The Priest's Confession" the lines "describing the relationship between the act and the actor—there can be no separateness"—set the context for the priest's self-exploration as he details a narrative of abuse that began with a twelve-year-old orphaned girl. The priest prays for deliverance, breaks his rosary, and envisions himself "a bead on God's own broken rosary." Alienated from his God, whom he calls "a stranger," the priest evades his culpability and posits God's abandonment of him, a childhood curse by the village witch, the universal existence of evil, and even the improbability that the orphan girl complies with his desire as ways to explain his behavior. He contemplates hanging himself in the belltower but returns instead to what he envisions as a normal domestic scene with a woman waiting to please him. "Life Story," subtitled "For Father Ritter and Other Priests Accused of Sexual Abuse," contains lines that succinctly say the act of rape produces another rapist: "To rape is to erase the other's identity," replacing it with yours. The molestation of a five-year-old boy begins a vicious circle of abuse and power that spins so rapidly that not even the death of Father Harrigan, named in the monologue, can reverse the activity. By age thirteen, the boy victim, who becomes a priest too, has been taught to capture other children. The circle of complicity that enables the boy victim's abuse includes his father, the priests who protect Harrigan by covering both his suicide and the pornography found in his room, the police in their noninvestigation of Harrigan, and the boy victim's mother. She finds irrefutable evidence of his boyhood abuse but refuses to confront its reality. The boy victim thus evolves into a full-fledged abuser, unable through flight and self-mutilation (severing a hand) to control his impulses. Only jail for a sex crime stops him. The monologues thus explore the lack of self-discipline, greed, and corruption as uncontrollable urges that lead to a destructive exploitation for the practictioner as well as the victim. In imagining and writing through the voice of public figures or those victimized by them, Ai can exercise the flexibility of a novelist in probing the rumor and suspicion that often swirl around notorious situations. Although the lengthy monologues lack the tension of the brief poems, that deficit is repaid through the full explorations of interior motivation, a feature that is absent in the short poems. Ai explores and reveals, but she does not presume a definitive explanation of corrupted or base human beings.

Images in Ai's work are relentlessly sharp and often shocking, but they are synchronous with the tone and violent character of the poems. For example, in "The County Midwife: A Day," a child being born is compared to "warehouse ice sliding down the chute." In another reference to death in "The Unexpected," birth will "crack you open with her sharp brown teeth." "Sleep Like a Hammer" in *Killing Floor* contains a particularly startling image of a son striking his father: "Your toes splay out, snap off like burned bacon." The poem chronicles a history of violence stretching back over the years and suggests a momentary mental loss in the seconds before the hammer strikes when the hitter sees his wife calling and running toward him. In "The Cockfighter's Daughter," "another sunrise breaks the night apart" to express the liberation a daughter feels after she has manipulated her father's death and now takes his ferocious killer rooster.

These blunt force images suggest Ai's facility with language. Numerous poems offer lines that do not lose their impact when divorced from the context of their respective poems. Such lines are worthy of memorization and can be found in many of Ai's poems: "I will sail us through the stormy seas of sleaze," from "Blood and Water" (William Jefferson Clinton); "I was afraid of what I might do," from "The Antihero" (Police Officer Terry Yeakey, a rescuer of victims of the Oklahoma City bombing); "God is like desire you cannot satisfy," from "Charisma" (the voice of David Koresh of the Branch Davidians in Waco, Texas); and "I am that which I fear," from "Life Story" (a poem about child abuse by priests).

Ai says her work is not influenced by anyone but that certain writers inspire her. She includes among them the Chilean poet, Pablo Neruda and Enrique Lihn, and Latin American novelist and short story writer Gabriel García Marquez. Ai's poems "Cuba, 1962" and "The Woman Who Knew Too Much" were both inspired by García Marquez's novel *One Hundred Years of Solitude*.

POETRY

Cruelty. Boston: Houghton Mifflin, 1973. (Out of Print)
Killing Floor. Boston: Houghton Mifflin, 1979. (Out of Print)
Sin. Boston: Houghton Mifflin, 1986.
Cruelty/Killing Floor. New York: Thunder Mouth Press, 1987.
Fate: New Poems. Boston: Houghton Mifflin, 1991. (Out of Print)
Greed. New York: W.W. Norton, 1994.
Vice: New and Selected Poems. New York: W.W. Norton, 1999.

REFERENCES

Field, C. Renee. "Ai." In *Dictionary of Literary Biography*. Vol. 120. Ed. R.S. Gwynn Detroit: Gale Research, 1992. 10–17.
Hadas, Rachel. "Ai." In *The Oxford Companion to Twentieth-Century Poetry in English*. Ed. Ian Hamiton. New York: Oxford University Press, 1994. 6–7.
Ingram, Claudia. "Writers of Mixed Ancestry." In *The Oxford Companion to Women's Writing in the United States*. Ed. Cathy N. Davidson and Linda Wagner-Martin. New York: Oxford University Press, 1995. 572.
Lee, A. Robert. "Ai." *The Oxford Companion to African American Literature*. Ed. William L. Andrews, Frances Smith Foster and Trudier Harris. New York: Oxford University Press, 1997. 10.
Matuz, Roger, ed. "Ai." In *Contemporary Literary Criticism*. Vol. 69. Detroit: Gale Research, 1992. 1–18.

MAYA ANGELOU

(1928–   )

Maya Angelou
Credit: North Carolina State University Communication Services

Although many poets illustrate extraordinary versatility in the arts, few are as accomplished as Maya Angelou. She has published essays, written television screenplays, directed a critically acclaimed feature-length movie, and been featured on a compact disc with the nationally recognized rhythm and blues duo Ashford and Simpson. She has been a dancer; an actress, earning a Tony nomination for her Broadway debut performance in *Look Away* (1973); and an Emmy nominee for best supporting actress in Alex Haley's *Roots* (1977). She wrote and directed the play *And Still I Rise*, performed in Oakland, California, in 1976. Her reading of "On the Pulse of Morning," commissioned for the first inauguration of President William Clinton in January 1993, increased her visibility to mainstream audiences. She frequently appears on television talk shows and in cameo appearances on various television dramas. She is a sought-after lecturer on the national and international circuits. Before being named to a lifetime appointment as Z. Smith Reynolds Professor of American Studies at Wake Forest University in Winston Salem, North Carolina, Angelou held writer-in-residence appointments at several universities, including the University of Kansas and Yale University.

Her numerous awards include a Yale University Fellowship, a Rockefeller Foundation Scholar in Italy Award, and Woman of the Year Award in Communications by the *Ladies' Home Journal*. Moreover, she received a Pulitzer Prize nomination for *Just Give Me a Cool Drink of Water 'Fore I Diiie* and a Golden Eagle award from the Public Broadcasting System for her documentary series *Afro-American in the Arts*.

Angelou has told her life story in five autobiographies, beginning with the publication of *I Know Why the Caged Bird Sings* (1969), the most engaging and well crafted of the five works. She spent her formative years in Stamps, Arkansas, with her paternal grandmother and her brother Bailey after her parents divorced. Born in St. Louis, Missouri, and christened Marguerite Johnson, her current name consists of the diminutive "Maya," bestowed by her brother during childhood, and the name of her first husband, the Greek Enistasious Angelos. Her father, Bailey, was a naval dietitian, and her mother, Vivian, was owner of a large boardinghouse in San Francisco in the 1940s. Having been separated five years from her mother, Angelou was returned to St. Louis to live with her. During that period she endured a traumatic rape by her mother's boyfriend and became mute for almost five years. In that condition, Angelou was then sent back to her grandmother in Stamps, where she eventually emerged from her shell of silence to embrace life again. Books and reading occupied a major role in her growing-up years. Although much of her childhood experience in Stamps has an idyllic quality of protection, Angelou also learned about being black, poor, and female, within the dignity of the black community. She graduated from Lafayette Training School in Stamps and again went to live with her mother, this time in San Francisco, California. Angelou attended high school and also an evening school where she studied drama and dance, two arts that she would pursue professionally. She graduated in 1945 and also in that year became a mother when her son, named Clyde Bailey Johnson, was born.

Between 1945 and her fairly short marriage to Enistasious Angelos in 1952, Angelou struggled to maintain her independence and support her son. She moved about in California working at various jobs such as cooking, waitressing, and being a chauffeur and salesperson, but always found time for reading. Her life seemed destined for failure as each job eventually failed or she fell in with unsavory men and rescued herself by returning to her mother. However, her luck changed in the 1950s when she began a stage career in dancing and singing at local clubs. She took singing lessons, employed a drama coach, and finally secured a part in a traveling production of DuBose Haywood's folk drama *Porgy and Bess*. She traveled internationally with the troupe for a year until her son's skin ailment required her return. Guilt about their separation made her vow that whenever she traveled again, so would he.

Events in the 1960s began to shape Angelou's career as a writer, social activist, and multitalented woman. John Oliver Killens, a respected novelist in the 1960s, read some of Angelou's work and deemed that she had talent but that it also needed work. He precipitated her move to Brooklyn, New York, for contact with the Harlem Writers Guild, a group that included African American novelists Paule Marshall and Rosa Guy. Angelou continued her singing for income as she endured the group's sharp critiques about her play *One Love, One Life*. Angelou heard Dr. Martin Luther King speak in Harlem trying to raise money for the Southern Christian Leadership Conference, the organization he and others founded to coordinate their civil rights work. Inspired, Angelou developed a successful revue as a fund-raiser, which led to her appointment as the northern coordinator for the organization. In New York the same year, 1960, Angelou met and married the South African freedom fighter Vasumzi Make, performed in the French playwright Jean Genet's play *The Blacks*, and moved with her son and husband to Cairo, Egypt. There, she took employment with an English news weekly, although she was inexperienced and had to teach herself about journalism. After her son's graduation from high school in Cairo, Angelou and her husband separated, and she and Guy (who had renamed himself) left Egypt for Ghana, West Africa.

Although she was making a life for herself in Africa, including learning several of its languages and working as an assistant administrator at the University of Ghana, Angelou continued her activism. On the day of Dr. King's march on Washington, she and other American blacks living in Ghana staged a supportive march to the American embassy. She also met Malcolm X in Ghana and returned to the United States in 1965 to work in his new organization, but he was assassinated two days after her return. Back home, in characteristic fashion, Angelou embraced several artistic tasks that would eventually result in writing becoming the focus of a multifaceted, energetic woman. In 1968, for example, she wrote *Black, Blues, Black*, ten one-hour programs for National Educational Television. Her friends, including the renowned novelist and essayist James Baldwin, encouraged her to write her life's story. Beginning her writing career in the 1970s, Angelou joined a chorus of African American women—Toni Morrison and Toni Cade Bambara, among them—who were publishing their first works to reach a wide audience in that decade. Random House brought out *I Know Why the Caged Bird Sings*, the first installment in Angelou's autobiographical series. She titled it from a line in Paul Laurence Dunbar's poem "Sympathy."

The decade of the 1970s was extraordinarily busy for Angelou with major writing projects and acting. Three volumes of autobiography, three books of her poetry, and her screenplay for *Georgia, Georgia* were published. Additionally, Angelou was nominated for a Tony Award for supporting actress in the play *Look Away* and nominated for an Emmy for her portrayal of Kunte Kinte's grandmother in Alex Haley's television miniseries *Roots*. Angelou spiritually married Paul De Deu in 1973. They later separated. *I Know Why the Caged Bird Sings* premiered as a film on CBS in 1979.

Public recognition at the highest levels began to pour in for Angelou's inspirational work. President Gerald R. Ford appointed her to the American Revolution Bicentennial Council in 1975, and President Jimmy Carter named her to the National Commission on the Observance of International Women's Year in 1977. In 1992, in London, she received a special tribute by a children's society that named their new facility for her, The Maya Angelou Child Protection Team and Family Center. Perhaps the capstone of recognition came in the form of Angelou being commissioned to compose and to read a poem for President William Clinton's inauguration in 1993. Among many other prestigious awards, the Spingard Medal, the highest honor the National Association for the

Advancement of Colored People (NAACP) awards, was given to Angelou in 1994.

Performance in the arts characterized Angelou's activities before she came to national prominence through publishing her autobiographical series and poetry. Her talent for performance became a valuable adjunct in the creation of poetry, but even more in its performance. In addition to writing poems, Angelou has been a primary force in sustaining poetry as an oral art form. Drawing on her ability as an actress and the power of her deep, enthralling voice, she performs programs of poetry ranging from the nineteenth-century work of Paul Laurence Dunbar to contemporary poets. She is, like Sonia Sanchez and Nikki Giovanni, a performance artist, but unlike them, she offers programs of poetry that are not limited to her own work, along with the inspiration of her own experiences. She effectively commands the stage, employing all of her majestic height, and mesmerizes audiences who fill auditoriums to capacity.

Like Langston Hughes's work, Angelou's poetry is mostly free of obscure symbols, and it appeals widely to a general audience. It is anchored by African American culture, particularly its music and history and its spirituals and linguistic expressiveness. Most of her poems are direct, the language is accessible, and brevity is a consistent quality. Many of her poems, like "Phenomenal Woman" and "Still I Rise," seem written with oral performance in mind.

Angelou has discussed her ritual for writing in numerous interviews. Her creative process requires the isolation of an impersonal hotel room rather than the familiarity of her own home. Her peripheral tools are a deck of cards for playing solitaire when ideas are elusive, a dictionary, *Roget's Thesaurus*, the Bible, cigarettes, and wine. Although she can type, she prefers the connection of the pen with paper. In writing poetry, she tries to find the natural rhythm of the poem, that is, the rhythm that seems logical for the content she envisions. After the rhythm is worked out, she creates the content.

Angelou's first published book of poetry, *Just Give Me a Cool Drink of Water 'Fore I Diiie*, anticipates the volumes that follow in its language, rhythmic rhyming, predominance of lyric forms, attention to black women, and emphasis on male and female relationships. Part I, titled "Where Love Is a Scream of Anguish," accurately forecasts the pain inscribed in several poems. In the image-laden "Late October," for example, the fall season signals an ending for lovers, while in "No Loser, No Weeper," the woman's soliloquy about hating to lose things ends with how much she'd hate to lose her lover.

The eighteen socially and politically concentrated poems in the second section of *Just Give Me a Cool Drink* are almost a rarity in Angelou's later volumes. Their thematic distinctiveness is perhaps due to the timing of the civil rights era consonant with their composition and publication dates. The poem containing the line that names the volume, titled "No No No No," is the lengthiest poem in the book and one of its harshest in language. An outraged persona says "no" to several current situations, such as ineffective missionaries in Third World countries. The persona has waited for many kinds of changes over long years, and dreams and hopes have dried up. The phrase "Just give me a cool drink of water 'fore I diiie" appears only once, after the first stanza, and is connected to the napalmed babies in Vietnam lifting their tongue for water from their killer's tears. This line suggests, then, that although hope is gone, some innocence remains that charity or grace may still exist, though evidence seems to defy such innocence.

And Still I Rise (1978), Angelou's third volume of poetry, consists of thirty-two poems in three sections. Its major theme of survival begins in the first section in "Phenomenal Woman," an uncharacteristically long poem. It is widely considered one of the best pieces in the volume. Its inspirational appeal with audiences when it is performed is likely due in part to its strong rhyme scheme and forceful but irregular rhymes. The phenomenal woman defies the petite beauty's form, and her attractiveness almost defies definition. Each of the poem's four stanzas is anchored by the speaker's attempt to explain the secret of her beauty in seven or eight lines that rhythmically repeat themselves. The beauty is physically visible in the arms, hips, eyes, waist, and feet, but it has a mysterious element that defies male comprehension or touch. The title poem of the volume, "Still I Rise," is thematically similar to "Phenomenal Woman" but is overtly historical. It recognizes the tradition of oppressive lies told about African Americans, but the collective response is sassiness and haughtiness. The poem celebrates a people's indefatigable spirit to overcome in its repeated phrase "I'll rise." The repetition of this phrase enforces the defiance that permeates the piece.

In *Shaker, Why Don't You Sing?* (1983), many poems concern the subject of romantic love. The most powerful in the volume, the title poem, conveys the deep loss of the rituals of romantic love, although the couple is still together. The pervasive metaphor of song is sustained by "croon," "canticle," "chanteys hummed," "anthem," and "perfect harmonies." "Family Affairs," a sharply imaged poem in the volume, continues Angelou's consistent attention to the concerns of women. It begins with a litany of fourteen chores. The speaker asks for succulence from nature, since that is the only thing that she can claim as belonging to her.

The poem read for President Clinton's inauguration, "On the Pulse of Morning," relies on images of nature and human inclusiveness for its quiet power. In equating the rock, river, and tree with the longevity of earth, they become witnesses to lost worlds and a history of human degradation. Drawing on the symbolic association of morning as a beginning, another opportunity exists by the side of the river. Referencing the spiritual "Down by the Riverside," with its line "ain't gon study war no more," people of the world are challenged to seek peace as in the old days when unity characterized existence. Inclusive in its roll call of nations, occupations, and the persecuted, the poem pleads to humankind to face history but to embrace a new destiny as if greeting a new day.

Angelou's productivity and promotion of African American poetry through her personal performances suggest that she has much more with which to delight and educate audiences fortunate enough to spend an evening with her or one of her books of poetry.

POETRY

Just Give Me a Cool Drink of Water 'Fore I Diiie. 1971. Rpt., New York: Random House, 1997.

Oh Pray My Wings Are Gonna Fit Me Well. New York: Random House, 1975. (Out of Print)

And Still I Rise. New York: Random House, 1978.

Shaker, Why Don't You Sing? New York: Random House, 1983.

Poems. New York: Random House, 1986.

I Shall Not Be Moved. New York: Bantam Books, 1991.

"On the Pulse of Morning" (presidential inauguration poem). New York: Random House, 1993.

The Complete Collected Poems of Maya Angelou. New York: Random House, 1994.

Phenomenal Woman. New York: Random House, 1994.

A Brave and Startling Truth. New York: Random House, 1995.

Even the Stars Look Lonesome. New York: Random House, 1997.

AUTOBIOGRAPHY

I Know Why the Caged Bird Sings. New York: Bantam Books, 1969.

Gather Together in My Name. New York: Random House, 1974.

Singin' and Swingin' and Gettin' Merry Like Christmas. New York: Random House, 1976.

The Heart of a Woman. New York: Random House, 1981.

All God's Children Need Traveling Shoes. New York: Random House, 1997.

RECORDINGS

Our Sheroes and Heroes. Los Angeles: Pacifica Tape Library, 1983. Maya Angelou interviewed by Susan Anderson. Cassette.

On the Pulse of Morning. New York: Random House Audio, 1993. Cassette.

And Still I Rise. New York: Random House Audiobooks, 1996. Cassette.

Black Pearls: The Poetry of Maya Angelou. Los Angeles, CA: GWP Records, 1998 Audio CD.

Making Magic in the World. Ukiah, CA: New Dimensions Foundations, 1998. Cassette.

The Maya Angelou Poetry Collection. New York: Random House, 1999. 4 Cassettes.

REFERENCES

Andrews, William L., Frances Smith Foster, and Trudier Harris, eds. *The Oxford Companion to African American Literature*. New York: Oxford University Press, 1997.

Chavalier, Tracy, ed. *Contemporary Poets*. 5th ed. Chicago: St. James Press, 1991.

Lisandrelli, Elaine Slivinski. *Maya Angelou: More Than a Poet*. Berkley Heights, NJ: Enslow Publishers, 1999.

Lupton, Mary Jane. *Maya Angelou: A Critical Companion*. Westport, CT: Greenwood Press, 1998.

Neubauer, Carol E. "Maya Angelou: Self and a Song of Freedom in the Southern Tradition." In *Southern Women Writers: The New Generation*. Ed. Tonnette Bond Inge. Tuscaloosa: University of Alabama Press, 1990, 114–42.

Williams, Mary E., ed. *Readings on Maya Angelou*. San Diego: Greenhaven Press, 1997.

When LeRoy Jones, in 1968, rejected his birth name and became Imamu Amiri Baraka, he followed a tradition of renaming to acknowledge a new self as many of his nineteenth-century black forebears had done, as well as the practice of renaming followed by converts to Islam. "Amiri" means a warrior or leader, and "Baraka," a gift or blessing, while "Imamu" means Mohammedan poet or priest. In 1974, however, Baraka dropped the first name, or spiritual title. Perhaps more than any writer associated with black cultural nationalism and the political revolution of the 1960s, Baraka has been a cultural warrior and a public presence. Through poetry, essays, plays, fiction, and music criticism, he has worked at institution building, at bridging the gap between the arts and the people, and at using the arts as catalysts to awaken black cultural pride. He is sought out as a knowledgeable and passionate commentator on the black cultural arts of the 1960s and as a spirited speaker and original performer of his own poetry.

Baraka came to national prominence in the 1960s through his award-winning drama, his poetry, and his demonstration of fierce leadership in and passionate commitment to political change for African American people. Along with several other prominent figures, his philosophy and his polemical poetry have been credited with being primary shapers of the period known as either the Black Arts Movement or Black Aesthetics. This emphasis on the revolutionary and propaganistic potential of the literary arts was intended to fuel or to complement the civil rights struggle in the 1960s. Black Aesthetics was a community-based art whose theories, critical positions, and standards were to originate within the black community.

Baraka was born to Coyette LeRoy and Anna Lois Russ Jones in Newark, New Jersey. (Baraka had recast his name "LeRoy" to the French spelling "LeRoi" during his high school years.) Anna Russ had attended Tuskegee Normal High School (before the institution became Tuskegee University) and Fisk University, although she did not graduate. Coyette LeRoy was a barber and postal worker from the South. Baraka was raised in a lower-middle-class family that included his maternal grandparents. He attended Rutgers University in 1951 on a science scholarship but then transferred to Howard University in 1952 and became an English major and philosophy minor. Baraka does not claim to have had an intellectually challenging experience at Howard, but he has credited Professor Sterling Brown for wonderful music classes that connected music and the history of black people and Professor Nathan Scott for conveying a love of Italian poet Dante Alighieri. Baraka left Howard University in 1954 and spent nearly three years in the air force, where he was stationed in Puerto Rico. It was during his postschool years, Baraka has said, that he became interested in learning.

In 1958 he settled in New York City, where he found the East Village section of the city congenial and its predominantly white Bohemian community supportive of his initial poetic impulses. He worked for *Record Changer* magazine and took graduate courses in comparative literature at Columbia University. In October 1958 he married Hettie Cohen, a young Jewish coworker at the magazine. Together they had two daughters. With her, he published and edited *Yugen*, a "little" literary magazine that brought Baraka in close contact with contemporary white "beat" poets Allen Ginsberg, Jack Kerouac, Robert Creeley, and Charles Olsen. This literary community influenced Baraka's early poetry, especially through its emphasis on self-awareness.

His first volume of poetry, *Preface to a Twenty Volume Suicide Note*, consisted of poems composed between 1957 and 1961. Several of the poems reflected Baraka's disenchantment with what he perceived as the seduction of the African American middle class by white values. The sun's radiating light, though traditionally a life-nurturing image, is one of the volume's dominant images. The speaker in many of the poems, for example, "The Turncoat," "The Insidious Dr. Fu Man Chu," and "The Death of Nick Charles," is all but paralyzed by his own stagnation and thus fixes upon death as the essential escape from a moribund civilization. In other poems, like "In Memory of Radio," "There *Must* Be a Lone Ranger," and "Look for You Yesterday, Here You Come Today," Baraka references popular culture from the comics, radio, and Hollywood. He nostalgically and ironically mourns the passing of the ideals they once offered. The images that convey the loss are vividly barren, and many of them use strong sexual images, a general characteristic of Baraka's poetry. The last poem in the volume is significant in view of Baraka's eventual metamorphosis from questioning his identity to affirming his blackness. Titled "Notes for a Speech," Baraka confronts his alienation from his cultural roots and identity as a child of Africa. Somewhat like Countee Cullen's poem "Heritage," the speaker does not know Africa as his homeland, as Africa does not recognize him. He does not know the color of Africa nor its language or culture and exists suspended between the lure of two cultures. Any meaningful connection with the motherland is thus doubtful.

Some critics judged his first volume as a good indication of Baraka's potential as a poet. *Preface* had some quiet poems as well as lyrical and reflective verse. Baraka used fluid structures that complemented the content of the poem, wrote without poetic language or clichés, and did not use conventional rhyme or meter. This first volume preceded the aggressive political position he later adopted. When the later poetry expressed his political stances, however, he was accused by mainstream critics of subverting his art for politics. In spite of this criticism, his poems were very popular in the black community.

Baraka has credited two twentieth-century American poets with influencing his work. Ezra Pound's writing influenced his understanding of how to shape a poem and to employ images, whereas William Carlos Williams's examples of using normal spoken language were useful. Jazz, too, has been a noted influence in Baraka's work. The playing styles of saxophonists John Coltrane and Charlie Parker suggested that disrupting and destroying predictible music structures could also be applied to predictible poetic structures.

In 1960 Baraka participated in a pivotal event that he later acknowledged as a turning point in his life. As part of a delegation of artists and scholars, he traveled to Cuba to commemorate Fidel Castro's coup of 1954. The political impact of the event awakened Baraka's own dormant political inclinations. The fervor of revolution in Cuba's youth ignited his own social consciousness. Action should be his goal, he concluded; thinking and writing alone were insufficient. The emergence of Third World nations in Africa in the early 1960s and the beginnings of the civil rights movement at home were other events that weighed in on Baraka's conclusions.

The Dead Lecturer, Baraka's second volume of poetry, continued to document the poet's developing artistic and political identity but also suggested an ongoing dialogue with the first collection. For example, Baraka continues his preoccupation with death, self-examination, and self-focus, apparent in *Preface*, through "A Poem for Willie Best," thematically connected to the ideas in "Notes for a Speech" (mentioned above) in its attempt to find a usable myth from the symbols of the African American past. Willie Best was an actor whose work stereotyped African Americans. Baraka's developing artistic identity was enhanced through the research and writing of *Blues People*, essays that Baraka worked on simultaneously with writing *The Dead Lecturer* poems. This artistic identity found an outlet through numerous references to music and its African American cultural traditions. "The Dance," for example, equated the self with the creation of musical form in direct lyrical language. The more complex five "Crow Jane" poems addressed the divide between Baraka's voice and Western and African American culture. These clever, allusive poems pair the Crazy Jane character from the poetry of the twentieth-century Irish poet and dramatist William Butler Yeats with a character Crow Jane from a blues song sung by Mississippi Big Joe Williams. These poems satisfy the volume's strategy of questioning traditions of Western art. Baraka indicates his movement toward those traditions of African culture that are alien to his American experience in the last line of "Crow Jane" as he calls on an African god, Damballah. Some scholars place the five "Crow Jane" poems among Baraka's most complicated work. *The Dead Lecturer* also contains the much-discussed poem "BLACK DADA NIHILISMUS," which calls for the destruction of Western civilization by violent means.

The changes in Baraka's artistic identity were reflected in his personal life. By fall 1965, he had left his Jewish wife and their children, along with his village friends, and moved to Harlem. The poems of *Black Magic*, a collection drawn from *Sabotage* (1961–1963), *Target Study* (1963–1965), and *Black Art* (1965–1967), reflected this period of metamorphosis in the poet's life and his embracing of black nationalism, although he wrote more drama than poetry between 1965 and 1970. *Black Magic* showed Baraka's complete withdrawal from white society and include two of his most anthologized and most widely discussed poems, "Black People" and "Black Art." The latter poem, in demanding that art should fuel political and violent action, had the language and incendiary tone that would become characteristic of the militant poetry of the decade. Among its images is an unidentified Negro leader on his knees in supplication to white America; the poem's message is the demeaning futility of patience and pleading. "Black Art" is representative of the models of Black Aesthetics poetry that challenged passivity and aimed to energize a black nation. It was criticized, however, for its anti-Semitic references.

Still another catalyst for Baraka's altering identity in 1967 was his year as a visiting professor at San Francisco State College. The thrust toward black nationalism was well under way on the West Coast and thus offered Baraka another model for personal and political potential. Moreover, by 1967, the poet had relocated from Harlem to his hometown of Newark, New Jersey, and remarried. His second wife, Sylvia, an African American woman, was an actress, painter, and dancer. Baraka's altered and charged state might have seemed fixed when, in 1968, he affirmed his identity through the name Imamu Amiri Baraka. However, he would continue with slight recastings of himself in the years to come. Sylvia, too, recast herself as "Bibi Amina." Baraka and Bibi Amina had five children.

For Baraka, the year 1967 still held additional life-altering episodes.

During the Newark riots, Baraka was beaten by the police and arrested for illegal possession of firearms. At his trial, Judge Leon Kapp read "Black People" as evidence of his guilt. Thus the poem became notorious in this connection. It was printed in newspapers and journals, not in the poetry sections but on the front pages. The poem offers a vision of black art as a catalyst for black people to return the violence that historically has been perpetrated against them. Baraka was convicted of a misdemeanor and imprisoned, but the conviction was overthrown during appeal.

In Harlem, Baraka had established the Black Arts Repertory Theatre, which became a model for black theaters in other cities, and in Newark, he continued this work by opening Spirit House, a black repertory theater and cultural center, and continued writing poetry. In *Black Magic*, Baraka redefined any perjorative associations with the term "black magic." *In Our Terribleness*, a volume of poems and prose selections in which *terribleness* is redefined to mean goodness and beauty, Baraka continued his spirit of inquiry in shaping art to political assertion. Appearing during the height of his black nationalist period, the volume also seemed to challenge the sufficiency of the poetic image by literally setting it against the visual images of photography.

In 1974 Baraka underwent yet another political transformation by deemphasizing black nationalism and became a socialist through accepting Marxist-Leninist thought. In this identity, capitalism was the greatest enemy of black people. The volume *Hard Facts: Excerpts* reflects this new position.

Baraka has continued to advocate social change and to use his art and voice as primary instruments to that end. He has also turned his talents to the service of poetry through editing anthologies of poetry. His status as a revered revolutionary poet and speaker in African American literary circles has remained constant. He remains a model for those poets who came to prominence with him in the turbulent days of the 1960s, when poetry by and for African Americans was revisioned in the hands of writers like Baraka, Sanchez, Madhubuti, and Rodgers. He has continued to remain antiestablishment in his poetry and in his dramatic mode of presenting it. His work has retained the political deftness that initially distinguished it.

POETRY

Preface to a Twenty Volume Suicide Note. New York: Totem Press (in association with Corinth Books), 1961. (Out of Print)
The Dead Lecturer. New York: Grove Press, 1964. (Out of Print)

Black Magic: Collected Poetry, 1961–1967. Indianapolis, IN: Bobbs, Merrill; 1969. (Out of Print)
It's Nation Time. Chicago: Third World Press, 1970. (Out of Print)
Spirit Reach. Newark, NJ: Jihad Productions, 1972. (Out of Print)
Hard Facts: Excerpts. Newark, NJ: Congress of Afrikan People, 1973. (Out of Print)
AM/TRAK. New York: Phoenix Bookshop, 1979. (Out of Print)
Selected Poetry of Amiri Baraka/LeRoi Jones. New York: Morrow, 1979.
Spring Song. N.P.: Printed Earth Editions, 1979. (Limited edition. Out of Print)
Raggae or Not! New York: Contact/Two Publications, 1982. (Out of Print)
Funk Lore: New Poems, 1984–1995. Los Angeles: Littoral Books, 1995.
Transbluesency: The Selected Poems of Amiri Baraka/LeRoi Jones (1961–1995). Ed. Paul Vangelisti, New York: Marsilio Publishers, 1995.

AUTOBIOGRAPHY

The Autobiography of Leroi Jones–Amiri Baraka. New York: Freundlich Books, 1984.
The Autobiography of LeRoi Jones. Chicago: Lawrence Hills Books, 1997.

SELECTED ANTHOLOGIES

(With Amini Baraka).*Confirmation: An Anthology of African American Women*. New York: Morrow, 1983.
Wise, why's y's. Chicago: Third World Press, 1995.

REFERENCES

Benson, Kimberly W. *Baraka: The Renegade and the Mask*. New Haven, CT: Yale University Press, 1976.
Harris, William J. "Amiri Baraka." In *African American Writers*. Ed. Lea Baechler and A. Walton Litz. New York: Charles Scribner's, 1991. 15–30.
———. *The Poetry and Poetics of Amiri Baraka: The Jazz Aesthetic*. Columbia: University of Missouri Press, 1985.
Hudson, Theodore R. *From LeRoi Jones to Amiri Baraka*. Durham, NC: Duke University Press, 1973.
Lacey, Henry C. *"To Raise, Destroy, and Create": The Poetry, Drama, and Fiction of Imamu Amiri Baraka (LeRoi Jones)*. Troy, NY: Whitston, 1988.
Miller, James A. "Amiri Baraka in the 1980s." *Callaloo 9.1* (Winter 1986): 184–92.
Reilly, Charles, ed. *Conversations with Amiri Baraka*. Jackson: University of Mississippi Press, 1994.

ARNA BONTEMPS

(1902–1973)

Arna Bontemps
Credit: Library of Congress

Bontemps was aware of the exciting potential and productivity under way in Harlem, New York, in the early 1920s before he traversed the country from California in 1925 to the city being called the Negro Capital of the World. The writers and writing of the era that emerged as the Harlem Renaissance were destined to shape the rest of Bontemps's professional life through his involvement in numerous genres. He subsequently became a teacher, librarian, editor, short story writer, novelist, dramatist, biographer, writer of children's poetry and fiction, and a poet for adults. He was prolific in these genres, collaborating with Langston Hughes to edit books of black poetry and folklore and alone editing a collection of slave narratives. Bontemps's introductions to the edited editions are scholarly and illustrative of his commitment to preserving the art and history of his community.

Bontemps was born in Alexandria, Louisiana, to Paul Bontemps and a teacher mother. The home where the poet was born is now the Arna Bontemps African American Museum and Cultural Arts Center. At age three, young Bontemps moved with his family to the Watts section of Los Angeles. A studious lad, Bontemps was encouraged in his love of reading by his mother, who died when he was twelve. He attended the predominantly white Seventh Day Adventist Church school San Fernando Academy in 1917. He graduated in 1923 from Pacific Union College, another church-run institution, having completed college in three years. Bontemps furthered his education in 1936 with postbaccalaureate work at the Graduate Library School, University of Chicago.

Bontemps married his wife Alberta Johnson, who was from Georgia, in 1926, and the couple subsequently had six children.

Bontemps felt the pleasure that success in literary endeavors could produce in 1921 when his college professor in northern California approved his assignment. When Bontemps found and read Claude McKay's poetry volume *Harlem Shadows* in the University of California at Los Angeles library in 1922 shortly after its publication, he told everyone he knew.

In 1923, Bontemps completed college but was unable to find a job except as an extra at the post office during the Christmas rush. He was then retained as an employee working a night shift, but he could see that his destiny might reiterate the lives of the men who worked around him. The monotonous job could become his life's work. Bontemps began raiding the public library for reading, and he began writing and then sending out poems to magazines. In his workplace, Bontemps met an-

other African American worker, Wallace Thurman, who was also sub-
mitting poems to magazines in New York. Thurman would flower into
a respected novelist.

When one of Bontemps's poem was accepted for publication and appeared in *Crisis* magazine, he left Los Angeles, destined for Harlem.
Through happenstance rather than self-promotion, Bontemps quickly became acquainted with several other young published writers, including
Countee Cullen and Langston Hughes. He and Hughes began written
correspondence in 1925 when Hughes sent him a poem, and they continued their letters until a few months before Hughes's death. Their
friendship also fueled their collaborative literary efforts; several of the
edited books they produced have become classics in black studies. In
Harlem, Bontemps also became acquainted with *Opportunity*, the journal
of the Urban League, which, like *Crisis*, sponsored literary competitions
and solicited and published new writing by black authors. Bontemps
published in *Opportunity* as well.

By the end of the 1920s Bontemps had written numerous prize-
winning poems but had not published a book of poetry. By that time,
he was also working on novels. His first, *God Sends Sunday*, was published in 1931. However, the stock market crash of 1929 was exerting a
debilitating force on the creativity that had flourished in Harlem earlier
in the decade. The physical proximity of artists within the Harlem community, a fact that many scholars consider when they rationalize the
period of the Renaissance, was affected because several writers, including Bontemps, left the cities for stable teaching jobs elsewhere. Bontemps
and his family moved south to Huntsville, Alabama, where he taught at
Oakwood Junior College, a small institution operated by the Seventh-
Day Adventists. In collaboration with Langston Hughes he began writing
children's books as well as many of his best-known short stories later
compiled under the title *The Old South*. His tenure with Oakwood ended
in 1934, and Bontemps and his family relocated to Los Angeles and then
to Chicago. In the latter city, he completed what is perhaps his best-
known novel, *Black Thunder*, the story of the slave rebellion of Gabriel
Prosser in Virginia in 1800. Upon completion of graduate school in 1943,
Bontemps became the librarian at Fisk University in Nashville, Tennessee, a position he held until 1972. However, in 1960 he was at Makerere
College in Uganda, Africa, and in 1969 he served as Yale Professor and
Curator of the James Weldon Johnson Collection. In 1963, he finally published *Personals*, a long overdue volume of poetry that contained only
twenty-three poems.

History and time are dominant themes in Bontemps's poems, but he treats them abstractly. He writes about black people's struggles with objectivity, relying on the broad image, the collective voice, and a distance achieved through referencing biblical events to establish the theme or the protest. The biblical references perhaps reflect Bontemps's many years of study in Seventh-Day Adventist church schools and the emotional control he might have learned through those experiences. His themes also look back to the past, to returning to an earlier period, to a lost love, or to a former place. References to Africa, often implied rather than direct, anchor his imagination in an ancestral past. The language of Bontemps's lyrics is direct, and the images of wind, mountains, darkness, rain, rivers, and trees are judiciously selected. Although Bontemps was knowledgeable about the poetry of other poets of the Harlem Renaissance, his work seems uninfluenced by them. He wrote reflective, quiet poems that illustrate an expansive intelligence looking back through the ages and assessing the arduous sojourn of African Americans since the Middle Passage.

"Nocturne at Bethesda" won the literary competition sponsored by *Crisis* in 1926, and "A Black Man Talks of Reaping" won the *Crisis* poetry award for 1926. Among his most anthologized pieces, the two poems illustrate the ideas that would engage Bontemps in numerous ways throughout his career. The place name Bethesda comes from the Bible (John 5:2–4) where it is a Hebrew name meaning "pool," and the pool has five branches. Sick and infirm people wait in the water for an angel to "trouble the water," after which the first infirm person entering it is healed. "Nocturne" is a poem of profound loss. Its reference to the biblical Bethesda as a site of miracles and hope is used to parallel the loss of golden days in the speaker's heritage as he tries to remember something that eludes him as he "wander[s] in strange lands." The reference to a place of healing suggests a sickness needing to be healed. The poem also suggests that some sicknesses are beyond the healing miracles. The speaker expects that after death if he can return, it will be to a place "beneath the palms of Africa." The poem implies that memory may be restored through death, and the speaker in eternity will finally recall those elusive scenes from his native land.

"A Black Man Talks of Reaping" uses the metaphor of sowing and harvesting to suggest the inequities between what black people have done and their noncommensurate rewards. More alarming, the fruit of the black man's labor, ironically, is enjoyed by his brother's sons, that is, his white brothers' sons. The result is that the sower's children are forced to scavage in unfamiliar territory and to "feed on bitter fruit." The metaphor of reaping also suggests the saying of one reaping what one sows.

In "Southern Mansion" the image called up by the title is not literally a part of the poem, but it is nevertheless part of the visual setting, a house situated at the end of a driveway lined by parallel rows of poplar trees. The poem looks backward across the years to a confrontation between slave owner and slave as the "years go back with a clank" and ghosts on the march trample down roses with the poplar trees as witness.

"The Return" is a love poem in which history and ancestral memory are central. Falling rain transports the speaker back through pain to remembered love, to a time when this rain transported the lovers back to a mythical African night to dance under spice trees. This poem suggests that the past holds an intangible something, an inarticulate happiness that persistently eludes the present.

Bontemps's awards include the Newbery Honor Book in 1949 for the children's book *Story of the Negro*, the Jane Addams Book Award in 1956 for *The Story Book of the Negro*, the Alexander Pushkin Poetry Prize from *Opportunity* magazine in 1926 and 1927, Rosenwald Fellowships in 1938 and 1942, and Guggenheim Fellowships in 1949 and 1954.

POETRY

Personals. London: Paul Breman, 1963.

SELECTED EDITED ANTHOLOGIES

(With Langston Hughes). *The Poetry of the Negro, 1746–1949*. Garden City, NY: Doubleday, 1949.
(With Langston Hughes). *The Book of Negro Folkore*. New York: Dodd, Mead, 1958.
American Negro Poetry. New York: Hill and Wang, 1963.

REFERENCES

"Arna Bontemps." In *The Oxford Companion to African American Literature*. Ed. William L. Andrews, Frances Smith Foster, and Trudier Harris. New York: Oxford University Press, 1997. 91–92.
Bontemps, Arna. "The Awakening: A Memoir." In *The Harlem Renaissance Remembered*. Ed. Arna Bontemps. New York: Dodd, Mead, 1972. 1–26.
Nichols, Charles H. *Arna Bontemps–Langston Hughes Letters, 1925–1967*. New York: Dodd, Mead 1980.

GWENDOLYN BROOKS

(1917–2000)

Gwendolyn Brooks
Credit: Atlanta University Center, Robert W. Woodruff Library
Photo credit: Griffith J. Davis

Gwendolyn Brooks's potential for becoming a poet was recognized and nurtured by her parents during Brooks's childhood. As early as age seven, she was writing poems and using rhyme. At age sixteen, she sent poems to James Weldon Johnson, a famous poet and novelist, who replied positively about her ability. Brooks attended a poetry reading by Langston Hughes at Metropolitan Community Church, and she also showed him her poems. Confirming Johnson's opinion, Hughes encouraged her to continue writing. Like Hughes, Brooks's poetry would be written primarily for her community, and through it she would become an activist for art. As she has written in the first installment of her autobiography, *Report from Part One*, she wanted her poems to "call . . . all black people in taverns, black people in alleys, black people in gutters, schools, offices, factories, prisons, the consulate . . . in pulpits, black people in mines, on farms, on thrones; not always to 'teach'—I shall wish often to entertain, to illume."

Brooks grew up in a home where love for one's culture and respect for other people were taught and practiced. She was born in Topeka, Kansas, on June 7, 1917, to Keziah Corinne Wims and David Anderson Brooks but grew up with them and her younger brother, Raymond, in Chicago. Her father had studied at Fisk University in Nashville, Tennessee, for a year, hoping to become a physician, and her mother was an elementary school teacher who enjoyed playing the piano in their home. Their focus was the development of their children. For Gwendolyn, they provided a place for her writing and freed her from normal children's chores so that she might write. Her father provided a desk for her writing materials and books. Her mother also coached her in the public recitation of Bible verses and poetry as early as age four and five. This practice suggests that Mrs. Brooks understood the value of orality in black culture. Instilling this value in young Gwendolyn assisted her ear for the rhythms and cadences of the black speech that became so vital in her adult poetry. Encouraged by her mother, Gwendolyn also wrote plays for young people's church programs. Her mother taught classes at the Carter Temple Methodist Episcopal Church, and Brooks and her brother attended Sunday school there.

Brooks graduated from Englewood High School in 1934 and from Wilson Junior College in 1936, where she earned the Associate of Literature and Arts degree. Unable to secure employment with *The Chicago Defender*, a black newspaper, Brooks briefly became a maid in a North Shore home. She then worked a few months in an unsatisfactory position as a secretary to a spiritual adviser specializing in patent medicines. His business was in the Mecca, an apartment building that later became the setting of her poem titled "In the Mecca." The sparse opportunities afforded to Brooks upon graduation bespeak the segregated era in which she lived.

Brooks met Henry Lowington Blakely II in 1938. Their spontaneous interest in each other was fueled, in part, by their common love of writing. They married in 1939 and had two children, Henry L. Blakely III and a daughter Nora, who like her mother writes poetry. Brooks's role as wife and mother competed with her ongoing attempts to become a poet. However, by 1945 when her first book of poetry, *A Street in Bronzeville*, was published, being a recognized poet seemed a certainty.

Besides her formal education and independent reading of both African American and mainstream poets, Brooks prepared to write poetry by enrolling in a modern poetry workshop at the South Side Community Art Center in 1941. Inez Cunningham Stark, an affluent white woman from Chicago and a board member for the prestigious *Poetry* magazine, taught the course. Brooks was joined in the workshop by fellow writer and friend Margaret Burroughs, also founder of the DuSable Museum in Chicago. Burroughs has said that she and the others recognized Brooks's distinctive talent.

Public recognition had already begun, however, through Brooks's first public award in 1943 at the Midwestern Writers' Conference. In 1950 she became the first black poet honored by the Pulitzer Prize for Poetry, awarded for her second book *Annie Allen* (1949). This award began what became a steady stream of honors for the poet: Poet Laureate of the State of Illinois; the National Endowment for the Arts Lifetime Achievement Award (which included $40,000, her largest cash award); the Jefferson Lecturer (the highest honor the federal government bestows for intellectual achievement in the humanities) chosen by the National Endowment for the Humanities; a Gwendolyn Brooks Cultural Center on the campus of Western Illinois University; and more than seventy honorary doctorate degrees. She was the first African American to win a Pulitzer Prize for any achievement, the first black woman appointed as Consultant in Poetry to the Library of Congress, and also the first one elected to the National Institute of Arts and Letters.

Brooks's productivity as a poet was consistent throughout her lifetime, beginning with her first published poem, "Eventide," printed in *American Childhood* when she was thirteen. She contributed numerous poems to black newspapers, including *The Chicago Defender*, and by age twenty had poems in two anthologies. She published four significant volumes of poetry—*A Street in Bronzeville, Annie Allen, The Bean Eaters* (1960), and *In the Mecca: Poems* (1968)—and a novel—*Maude Martha* (1953)—in the first twenty years of her formal writing career. Her work is recognized by scholars and critics for its attention to the connection between form and content, for its uniqueness of language, and for its ability to imbue ordinary experiences and people with the richness and complexity they deserve.

The sonnet, ballad, elegy, mock heroic, and lyric are evident among the forms of her poetry. However, she is not content to use them without adding her distinction, thus individualizing and transforming them. The traditional Shakespearean or Petrarchan sonnet, for example, as used by Brooks, is rarely true to its original form, a fact illustrated in her celebrated sonnet sequence of twelve poems titled "Gay Chaps at the Bar" in *A Street in Bronzeville*. The traditional subject of the sonnet has been love, but in Brooks's "Gay Chaps," it is war. In another challenge to tradition, in Brooks's "The Anniad" in *Annie Allen*, the author looks back to an eighteenth-century British structure, the mock heroic poem, but alters the traditional stanzaic forms and rhyming patterns, thus stamping the form with her distinctive signature.

Having chosen Chicago's black South Side community as her milieu marks Brooks as an urban poet. The variety and vitality of the experience there provided her work with numerous subjects, themes, and issues. Marriage, poverty, survival in old age, racism, love, coming of age, and endangered young black men are among her numerous concerns, particularly in the early poetry. "The Bean Eaters," for example, engages old age, marriage, and poverty in a slow-paced poem about a couple whose survival in old age is chiefly motivated through memories and the accumulated minutiae of life. The vitality of black life hemmed in by the narrowness of segregated America, which breeds poverty and other sickness, forms the motif in several poems. In "kitchenette building," for example, the mood of the people is described as gray, and the concept of a dream is unsettling. Having a dream is remote, unlike the tangible reality of paying rent or feeding a family. In "the rites for Cousin Vit," where the woman's funeral is the occasion for the poem, the coffin is incapable of retaining her bigger-than-life presence even in death. Brooks creates identities for many of the dispossessed black people who are part of her poetry. "Of De Witt Williams on the way to Lincoln Cemetery" constitutes an informal eulogy for the undistinguished young man, a migrant from Alabama to Illinois who lived too fast in the impersonal city.

Brooks's work includes several poems that address social rejection experienced both within and without the black community because of a person's dark skin. In such poems, the receiver of this social abuse is most often a child, as if the experience of repulsion is an additional painful rite of passage. Such poems include "the ballad of chocolate Mabbie," "The Life of Lincoln West," and "Ballad of Pearl May Lee," though in the latter poem, Pearl May Lee is not a child but a rejected woman. Although the pain of rejection is dramatized against childhood innocence in "chocolate Mabbie" and "Lincoln West," Lincoln finds a cause for celebration in the distinctiveness of his black skin. Considered ugly by everyone, one day Lincoln hears white men identify him as a real African specimen, undiluted by miscegenation. Although they single out stereotypical features, and their remarks are not intended as complimentary, Lincoln, ironically, misunderstands the import of their words. What he seizes upon is that he is distinctively real, and that knowledge provides him solace from the stares and whispers. Ironically, for Lincoln, an intended negative becomes affirmingly positive.

Brooks's consciousness about social inequities in black America, while apparent in her early volumes, becomes more pronounced in the work published on the eve of the civil rights decade of the 1960s and in its aftermath. Her usual control and terseness in structure, language, and event are evident, but irony and understatement play increased roles. In "A Bronzeville Mother Loiters in Mississippi. Meanwhile a Mississippi Mother Burns Bacon," the Emmett Till murder in Money, Mississippi, and the not-guilty jury decision are the background, but the persona is the white Mississippi mother and wife of one of the murderers. As is often her technique, Brooks avoids direct, angry rhetoric. In the ballad, she illustrates the growing conscience of the Mississippi mother and wife who eventually silently understands that she and her children are not in the household of the protective fairy prince of her fantasy. Instead, they live with the dark, murderous villain. Implied but not stated is the irony that as a white woman in the South in the late 1950s she is condemned to silently live with this knowledge that will smear every facet of her life and her children's lives. In "The Last Quatrain of the Ballad of Emmett Till," the brief poem offsets the knowledge of the Mississippi mother with the frozen emotions of the Bronzeville mother. The numbing grief of the slain boy's mother is communicated through quietly understated images.

Another turbulent event, the desegregation of a southern high school in Arkansas, is the setting for "The Chicago Defender Sends a Man to Little Rock." Instead of a focus on the specifics of racist opposition, however, the poem depicts people with ordinary social and civic activities.

The reporter concludes that the white people in Little Rock are like most people in spite of their frenzied determination to keep racial separation in the schools. The poem, thus dependent on dramatic irony for its power, also suggests that ordinary people in other places also have the capacity for uncontrollable unreasonableness in matters of race.

Brooks's volumes published after 1967 reveal her participation in the Black Arts aesthetic of the time. Briefly defined, Black Aesthetics was part of a cultural nationalism that championed creative work originating within the black community. Such work should be pitched for the black community and should reflect its language, values, experiences, and images. Although black people had always been at the core of Brooks's work, her early poetry had successfully showcased her command of European poetic forms and techniques. Black 1960s poets abandoned standard poetic forms for unorthodox ones infused by sound and distinguished by their visual arrangement on the page. While Brooks did not drastically relax formal structures, she engaged in some release of them. Her more noticeable alteration was in the content of her poems. They revealed Brooks's spiritual kinship with the younger poets and with the role poetry might play in the political liberation of black people. Aside from her poetry composition, Brooks showed her kinship with the liberation causes in another significant way: Consistent with the Black Arts Movement's belief that the community should control the dissemination of black art, Brooks switched from a major New York publisher to the small, black-founded Broadside Press in Detroit, which Dudley Randall had initiated. Later, Brooks switched to Third World Press in Chicago, founded by black poet and educator Haki Madhubuti. Brooks also published her own work in later years, having founded The David Company, a press that she named for her father.

Although her subjects in the 1960s remained the same, she expanded her poetry to reflect a black consciousness consistent with that turbulent era and adjusted it to make her anger more visible. She also continued to use those elements distinctive to the black community such as the folk, jazz and blues rhythms, and black speech patterns. *In the Mecca* is the volume that marks the departure between Brooks's early work and her reordered focus. The lengthy title poem of the volume chronicles the lives of tenants in the Mecca, a showcase building designed by a famous architect as an apartment building for the white elite. Flight by the elite to the city's Northside meant the building became the home of poor blacks on the Southside. These tenants for whom the American dream is a mirage are shown in the poem as America's disinherited. In "The

Blackstone Rangers" Brooks calls attention to the street gangs that cities spawn, who prey on their own communities. She suggests their intense isolation in the arresting line: "Their country is a Nation on no map." *Riot* (1969) is a poem in three parts. The first part is a consummate narrative and a perceptive juxtaposition of the haves and have-nots, the isolated wealthy and the angry black masses. *Riot* is one among several of Brooks's poems that show white Chicagoans as symbols of wealth and as part of the social problems that gave rise to the riots of the 1960s. The irony is that the persona, John Cabot, is killed still holding on to his misconceptions and his ignorance of what fueled the riot.

Brooks, though internationally known, continued to live modestly on the Southside of Chicago with her husband. She continued to address vital issues of the black community in America but also extended her reach to include South Africa before the dismantling of apartheid. Her poem "The Near-Johannesburg Boy" is one example of her expanded geographical concerns. The most basic human needs such as love, death, psychologically healthy children, and racial equality remained most engaging to her, and she continued to address these subjects through the particular vision of her poetic eye until her death.

POETRY

A Street in Bronzeville. New York: Harper and Row, 1945. (Out of Print)
Annie Allen. New York: Harper and Row, 1949. (Out of Print)
The Bean Eaters. New York: Harper and Row, 1960.
Selected Poems. New York: Harper and Row, 1963. (Out of Print)
In the Mecca: Poems. New York: Harper and Row, 1968. (Out of Print)
Riot. Detroit: Broadside Press, 1969.
Aloneness. Detroit: Broadside Press, 1971.
Family Pictures. Detroit: Broadside Press, 1971.
The World of Gwendolyn Brooks. New York: Harper and Row, 1971. (Out of Print)
Beckonings. Detroit: Broadside Press, 1975.
Primer for Blacks and Young Poet's Primer. Chicago: Brooks Press, 1980.
To Disembark. 1981. Rpt., Chicago: Third World Press, 1992.
The Near-Johannesburg Boy, and Other Poems. Chicago: David, 1986.
Blacks: The Collected Poems. Chicago: David, 1987.

AUTOBIOGRAPHY

Report from Part One. Detroit: Broadside Press, 1972.
Report from Part Two. Chicago: Third World Press, 1996.

EDITED ANTHOLOGIES

A Broadside Treasury. Detroit: Broadside Press, 1971. (Out of Print)
Jump Bad: A New Chicago Anthology. Detroit: Broadside Press, 1971. (Out of Print)

RECORDINGS

Lemonade Suite. Bloomington: Indiana University Audio-Visual Center, 1981. Videocassette.
Poets in Person. Chicago: Modern Poetry Association, 1991. Cassette.

REFERENCES

Bloom, Harold, ed. *Gwendolyn Brooks*. Philadelphia: Chelsea House, 2000.
Bolden, Barbara Jean. *Urban Rage in Bronzeville: Social Commentary in the Poetry of Gwendolyn Brooks*. Chicago: Third World Press, 1999.
Kent, George E. *A Life of Gwendolyn Brooks*. Lexington: University Press of Kentucky, 1990.
Madhubuti, Haki R., ed. *Say That the River Turns: The Impact of Gwendolyn Brooks*. Chicago: Third World Press, 1987.
Melhem, D.L. *Gwendolyn Brooks, Poetry and the Heroic Voice*. Lexington: University Press of Kentucky, 1987.
Mootry, Maria K., and Gary Smith, eds. *A Life Distilled: Gwendolyn Brooks: Her Poetry and Fiction*. Urbana: University of Illinois Press, 1987.
Shaw, Harry B. *Gwendolyn Brooks*. Boston: Twayne, 1980.
Smethurst, James Edward. "Hysterical Ties: Gwendolyn Brooks and the Rise of a 'High' Neomodernism." In *The New Red Negro: The Literary Left and African American Poetry, 1930–1946*. New York: Oxford University Press, 1999. 164–79.
Watkins, Mel. "In Memoriam: Gwendolyn Brooks." *Black Scholar* 31.1 (2001): 51–54.
Wright, Stephen Caldwell, ed. *On Gwendolyn Brooks: Reliant Contemplation*. Ann Arbor: University of Michigan Press, 1996.

STERLING BROWN

(1901–1989)

Sterling Brown
Credit: Prints and Photographs Collection, Moorland-Spingarn Research Center, Howard University

Brown's seven poems in fellow writer Countee Cullen's famous anthology *Caroling Dust* in 1927 place him squarely amid the productive writers of the Harlem Renaissance. However, his poetic temperament—his embracing of the unadorned and honest language of unassuming rural people and their stories of pain, joy, and resilience—distances him from most writers of that period with the notable exceptions of Langston Hughes, James Weldon Johnson, and Zora Neale Hurston. Perhaps because Brown's period of greatest productivity occurred between 1930 and 1940, he is more closely linked with the post–Renaissance poets, including Margaret Walker and Robert Hayden. Brown's reputation rests on his poetry and his highly respected scholarship in African American literature and culture.

Brown was born in Washington, D.C., to the Reverend Sterling Nelson John Brown and Adelaide Allen Brown, as the only brother to five sisters. Both parents were college educated, his father at Fisk and Oberlin Theological Seminary, and his mother at Fisk as well, where she was valedictorian of her class. Born in slavery in Roane County, Tennessee, in 1858, Reverend Brown became a professor in the School of Religion at Howard University in 1892, and he pastored an influential church in the city. His son was later to say that his father held two jobs but still made no money.

The younger Brown's conditioning as a scholar began in his early environment on Howard University's campus and in his parents' home where he was surrounded by books and his mother's love of music and literature. She read Longfellow and Robert Burns to her son but also recited the dialect poems of Paul Laurence Dunbar. In addition to his mother as an early influence, Brown enjoyed the influence of literature teachers during his high school and college years.

He attended Lucretia Mott Elementary School and Dunbar High School, both segregated institutions in Washington, D.C. Brown received an excellent education, particularly at Dunbar, which boasted accomplished teachers with masters and doctorate degrees because segregation closed to them most other respectable professions aside from law and medicine. He won a scholarship to Williams College in Williamstown, Massachusetts, and entered at age seventeen. Brown and three other black males were not housed with the other students. The college circulated the idea that their black students would be happier together and put them together in a private home. In spite of the racial isolation fostered by the college, Brown participated in campus life by playing tennis in which he won national competitions and serving on the debating team. He joined Omega Phi Psi fraternity, traveling to Boston for the initiation. He was awarded a Phi Beta Kappa key in 1921 and graduated in 1922. He attended Harvard University in 1923, graduating with the master's degree, and returned in 1931 for the doctorate, which he did not complete.

Recognizing his talents, some friends discouraged Brown from embracing teaching as his profession, and his father discouraged him from coming to Howard immediately after earning his master's. Convinced that teaching was his calling, however, Brown took a position at Virginia Seminary in Lynchburg where he taught for three years. Before joining the English faculty at Howard University in 1929, where he would work for forty years, Brown also taught at Lincoln University in Missouri (1926–1928) and at Fisk University (1928–1929). In 1927 Brown married Daisy Turnbull, who had graduated from Virginia Seminary and College before his arrival there.

The decision to work in Lynchburg was fortuitous on a personal as well as a professional level. In Lynchburg, Brown discovered a black folk community participating fully in the spirituals, tales, and stories of the oral tradition from which Paul Laurence Dunbar had mined his work. Brown smoothly blended into the life of the community and absorbed its character, speech, and folkways. In fact, he later said he was like a "sponge" in learning the local folklore. Many of the people he met became subjects for numerous poems. What he observed and liked in Lynchburg coalesced in significant ways with what Brown was responding to in the modern American poetry of the early 1920s. As an undergraduate at Williams College, Brown had begun writing poetry. He embraced, in particular, certain elements of the Imagists, a group in which H.D. Dolittle, Amy Lowell, and Ezra Pound were prominent. The Imagists advocated simple direct language in poems, a controlling image, and the liberty to choose any subject for their work. Other modernist poets whose work Brown admired included Robert Frost, A.E. Housman, Vachael Lindsay, and Edwin Arlington Robinson, though he was not completely at ease with Lindsay's attempt to describe the Negro. Robinson's technique, however, of creating a series of personalities was very attractive to Brown.

Drawing on modernist techniques that appealed to him, and seeking to represent with accuracy and respect the folk culture he found in Virginia, Brown turned to writing folk poetry. His work is complete in a way that distinguishes it from similar work by Langston Hughes and Paul Laurence Dunbar. Through involvement with the folk in Lynchburg as well as in urban barbershops and other venues where the unlettered were to be found, Brown listened to their speech and their stories and noted their perspective on the hand that life had dealt them. He responded to their irony or sarcasm or stoicism as completely as he did to their exuberance, resilience, or patience. In recognizing their joys as well as their pains, Brown's work conveyed a scale of human emotion that earned him praise. In contrast, Dunbar's folk poems had been accused of being patronizing because they failed to reference black hardship. As a scholar, Brown also read the folklore of other nations, including Germany, France, and Ireland, and noted its use in the literature. Thus he could approach the African American folk tradition through its shared fate with other groups.

Brown's investigation of and immersion in the black oral tradition proved fruitful in his first book of poems, *Southern Road* (1932), with an introduction by James Weldon Johnson. The volume established Brown as an authentic artistic voice for the African American folk experience in all its variety, moods, and forms. The poetry is remarkable for its capture of rich vernacular speech represented as the poet knew it was spoken, not as it had been imagined in some work by earlier writers. As much as any other feature, *Southern Road* illustrates the poet's attention to individuals. No reader can think that the folk experience is a monolithic one, for the poems encompass the full range of human emotions, although the blues as a condition of life and the blues as a music form permeate all four sections of the volume. In "Maumee Ruth" the speaker traveled a rocky blues road, but in "Ma Rainey," one of his best-known poems, Brown celebrates the appeal of that legendary early performer of blues music to her own community. Brown's motif of travel, contained in the book's title and confirmed by poems such as "Odyssey of Big Boy," "Long Gone," "Memphis Blues," "Children of the Mississippi," and "New St. Louis Blues," suggests the breadth of the folk experience that can be found throughout the South.

Numerous poems speak specifically to hardship in the lives of black men. In the ballads "Johnny Thomas" and "Frankie and Johnny" black men die. Forces in Johnny Thomas's life such as a poor education, an abusive father, gambling, women, theft, imprisonment, and the conflicts found there lead to his violent death in prison. In "Frankie and Johnny," an old ballad, Johnny, a hardworking farmer, and a mentally impaired white girl begin a liaison that leads to his lynching. In the ballad "Sam Smiley," a veteran who has been schooled in the methods of killing as a result of military service, revenges the death of the black woman he loved by killing the white man whose involvement with her precipitated her death. Sam, too, dies by mob violence. The misfortune and deaths in these poems and others are balanced by the Slim Greer travel ballads where skills and stealth assure Slim's survival to turn his escapades into bragging rights. In "Slim Greer," for example, Slim passes for white in Arkansas with a white woman until his facility at blues piano playing betrays his racial identity. In "Slim in Atlanta," Brown illustrates the absurdity of laws designed to constrain black people by positing a law that restricted black people from laughing outside. They could only laugh confined within a phone booth. "Strange Legacies" extols heroes and their resilience in tough times. It begins with the boxer Jack Johnson and his ability to take his punishment "like a man," like the legendary railroad builder John Henry, but ends with a nameless couple who, in spite of environmental deficits and economic exploitation that bring misery, will continue trying. In perhaps the most frequently anthologized poem of the *Southern Road*, "Strong Men," a historical overview of the black "blues" producing experience in America is illustrated against the resilience of the community, a resilience communicated through its music, particularly the folk spirituals.

The title poem of *The Last Ride of Wild Bill* (1975) is the longest of the pieces. They showcase Brown's exceptional narrative and rhythmic abilities alongside the folk tradition of extolling the unsung, ordinary community hero through the tradition of the exaggerated tale or the "lie." His figures illustrate self-actualization as the cultural will, and the range of cultural heroes is notable. In the title poem, whose figure is named for the legendary hero of the Old West, Wild Bill is a numbers runner who wantonly challenges the law. However, Crispus Attucks McCoy, named for the historic Crispus Attucks, the first man to die in the Revolutionary War in a Concord, Massachusetts, battle, is a more ordinary man who is driven to violence by the cumulative insults in ordinary events. "Elder Mistletoe," a country minister, had the patience of Job until his congregation sought to cheat and insult him for four years. His defiance is his speech to them and his wearing of mistletoe pinned on the lower edge of his coat, his Christian way of turning the other cheek. The common element in these poems is the men's bold resistance to the establishment when their death is the probable end. *No Hiding Place*, whose title comes from a folk spiritual, was not published independently but was included in Brown's *Collected Poems* (1996). It includes a few of Brown's poems that are frequently anthologized, such as "Old Lem," "Southern Cop," and "Remembering Nat Turner."

Brown remains highly praised for his spirited defense and championing of folk culture. In the 1960s when many older writers, Hayden, for example, were denigrated for poetic conventionalism, Brown's work was still applauded because of its grounding in the resistance of ordinary folk, the forerunners of those who were braving the water hoses and jails of southern cities. Brown's extensive scholarship on African American poetry and culture is equally important to his merit. He persistently and quietly promoted the value of folk culture, including blues and jazz, through his teaching and writing at Howard University, when his interests were not generally shared nor valued there. Nevertheless, his impact on the field of poetry and on his many students, several of whom became famous in their own right, is testament to his persistence. Brown's significance in poetry was acknowledged through *The Collected Poems* being awarded the Lenore Marshall Poetry Prize in 1981.

POETRY

Southern Road. New York: Harcourt, Brace, 1932. (Out of Print)
The Last Ride of Wild Bill and Eleven Narrative Poems. Detroit: Broadside Press, 1975.
The Collected Poems of Sterling A. Brown. Ed. Michael S. Harper. Evanston, IL: Northwestern University Press, 1996.

EDITED ANTHOLOGY

(With Arthur P. Davis and Ulysses Lee). *The Negro Caravan*. New York: Dryden Press, 1941. Manchester: Ayer, 1969.

OTHER

A Son's Return: Selected Essays. Boston: Northeastern University Press, 1996.

REFERENCES

Bell, Bernard. *The Folk Roots of Contemporary Afro-American Poetry*. Detroit: Broadside Press, 1974.
Collier, Eugenia. "The Mythic Hero in Sterling Brown's Poetry." In *The Furious Flowering of African American Poetry*. Ed. Joanne Gabbin. Charlottesville: University of Virginia Press, 1999. 25–37.
Gabbin, Joanne V. *Sterling A. Brown: Building the Black Aesthetic Tradition*. Charlottesville: University of Virginia Press, 1985.
Sanders, Mark A. "The Ballad, the Hero, and the Ride: A Reading of Sterling A. Brown's 'The Last Ride of Wild Bill.' " In *The Furious Flowering of African American Poetry*. Ed. Joanne Gabbin. Charlottesville: University of Virginia Press, 1999. 118–34.
Smethhurst, James. " 'The Strong Men Gittin' Stronger': Sterling Brown and the Representation and Re-creation of the Southern Folk Voice." In *The New*

    Red Negro: The Literary Left and African American Poetry, 1930–1946. New York: Oxford University Press, 1999. 60–92.

Sterling Brown: A Special Issue. *Callaloo* 21.4 (1998): 775–1075.

Yarborough, Richard, ed. *A Son's Return: Selected Essays of Sterling A. Brown.* Boston: Northeastern University Press, 1996.

LUCILLE CLIFTON

(1936–)

Lucille Clifton
Credit: BOA Editions

Lucille Clifton's first book of poetry, *Good Times*, published in 1969, chronologically places her first publication alongside those of Nikki Giovanni and Sonia Sanchez, poets whose reputations were initially based on the pertinence of their work to the Black Arts Movement of the 1960s. However, Clifton's *Good Times* poems did not promote a black revolution through their content or structure. The title poem, "Good Times," written from a child's perspective, celebrates economic solvency within a family. Bills are paid, food is prepared, and relatives are singing, dancing, and enjoying each other; but lurking behind the good times is the threat of those other times. The remaining twenty-seven poems in the volumes are quiet, thoughtful, short lyrics, many of them untitled. Only nine short poems near the end of *Good Times*, told through the perspective of two young boys, acknowledge the burning and looting that were part of the civil rights conflict. In these nine poems, Clifton perceptively connects the civil rights struggle of the 1960s with a historical antecedent by referencing the heritage of the buffalo soldiers who, during the post–Civil War years, were the ninth and tenth all-black calvary units in the U.S. Army. Bridging these historical times has the effect of anchoring the poems in a timeless struggle. During the decade of her first publications, Clifton felt her poems on a variety of subjects were out of step with the protest poetry that characterized the era. These publications and subsequent ones have established Clifton as an individualistic poet whose work is always current as it adroitly and insightfully engages all that it means to be human.

Unlike Giovanni and Sanchez, who began publishing and became popular as very young writers, Clifton had six children under the age of ten and had been writing poetry for twenty years when *Good Times* appeared. Ishmael Reed, black novelist and essayist who was raised in Buffalo, New York, assisted in bringing Clifton to public notice by showing some of her work to Langston Hughes. Hughes then published a few of Clifton's poems in his anthology *Poetry of the Negro, 1746–1970* (1970). Robert Hayden, also a well-respected poet, arranged for Clifton to present her work to the YW–YMCA Poetry Center in New York after Clifton sent him samples of her writing in 1969. She also began in the same year a position as literature assistant for the Central Atlantic Regional Educational Laboratory in Washington, D.C.

Clifton attributes her literary talents to her parents, Samuel Louis Sr. and Thelma Moore Sayles. They lived in Depew, New York, a small steel mill town with a heavy concentration of Polish residents. Buffalo, the nearest large town, was twelve miles away. Clifton's father was an oral storyteller and her mother, a folk poet. The Sayles chose the name Thelma Lucille for Clifton but always called her Lucille, the name of her father's mother and his sister. One of Clifton's childhood memories is of her father walking to Buffalo and back to purchase a dining room set on the credit plan. They were the first family in their community to own one.

Clifton's own family history, community, connections among generations, spiritual links, and the indomitable survival skills of black women and families have been her ongoing subjects as she has written poetry that over time has established a fine literary reputation. In addition to her poetry, Clifton, who describes herself as being called to write, has also written plays, nineteen works of juvenile fiction, and a memoir titled *Generations* (1976). Clifton pays homage to her father's narrative ability in *Generations*, which she dedicated to Samuel Sayles Jr. because in it she lyrically records the family history that he had kept alive over the years. Her title conveys the family connections that are special to Clifton and that she has made a prominent component in her poetry. The memoir also documents her great-great-grandmother, Caroline Donald, called "Mammy Ca'line," born in Dahomey, Africa, in 1822. She was captured and enslaved in Virginia. During Reconstruction, Mammy Ca'line's daughter, Lucille (Clifton's namesake), was the first African American woman legally hanged in Virginia for killing the white father of her son. Clifton's poetry acknowledges and affirms this female ancestry in various ways, including a character called "Mammy Caline."

Clifton's father, Samuel, from Virginia, and her maternal grandfather from Georgia were friends before her parents married. The men left the South on the same train to Depew, lured by recruiters offering work to black men and a train trip to the employment. Other family members from both sides followed. Thus when Clifton's parents married, the second marriage for Samuel, their children grew up among a clan of transplanted black southerners and in a close-knit community. Clifton's parents moved to the larger town of Buffalo when she was a young girl, and her maternal grandparents soon followed. Although her father worked at the steel mill, the family's economic condition was tight, and family life for Clifton's mother Thelma was sometimes difficult. Thelma also experienced epileptic seizures, which become the subject in several of Clifton's poems. Clifton admired her mother and considered her a magic woman because she could decorate the house with items that other people might throw away, and she could open locked doors with little objects. Clifton's mother urged her to get away from Buffalo and to have what the mother considered a natural life.

Clifton's opportunity to leave her community came when she graduated at age sixteen and was awarded a scholarship to Howard University. As the first member of her family to attend college, her Buffalo community was justly proud of her scholarship. However, Howard University was not a nurturing experience for Clifton, who felt out of place with many of the upper-class, color-conscious young women she encountered there. Nevertheless, Clifton capitalized on being from New York and on being a drama major, the two factors that provided her with some social leverage. After two years, she returned home to disappointed parents, having lost her scholarship, and declared her intention to write poetry. In 1955 Clifton transferred to Fredonia State Teachers College in New York, where she graduated. Her earliest paid employment was not in the arts but in the modest position of a claims clerk in the unemployment office in Buffalo, New York, in 1958. That same year, she wed Fred James Clifton, a philosophy professor at the University of Buffalo. Throughout most of the 1960s her primary role was mother and wife. Her husband died in 1984.

Although Clifton has not always been widely known as a poet, her work is highly regarded and is increasingly being read by an enthusiastic audience. The cluster of significant prizes she has earned in recent years, in addition to earlier ones, illustrates the appeal of her work. Clifton has received honorary doctorates, a Pulitzer Prize Committee Citation in 1970, the Juniper Prize awarded by the University of Massachusetts Press for a volume of original poetry in 1980, and a Pulitzer Prize nomination in 1980. She was named poet laureate of Maryland in 1979. Additionally, she won an Emmy Award from the American Academy of Television Arts and Sciences and two fellowships from the National Endowment for the Arts. She received the Shelley Memorial Prize, the Charity Randall Citation, and a Lannan Literary Award. In 1996, Clifton became the only poet ever to have two books—*Next: New Poems* and *Good Woman: Poems and a Memoir, 1969–1980*—chosen as finalists for the Pulitzer Prize in the same year. She was appointed a chancellor of the Academy of American Poets in 1999 and elected a fellow of the American Academy of Arts and Sciences. The Getty Museum comissioned her to write a poem that has been etched in marble and is on perpetual display. In 1999 Clifton won the Lila Wallace Reader's Digest Writer's Award. In 2000 *Blessing the Boats: New and Selected Poems 1988–2000* won a National Book Award.

Like many contemporary poets, Clifton has been writer-in-residence or a visiting professor at numerous universities. Following the critical acclaim of *Good Times* she began teaching at Coppin State College in Baltimore, and in 1972, she was invited to Columbia University School of the Arts as a visiting professor. She has also taught at the University of California at Santa Cruz, and at the American University in Washington, D.C., and has been the Blackburn Professor of Creative Writing at Duke University. Clifton's academic home is St. Marys College of Maryland, where she is Distinguished Professor of Humanities.

In an interview with Charles Rowell in the journal *Callaloo*, Clifton affirms her love of writing poetry, her clarity of purpose, and her motivation. She writes from the perspective of being human, black, and female. She believes that her experiences are also part of the human story, so if they are omitted, then the story is incomplete. Clifton writes with a completeness of self. She believes that poetry is not an intellectual exercise, limited to the brain, but that it must encompass all of one's emotions, intuitions, and fears. Her poems can be enjoyed and understood without a reader knowing her race, but she feels that understanding her work is enhanced if her racial identity is known. Her language is deliberately simple, she has said, because she doesn't believe truth or intellectual honesty demands needless complexity.

Some of Clifton's most compelling poetry reflects her exploration of intergenerational connections. The subjects in some of her poems are literal physical links such as the intriguing fact of Clifton, her daughter, and her mother being born with six fingers on their hands; Clifton and her mother both being poets (though her mother was unpublished); and the notoriety of Clifton's female namesake. In "lucy and her girls" Clifton draws images from nature to show that the interdependency of mothers and daughters is natural. This connection is conveyed in several poems in *Two-Headed Woman* (1980), whose title uses a phrase in African American culture that refers to a conjurer or root worker, a person enabled with supernatural abilities. Clifton, in fact, has acknowledged that she heard her mother speaking to her from beyond the grave. The poems in the third section of *Two-Headed Woman* titled "the light that came to lucille clifton" reflect this experience, especially "testament," "perhaps," and "to joan," which alludes to Joan of Arc's hearing of voices. Other poems such as "february 13, 1980" and "poem on my fortieth birthday to my mother who died young" are informed by Clifton's relationship with her mother, but they also recognize the poet as a separate person. The volume *The Book of Light* (1993) also includes poems recognizing links between the women of Clifton's family. These include "daughters" and the oblique allusions in "it was a dream" and "thel."

The will to survive in black women, an ongoing subject in Clifton's work, is a quality that Clifton herself has illustrated as a survivor of breast cancer and of kidney failure and a kidney transplant. Nine brief poems referencing the cancer's diagnosis and treatment, including Clifton's mastectomy, appear in *The Terrible Stories* (1996) in a section ironically titled "From the Cadaver." "Amazons" identifies Clifton's sisterhood with Audre Lorde, a lesbian poet whose struggle with breast cancer ultimately ended in death. The poems in "From the Cadaver" range in emotion from bittersweet to an uneasy truce with the result of mastectomy, a scar that will be called a ribbon. They offer no self-pity, however. Rather, "hag riding" and "scar" affirm one woman's tenacity for living through the image of her riding life. She refuses to be thrown off, and she will not fall off.

Although several lyrical poems in *The Terrible Stories* communicate Clifton's stamina, she eloquently examines African American historical issues in a section of the volume titled "A Term in Memphis." Living in Memphis, Tennessee, for a semester where considerable racial violence had at one time occurred provoked Clifton's inquiry about the South in an unprecedented way. Several poems imaginatively consider relationships between the past and present, between African ancestors and their New World descendants, and between the Mississippi River and the state of that name. A similar thematic connection is maintained in the volume *Next* (1987) where Clifton writes about African slaves, present and past victims of war, and those close to the poet who have died young.

Clifton's occasional poems often convey her subtle sense of humor. Several unabashedly celebrate certain physical features of black women that have been disparaged in American culture. These include "homage to my hair" and "homage to my hips" in *Two-Headed Woman*. "[T]hem and us" in *The Book of Light* offers an example of Clifton's insightful humor in pointing out the psyche of "them" who believe that Elvis still lives while black people understand through their painful history about the inexorable nature of death. Thus they are certain about dead Elvis but remain on the lookout for Marvin Gaye.

The nineteen new poems in *Blessing the Boats: New and Selected Poems 1988–2000* are tightly integrated and thematically specific works. Clifton begins by advancing the idea that the world is somehow in reverse, that irrationality has displaced rationality. When birds weep, squirrels are attentive, dogs look away in pity (in "the times") or "birds begin to walk," and "crows . . . stand in the road and watch" (in "signs"), these are the signs of a world in reverse. Nature is, in effect, alerting us, and we should know how to interpret the meaning of these signs. The primary indication of human irrationality, blatant violence, is exposed through its varying forms against children and adults. Against this primary theme, several other poems engage the possibility of salvation, hope, and transformation under mystical circumstances. Death, grief for the world, and persistent evil as subjects in the last of the new poems, however, suggest that given the overwhelming evidence of ongoing violence, Clifton is unable to envision a radical transformation for America's society. While these subjects may seem dark or pessimistic, Clifton varies the way she engages them, thus diffusing their impact.

Her strategy in the new poems of *Blessing the Boats* integrates the general subject of violence with a specific incidence of it, as if to prevent a numbing disconnection that can occur when violence is discussed in a way that allows it to be distant from our own experiences. Thus in the first poem, "the times," is the line "another child has killed a child." The violence engages the speaker, but the absence of names and geographical specificity also allows her psychological self-distancing. Additionally, the speaker initially expresses relief that the victim and perpetrator are not of her racial group. However, she shortly concludes that any child victim of violence is her child. "[T]he times" thus establishes Clifton's attitude that no citizen can dismiss or distance the violence that is happening all around him or her. In "moonchild," the violence is specific as the speaker recalls herself as an innocent, giggling ten-year-old girl being inducted into unmentionable knowledge by learning about French kissing from her father rather than experimention with her male peers. In "donor," an adult woman recalls the violence she used thirty years earlier trying to dislodge a fetus, but the baby persisted. The poem's title refers to a kidney being given to the mother who tried to sabotage the fetus. The donor is that daughter who refused the mother's efforts to abort her. A different kind of violence is the subject of "dialysis," a poem obviously based on Clifton's personal medical history. This is violence done to the body by cancer first and now by the failing organs that "refused to continue . . . after the cancer."

The violence of racism is the subject of several poems—"libation," "the photograph: a lynching," "jasper texas 1998," and "alabama 9/15/63." The first poem pays homage to a historically based physical and psychic fragmentation when the speaker pours a small amount of whiskey on the ground in homage to an imaginary old man, a physically and emotionally scarred victim who lived in slavery. "[L]ibation" thus sets the general stage for the continuing spiral of racially inspired violence across the years—a lynching, the story of James Byrd's vicious dismemberment in Jasper, Texas, in 1998, and the bombing deaths of the four girls in Sunday school in Birmingham, Alabama, in 1963. Acts of racist violence also visit psychological violence on the family members, a fact expressed by referring to James Byrd's daughters in the poem about him. Then there is the personal violence that people inadvertently or deliberately practice against themselves. The speaker in these poems offers specific personal instances—her father's work, her Aunt Blanch who attempted to roll her body "into the street," and a brother who seemed to will his death.

Against these public and more private forms of violence, however, Clifton seems to hold out hope for diminishing its epidemic quality as she suggests in "study the masters." And in three poems titled "lazarus" on the first, second, and third days, Clifton alludes to the biblical story of a man being raised from the dead. She suggests in these poems that transformation, presumably from the violent and worrisome state of the world, is possible. The Lazarus of the third day has extremely heightened senses, as he can hear and see nature unfolding. He orders his sisters away "from the door to my grave," a line that conveys the subject's returning from death to life. Whatever the possibilities, however, one certainty is death.

That certainty informs the last three poems that blend the poet's private experience and her concern for the world in which she lives. "birthday 1999" offers the haunting image of a train coming closer, like the carriage for Emily Dickinson's speaker. The train has a "cracked set labeled lucille." In "grief" Clifton alludes to herself and perhaps other women in her family by including their distinctive trait of being born with twelve fingers. The poem acknowledges the grief of the world from creation to present time. The last of the new poems, "report from the angel of eden," makes use of the biblical story of Creation to say that evil was created along with the world. One angel, who resists joining those angels who introduce evil, asks what will happen to paradise. The poem offers no answer, but the title poem, "blessing the boats," offers a nebulous possibility for individual survival where no concrete answer exists for ending the violence and grief that plague us. "[B]lessing the boats" uses the metaphor of an incoming and outgoing tide and asks for transport in innocence. Its message is to "open eyes to water waving forever in innocence sail thru." It seems a fitting conclusion to the subjects Clifton has explored in these new poems. Violence and innocence are opposite poles, similar to the position the Lazarus of her poems finds himself in on the second day, when he hears voices calling to him from both ends of his existence. People can gravitate to either end of this pole, but the gravitation toward violence surely means death and grief in its physical or metaphysical permutations. But like Lazarus, one can ride the tides and sail through this to that.

Winning the National Book Award for *Blessing the Boats* significantly singles out Clifton's work. This award, as has others she has won, recognizes the overall excellence of her poetry. Clifton writes with directness, honesty, humor, economy, and profound concern for the individual life. Like Robert Frost's work, the apparent simplicity of her poems is often shrouded in metaphysical and philosophical questions that can engage readers on many levels without entangling them in abstruse literary allusions. Many of her poems can be read as investigations about her own life and family through which she seeks an understanding of larger humanity. Clifton's biography, about which she has been quite revealing, confirms this association. Using the self as a means for personal revelation while simultaneously exploring the humanity that unites us all is a task that has animated the work of many previous generations of fine poets.

POETRY

Good Times: Poems. New York: Random House, 1969. (Out of Print)
Good News about the Earth: New Poems. New York: Random House, 1972. (Out of Print)
An Ordinary Woman. New York: Random House, 1974.
Two-Headed Woman. Amherst: University of Massachusetts Press, 1980. (Out of Print)
Good Woman: Poems and a Memoir, 1969–1980. Rochester: BOA Editions, Limited, 1987.
Next: New Poems. Rochester: BOA Editions, Limited, 1987. (Out of Print)
Quilting: Poems 1987–1990. Brockport, NY: BOA Editions, 1991.
The Book of Light. Port Townsend, WA: Copper Canyon Press, 1993.
The Terrible Stories. Rochester: BOA Editions, Limited, 1996.
Blessing the Boats: New and Selected Poems 1988–2000. Rochester: BOA Editions, Limited, 2000.

MEMOIR

Generations. New York: Random House, 1976. (Out of Print)

REFERENCES

Holladay, Hilary. " 'I am not grown away from you': Lucille Clifton's Elegies for her Mother." *College Language Association Journal* 42.4 (June 1999): 430–44.
Hull, Akasha [Gloria]. "Channeling the Ancestral Muse: Lucille Clifton and Do-

lores Kindrick." In *Female Subjects in Black and White: Race, Psychoanalysis, Feminism*. Eds. Elizabeth Abel, Barbara Christian, and Helen Moglen. Berkeley: University of California Press, 1997. 330–348.

Madhubuti, Haki. "Lucille Clifton: Warm Water, Greased Legs, and Dangerous Poetry." In *Black Women Writers 1950–1980*. Ed. Mari Evans. New York: Anchor, 1984. 150–160.

McCluskey, Audrey T. "Tell the Good News: A View of the Works of Lucille Clifton." In *Black Women Writers 1950–1980*. Ed. Mari Evans. New York: Anchor, 1984. 139–49.

Peppers, Wallace. "Lucille Clifton." In *Dictionary of Literary Biography*. Vol. 41. Ed. Trudier Harris and Thadious Davis. Detroit: Gale Research, 1985. 55–60.

Rowell, Charles H. "An Interview with Lucille Clifton." *Callaloo* 22.1 (1999): 56–72.

WANDA COLEMAN

(1946–   )

Wanda Coleman
Credit: Black Sparrow Press

The author of poetry and fiction, Coleman has worked as a medical secretary, magazine editor, journalist, and scriptwriter. She has been the recipient of several prestigious awards. Coleman's outstanding work as a staff writer for NBC won an Emmy Award for best writing in a daytime drama from the Academy of Television Arts and Sciences in 1976 for the daytime series *Days of Our Lives*. In 1981–1982, she received a National Endowment for the Arts Fellowship, and in 1984 she was awarded a Guggenheim Fellowship for poetry. *Bathwater Wine* (1998), in competition with 200 other volumes of poetry, was selected as the winner for the 1999 Lenore Marshall Poetry Prize, a cash prize of $10,000 given annually by the Academy of American Poets and *The Nation* magazine. Coleman is only the second black poet to win the award (Sterling Brown was the first), and the sixth woman in the twenty-five years of the award's existence.

The pathway to these recognitions, however, has been an arduous one for Coleman. Unlike many contemporary writers, she came to writing primarily without mentors. She attended California State College at Los Angeles (now California State University) in 1964 and Los Angeles City College in 1967. Whatever guidance she experienced came through her participation in several workshops. After the 1965 Watts riots she was involved in an arts studio and later attended a workshop called Writers West. When Writers Guild of America, West, opened to minorities, she went there. Mostly, Coleman was sustained by her own drive and by her desires for her children. In the early years of her writing, in fact, Coleman had to choose between freelance journalism, editing, and poetry. Poetry often took the back seat because journalism at least paid when she could get assignments.

Coleman was born in the California community of Watts, in the south central section of Los Angeles, the oldest of two brothers and a sister. In spite of the community's reputation for violence and unemployment, Coleman has said that her parents, George and Lewana Scott Evans, and their neighbors were decent, hardworking, and law-abiding people. Her father operated a sign shop but also worked as a janitor for RCA Victor in the evenings. Her mother also worked outside the home. She saw her community gradually become the economically blighted site that dominates the public image of Watts, but her childhood memories of growing up there are positive, in spite of her parents' financial struggles. Coleman was one of the smart students at John C. Fremont High School. Oratory was her forte, and she competed on a team with five other black students in the public speech and debate society's national program of high school competitions. She was dubbed "the professor," and no one invited her to the senior prom because of her intelligence. Coleman also felt the rejection of being dark-skinned and physically large, but her close relationship with her mother offered compensation. Reading offered additional solace from the isolation she experienced from her peers. In an essay, Coleman has written about her father taking her to the library with him where she could briefly rummage through adult fiction. But it was the gift from her cousin of *The Adventures of Alice in Wonderland and Through the Looking Glass* when she was twelve years old that gave her a situation and character to apply to herself. Lewis Carroll's "Jabberwocky" became her favorite poem, which she memorized along with a handful of others. Alice's stepping through the mirror, according to Coleman, provided her a means for seeing herself. After high school, Coleman sporadically attended college, but financial considerations were a primary deterrent to its completion.

Coleman met her husband, a young man of English Irish descent, when he came to the area in the early 1960s along with Jesse Jackson and Stockley Carmichael as troubleshooters for the Student Nonviolent Coordinating Committee (SNCC). By 1965 they were married and starting their family. By 1969, she had two children but was divorced. She and the children subsisted off unemployment insurance. She remarried twice more, the third time in the 1980s, and also had another child. Her three children are Anthony, Tunisia, and Ian Wayne Grant.

Coleman's poetry is informed by an autobiographical impulse, and most of her settings are based in her south central Los Angeles community of Watts. Her themes encompass the highs and lows of male and female relationships, economic powerlessness, and sexual inequities. She writes about the particular isolation, alienation, and harassment experienced by black women as a result of not meeting the idealized images of beauty in American culture. She reveals her home life with her three siblings and her toiling parents. Her interest travels outside her parents' home to encompass the young people with whom she grew up and went to school. She writes of neighborhood boys' lives misdiagnosed and killed off by the larger society. She writes of drugs, alcoholism, and the desert of economic opportunity that Watts became, especially after the riot in 1965. The disappointments of a struggling, working mother between husbands or lovers, interracial unions, society's response to them, and the problems of interracial children also are thematic interests in Coleman's poetry.

Although personal experience seems to be the driving force behind most of Coleman's poetry, her work is not narrowly self-centered. When Coleman uses an incident or emotion that she experienced, she fashions a poem that addresses the issue in the lives of many women who share certain characteristics with her. Her experiences, her family, and the community are largely representative. For example, the father called "Daddyboy" in the poem "Strappling" is any father playing with his children by tossing them almost to the ceiling and playing horse by carrying them on his back through the house while "mommygirl" looks out at them from the kitchen. "By Watching Daddy I Learn About Men & Stuff," also a poem where the father's activity is central, is representative of lessons being learned through observation. The poem is structured as a random list of what the observing girl learns, but perhaps the most important fact is the last, that "few women speak the language of men." Coleman's matrilineal ties are strong as well, but she has numerous poems either about or inspired by her father, including his deteriorating illness and his grave site.

Coleman effectively sprinkles specific detail throughout her poems, especially when her objective is to enhance the image of Watts as the physical site. Thus, she includes street names, the names of local hangouts, and games that her father and other men played during their recreational time. However, Coleman is equally effective writing in the abstract. "Flight of the California Condor," for example, details white flight from her neighborhood and her school and its subsequent peopling by immigrants of color. With stealth and restraint, however, she uses the metaphor of birds and never mentions race.

The "birds" that Coleman creates in "Flight of the California Condor" suggests her wry sense of humor. It is pervasive even when it is subdued, but its sharpness is nevertheless present. This level of wit is often obvious in poems that address subjects of sadness, such as in "Things No One Knows," a litany of the effects of immediate poverty and self-pity. Coleman's particular brand of humor emerges in lines such as "even my begging cup has mold sprouting in its well." Another source of humor is located in black urban vernacular language that Coleman massages into other uses, as in American sonnets, number 35: "usta be young usta be gifted—still black."

In structuring her poems, Coleman most often creates the form she wishes the poem to have. Very little of the traditional will be found, especially in her later books. In *Bathwater Wine*, section three is titled "More American Sonnets" (26–86), but they are written in free verse and of varying line length, but mostly fourteen or fifteen lines. Also in this collection, Coleman includes numerous prose poems in the last section and a few appear as well in *Hand Dance*.

Coleman's range as a poet defies containment. Her interests, cares, experiences, pains, and joys touch the universe, and she is capable of its interpretation. Perhaps her greatest achievement is her ability to make art out of her life and, in the process, to create art from the lives of others. Coleman sings everyone's blues and celebrates their jubilation as well.

POETRY

Mad Dog Black Lady. Santa Rosa, CA: Black Sparrow Press, 1979. (Out of Print)
Imagoes. Santa Rosa, CA: Black Sparrow Press, 1983.
Heavy Daughter Blues: Poems & Stories 1968–1986. Santa Rosa, CA: Black Sparrow Press, 1987; 1991.
African Sleeping Sickness: Stories and Poems. Santa Rosa, CA: Black Sparrow Press, 1990. (Out of Print)
Hand Dance. Santa Rosa, CA: Black Sparrow Press, 1993.
American Sonnets. Kenosha, WI: Membrane Press, 1994.
Bathwater Wine. Santa Rosa, CA: Black Sparrow Press, 1998. (Out of Print)
Mercurochrome: New Poems. Santa Rosa, CA: Black Sparrow Press, 2001.

CHAPBOOK

Art in the Court of the Blue Fag. Santa Rosa, CA: Black Sparrow Press, 1977.

ESSAYS

Native in a Strange Land: Trials and Tremors. Santa Rosa, CA: Black Sparrow Press, 1996. (Out of Print)

REFERENCES

Ciruaru, Carmela, ed. *First Loves: Poets Introduce the Essential Poems That Captivated and Inspired Them*. New York: Scribner, 2000. 58–61.
Stanley, Sandra K. "Wanda Coleman." In *The Oxford Companion to African American Literature*. Ed. William L. Andrews, Frances Smith Foster, and Trudier Harris. New York: Oxford University Press, 1997. 60.

JAYNE CORTEZ

(1936–   )

Jayne Cortez
Credit: Jayne Cortez

Cortez is widely known for her performance poetry accompanied by jazz. While this mode of presenting poetry was a popular practice for bring the art form directly to the community in the 1960s, the practice lapsed. Cortez, however, has persisted in perpetuating the marriage of these two complementary art forms. Since her first published volume of poetry, each succeeding volume has illustrated the influence of musical rhythms and musicians on her poems as she has explored numerous other issues.

Cortez was born in Fort Huachuca (WaCHOO-ca), Arizona, where her father was stationed at the army base. She was the middle child between an older sister and a younger brother. The family moved when Cortez was seven, relocating to the Watts community in Los Angeles, where she was reared. Cortez wanted to be an actress and attended Compton Junior College. However, she put her aspirations aside and married jazz musician Ornette Coleman in 1954 at age eighteen. Their son, Denardo Coleman, was born in 1956. Cortez subsequently remarried Melvin Edwards, an illustrator, and studied drama at the Ebony Showcase in Los Angeles in 1960.

Between 1964 and 1970 Cortez worked as artistic director of the Watts Repertory Theatre Company, which she cofounded. Her directing of plays, acting, and reading her poetry provided a creative stimulus, and in 1964 she began recording her poetry with music. Similarly, the civil rights movement provided immeasurable influence on her creativity and personal politics. The thrust for civil rights in the southern states propelled Cortez to Mississippi where she worked with Fannie Lou Hamer on voter registration. In 1967 Cortez moved to New York. She eventually became writer-in-residence at Livingston College at Rutgers University in New Brunswick, New Jersey, from 1977 to 1983. In 1980 Cortez organized her own band, The Firespitters, to accompany her work. She has recorded six compact discs of poetry accompanied by jazz. Denardo Coleman performs as a drummer with the band his mother created.

Cortez entered the literary world during the cultural and civil rights fervor of the 1960s. The political and social concerns that marked the writing and thinking of that era and the new style of writing poetry were evident, in part, in Cortez's work. However, she always illustrated an intensely individual style of expressing the issues and themes that dominate her work. Spontaneity is a hallmark of Cortez's style, although it is perhaps unapparent as the work appears on the page. However, in a brief foreword to *Poetic Magnetic* (1991), Cortez admits that during a recording session for her poetry, to which she brings prepared material, she creates the real structure while she is working. During her performance, she also composes "on the spot." She views her working through music as a way of extending the role of the poet through extending the possibilities of technology. "I am trying to move this combination of poetry, music, and technology to a higher poetic level. It's the poetic use of music, the poetic use of technology, the poetic orchestration of it all," she has said (*Poetic* 6).

Cortez primarily writes praise poems, broadly explained as poems influenced by the structure and mood of blues and protest poems. Her broad sociopolitical agenda reflects the range of her concerns from the individual to the worldly. She writes about loss, exploitation, greed, corruption, fraud, commercial silliness, and the murdering of children through the narcotics supplied by drug dealers. Love and women's sexuality are also among her subjects. The style of the poem seems chosen to fit its content, but Cortez does not use conventional forms such as the sonnet or the villanelle, a French verse form of nineteen lines divided into five three-line groupings and a final four-line stanza, with a recurring, intricate rhyming pattern in certain lines. Her geographic and cultural visions cover a broad map that is reflective of her extensive travel in Africa, Latin America, Europe, Canada, and South America. Overall, many allusions in Cortez's poetry reflect her travels and interests, but her references to African culture are particularly apparent. In fact, in 1973 when she published *Scarifications*, a descriptive word for the decorative and facially identifying marks characteristic of some African people, Cortez changed the name of the publishing company she had founded and rechristened it Bola Press. Bola in Yoruba, a Nigerian language, means "successful."

Jon Woodson links Cortez's work to American surrealist poets in their employment of African art, blues, and jazz and to the writing of the Negritude poets. The Negritude poets—black European-educated students that included Léopold Sédar Senghor of Senegal, West Africa, and Aimé Césaire of Martinique in the French Caribbean—initiated a literary movement in the 1930s to reclaim and recenter their respective African cultures that had been decentered by European colonialism. Woodson's comparison of Cortez to the work of the Negritude poets suggests that he identifies several qualities in her work that are focused by a commitment to African cultural memory.

However, Cortez also firmly grounds herself in the underspaces of African American experience, particularly by the setting and quality of life implied in the title of her first collection of poems, *Pissstained Stairs and the Monkey Man's Wares* (1969). The volume's title appears in the poem titled "Lead," a reference to the blues singer Leadbelly. The poem is not specifically about the singer, but it suggests the place and value of blues in an environment characterized by poverty and commercial exploitation. Because blues and jazz have been art forms that have chronicled and communicated various permutations of African American experience that differentiate it from mainstream experience, Cortez pays homage to these musical chroniclers in this first volume. She includes Charlie Parker, Huddie "Leadbelly" Ledbetter, Dinah Washington, Ornette Coleman, Billie Holiday, John Coltrane, and Theodore "Fats" Navarro, better known as Fats Waller. Cortez practices visual aerobatics with some of the poems, a technique reflective of the 1960s black poet's flair for disrupting poetic convention. For example, "Dinah's Back in Town" is printed as if the right-page margin is the top margin; thus the book has to be turned ninety degrees for conventional placement of the reading material. In several other poems, the title is printed alongside the left-page margin rather than at the top of the page. Cortez's language in this volume and in her others is representative of a distinctively black spoken language, often with a hard urban edge. The language is unflinchingly direct when it needs to be so, when Cortez's subjects reflect the way human life can be wasted as she does in "A Gathering of Fishes Dried with Salt Waiting to Wiggle in the Net of Life." This poem tells about a girl at sixteen who has experienced too much of the wrong side of life. Another poem, "Race," engages black male homosexuality. According to the poem's speaker, same-sex preference is a threat to black people as a racially defined group.

In her second volume, Cortez expands her aesthetic and her thematic concerns. Whereas the first volume had been focused by its attention to musicians and to specific instances of communal loss and pain, *Festivals and Funerals* (1971) reflects broader concerns. The title poem, for example, "Festivals & Funerals," mourns the deaths of black leaders Patrice Lumumba and Malcolm X in Africa and in America, respectively. It recognizes other kinds of death, too, brought about through poverty, drugs, and violence. The balancing of "festivals" against "funerals" in the title suggests stasis and equality; any celebration is balanced by death. We die when leaders die ("our flesh of a flesh is Lumumba our flesh Lumumba"), and the results of fear and sadness are not relieved in words but in the blues. The speaker in "Watching a Parade in Harlem 1970" evaluates the event through a politically astute perspective as he designates it an example of the "corroded culture of colonialism." The speaker slices through the superficial gaiety to arrive at the very core—an illus-

tration of the dominant over the weak with the victim being unknow-
ingly coerced into admiration for his or her oppressor. "African Night
Suite," apparently inspired by Cortez's travels to Africa, merges African
and African American perspectives in a poem that affirms the experience
of both. The speaker begins by requesting of Africa that her sight be
released from "the mercenaries of illusion," presumably American. In a
transcendent moment, the speaker renounces the pains of black American history and surrenders her "shadow of sorrow" to become a receptive African woman to her ancestral history. But the memory that
repositions the speaker within her heritage is incomplete without that of
the translantic migration and its cultural and physical disruptions. Cortez renders this part of the poem through a collage of surrealistic images
of weapons and death. However, people survived, and the survivors are
imagined as birds receiving both African and American cultures.

   In subsequent volumes, Cortez plays variations on the themes and
styles that she established in her first two volumes. She writes about the
city dweller, politically charged events during the Vietnam conflict, the
massacre at Attica prison, the ongoing struggle for liberation of African
nations, the escalating problems of South Africa, and American police
brutailty. She increases her use of irony and continues to refine her poetic
form. Jazz continues to inform her work, as in "Rose Solitude" for Duke
Ellington, and she is always aware of heroes and heroines in areas other
than in music.

   Somewhere in Advance of Nowhere (1996) offers full evidence of a poet
who has been writing for close to thirty years. It is a volume richly
evocative of the ideas and techniques that have previously engaged Cortez, particularly in her recognition of the international. The volume begins, for example, with a three-part poetic homage to the Cuban poet
Nicholás Guillen, inspired, in part, by Cortez's visit to Cuba in 1985
where she was among a group of American writers and a sculptor invited to visit with Nancy Morejon and Guillen. Cuba feels like West
Africa to her: She recognizes the dilapidation that is visible to an American eye, but she can see beyond the superficial to a natural physical
beauty and to a beauty of spirit. In the second part of the homage, titled
"Aduepe," a word meaning "thanks" in the Yoruba language of Nigeria,
Cortez finds the Cuba of Guillen's poetry but not the man himself. Referencing rhythms and images of dance, Cortez suggests the glorious
richness and completeness of Guillen's work. She employs an exhilarating catalog to evoke the energy of his work: "I stood in the stadium of
his staccato yelping poetry and heard messages coded and covered with
drum heads from Oyo." The last of the three tribute poems, the shortest

and most direct, details Cortez's meeting Guillen, finally, with a delegation of African American poets in 1985. The overall tone of this volume is characterized by an exhuberance about life and the small natural beauties of earth. It recognizes the persistent nature of change through recognizing that in 1985 political change is afoot in Pretoria, South Africa, and in Haiti, where in both places the original inhabitants are reclaiming what was taken away from them, unlike, however, the original inhabitants of Arizona. In fact, Cortez retains a critical edge for American problems as expressed in "New York City Pigeons" and "1988 Now What."

Cortez's immersion in her music-centered art has been consistent since the beginning of her career. Her work continues to illustrate the perfect joining between the complementary arts of poetry and music and a profound respect for poets who have inspired her. Cortez's voice is a vital component in the chorus of African American poetry.

POETRY

Pissstained Stairs and the Monkey Man's Wares. New York: Phrase Text, 1969. (Out of Print)
Festivals and Funerals. New York: Bola Press, 1971. (Out of Print)
Scarifications. New York: Bola Press, 1973. (Out of Print)
Mouth on Paper. New York: Bola Press, 1977. (Out of Print)
Firespitter. New York: Bola Press, 1982. (Out of Print)
Mervilleux Coup de Fondre Poetry of Jayne Cortez & Ted Joans. Paris: Handshake Editions, 1982. (Out of Print)
Coagulations: New and Selected Poems. New York: Thunder's Mouth Press, 1984. (Out of Print)
Poetic Magnetic. New York: Bola Press, 1991. (Out of Print)
Somewhere in Advance of Nowhere. New York: High Risk Books, 1996.

RECORDINGS

Maintain Control. New York: Bola Press, 1986.
Everywhere Drums. New York: Bola Press, 1990.
Cheerful & Optimistic Poetry and Music. New York: Bola Press, 1994.
Taking the Blues Back Home: Poetry & Music. New York: Harmolodic/Verve, 1996.

REFERENCES

"Jane Cortez: Supersurrealist Vision." In *Heroism in the New Black Poetry.* Ed. D.H. Melhem. Lexington: University Press of Kentucky, 1990. 181–95.
Redmond, Eugene B. *Drumvoices: The Mission of Afro-American Poetry, a Critical History.* Garden City, NY: Anchor/Doubleday, 1976.
Woodson, Jon. "Jane Cortez." In *Dictionary of Literary Biography.* Vol. 41. Ed. Thadious Davis and Trudier Harris. Detroit: Gale Research, 1985. 69–74.

Countee Cullen

(1903–1946)

Countee Cullen
Credit: Atlanta University Center, Robert W. Woodruff Library, Cullen-Jackman Memorial Collection
Photo credit: Carl Van Vechten

ullen was the poster poet of the great period of productivity during the 1920s, the Harlem Renaissance, also known as the New Negro Movement, a period of artistic productivity physically centered in Harlem, New York. Cullen won poetry contests, published two well-regarded volumes of poetry, received a master's degree from Harvard University, and married the daughter of W.E.B. Du Bois, one of the founders of the National Association for the Advancement of Colored People (NAACP) and editor of its journal, *The Crisis*. Unlike many of the writers who made their way to Harlem during the great migration, Cullen had grown up in New York as the adopted son of Reverend and Mrs. Frederick A. Cullen of the Salem African Methodist Episcopal Church.

Some confusion exists about Cullen's place of birth, which has variously been given as Louisville, Kentucky, Baltimore, Maryland, and New York City. By some accounts, his mother, Elizabeth Lucas, named him Countee LeRoy, and he was raised by his paternal grandmother, Elizabeth Porter, until her death in New York in 1918. What is certain is that the Cullens unofficially adopted Countee in 1918, and he grew to adulthood in their middle-class home. Reverend Cullen was a political and social activist as well as a respected minister, and his home provided a developing Countee with a view of black leadership, of fighting racial injustice, and of masculine gentility. Reverend Cullen went with a group of black citizens who met in 1919 with President Woodrow Wilson to seek his intervention in the treatment of black World War I veterans, thirteen of whom had been executed in Texas. Undoubtedly, Reverend and Mrs. Cullen's home also advocated educational achievement for Countee and encouraged his propensity for writing.

Having begun writing at an early age, Cullen published a poem in his DeWitt Clinton High School magazine in 1921 and was vice president of his class and, like many other black poets, editor of his school newspaper and its literary magazine, the *Magpie*. After his graduation in 1922, he attended New York University, where his scholarship earned him a Phi Beta Kappa key. He began gaining attention for his writing by winning several prizes, especially in 1925. *Poetry* magazine awarded him its John Reed Memorial Prize for "Threnody for a Brown Girl"; he won the Spingarn contest in *Crisis* magazine with "Two Moods of Love" and second prize in the poetry contests of *Palms* and *Opportunity*. Cullen's first book of poetry, *Color*, was published in 1925 by Harper and Row, a major New York publisher. Also in 1925, Cullen entered Harvard University to study for the M.A. degree in creative writing, which he earned in

1926. Boston-born poet of African Caribbean ancestry William Stanley Braithwaite, who promoted American verse through annual yearbooks of poetry culled from magazines, included Cullen's early work in his annual anthologies and commended the young poet's outstanding ability.

Color was divided into three sections titled "Color," "Epitaphs," and "Varia." "Epitaphs" offered poems on Cullen's model poet, nineteenth-century British Romantic John Keats, and on Paul Laurence Dunbar, among others; "Varia" contained a poetry miscellany including "She of the Dancing Feet Sings" and "To John Keats, Poet. At Springtime," both frequently anthologized works. "Color," the first section, contained most of Cullen's most widely known and anthologized poems including "A Brown Girl Dead," "To a Brown Girl," "Simon the Cyrenian Speaks," "Incident," "Heritage," and "Yet Do I Marvel." "Incident" represents the memory of an eight-year-old traveler to Baltimore who innocently said "Hello" to a fellow white traveler who was not a bit bigger but who called the innocent "nigger." That memory overwhelmed any others about the trip. This brief poem succeeds not only because Cullen presented a dramatic incident of one child destroying the innocence of another child but also because he fashioned the rhyme to reflect the verbal agility of the children involved. It becomes both telling and cruelly ironic, then, that a white eight-year-old could so damagingly injure his black age mate.

"Heritage," dedicated to Cullen's close friend Harold Jackman, is one among several of Cullen's poems that interrogated the meaning of an Africa lost to many black Americans. Beginning with the question "What is Africa to me," the narrator indicates many misconceptions of the continent through a mix of images romantic and realistic and Christian and pagan. That ancient place, the poem suggests, is physically and culturally inaccessible.

In 1926, Cullen served as assistant editor to Charles Johnson at *Opportunity* magazine, the official publication of the Urban League. The editorship placed Cullen in an influential place at a significant time in black literary history, for the position provided him a public platform for his views, the opportunity to promote other writers if he chose, and a place for reviewing other writers. One of his most provocative and perhaps famous reviews was the one of Langston Hughes's *The Weary Blues* (1926), where Cullen cautioned Hughes against becoming a racial artist. Hughes reciprocated with the same phrase in his famous essay "The Negro Artist and the Racial Mountain."

Cullen's perspective concerning writing Negro poetry, the term iden-

tifying black Americans in the 1920s, incited discussion and some outrage in his day, which has persisted and shadowed the critical
appreciation of his work. The 1960s poets of the Black Aesthetic Movement were particularly intolerant of Cullen's viewpoint. Cullen, like William Stanley Braithwaite, believed that art should be free of any
restrictions occasioned by race. Unlike Hughes who urged poets to cull
Negro life at all levels for their inspiration and subjects, Cullen did not
accept the idea that his poetry should always treat racial themes. He
rejected the idea that his art should always argue against social injustice
for the Negro or be limited to Negro subjects, whatever someone thought
those subjects were. Thus, he resisted being labeled as writing "Negro
poetry" merely because he was a Negro. In "Yet Do I Marvel," one of
Cullen's most frequently anthologized sonnets, he addresses this dilemma, though the poem leaves the question of whether Cullen was
writing about himself or more generally about black writers. The poem
begins with examples of the various confounding puzzles in human existence that God could explain should he "quibble" to do so. He could
explain why moles are blind, why humans must die, and why Tantalus
and Sisyphus, two mythological beings, received their respective pun-
ishments. The last of these puzzles that God might explain is "To make
a poet black, and bid him sing!" The profound nature of the inquiry,
suggested by the comparisons, confirms the weight of this race and art
problem for Cullen. It must have been bitterly ironic for him, then, that
the poems where race is a significant component are the poems that have
secured his literary reputation.

Cullen's productivity peaked in the 1920s when in 1927 he published
his second volume *Copper Sun*, his third volume *Ballad of the Brown Girl*,
and edited the anthology *Caroling Dusk: An Anthology of Verse by Negro
Poets*. Like James Weldon Johnson's 1922 anthology *The Book of American
Negro Poetry*, Cullen's book was significant because it packaged for the
public the young voices that have become known as the major poets of
the Harlem Renaissance. The young editor also articulated his position
about his poetry and his poetic models. Unfortunately, none of the 1927
volumes surpassed the success of *Color*, which had sold 2,000 copies.
Ballad of the Brown Girl, a single long poem, was offered as a separate
volume. It told of a girl of African descent and a white girl and their
relationship with a white man, a love triangle, in other words, made
more dramatic by race and their tragic deaths. Cullen had based it on a
British ballad where the term "brown girl" referred to a peasant. Written
while Cullen was a sophomore at New York University, the poem had
won second place in the national Witter Bynner poetry contest for un-

dergraduates. *Cooper Sun* contained the poem "From the Dark Tower," which was also the title of the column Cullen wrote in *Opportunity*. The poem addresses the tireless work of black people in America and the benefit it has been to others. Somewhat optimistically, it also envisions a change in the future. Some other poems are thematically linked by love, a subject Cullen explored in many poems.

Like his models, the British Romantic poets, particularly John Keats, Cullen was traditional in style, writing ballads, sonnets, and lyrics. This position set him apart from several of his literary contemporaries whose poetry was more modern in its form and subject matter. Hughes, for example, was interested in exploding the conventional boundaries of poetic form and content and creating his own poetic forms. Critics have theorized that Cullen's inability or refusal to embrace the modern was responsible for his withdrawal from writing in the last two decades of his short life.

In April 1928, Cullen married Nina Yolande Du Bois, the daughter of W.E.B. Du Bois, in the social event of the year. Attended by all the important writers and dignitaries of the city, nevertheless, the marriage was short-lived, and the couple divorced in 1930. In the year of his marriage, Cullen also won a Guggenheim Fellowship for poetry, which supported his travel to France. He enjoyed France and returned there during summers in the 1930s until the beginnings of World War II. He also traveled to other locations in Europe in the 1920s and to Palestine. Cullen remarried in 1940 to Ida Mae Roberson.

Although Cullen's perspective about his art was controversial, he was not known for writing controversial poems. However, the title poem in *The Black Christ and Other Poems* (1929) might have raised eyebrows. The title poem is a long narrative poem that begins with the narrator's coming to God, in spite of stumbling blocks. The narrator's brother had experienced an innocent relationship with a white woman but had nevertheless been murdered by a white mob. Although the dying brother had acquired the glow of saintliness, the surviving brother is outraged that God has permitted this injustice. Their mother's faith remains steadfast, however, and the doubting brother returns to the Christian fold. The end of the poem suggests that the family will enjoy an earthly paradise. Several other poems in the volume address racial subjects. Notably, "To Certain Critics" defends Cullen against critics who found his protest too genteel.

Cullen had been a major poetic voice of the period called the Harlem Renaissance, but when the depression arrived in the 1930s, he was affected as other 1920s writers were. Like other poets Arna Bontemps and

James Weldon Johnson, Cullen turned to teaching. In 1934 he began teaching English and French at Frederick Douglass Junior High School in New York City, the occupation that he kept until 1946. On at least two occasions, Cullen declined positions in black colleges in the South, preferring to avoid the strictness of southern racial segregation. Cullen continued to write during the 1930s as well. *The Medea and Some Poems* (1935) was a translation of *Medea* with additional poems. More than any other form of writing, Cullen wrote for children during this period of his life. *The Lost Zoo* was stories in verse, and he wrote short stories as well. He died unexpectedly in 1946 of uremic poisoning. *On These I Stand: An Anthology of the Best Poems of Countee Cullen* (1947), selected by the poet, was published posthumously. Cullen chose a very significant number of them from his first volume *Color*.

One of Cullen's beliefs that has been problematic for scholars was his preference for being labeled a poet and denying the racial component. He stated his position in the foreword to *Caroling Dusk*, which he subtitled *An Anthology of Verse by Negro Poets* rather than "of Negro Verse." He felt that since Negro writers are heir to the traditions and heritage of the English language, and to none other, that their work will conform to the times in which they live. He asserted that the label "Negro Poetry" carries the expectation of a monolithic or standardized poetry written by poets of African ancestry. He wanted his work freed from the *expectation* of racial art, preferring that his work be evaluated only for its qualities of art. Paradoxically, Cullen's poetry meets the definition of black poetry that he so vehemently rejected. Although he has poems whose content has nothing to belie the author's race, most of them are written from a point of view that is critical of racial practices against black people.

POETRY

Color. New York: Harper & Brothers, 1925. Rpt., Manchester: Ayer, 1975.
Ballad of the Brown Girl. New York: Harper & Brothers, 1927. (Out of Print)
Copper Sun. New York: Harper & Brothers, 1927. (Out of Print)
The Black Christ and Other Poems. New York: Harper & Brothers, 1929. (Out of Print)
The Medea and Some Poems. New York: Harper & Brothers, 1935. (Out of Print)

ANTHOLOGIES

Caroling Dusk: An Anthology of Verse by Negro Poets. New York: Harper & Brothers, 1927. (Out of Print)
On These I Stand: An Anthology of the Best Poems of Countee Cullen. New York: HarperCollins Publishers, 1947. (Out of Print)

COLLECTED WORK

My Soul's High Song: The Collected Writings of Countee Cullen, Voice of the Harlem Renaissance. Ed. Gerald Early. New York: Doubleday, 1991.

AUTOBIOGRAPHY

One Way to Heaven. New York: Harper & Brothers, 1932. (Out of Print)

RECORDING

To Make a Poet Black: The Best Poems of Countee Cullen. Caedmon, 1971. Read by Ossie Davis and Ruby Dee.

REFERENCES

Baker, Houston A., Jr. *A Many-Colored Coat of Dreams: The Poetry of Countee Cullen.* Detroit: Broadside Press, 1974.

Bronz, Stephen H. *Roots of Racial Consciousness: The 1920s: Three Harlem Renaissance Writers.* New York: Libra Publishers, 1964.

Davis, Arthur P. *From the Dark Tower: Afro-American Writers 1900–1960.* Washington, DC: Howard University Press, 1974.

Huggins, Nathan Irvin. *Harlem Renaissance.* New York: Oxford University Press, 1971.

Lewis, David Levering. *When Harlem Was in Vogue.* New York: Knopf, 1981.

Shucard, Alan R. *Countee Cullen.* Boston: Twayne, 1984.

———. "Countee Cullen." In *Dictionary of Literary Biography.* Vol. 51. Detroit, MI: Gale Research, 1987. 35–46.

Wagner, Jean. *Black Poets of the United States: From Paul Laurence Dunbar to Langston Hughes.* Trans. Kenneth Douglas. Urbana: University of Illinois Press, 1973.

TOI DERRICOTTE

(1941–   )

Toi Derricotte
Credit: University of Pittsburgh Press
Photo credit: Adrienne Heinrich

Toi Derricotte's poetry is increasingly finding a broader audience as a result of her productivity and the caliber of prizes recognizing her work. Derricotte's primary subjects—violence, motherhood, the tortured self, and victimization—and her manner of balancing personal experiences against their broader implications in the public venue also have increased her visibility to scholars and readers focusing on women's studies. In addition to writing and teaching creative writing at the university level, Derricotte's commitment to poetry as an art form is apparent in her role as cofounder (with Cornelius Eady) of Cave Canem. The program was conceived in 1996 as a way to support emerging poets by bringing them in contact with skilled, well-published poets in workshops held at scheduled retreats.

Derricotte was born in Detroit, Michigan, to Benjamin Sweeney Webster, a mortician and salesperson, and Antonia Banquet, a systems analyst. Derricotte grew up in their home in Conant Gardens, the first black middle-class suburb in Detroit. Her paternal grandparents, owners of a funeral home, also lived in Detroit. Derricotte had an ambivalent relationship with her grandmother, whom she has described as a powerful, beautiful, and charismatic woman. In fact, the title of Derricotte's first book, *The Empress of the Death House* (1978), and several of its poems evoke her paternal grandmother and their relationship. In her parents' home, Derricotte's coming-of-age years were turbulent; the fractured relationship between her parents and her treatment in their household are among the personal experiences that she scrutinizes and exposes in many of her poems. Derricotte attended Girls Catholic Central, where, she has said, the girls were taught to repress their sexuality. At Wayne State University, Derricotte studied special education and received a B.A. degree in 1965. In 1984 at New York University she was awarded an M.A. degree. Derricotte's first marriage to artist Clarence Reese ended in divorce in 1964. Her second marriage in 1967 to Bruce Derricotte, a banking consultant, also ended in divorce. She has a son, Anthony, born when Derricotte was a junior undergraduate student. His birth is the subject of her volume *Natural Birth* (1983).

Derricotte began her career as a teacher in Detroit and New Jersey in the 1960s after completing her studies at Wayne State. She moved to New York City in 1967, where her poetry resurfaced when she was twenty-seven years old. Her first major publication appeared in the *New York Quarterly* (1972). In 1974 she became a poet-in-residence for the Poet-in-the-Schools program of the New Jersey State Council on the Arts. She also taught at the Duke Ellington High School, a black arts institution in Washington, D.C. As a result of her success as a poet and a writer of memoir, Derricotte has became a frequent lecturer and visiting professor at numerous colleges and universities.

Derricotte began writing poetry secretly and did not reveal that she was doing so until she was fifteen years old. When she visited the Chicago Museum with her cousin, a medical school student, where they saw exhibits of fetuses and embryos, the experience provoked her to share her poems. However, the cousin's rejection of their subjects motivated her once again to retreat into writing secretly.

In an interview with Charles Rowell, Derricotte explained that during her first poetry-writing workship in New York, her reading of Sylvia Plath's poem "Daddy" provided the revelation that poetry could offer an appropriate site for expressing women's anger. In Derricotte's formal education the traditional poetry of high school and college classrooms, which was mostly the writing of white men, had failed to communicate all of its potential. The institutions she attended had not taught African American poetry.

In Derricotte's first book, *The Empress of the Death House*, she addresses a series of poems to Anne Sexton, whose work is representative of confessional poetry and women's subjectivity. Although Derricotte's poetry distantly echoes Sexton's emphasis, Derricotte's work strongly reflects the autobiographical impulse in African American literature, an impulse traceable to the eighteenth- and nineteenth-century slave narratives. Derricotte's *The Empress* engages near-taboo subjects including women's anger about what has happened to them as children when they had no voice with which to speak out, violence in the family that touched girls or their female relatives, and sexual matters. The book begins with death in the poem "Sleeping with Mr. Death" but ends with "Unburying the Bird," which is a resurrection. "Unburying the Bird" is based on an incident from the poet's childhood experience when she literally buried a dead bird. The poems in the volume speak to the emotions that surface and grow during childhood, but unexplored and unvoiced, they lie indefinitely unless the subject unearths them. For example, Derricotte's grandmother is part of the past. Literally associated with death through her ownership of a mortuary, the grandmother occupies a significant niche in Derricotte's exploration of self and family members. The grandmother's refusal to send her Cadillac to the suburbs for Derricotte and her mother meant they were forced to stand in the cold waiting for a city bus. The poem is a means of exploring the control exerted by the grandmother along with the feelings of isolation and rejection her behavior inspired.

Derricotte's second volume, *Natural Birth*, a book-length poem of her giving birth as an unwed mother, was not written until her son was seventeen years old. The poems reveal secrets hidden because of personal shame, explore different kinds of victimization that women experience, and probe painful feelings of isolation and alienation. Derricotte also questions the ways that women are vulnerable in American culture, and she analyzes the roles their personal relationships often play in the process.

Thus *Natural Birth* is a volume of self-exploratory poems. As the daughter of a middle-class family with rigid values, Derricotte's pregnancy without marriage was an event to be hidden. In the ten poems that comprise *Natural Birth*, Derricotte rips through the secrecy and exposes a vunerable, isolated young woman, but one who is also idealistic and determined. The sections titled "Natural Birth," "Postpartum," and "In Knowledge of Young Boys" chronicle the last two months of Derricotte's pregnancy. Scheduled to live at a home for expecting women between her seventh and ninth months, Derricotte unexpectedly had to reside with a private family until space became available at the home. "November" describes Derricotte's observation of and attempt to understand that passionless family, especially its mother, with whom she temporarily lives. Although they treat her kindly, Derricotte feels isolated. "Holy Cross Hospital" explains Derricotte's interaction with the other "children swollen as [herself]"; she still feels pretty and strong, and she is idealistic and romantic in her pledge to keep the baby, to attend school at night, and to give birth without drugs. "November" and "Holy Cross Hospital" are prose poems with strong narrative features. Beginning in "Maternity" and "10:29," however, Derricotte alters the fluid narrative lines to incorporate strong images and to bend the language so that it communicates the process of labor, not only its pain but also its intense and fluctuating emotions.

In "10:29," "Transition," and "Delivery" are the central poems of the volume because they cover the quickening of labor through the baby's appearance into the world. Their significance is signaled by alterations in Derricotte's language, style, and images. In "10:29," for example, stanzas of short, choppy lines describe the shock of pain: "fall asleep. two minutes. can't stand the pain." Derricotte's intense awareness of what is happening around her and of time's slow gait contrasts with what she feels. Her images of expansion and closure and of inside and outside intensify the reader's perception of a young woman whose pain pulls her inside herself where she is alone. Derricotte must also fight the doctor's cocky attitude that he *will* administer drugs to ease the delivery. She conveys his indifference to her wishes and his disregard of her discomfort through imagery that transforms his medical instrument into a "hammer." Discussing this poem in an interview, Derricotte says she composed twenty-three pages of it in one sitting, but it took five years to pare those pages down to the poem that appears in the volume.

In "Transition," the pain of birth has obliterated individuality: the experience of childbirth, in addition to producing a baby, produces *a woman*. Derricotte merges with a new self, one capable of getting this job done in short order. "I had lived through to another mind." In "Delivery," which details the final step of the birth process, when the physician still insists on using drugs, Derricotte thinks that perhaps the baby needs that kind of assistance. But the needle will not penetrate her back for the spinal. To convey the final steps of the natural birth, the poet manipulates the rhythm of the language so that it conveys the undulating movement of waves. The vital imagery juxtaposes the woman with herself and with elements of nature for the purpose of communicating the most intense self-communion and awareness.

The anticlimatic style of the poems at the end of the volume chronicles the patient's removal from the delivery room, a visit from the baby's father, and the changed relation to the other girls once the baby was born. The final, unexpected poem in the process of birth that Derricotte has so minutely detailed, "In Knowledge of Young Boys," speaks to the intimacy of a mother's knowing the unborn child before it knows anything about itself. Using the image of a mute oak tree, the poem ends on a note of strength for both mother and son.

As *Empress of the Death House* and *Natural Birth* suggest, Derricotte's poems balance well between the abstract and the concrete. Her images create startling effects that anchor content and symbol. The personal experience is inseparable from her poetry, and Derricotte rather fearlessly explores and exposes subjects that still might be considered private terrain. She continues these practices to some degree in *Captivity* (1989) and *Tender* (1997). *Captivity*, more directly than her previous volumes, addresses the consequence of racism in the community and in the home. In "Blackbottom," for example, Derricotte addresses what people miss when they "escape" an all-black community for the status and security of the suburbs, using her own family's move as the specific example. "On the Turning Up of Unidentified Black Female Corpses" is representative of the poems that use a specific incident to highlight larger questions. Are resources expended to their fullest capability when black women's bodies are found rather than white women's? Second, how can black women keep themselves safe? The poem ends enigmatically: A part of the speaker wants to escape reality, but another part "turns my sad black face to the light." The reader must conclude what reality the light illuminates for the speaker.

Derricotte's strong poems are often poems about family, and two of them appear in *Captivity*. "Christmas Eve: My Mother Dressing" details the poet's mother's preparation for festivity. Although the mother's beauty is the subject of the poem, it is not a vital and vibrant beauty. Instead, the beauty, as it is communicated through images, is a trap and a mask put on by the application of facial makeup. The mother's decorative hair pins are likened to insects. The blotches on her chin resulting from hair removal looked "as if acid were thrown from the inside." She leaves off being the "slave of the house" to become "the woman." However, her beauty, at best, is ambiguous, an exterior beauty only applied with cosmetic aids. "Christmas Eve: My Mother Dressing" depicts the mother's beauty as static, even staged. "Poem for My Father" also suggests that the father, too, is mostly someone else, a man emotionally dead. Although "[he] walked in [his] body like a living man," he was not. The poem is shot through with the father's activity that bespeaks his raging anger and violence against both his daughter and his wife. Some of the poem's content suggests that the source of the anger and violence stemmed from the anger, fear, and disappointment that "pretty ben" himself experienced in his family. While the poem does not offer reconciliation, it does seem to acknowledge the emotional dichotomy of the man in the last lines as she entreats her father to: "come back in love, come back in pain."

Unlike *Captivity*, Derricotte's *Tender* reflects a concept that the poet sets out in the brief preface. The volume should not be read from beginning to end. The title poem is the center of a wheel and each subdivision in the volume "radiat[es] out from that center." "Tender," a brief six-line lyric, speaks to a person's emotional fragility through language that evokes a hog killing. Within this concept, the numbered subdivisions reflect a journey inward, beginning broadly with a historical perspective generated by a visit to a former Portuguese slave fortress, Elmina Castle, in Cape Coast, Ghana. Subdivision three of the volume offers several poems—"Black Boys Play the Classics," "Workshop on Racism," "Bookstore"—that address children's and adults' experiences of being black in urban America. "Family Secrets" and "Passing" address physically looking white when Derricotte identifies as a person of African descent, the subject that occupies Derricotte's memoir *The Black Notebooks* (1997). The remaining poems work through various fragile, introspective postures on the rugged course to self-realization.

Derricotte's work has been recognized by several important awards. She has received two National Endowment for the Arts Awards (1985, 1990). She has received the United Black Arts, USA, Inc. Award, the Lucille Medwick Memorial Award from the Poetry Society of America, a Pushcart Prize, and a Folger Shakespeare Library Poetry Book Award. Readers are likely to continue responding to the earnest questions and difficult issues that Derricotte explores in her work.

POETRY

The Empress of the Death House. Detroit: Lotus Press, 1978.
Natural Birth. New York: Crossing Press, 1983.
Captivity. Pittsburg: University of Pittsburgh Press, 1989.
Tender. Pittsburg: University of Pittsburg Press, 1997.

MEMOIR

The Black Notebooks. New York: W.W. Norton, 1997.

REFERENCES

Hernton, Calvin C. "Black Women Poets: The Oral Tradition." *In The Sexual Mountain and the Black Women Writers.* Ed. Calvin C. Hernton. New York: Anchor Books, 1987. 119–55.
Raz, Hilda. *The Kenyon Review* (Spring 1991): 175–179.
Richardson, James W., Jr. "Toi Derricotte." In *The Oxford Companion to African American Literature.* Ed. William L. Andrews, Frances Smith Foster, and Trudier Harris. New York: Oxford University Press, 1997. 210.
Rowell, Charles H. "Beyond Our Lives: An Interview with Toi Derricotte." *Callaloo* 14.3 (Summer 1991): 654–64.

RITA DOVE

(1952–   )

Rita Dove
Credit: Rita Dove
Photo credit: Fred Viebahn

Rita Dove soared to literary acclaim through recognition earned for *Thomas and Beulah* (1986), her third volume of poetry and winner of the Pulitzer Prize in 1987. As winner of this award, Dove became the second black writer so recognized, the first having been Gwendolyn Brooks in 1950. Dove has shown herself as a multitalented writer, having published a collection of short stories, *Firth Sunday* (1985); a novel, *Through the Ivory Gate* (1992); and a verse drama, *The Darker Face of the Earth* (1994).

The oldest of four children, Dove was born in Akron, Ohio, on August 28, 1952, to Elvira Elizabeth Hord, a housewife, and Ray A. Dove, the first black chemist at the Goodyear Tire and Rubber Company in the city. They were a first-generation middle-class family, a status that groomed Dove for academic success. Her grandfather had migrated from Tennessee to Akron, Ohio, in the 1920s, where he found employment. He died when Dove was only thirteen. She was given the responsibility of spending weekends with her grandmother to provide her comfort during her grief. The grandmother shared many of her memories with Dove. These memories became the nucleus for Dove's award-winning volume *Thomas and Beulah*, the poetry sequence based on her grandparents' lives.

When Dove graduated from high school in 1970, her ranking among the top 100 high school seniors of the year secured her designation as a "Presidential Scholar." She earned a bachelor's degree from Miami University at Oxford, Ohio, as a National Achievement Scholar and graduated summa cum laude in 1973. Dove had considered becoming a lawyer but found herself increasingly drawn to writing and literature. By her junior year at the university, she had decided to become a poet. During 1974–1975, with a Fulbright scholarship she attended Tübingen University in West Germany. While there, she studied expressionist drama, the Austrian-German poet and novelist Rainer Maria Rilke (1875–1926), and the Romanian-born French poet and translator who wrote almost exclusively in German, Paul Celan (1920–1970). Perhaps not surprisingly, many of the qualities that scholars applauded in Rilke's poetry have been applauded in Dove's work: a precise, lyrical style, symbolic imagery, and spiritual reflection.

In 1977 Dove earned the M.F.A. in creative writing from the Iowa Writers' Workshop at the University of Iowa. Her thesis was the basis for the volume of poems *The Yellow House on the Corner* (1980), whose title suggests domesticity and familiarity but also liveliness. In her academic preparation Dove objected to the artificial separation of fiction and poetry, although she recognized its utility in curriculum structuring.

In 1979, she married the German-born writer Fred Viebahn, a fellow student at the Iowa Writers' Workshop, and they have a daughter, Aviva Chantal Tamu Dove Viebahn.

After Dove's first volume of poems was received with notable critical attention, her career moved rapidly in teaching opportunities, fellowships, and other forms of public notice. In 1981, she joined the English faculty at Arizona State University, Tempe, and in 1982 became writer-in-residence at Tuskegee Institute. In 1988, she enjoyed a Bellagio residency sponsored by the Rockefeller Foundation and was also a Mellon Fellow, during which she spent time at the prestigious National Humanities Center in North Carolina. She accepted a teaching position with the University of Virginia in 1989, but the next three years until (1992) were primarily spent at the Center for Advanced Studies there. In 1993, the University of Virginia advanced her to an endowed chair as Commonwealth Professor of English, where she has remained. She currently lives near Charlottesville, Virginia, with her husband and daughter.

The honors Dove has received are further confirmation of her national prominence and of the high critical regard extended to her poetry. In 1983–1984, she received a fellowship from the Guggenheim Foundation, and in 1986, the Lavan Younger Poets Award from the Academy of American Poets. Her alma maters, Miami University and Knox College, respectively, awarded her honorary doctorate degrees in 1988 and 1989. In 1993, the National Association for the Advancement of Colored People (NAACP) awarded her the Great American Artist Award, and she became the first African American poet laureate. In 1994, in addition to numerous honorary doctorate degrees, Dove received the Renaissance Forum Award for Leadership in the Literary Arts from the Folger Shakespeare Library and the Carl Sandburg Award from the International Platform Association. Additionally, Dove received the 1996 Heinz Award in the Arts and Humanities, one of the largest cash prizes in the world; and the 1996 Charles Frankel Prize National Humanities Metal, the U.S. government's highest honor for writers and scholars. In 1997, Dove received the Sara Lee Frontrunner Award and the Barnes and Noble Writers for Writers Award. In 1998, the recognition continued with the Levinson Prize from *Poetry* magazine, and in 1999, the John Frederick Nims Translation Award (together with Fred Viebahn), also from *Poetry*. *On the Bus with Rosa Parks* (1999) was nominated for the Year 2000 National Book Critics Circle Award.

Dove was also a judge for several prestigious poetry competitions in

1991, including the Walt Whitman Award of the Academy of American Poets, the Pulitzer Prize for Poetry, and the National Book Award Poetry Panel.

Dove has served on various committees and boards that promote poetry and other arts. For example, she has been a panel member and chair of the poetry grants panel of the National Endowment for the Arts as well as on the board of directors of the Associate Writing Programs. She also holds a contributing and advisory editor position with *Callaloo*, a significant journal of criticism and art, with the *Gettysburg Review*, and with *TriQuarterly*. Moreover, she is a commissioner for the Schomburg Center for Research in Black Culture in New York.

Many elements in Dove's poetry are critically acclaimed. For example, her technical accomplishment has earned her comparison to Gwendolyn Brooks. Dove incorporates many literary traditions from her past predecessors, including conventional forms, but has distinguished herself and illustrated originality in her ability to depart from tradition. As a modern African American poet, Dove is heir to the 1960s legacies of protest poetry and the Black Arts or Black Aesthetic Movement of that era. Her poem "Upon Meeting Don L. Lee, in a Dream" has been cited as her poetic statement of departure from the traditions that he represented and advocated in the 1960s and early 1970s. Images of destruction and ineffectiveness characterize the older poet, whereas those of nurture and survival protect the poem's speaker.

In the essay "The House That Jill Built," Dove explains that at one time her method of writing was labor intensive since she worked at completing a poem from its beginning to its end. Simultaneously with discovering colored plastic theme sheet-sized folders, however, she has chosen to use them for enclosing incomplete poems. She matches the mood of the poem to the color of the plastic. When she's ready to write, she chooses a folder that suits her mood of the moment. This method allows her to have several poems under composition at once.

Like most poets, Dove writes on numerous subjects. In *The Yellow House on the Corner*, divided into five sections, a reader finds numerous poems focused on women, love, romance, international travel, and slavery. Ten poems about slavery form the center of the volume as section three. Thematically, they are united by the various ways that captives seek freedom. "Belinda's Petition," for example, invites comparison to the battle against tyranny recently won by the colonies as the slave woman requests her own freedom. "David Walker (1785–1830)" acknowledges this historic figure's protests against the institution and his death because of it. "Pamela," a narrative poem, reveals a slave woman's walk into freedom one afternoon, her feelings of liberation, of using the night stars for direction, and of being caught. The poems titled by individual names give identity to members of the group, while those otherwise titled call attention to numerous conditions within the institution. "The Abduction," narrated from Solomon Northrup's perspective, details his kidnapping, an act that reversed his status as a free man with identifying papers to that of chattel. "The Transport of Slaves from Maryland to Mississippi" tells of an attempted escape in 1839 by a wagonload of captives who in their freedom effort killed two white men. Their freedom, ironically, was short-lived when a slave woman helped the Negro driver ride for help.

Thomas and Beulah details another form of bondage. On its cover is a deliberately chosen photograph that shows a circa 1940s-styled black and white snapshot of a smartly dressed couple solemnly posing against an automobile with houses visible in the background. While the couple posing accurately foreshadows the volume's concern with romance and family, the stark color contrast also accurately forewarns of the austerity that characterizes the poems. The unity that has been glimpsed in Dove's previous work is given full rein here in selections that chronicle the poet's grandparents' courtship and marriage. Cautioning the reader that the poems tell both sides of a story and should be read sequentially, the volume is divided into two parts. Thomas's section, titled "Mandolin," has twenty-three poems, beginning with a fateful and life-plaguing night when his best friend, Lem, drowned, somewhat mysteriously, by falling or jumping from a boat. Beulah's section, titled "Canary in Bloom," offers twenty-one poems thematically unified by her courtship, married life, and widowhood. As the poems chronicle the intersecting of Thomas and Beulah's dissimilar personalities, Dove illustrates her enviable ability to select the telling detail—a color, a physical characteristic, or a spoken phrase. She also avoids sentimentality and sidesteps nostalgia by looking dry-eyed at life-structuring events: Thomas's leaving Tennessee in 1919, arriving in Akron, Ohio, in 1921, his marriage to Beulah in 1924, the birth of the first of four daughters in 1926, the depression of the 1930s, Thomas's working years, Beulah's life as a wife and mother and her adjustment to those roles, their grandchildren, her work as a hat maker, the beginnings of Thomas's illness, his subsequent death, and Beulah's death in 1969.

In *Thomas and Beulah*, as in her other volumes, Dove expertly integrates symbols and images through the poems, not only as unifying devices but also for intensifying meaning and emotion. For example, the mandolin that Thomas plays and that identifies his section is expressive of his lifelong blues for his friend Lem's death. Music becomes his emotional salvation, including, briefly, church music. Additionally, his music production suggests his appeal as a lady's man before he meets and courts Beulah. As Lem's death haunts Thomas, a haunting not shared with his wife, the mandolin, music, and images of boating and water reappear. With water established as a means of death, its prominent reappearance in imagery during Thomas's courtship and wedding night with Beulah signals different kinds of death in their union together. The descriptive darkness of water pitching a boat in "Refrain," the poem following his engagement, and the image of Thomas having drunkenly raised a mast and tied himself to it are ample forewarning that their marriage will not mirror romantic idealism. Moreover, it will not displace the guilt that has pursued Thomas since Lem's death. The recurring image of yellow strongly links the two sections as the yellow scarf that Thomas wore and gave to Beulah links the two of them. She owns a yellow singing canary in "The House on Bishop Street." Her life with Thomas, however, and the experience of caring for four girls is not merry and bright, a truth revealed in the poem "Daystar." The image of the dancing ballerina in "The Oriental Ballerina," the poem about Beulah's death, conveys the lightness that has been miserably absent in Beulah's life.

There are, of course, pleasant episodes in their long relationship, as suggested in "Summer Greens" and "Promises" in Beulah's section of poems and in Thomas's "The Satisfaction Coal Company," "Gospel," and "Roast Possum."

Grace Notes (1989) is as deliberately named as Dove's previous books. She has admitted to numerous influences in the choice of its title, including the multiple definitions of *grace*, of *notes*, and of *grace notes*. She also wished to move beyond the large scope of *Thomas and Beulah*, though a few of its poems—"Summit Beach, 1921," "Silos," and "Quaker Oats"—are seemingly connected by theme, tone, and content to that volume. Tight unity and subtle grace are finely woven into the diverse poems of *Grace Notes*. Travel references, both literal and metaphorical, domestic and international, are apparent in "Backyard, 6 A.M.," "Watching *Last Year at Marienbad* at Roger Haggerty's House in Auburn, Alabama," and "The Other Side of the House." In a slight departure from the usual, "The Island Women of Paris," a humor-tinged tribute to the distinctive beauty of Caribbean women, acknowledges their smooth physical movement about the city. Numerous poems position children's experiences as central including "Fifth Grade Autobiography," "Flash Cards," "Hully Gully," "Sisters," and "After Reading *Mickey in the Night*

Kitchen for the Third Time Before Bed." This focus on children's experiences in so many poems suggests that the center of Dove's next volume, *Mother Love* (1995), had begun its shaping in the poet's mind. It suggests, too, that, increasingly, Dove is adopting a reflective posture and drawing from her own coming-of-age experiences and from those of being a mother herself.

Unlike the other volumes of poetry, Dove provides an introduction to *Mother Love*. Suggesting that the restrictive form of the sonnet conveys an inviolate world, Dove summarizes the ancient myth of Demeter and her daughter Persephone as illustrative of a world gone berserk. Demeter's grief at her daughter's capture by the king of the underworld caused her to neglect her duties as goddess of agriculture, and as a result, crops suffered. She began to wander the earth disguised as a mortal. Finally, Zeus's intervention persuades Hades to return Persephone. On her return, however, she eats a pomegranate, an action that dictates her cycle of return to Hades each year. This myth explains fall and winter seasons as the periods of Demeter's grief. Acknowledging homage and counterpoint to Maria Rilke's *Sonnets to Orpheus*, Dove writes sonnets from the perspective of both Demeter and Persephone. Dove borrows both the Shakespearean and Italian sonnet forms, but she also departs from them in some poems. Moreover, the volume moves beyond the myth by converting it to a paradigm to explore contemporary seductions awaiting innocent girls blossoming into young women. One of the most intriguing poems is the title poem, "Mother Love."

On the Bus with Rosa Parks continues Dove's success and illustrates the poet's deepening ability to refine voice, image, metaphor, and theme in a single volume. Dove's facility with creating convincing voice and character shines in this volume in the interrelated poems of section one, "Cameo,"a small grouping that moves through fifteen years in the family's existence together. The precocious son is perhaps most intriguing, having already acquired an unjustified disdain for women and an unwavering determination to circumvent the life path that awaits black men.

Several poems in the volume address innocence and discovery, particularly in the section "Freedom: Bird's-Eye View." Dove withholds the subtle surprise of discovery in poems where, paradoxically, the discovery is the resounding conclusion to the poem. In "Parlor," for example, the girl discovers her grandmother's key to solace only after her death. "The First Book" and "Maple Valley Branch Library, 1967" chronicle the movement from innocence to knowledge not in an awakening girl's body but in her intellect. The last section of poems also bears the name of the book. Dove guards against overburdening these poems with the rhetoric or tension that Rosa Parks's resistance on the bus in Montgomery, Alabama, subsequently caused. The poems engage the atmosphere that was fast making life in Montgomery "intolerable" for its black citizens, however, and they convey movement and planning toward Rosa Parks's selection as the chosen one. In Dove's notes at the section end, she explains that the context for "Claudette Colvin Goes to Work" is a fifteen-year-old girl's refusal to relinquish her seat on a city bus on March 2, 1955, several months preceding the act by Rosa Parks. Dove does not construct the bus incident as the focus, choosing instead an indirect reference. The numbing adult work that has already claimed the cheery adolescence of Claudette Colvin and the implied death of her dreams is centered instead. In "Rosa," the act of refusing to relinquish the bus seat is accomplished in a short lyric in the paradoxical line "Doing nothing was the doing."

Dove's accomplishments are indicative of the creative paths that await her. She has illustrated her interest in transcending tradition even as she employs it. Her readers should be prepared to expect increasingly bold and stunning work from her in a variety of genres.

POETRY

The Yellow House on the Corner. Pittsburgh: Carnegie-Mellon University Press, 1980. (2nd edition)
Museum. Pittsburgh: Carnegie-Mellon University Press, 1983. (Out of Print)
Thomas and Beulah. Pittsburgh: Carnegie-Mellon Press, 1986.
The Other Side of the House. Photographs by Tamarra Kaida. Temper, AZ: VARI Studios Pyracantha Press, 1988. (Out of Print)
Grace Notes. New York: W.W. Norton, 1989.
Selected Poems. New York: Vintage Books, 1993.
The Darker Face of the Earth. Ashland, OR: Story Line Press, 1994, 1996. Verse drama.
Mother Love, New York: W.W. Norton, 1995.
On the Bus with Rosa Parks. New York: W.W. Norton, 1999.

CHAPBOOKS

Ten Poems. Lisbon, IA: Penumbra Press, 1977. (Out of Print)
The Only Dark Spot in the Sky. Tempe, AZ: Porch Publications, 1980. (Out of Print)
Mandolin. Athens, OH: Ohio Review, 1982. (Out of Print)

RECORDINGS

Rita Dove. Kansas City, MO: University of Missouri, 1985. Cassette.
Poets in Person. Chicago: Modern Language Association, 1991. Cassette.
Selected Poems. New York: Random House, 1993. Cassette.

REFERENCES

Corn, Alfred. Rev. *Grace Notes*, by Rita Dove. *Poetry* 157. 1 (October 1990): 37–39.

Costello, Bonnie. "Scars and Wings: Rita Dove's *Grace Notes*." *Callaloo* 14 (Spring 1991): 434–438.

Georgoudaki, Ekaterini. "Rita Dove: Crossing Boundaries." *Callaloo* 14 (Spring 1991): 419–33.

Hunters, Jeffery W., and Jerry Moore, eds. *Black Literature Criticism. Supplement.* Detroit: Gale Research, 1999. 109–28.

Jones, Kirkland. "Rita Dove." In *Dictionary of Literary Biography.* Vol. Ed. R.S. Gwynn. 120. Detroit: Gale Research, 1992. 47–51.

McDowell, Robert. "The Assembling Vision of Rita Dove." *Callaloo* 9.1 (Winter 1986): 61–70.

Rampersad, Arnold. "The Poems of Rita Dove." *Callaloo* 9.1 (Winter 1986): 52–60.

Serafin, Steven R., ed. *Modern Black Writers.* Vol. 12. New York, Continuum, 1995. 190–98.

Vendler, Helen. "An Interview with Rita Dove." In *Reading Black, Reading Feminist.* Ed. Henry Louis Gates Jr. New York: Meridian, 1990. 481–91.

PAUL LAURENCE DUNBAR

(1872–1906)

Paul Laurence Dunbar
Credit: The National Portrait Gallery, Smithsonian Institution

Dunbar holds the distinction of being the first African American poet to enjoy a national and international reputation. Dunbar was also the first black writer to support himself solely by his writing. Although he wrote excellent poems in standard English, his dialect poetry was selected by nineteenth-century American critics as the medium that most captured the joys and sadness of black southern folk life. His work included short stories, librettos for musicals, essays, and four novels, but his reputation as a writer is dependent on his poetry.

Dunbar was born in Dayton, Ohio, to former slaves Joshua and Matilda Glass Burton Murphy Dunbar. Matilda, previously married during slavery, had two sons from that marriage, William and Robert, who moved to Chicago. Joshua Dunbar had escaped from slavery in Kentucky via the Underground Railroad and made his way to Canada. During the war, he served in the Fifty-fifth Massachusetts Regiment, Company F, and fought for the Union army. Joshua returned to Ohio after the war where he became a plasterer. Both Joshua and Matilda taught themselves to read. Joshua loved history and Matilda enjoyed literature. The couple divorced in 1876 when Paul was only four years old, and Joshua died when Paul was eleven.

As Matilda raised her son Paul, she transmitted her love of literature to him and told him many of the stories about slavery that were later integrated into his writing. Dunbar, the only black student in his high school, excelled in his studies and activities. He was editor in chief of the *High School Times* and president of the literary club, the Philomathean Society. He wrote the class poem and delivered it at his graduation in 1891 and was editor and founder of a short-lived newspaper for African Americans, the *Dayton Tattler*. His classmate Orville Wright, who would become famous with Wilbur as inventor of the modern airplane, printed Dunbar's paper.

After graduation, Dunbar's hope of becoming a lawyer died in the reality of his poverty. He had to seek work, but in the Midwest in 1891, a black high school graduate found all doors to lucrative employment closed. Dunbar finally got a job as an elevator operator in the Callahan building, earning $4 a week on which he supported himself and his mother. He published short poems in midwestern newspapers but received little or no compensation.

The prospect of becoming a world-renowned writer or member of any profession was bleak for Dunbar. However, in 1892, his high school English teacher asked him to deliver the welcome address to the Western

Association of Writers convening in Dayton. Instead of a traditional speech, he composed a twenty-six-line poem, presented it, and left. Dunbar's youth and race impressed the audience more than his poem, and the exposure proved invaluable. Dr. James Newton Matthews sought Dunbar out at the Callahan building, requested a few of his poems, and quoted them in a press letter a few weeks later. This deed brought him to the attention of James Whitcomb Riley, a regional poet who had used the Hoosier dialect in his work and with whom Dunbar would later be compared. Riley wrote Dunbar to commend the young poet's writing.

Perhaps emboldened by these responses, in 1893 Dunbar approached the office of the United Brethren Publishing House to have his first volume of poetry privately printed, but he was rejected when he did not have $125 to pay for the books. Having heard about Dunbar's writing, the business manager, William Blacher, intervened and promised to stand for the money. The company thus printed 500 copies of Dunbar's first book, titled *Oak and Ivy*. He sold them from his job site and after readings charged $1 per copy. The volume contained the much-lauded "Ode to Ethiopia," an affirmation of racial pride that cites the contributions of blacks in building America and their achievements during Reconstruction. It also contained "Sympathy," Dunbar's most anthologized poem after "We Wear the Mask." "Sympathy," a lyric in which the speaker identifies with restrictions but also with an everlasting hope for freedom in a caged bird, is also the source of Maya Angelou's famous autobiography *I Know Why the Caged Bird Sings*. Other titles cited as the best in the volume are "To Ol' Tunes," "A Drowsy Day," "October," and "A Career."

Another benefactor, Charles Thatcher, an attorney in Toledo, Ohio, offered to finance Dunbar's college education, but Dunbar respectfully declined because his mother was dependent on his earnings. Nevertheless, Thatcher remained a friend and supporter throughout the poet's career. Frederick Douglass also became a supporter when Dunbar visited Chicago in 1893. As minister to Haiti, Douglass had authority over the Haitian exhibit at the World's Columbian Exposition Fair, and he arranged a reading of Dunbar's standard English verse at the "Colored Folk's Day." Not only did Dunbar's poetry gain acceptance, but he met and conversed with other black writers.

Dunbar's second volume of poems, *Majors and Minors*, appeared in 1895. Its poems numbered ninety-three, some from the first volume, though Dunbar preferred not to include an excessive number of poems from previous publications in a new book. *Majors and Minors*, diverse in its styles and themes, included the standard favorite "When Malindy

Sings," a tribute to Dunbar's mother's singing. The volume consisted of poems in standard English, the "majors," and poems in black and white southern dialect, the "minors." This volume was also published with the help of a white benefactor, the psychiatrist Dr. Henry A. Tobey. *Majors and Minors* was reviewed in *Harpers Weekly* by the most eminent critic in American letters, William Dean Howells.

Howell's positive review, widely reprinted and analyzed, brought national and international attention to Dunbar's work. Simultaneously, however, Howell's review imposed restrictions on Dunbar from which the poet was never able to break free. His comments on Dunbar's dialect poems provided the lens through which others would see Dunbar. Howell praised the dialect poems to the exclusion of the numerous poems in standard English. The dialect poems, according to Howells, captured the humor and pathos of the Negro folk population in the South and genuinely showed them as they really were. He praised Dunbar's capacity for his depth of feeling and his ability to avoid sentimentality in rendering a folk portrait.

After Howell's review, journals and newspapers wanted only to publish dialect poems, and they rejected Dunbar's submissions of poems written in standard English, although more than half of his output was in standard English. A year after Howell's review, Dunbar realized what he called the "irrevocable harm" of Howell's paradoxical praise. Although Dunbar's dialect poems were popular performance pieces among African American schools and communities, Dunbar's critical standing with Harlem Renaissance writers as well as other generations of black scholars has fluctuated with the political and social climate of the time. The problem with dialect poetry can be explained as its perceived affirmation of certain stereotypical traits such as the lazy tongue incapable of speaking standard English, the black population's acceptance of the status quo without protest, and the poetry's seeming confirmation of black people's perennial joy regardless of economic and political circumstances. Dunbar's work did not introduce the use of dialect. Contemporary white southern poets Sidney Lanier and Joel Chandler Harris were using it as well as nineteenth-century black poets James D. Corrothers and James Campbell, so-called invisible poets by later scholars because their work was not widely known. Campbell, in fact, was the first black poet to use dialect consistently in his poems.

When Dunbar's complete poems were published in 1914, a reviewer in the *New York Times Book Review* expressed surprise by the "unexpected excellence" of much of Dunbar's standard English poetry. Later critics and the general reader have preferred the standard English work, as

Dunbar himself did. "The Poet," a lyric of two stanzas, succinctly expresses Dunbar's disappointment that a poet sang of profound life and love, but the public preferred only "a jingle in a broken tongue." "We Wear the Mask," a three-stanza lyric, has become a classic that recognizes the dual nature that black people often had to display. Comic and tragic theater masks were the images that conveyed the necessity to hide true feelings beneath a mask that "grins and lies."

Paradoxically, Dunbar's popular dialect verse proved both his bane and his ticket to prosperity. The bestselling volume that in four years sold over 12,000 copies, *Lyrics of a Lowly Life* (1896), offered 105 poems, many in dialect verse, and contained an introduction by William Dean Howells. Howells asserted that Dunbar presented Negro life "aesthetically and express[ed] it lyrically" and that he brought objectivity, humor, sympathy, and truthfulness to his subjects. *Lyrics* was brought out by a major New York publishing house, which guaranteed a national audience, and Dunbar was given a $400 advance and a regular monthly salary. To assist marketing, Dunbar's benefactors arranged for him to have a professional manager who arranged a trip to New York for public readings.

The success of *Lyrics* created many possibilities for Dunbar, and his future finally looked promising professionally and personally. He continued to write poetry, fiction, essays, and lyrics for musical theater production. He also continued correspondence he had begun in 1895 with Alice Ruth Moore, a New Orleans teacher, poet, and short fiction writer whom he had not met and who published in the 1890s as he did. Dunbar's manager arranged a six months' reading tour in London in 1897. At the tour reception Dunbar finally met Alice Moore, and they became engaged that same evening. When he returned, he acquired a job as an assistant clerk in the reading room at the Library of Congress, earning an annual salary of $720. He worked there for a year and a half before resigning to devote more time to his writing. He and Alice married secretly in March of 1898, because Alice's family objected to his black skin and to his involvement as a lyricist for minstrel shows, those burlesque variety shows begun by white performers made up in blackface but also performed in later years by black groups. In the same year Dunbar also visited the South for the first time. Booker T. Washington invited the poet to visit Tuskegee Institute, the educational facility he founded in Tuskegee, Alabama. While there, Dunbar wrote lyrics for the school song. The only negatives that tempered Dunbar's successes were his failing health and the disregard for his standard English poems.

Between 1897 and 1899 Dunbar continued to write in a variety of genres and to enjoy his national and international popularity. The volumes of poetry published during the period were well received, but the earlier work was considered his best. In 1899, en route to a poetry reading in New York where Governor Theodore Roosevelt was scheduled to introduce him, Dunbar became ill and was diagnosed first with pneumonia. He was later diagnosed with tuberculosis, the illness that would end his life in a few years. Acting on his doctor's recommendation for changing his environment, he and his wife went to the Catskills for a few weeks. In the spring of 1900, the Dunbars, including his mother, moved to Harmon, Colorado, for his health, but little change occurred. They returned to Washington. The illness and other matters placed stress on their marriage, and in 1902, the couple separated. Dunbar and Alice unsuccessfully tried to reunite in 1903. His last years were spent in Dayton in the home he had bought for himself and his mother, who survived his death. Dunbar was buried in Woodland Cemetery in Dayton, Ohio, also the final resting place, very near his site, of classmates Orville and Wilbur Wright. Dunbar's grave is marked by a large, simple upright stone identifying him as a poet.

POETRY

Oak and Ivy. New York: Dodd, Mead, 1893. Irvine, CA: Reprint Services Corporation, 1993.

Majors and Minors. New York: Dodd, Mead, 1895. Manchester: Ayer, 1977.

Lyrics of a Lowly Life. New York: Dodd, Mead, 1896. Secaucus, NJ: Carol Pub. Group, 1993.

Lyrics of the Hearthside. New York: Dodd, Mead, 1899. Manchester: Ayer, 1977.

Poems of Cabin and Field. New York: Dodd, Mead, 1899. Manchester: Ayer, 1991.

Candle-Lightin Time. New York: Dodd, Mead, 1901. New York: AMS Press, n.d.

Lyrics of Love and Laughter. New York: Dodd, Mead, 1903. Irvine, CA: Reprint Services Corporation, 1993.

When Malindy Sings. New York: Dodd, Mead, 1903. Manchester: Ayer, 1977.

Li'l Gal. New York: Dodd, Mead, 1904. New York: AMS Press, n.d.

Chris'mus Is a Comin', and Other Poems. New York: Dodd, Mead, 1905. (Out of Print)

Howdy, Honey, Howdy. New York: Dodd, Mead, 1905.

Lyrics of Sunshine and Shadow. New York: Dodd, Mead, 1905.

A Plantation Portrait. New York: Dodd, Mead, 1905. (Out of Print)

Joggin'erlong. New York: Dodd, Mead, 1906. Manchester: Ayer, 1991.

The Complete Poems of Paul Laurence Dunbar. New York: Dodd, Mead, 1913. New York: Dodd, Mead, 1980.

Speakin o' Christmas, and Other Christmas and Special Poems. New York: Dodd, Mead, 1914. New York: AMS Press, n.d.

I Greet the Dawn: Poems by Paul Laurence Dunbar. New York: Atheneum, 1978.

Four Collections of Poetry: Howdy Honey Howdy, Li'l Gal, Poems of Cabin & Field, & When Malindy Sings. Manchester: Ayer, 1991.

Three Collections of Poetry: Joggin'erlong; Lyrics of Sunshine & Shadow; Majors & Minors. Manchester: Ayer, 1991.

RECORDING

Margaret Walker Alexander Reads Poems of Paul Laurence Dunbar and James Weldon Johnson and Langston Hughes. Folkways Records, 1975. Sound Disc.

REFERENCES

Braxton, Joanne M., ed. *The Collected Poetry of Paul Laurence Dunbar*. Charlottesville: University Press of Virginia, 1993.

Dunbar, Paul Laurence. *The Paul Laurence Dunbar Reader*. Ed. Jay Martin and Gossie H. Hudson. New York: Dodd, Mead, 1975.

Rauch, Esther Nettles. "Paul Laurence Dunbar." *In African American Writers*. Ed. Lea Baechler and A. Walton Litz. New York: Charles Scribner's Sons, 1991. 87–102.

Revell, Peter. *Paul Laurence Dunbar*. Boston: Twayne, 1979.

Wagner, Jean. "Paul Laurence Dunbar." Trans. Kenneth Doughlas. In *Black Poets of the United States: From Paul Laurence Dunbar to Langston Hughes*. Ed. Jean Wagner. Chicago: University of Illinois Press, 1974. 73–121.

CORNELIUS EADY

(1954–)

Cornelius Eady
Credit: G.P. Putnam's Sons
Photo credit: Miriam Berkley

Cornelius Eady, born in Rochester, New York, attended Monroe Community College and Empire State College. He began writing around age twelve and seriously in his twenties. His high school English teacher encouraged his efforts, but his parents were not readers or writers. In addition to poetry, Eady writes music and has completed two musical theater pieces. When *Victims of the Latest Dance Craze* (1986) won the Lamont Award, his work came to the attention of a much broader audience.

Eady held numerous positions before his teaching at City College. He hosted and coproduced a monthly poetry program on WBAI in New York City and worked in the Poet-in-the-School programs in New York and Vermont. In Virginia he was artist-in-resident in Richmond and at the University of Virginia's Young Writer's Workshop. From 1982 to 1984 he was Margaret Banister Writer-in-Residence at Sweet Briar College. Married for more than twenty years, Eady has no children.

Eady has amassed significant recognition for his poetry through honors that include a National Endowment for the Arts Fellowship, a Guggenheim Fellowship, a Lila Wallace-Reader's Digest Writer's Award, a Rockefeller Foundation Fellowship, and the Prairie Schooner Strousse Award. *Victims of the Latest Dance Craze* won the 1985 Lamont Prize from the Academy of American Poets, and *The Gathering of My Name* (1991) was nominated for the Pulitzer Prize in Poetry in 1992. Eady and poet Toi Derricotte are the founders of Cave Canem, a retreat and workshop designed to bring aspiring African American poets together with seasoned, published ones.

Music, dance, and family are the central motifs in Eady's work, but he also writes about relationships, loss, and survival. His poems suggest that life in its infinite permutations is a dance; and as such, it is inspiration and ritual, and it holds the fulfillment of promise. Dance needs music, and music requires a source. Thus it is through music and dance that Eady can explore the vast reaches of the human experience and perhaps reach a few conclusions. Eady has said that his favorite poem "Between the Walls" by mainstream, modernist poet William Carlos Williams always reminds him that the poetic is found in everyday speech and occurrences. Eady's work illustrates that he has considerable talent for converting the sights and sounds of observed life experiences into lyrical transformative poems that then have much to teach and to show to others.

You Don't Miss Your Water (1995), twenty selections of poems and short prose about a son's relationship to his unconventional father, illustrate Eady's use of family, specifically a father, as a way to explore human relations. Each poem in the book is taken from a song title. Eady has said that he wanted to use the idea in the songs as an anchor for the poems. However, if readers are unaware of the song lyrics, they do not necessarily lose any meaning in the poem; conversely, if they know the lyrics, their reading is clearly more enriched. The book title itself is taken from a song. Since the book explores a son's relationship with his father, who dies, the idea is explicit that loss by death, even in a difficult relationship, is nevertheless painful. One poem, "A Little Bit of Soap," explores the subject of skin tone for African Americans from the ironic perspective that lighter is nicer. Thoughtlessly, the African American father conveys this idea to his young son, saying that when the son was a baby he was pretty with a light-colored skin. As the skin darkened with age, the father directed that it should be washed more frequently. The title "A Little Bit of Soap" performs doubly ironic duty here. It suggests a father's low self-esteem and his callous attitude in communicating to his son that his complexion is unacceptable. But Eady also has selected a song that, when its lyrics are recalled, conveys the pain of that father's conclusion. No amount of soap can erase the pain of the father's words. As in the original song, soap could never erase the tears of lost love. Another poem about the father, however, "One Kind Favor," offers a sympathetic image of a man dying, one whose memory reverts to things that might offer him comfort, such as going home to Florida, putting on his regular clothes instead of a hospital gown, or pulling on his own shoes. The motivation for "Paradiso," also the dead father, is a lecture about the Italian poet Dante when the speaker is in Italy. The speaker considers his father's reappearance in the eternity of Christiandom and poses three possible images. One of them might be the shape of the man who visited his mother weeks after the funeral, presumably a reference to a ghost visitation. Somewhat uncharacteristically, "Paradiso" contains the hauntingly lyrical idea that music and language are sites of pain and peace. *You Don't Miss Your Water* became the basis for an off-Broadway theater production.

In *Victims of the Latest Dance Craze*, the title poem sets the pace and direction of the volume. In it, dance touches and positively transforms everyone. It elicits memory, inventiveness, and vision; it miraculously reinvigorates, as in "The Ballet Called John the Baptist," where homeless old people remember and dance. The constant motion of these poems invites readers to think about movement differently and to consider dance as a part of motions that are not normally thought of as dance.

For example, "Aerial Ballet" is told from the perspective of a star falling over New York City. "The Dance of Eve" is a reimagining of Eve and Adam. When she walks toward him with the red apple, neither of them knows what "[H]er body is trying to promise." The suggestion that it is dance, given the focus of the poems, is richly ambiguous. "Poet Dances with Inanimate Object" ends saying that absolutely nothing is "safe from the dance of ideas."

The Autobiography of a Jukebox, as its title suggests, has music at its core. The jukebox—physically a bulky but colorful holder, a repository for songs on records or compact disks that listeners can call up and hear by depositing the appropriate coin—is the repository of a family's life in Eady's book, and blues is the tune to which their lives have danced. In the first eighteen poems focused on family, the theme is literal and spiritual loss and the narrative is a blues tongue. The poems voice the speaker's sympathetic inquiry primarily into situations of his mother's life but also into the blues existence that enveloped his sister, his cousin, himself, and even the father who is responsible for so much of the heartache and disappointment.

These poems suggest that disappointments accumulate to total blues. They include the mother's choosing the better of two men but nevertheless choosing unwisely, having a large amount of money made on numbers taken by her husband and cousin, and pleading for state assistance when for whatever reason her husband's provisions are insufficient. The mother's physical appearance, in fact, becomes a portrait of the blues: The hardness that squeezes her eyes and pinches her mouth "is what the blues looks like." The unmarried sister's destiny echoes her mother's through her dream escape. When the getaway is achieved, in "Buked and Scorned," the mother and sister depart together, leaving the empty house a surprise for the husband's return. Eady collapses the spiritual with the lines "I been buked and I been scorned" and the blues in this poem, his affirmation that the two art forms spring from the same wellsprings of human pain. "I'm Walkin," the poem placed before "Buked and Scorned," about departure, had been the father's threat. The emotional punch of this family's blues, as communicated in the poems, does not directly tumble the son, though he registers and records it. He describes how he learned to write "[i]n that house, on a cot in a small, blue room."

While no redemption is offered for the father, there are poems that offer glimpses into his background. Without completely evoking the discrimination practiced against black men in the workplace, Eady offers an employment incident that his father handled. In "I Don't Want Nobody to Give Me Nothing (open up the door, I'll get it myself)" when a white worker poses trouble at the father's job, he handles it diplomatically with words. But the poems that suggest his father's diplomacy are exceptions. In "King Snake," for example, the father as a young man in the South handled and sold rattlesnakes. When a dispute once involved a white customer who summoned the sheriff, the grandfather merely stood in the door with a shotgun to protect his son, illustrating another version of diplomacy. Muddy Waters, the son writes, might have written the episode into a song that elevated the feat into legend: "When my daddy was a young boy, he played with rattlesnakes."

The three other sections of *The Autobiography* branch into the community and then return in "Small Moments" to lyrical, occasional poems. Section two, "Rodney King Blues," offers seven poems informed by the videotaped brutality to which he was subjected. "Dread" is the only poem in this blues-infused volume that is written in a blues structure. The concluding poem of the section, it addresses the constant expectation of violence under which black men and boys live. Section three, "The Bruise of the Lyric," offers poems on jazz musicians and Chuck Berry. The last poem of the book, "Hard Times," intentionally evoking poet Etheridge Knight, alludes to Knight's blues near the end of his life when he was living in a shelter in New York. In this poem, Eady illuminates the reason for using song titles for most of the poems in this volume. In the poetry of their music African American lyricists and musicians have recorded the experiences of all of us at some time or other. Often, the specificity is alarming because it signals the pervasiveness of pain, disappointment, and heartache among all human beings. In "Hard Times" Cornelius Eady writes that, although he bears no resemblance to Knight, except in skin tone, following a *Village Voice* article about Knight living in a shelter, people mistook Eady for Knight for months.

Eady's most recent volume, *Brutal Imagination* (2001) illustrates the increasing range of his art. He addresses the irony and the perverseness of invention; he writes in the voice of the kidnapper whom Susan Smith imagined and offered to the public as the abductor of her two sons. She spun a monster out of her head and offered up a black man for the law to pursue. Her notorious accusation reerected racial bars and unearthed stereotypes. In *Brutal Imagination* Eady assumes the point of view of Susan Smith's invented villain through a dazzling, provocative combination of drama and poetry. Eady focuses on the lie and its easy acceptance and in the process creates a narrator with imagination, personality, and widsom: He says he is not the "hero" but "only a stray thought, a solution." In this first part of his two-song cycle, Eady also summons earlier personalities created by white writers, including Uncle Tom, Uncle Ben, Jemima, and Steppin Fetchit. The second part of the cycle, the "Running Man Poems," the basis for a libretto for the jazz opera so named, was a finalist for the 1999 Pulitzer Prize. Presented at the HERE Performing Arts Space in New York in winter 1999, the poems offer the life of a black southern man who ventures into the city and who has died.

POETRY

Kartunes. Warthog Press, 1980.
Victims of the Latest Dance Craze. Chicago: Ommation Press, 1986.
BOOM BOOM BOOM. Brockport, NY: State Street Press, 1988. (Out of Print)
The Gathering of My Name. Pittsburgh: Carnegie Mellon University Press, 1991.
You Don't Miss Your Water. New York: Henry Holt, 1995. (Out of Print)
The Autobiography of a Jukebox. Pittsburg: Carnegie Mellon Press, 1997.
Brutal Imagination. New York: G.P. Putnam's Sons, 2001.

REFERENCES

Miller, E. Ethelbert. "An Interview with Cornelius Eady (1995)." In *African American Literary Criticism, 1773 to 2000*. Ed. Hazel Arnett, Ervin. New York: Twayne, 1999. 453–460.
Peters, Erskine. "Cornelius Eady's *You Don't Miss Your Water*: It's Womanist/Feminist Perspective." *Journal of African American Men* 2.1 (1996) 15–31.

MARI EVANS

(n.d.–)

Mari Evans
Credit: Mari Evans
Photo credit: Derek Phemster

W ords and language have always been a part of Mari Evans's life. Poetry is only one of the genres in which she has excelled. Many of Evans's poems are mainstays in anthologies of African American literature and have been translated into various foreign languages. She came to national attention as part of the vanguard of black poetry in the 1960s and early 1970s, but she came to poetry writing indirectly, she has said, because she had phrases that she didn't want to lose.

Evans was born in Toledo, Ohio, to working-class parents. After high school, she studied fashion design at the University of Toledo but changed her interest. Evans's work experience is extremely varied. She has worked in television, including five years (1968–1973) as a producer, writer, and director of *The Black Experience* at WTTV in Indianapolis. Evans is also a playwright, having written a choreopoem, *River of My Song*, a one-woman theater piece, *Boochie*, and a one-man piece, *Portrait of a Man*. She is also playwright, composer, and lyricist for the musical *EYES*, adapted from Zora Neale Hurston's novel *Their Eyes Were Watching God*. Moreover, she has written six books for young people. She is the editor of *Black Women Writers (1950–1980*, a highly regarded collection of essays that also includes brief introductory essays by the authors featured.

Evans has taught at numerous universities and consulted and lectured nationwide. She is former distinguished writer and associate professor at Cornell University's Africana Studies and Research Center and has taught at Indiana University, Purdue University, Northwestern University, Washington University in St. Louis, Spelman College in Atlanta, and the State University of New York at Albany. Evans, divorced with two sons, lives in Indianapolis.

Evans has received numerous awards and honors. A partial list includes being named a John Hay Whitney Fellow (1965); a MacDowell Fellow at the prestigious MacDowell Colony (1975); Outstanding Woman of the Year (1976) from Alpha Kappa Alpha Sorority, graduate chapter; Copeland Fellow at Amherst College (Massachusetts, 1980). She won a Woodrow Wilson grant (1968), the Builder's Award from Third World Press (1977), Black Liberation Award, Kuumba Theatre Workshop Tenth Anniversary Award (Chicago 1978), National Endowment for the Arts Creative Writing Award (1981–1982), Alain Locke–Gwendolyn Brooks Award for Excellence in Literature (1995), Gwendolyn Brooks Center for Black Literature and Creative Writing Award for Longterm Contributions to Black Cultural Arts (1996); and the National Coalition of 100

Black Women, Indianapolis chapter, Award for Excellence in Arts and Culture (1998). In 1997 Evans was honored with her photo on a Ugandan postage stamp.

Clarity and technique are major characteristics of Evans's poetry. Rather than obscure diction or allusion, Evans's lyrics, although often brief and thoughtful ideas or emotions, may be grasped through straightforward reading. The form or physical appearance of the printed poem on the page is a distinctive part of Evans's technique in gaining a reader's attention. To her, the visual aesthetic is as important as what the poem communicates. The persona is also a major component in promoting the realism of the poem, for the speaker's emotion often evokes familiarity with the reader's experiences. The speaker is chosen from different socioeconomic groups, which adds to Evans's ability to engage a wide spectrum of readers.

Like Gwendolyn Brooks, Mari Evans acknowledges the generosity of Langston Hughes in encouraging her early work and motivating the essential self-confidence that preceded her embracing writing as a profession. Armed with this confidence, Evans consciously set about learning the craft of writing and bending herself to its rigorous demands; in other words, she became disciplined. Evans also has followed an artistic position articulated by Hughes in his influential 1926 essay "The Negro Artist and the Racial Mountain," where he stated his intention to direct his work first to African American readers. Through content, diction, voice, and image, Evans also targets her work primarily to the same readers; if others appreciate and understand her work, she is pleased. Another significant person whom Evans recognizes as inspirational is her father. As early as fourth grade, when she wrote a short story, her father's noting its composition date and prominently displaying the story at home left an indelible impression.

Evans's *I Am a Black Woman* (1970), her most widely known volume of lyrics, places emphasis on the personal, including romantic love, and the political. The title poem has become a favorite piece for recitation by college oral performance groups and has often inspired original choreography. The fifteen to twenty revisions that Evans said the poem required appear to have been worth her effort. "I Am a Black Woman" communicates a collective historical consciousness through progressive images of loss. The images date from the Middle Passage through the Vietnam conflict up to the confrontations of the civil rights movement and situate black women in history with black men. These centuries of hardship have produced the indestructible strength affirmed by the last stanza and made black women a source of regeneration. As a unifying strategy for the volume, the last stanza of "I Am a Black Woman" is repeated as the volume's conclusion.

The ninety-three poems in five sections in *I Am a Black Woman* are prefaced by stark and disarming black and white photographs that range from the private and personal to the communal. The first section of poems concerns romantic love, and Evans uses only two speakers. The first section continues in the second, in the lament for the lover who has gone. The poems of the third section involve children, while the fourth section emphasizes distinct personalities in the working-class community. The fifth section, also the lengthiest, moves the community to unity and strength. Among the best known and most effective poems of the volume are the following. "Where Have You Gone," a terse, dramatic situation, is made bittersweet by the speaker's diction when the lover walks out, taking everything precious, including the rent money in one pocket and the woman's heart in the other. "The Friday Ladies of the Pay Envelope," an image-driven lyric, depicts "limpworn" maids reduced by life's conditions to merely waiting for their paychecks on Friday. Although the pay they have earned is their lifeblood, the manner of its delivery markedly undermines any sense of accomplishment. "When in Rome" ironically and humorously recalls the saying, "When in Rome, do as the Romans do." This poem subordinates the maid's voice as she is subordinated in the home of her employer by relegating her colloquial responses to parenthetical positions *beneath* the words of the employer. The employer welcomes the maid Mattie to the food in the refrigerator, except her expensive anchovies, but the employer's choices are displeasing to Mattie who is dissatisfied with eating like the Romans and hopes to live until she arrives home to her own choices. "Vive Noir!"—a lengthy anomaly among Evans's short lyrics—captures primary economic and social goals of the 1960s era to eliminate inner-city ghetto conditions. Packed with black urban idioms, "Vive Noir," a French phrase meaning long live black, chronicles the metaphorical and literal escape from inner-city communities into the mainstream of America. Chronicling the history of black labor in the nation, the speaker plans to occupy those spaces that his labor has produced and to move into the positions of power as well. Although light humor underscores the content through the speaker's diction, the end of the poem concludes with increased humor. Angels, bunnies, and fairies will be black; it will be a crime to be anything but black, and being white will be a lifetime "J.O.B." The physical gymnastics of "Vive Noir" on the page are also more extreme than the other poems in the volume as if to suggest the energy and determination of the content.

Nightstar (1981) includes poems on the subject of the self, music, love lost, and poems written as a blues. The diction runs the gamut from standard usage to black urban vernacular; some poems that are not written in the blues idiom are infused with a blues feeling, as in "Maria Pina and the B&G Grill"—the sadness of women whose men are killed by violence, the loneliness of women who only know love through its physical act. "On the Death of Boochie by Starvation" is a poem that juxtaposes the victim with "they" who are engaged in acts of conjure. Juxtaposition is indicated by the placement of stanzas on the page. When Evans's poems are angry, her images are often sharp, her language clipped as in the brief poem "The Expendables," where people of other nations are killed and the news reports light casualties. In "Face on the Sunwarmed Granite," a black boy is killed for protesting, shot while he lies on the ground. The killer and victim are identified by Christian names and given personal characteristics to bring home the reality of the poem. The individual consistently emerges throughout this volume, from the opening poem "Conceptuality" to "Odyssey"—the power of memory, heritage, and ancestry in the service of revenge. The volume celebrates strong men, those internationally known, like Malcolm X in "El Hajj Malik Shabazz," or those unknown by most, like "The Nigger Who Is Now Hunting You" and James Everett, the protester in "Face on the Sunwarmed Granite."

In her later work as in the initial volumes, Evans has retained and engaged an acute response to those often illogical events that pattern and shape African American experiences. Nevertheless, the style through which she exposes them is never bitter or vituperative but is characterized by a winning lyricism that is always thought provoking.

In the 1980s Evans edited an important collection of essays, *Black Women Writers (1950–1980): A Critical Evaluation*. The collection is distinguished by its inclusion of poets and novelists and its organization, which includes an essay by each writer on her work followed by two essays about that writer. Additionally, Evens has continued to produce literature for African American children. She continues to be a sought-after lecturer and reader across the country.

POETRY

I Am a Black Woman. New York: William Morrow, 1970.
Singing Black. Indianapolis IN: Reed Visuals, 1979. Bpt. East Orange, NJ: Just Us
    Books, 1998.
Nightstar: 1973–1978. Los Angeles: CAAS Publications, 1981.
A Dark and Splendid Mass. New York: Harlem River Press, 1992.

REFERENCES

Dorsey, David. "The Art of Mari Evans." *In Black Women Writers (1950–1980): A Critical Evaluation*. Ed. Mari Evans. New York: Doubleday, 1984. 170–189.

Edwards, Solomon. "Affirmation in the Works of Mari Evans." In *Black Women Writers (1950–1980): A Critical Evaluation*. Ed. Mari Evans. New York: Doubleday, 1984.

Metzger, Linda. *Black Writers*. Detroit: Gale Research, 1988. 188–191.

Peppers, Wallace. "Mari Evans." *In Dictionary of Literary Biography*. Vol. 41. Detroit: Gale Research, 1985. 117–123.

Nikki Giovanni

(1943–   )

Nikki Giovanni
Photo credit: Mari Evans

Nikki Giovanni sparkled onto the black literary scene in 1968, a young Fisk University graduate, and joined her young, energetic, and angry voice with others who were using their poetry to forge social and political change in black America. Charged by the revolutionary fervor of that decade, Giovanni took her poetry directly to the people through performance. Also, she began an extensive schedule of national and international readings and recorded her work with choirs. Her popularity and appeal were almost instant. Within ten years of her first published volumes, she was proclaimed a "star" and "the Princess of Black Poetry." But like other black writers whose poetry was deemed revolutionary, critical opinions differed about the quality of her work. Nevertheless, Giovanni's audience appeal has persisted for thirty years, and her work is taught in colleges and universities. In addition to writing poetry for adults and children, Giovanni has written an autobiography and a collection of essays and edited an anthology of black women poets.

Born in Knoxville, Tennessee, as Yolande Cornelia Giovanni, Jr., on June 7, 1943, the second daughter of Yolande and Jones Giovanni, her family moved to Cincinnati, Ohio, when Giovanni was two months old. Yolande and Jones's decision to relocate north was their effort at shielding their family from racial discrimination. Although both were college graduates, their options in segregated Knoxville were limited to teaching or, for Jones, menial jobs such as hotel bell hop or janitor. Jones began in Cincinnati by being a house parent at Glenview School, then teaching, and finally he became a probation officer. Yolande, who had initially taught school, began work at the Welfare Department. These changes in employment enabled a degree of financial security and the family moved to the black community of Lincoln Heights. Nikki Giovanni's formal education thus began in Cincinnati. Before the family moved to Lincoln Heights, she entered kindergarten and completed third grade at St. Simon's, an all-black Episcopal church.

Giovanni's poetry, especially her signature poem "Nikki-Rosa," confirms that her parents energetically worked to provide a nurturing, loving, and happy environment for their children. Nevertheless, tensions developed in the house, and Jones Giovanni became abusive. Illustrating the independent spirit that has continued to characterize her, Giovanni at age fourteen asked to live for the summer with her maternal grandparents John Brown and Emma Louvenia Watson in Knoxville, Tennessee.

The nurturing environment that Nikki Giovanni had initially enjoyed with her birth parents continued unabated in her grandparents' home where she lived from 1957 to 1960. Her grandfather, a graduate of Fisk University in Nashville, Tennessee, was nicknamed "Book" because he was a Latin teacher and scholar. Giovanni has credited Emma Louvenia Watson with being one of the most influential women in her life. In their segregated Knoxville community, Ms. Watson worked tirelessly as a community volunteer, a church worker, and political activist. In fact, the Watsons had fled Georgia years earlier because Ms. Watson had spoken out against blatant discrimination, and the family feared racist reprisal. She involved the young Nikki in fighting for the rights of full citizenship.

In Knoxville, Nikki attended Austin High School during her ninth, tenth, and eleventh grades. There she met two other women who were instrumental in shaping her educational development. Her English teacher, noting that she needed intellectual challenge, introduced her to African American writers and required her to write reports on what she read. Along with her French teacher, the two teachers encouraged her to apply for early admission to Fisk University. A young Nikki thus left high school at the end of her eleventh year and entered the university at age seventeen. Her first college experience produced conflict between the self-determined granddaughter of Louvenia Watson and the estab-lished protocol for women at the university. Fisk released her from en-rollment after completion of her first semester, presumably because she failed to seek permission from the Dean of Women to return home for the Thanksgiving holidays.

Giovanni's grandfather died in Knoxville shortly after her release from the university. She went to Cincinnati and worked at odd jobs, but she returned to Fisk in 1964 to continue her study as a history major. As her high school English and French teachers had recognized, the new Dean of Women, Blanch McConnell Cowan, also saw something special in Giovanni. Cowan purged the record that had been accumulated against Giovanni by the other dean and became her supporter and mentor. The activism that Giovanni's grandmother had modeled found expression in Giovanni's involvement at Fisk during those turbulent 1960s. Giovanni spearheaded the reinstatement of the Student Nonviolent Coordinating Committee (SNCC) on campus and involved herself with radical student views. Her creativity was fueled by a workshop with the famed novelist John Oliver Killens, and she also edited the university literary magazine. Giovanni graduated with honors in 1967. Her beloved grandmother died shortly afterwards, having been emotionally devastated by the destruc-tion of her Mulvaney Street and home in the name of urban renewal, a fate that befell many African American communities.

The years 1967 and 1968 proved pivotal ones for Giovanni. She moved back to Cincinnati and lived independently. As one way of assuaging her grief for her grandmother, she wrote most of the poems for her first volume of poetry, *Black Feeling, Black Talk*. She continued the activism begun at Fisk and the philosophy of community involvement fostered by her grandmother by organizing the first Black Arts Festival in Cincinnati. It was a resounding success that resulted in the formation of a Black Theater group in the city. She also attended the Detroit conference of Unity and Art where meeting the new president of SNCC, H. Rap Brown, initiated her ongoing close involvement with key figures of the Black Arts Movement. In 1968 Giovanni entered the University of Pennsylvania School of Social Work with a Ford Foundation Fellowship, but she withdrew after only one semester. She had worked at People's Settlement House in Wilmington, Delaware, while enrolled at the university, and she continued that work. When Martin Luther King was killed she left Delaware and drove all night in order to attend his funeral. During the spring and summer of 1968, she wrote the poems that became *Black Judgement*. Giovanni moved to New York City in the same year and gave graduate school a second try, this time at Columbia University in the School of Fine Arts. She encountered a traditional department that could not accept the way she wrote. She resigned from their program and borrowed enough money to publish *Black Feeling, Black Talk*.

A book party for *Black Feeling* in 1969, held at the famous Birdland jazz club, attracted the attention of the *New York Times*, which carried a story with photographs. This attention helped generate the sale of 10,000 copies in less than a year. A grant from the Harlem Council of the Arts assisted Giovanni's publication of her second book, *Black Judgement*. In 1970, a major New York publishing house, William Morrow, published both of Giovanni's volumes under the title *Black Feeling Black Talk/Black Judgement*.

Because much of the black poetry of the 1960s addressed social issues in revolutionary tones and language, the performance of the work, often with musical accompaniment, took on additional significance. Giovanni gained a national audience and became a household name through her frequent appearances on the television program *Soul*. Her performance with the New York Community Choir, released as *Truth Is on Its Way* in 1971, won the Best Spoken Word Album and was listed on the hit charts. Giovanni's initial performance with the choir, before 1,500 people, was testament to her visibility and popularity. In 1971, the importance ascribed to her work was evident when *Mademoiselle* magazine selected her to receive its "Highest Achievement Award." Just two years later, *Ladies'*

Home Journal selected Giovanni for one of its eight Women of the Year Awards. The ceremony was held at Washington's Kennedy Center and televised nationwide.

As Giovanni's popularity soared, and she was noticed and applauded by mainstream organizations, her work incurred the criticism that she was backing away from her initial militancy, especially when *My House* (1972) was published with its lyrical monologues and its emphasis on existence as divided between private and public. Her first three volumes had struck responsive chords with other black cultural nationalists also writing poetry, such as Haki Madhubuti (then named Don L. Lee). From her earliest volumes, however, Giovanni's themes were inclusive. That is, she was never exclusively a promoter of black revolution and social issues in her poetry but addressed numerous other ideas and themes. In fact, two-thirds of the poems in her first two volumes were brief and introspective lyrics. Among the poems of *Black Feeling, Black Talk*, more than half of them address nonrevolutionary concerns. Her themes were blackness, womanhood, fathers, mothers, children, romantic love, and dreams. Collectively read, her poems also suggest her belief that individuals are more important than ideas.

By 1969, in fact, she had distanced her work from the dictum that all black poetry of the era was required to promote revolution. One of her most popular poems, "Seduction," pokes fun at the concentration on social change to the exclusion of other important concerns. The male character in the poem spouts the rhetoric of revolution in the house with "Nikki," the partner in the poem, while she is disrobing both of them. When he notices their states of undress, his final line in the poem is a stunned, "isn't this counterrevolutionary?"

Among the poems in Giovanni's early volumes that fit the militancy of the times are "The True Import of Present Dialogue Black vs. Negro," "For Saundra," and "Poem (No Name No 3)." The short repetitive questions of "can you kill" in the initial eight lines of "The True Import" are designed for shock and attention. The most important query in the poem is whether the enslaved mind of the "negro" can be killed. The poem points out that through the black man's participation in the life of the United States, its conflicts in Japan, Africa, and Vietnam, for example, political killing is common. This time the killing will be for the liberation of black men, figuratively and literally. "For Saundra" points out that the politically charged times do not lend themselves to traditional poetic images like trees and blue skies, but the times do suggest readying one's gun and kerosene supply. "Poem" issues an urgent plea to join the revolution because white retaliation is inevitable and already apparent in what has happened to outspoken black leaders like Malcolm X and LeRoi Jones (black cultural nationalist and poet legally charged and jailed in Newark during the 1967 riots). This poem, similar to "The True Import," urges "negroes" to action. Giovanni strategically places that word, written in lowercase on a single line, to draw distinction between those mentally conditioned to wait and the black person fighting for change.

On the other hand many of Giovanni's most respected nonmilitant poems, often cited as her best efforts, appear in the early volumes. "Nikki-Rosa," the name given to Giovanni by her sister, offers the well-quoted line, "Black love is Black wealth." The poem draws incidents from the poet's childhood experiences to say that growing up without material wealth does not equal a miserable childhood in the black experience. "Knoxville, Tennessee" also draws from lovely childhood memories of the time that the poet spent with her maternal grandmother. An extensive list of foods grown in southern gardens along with the warm colors of summer comprises the content of the poem. "Kidnap Poem" and "Ego Tripping," both in *Re: Creation*, illustrate Giovanni's sense of playfulness. "Kidnap" is a lyric that names several techniques of poetry that might be used to ensnare someone. To affirm the poem's playful tone, the poet divides the word "kidnap," placing the word "kid" in a crucial position at the end of a concluding line. "Ego Tripping," a favorite performance piece for spoken word groups, reflects the oral tradition of the toast, an urban black folk narrative that is elaborate and exuberant and characterized by exaggeration and bravado. "Ego" is pure hyperbole, the bigger-than-life exploits and abilities of an African-born mythic woman. Narrated in the first person, the persona is the mother of many great sons including Hannibal and Noah, and her smallest actions—blowing her nose and producing oil, for example—have consequences. Giovanni's playfulness is again evident in this poem where world-building greatness concludes with understatement: The woman can fly like a bird. Angelou's similarly popular poem "Phenomenal Woman," structured like a toast as well, is most probably indebted to Giovanni's "Ego Tripping."

Black music and its rhythms are also significant in Giovanni's poetry. "Master Charge Blues," for example, is a blues-structured poem. "That Day" in *Cotton Candy on a Rainy Day* (1978), has been set to music in a bluesy jazz style. Several poems include references to specific songs and performers as in "Beautiful Black Men" and "Revolutionary Music" in her first volume and "Poem for Aretha" in *Re: Creation*.

Although images abound in Giovanni's work, her poems do not employ difficult-to-determine symbols or abstruse metaphors or other techniques that can make poetry intellectually challenging. Most readers find it easy to read and understand because the content often addresses ordinary human experience in direct language that is drawn from ordinary black speech patterns. This is not to say that Giovanni is not serious about her poetry. Poems titled "Poetry" and "Poetry Is a Trestle" are devoted to her examining or questioning the craft of poetry or its effect. "A Poem Off Center," a recognition of the relationship between gender and writing, seems also directed to Giovanni's critics who have suggested that she pandered to the demands of the moment. She emphasizes in interviews that her work is always an attempt to confront and to express the truth. In an interview with Virginia Fowler, Giovanni says that voice is the most important quality of her poems. She works at making the voice consistent in her numerous poems, at keeping it purely hers, but she also wants the voice to reflect her maturity over the years. The idea of the poet's subjective or personal voice in his or her poem strongly contradicts the generally taught supposition that writers create objective voices who speak in their poetry.

Regarding her work, Giovanni speaks of connections and tradition rather than influences. Ideologically, she feels connected to Langston Hughes. He wrote what he believed, freed from ideologies of the time, as Giovanni tries to do. He performed his poetry with jazz, and she has used music in poetry performance. Also, his poetry had the qualities of the spoken word that are significant to Giovanni.

Giovanni beings an indomitable spirit to her work and to personal adversity. For example, when her father had a stroke in 1978, she returned to Cincinnati with her son, Thomas Watson Giovanni, who had been born in 1969, and cared for her parents. This decision illustrated her commitment to family at the same time as she maintained a schedule of personal appearances and writing. In 1984, when she disagreed with artists boycotting South Africa, she received death threats. Her personal mettle was required again in 1995 when she was diagnosed with lung cancer and underwent successful surgery.

Giovanni has been a phenomenal success by most standards. In addition to her writing, personal appearances, recordings, editing, and travel, she has been teaching since 1969, beginning at Queens College in New York and then at Rutgers. In 1984–1985, she was a visiting professor at Ohio State University, and Mount Saint Joseph's College from 1985 to 1987. Since 1987, she has been a faculty member at Virginia Polytechnic Institute and State University in Blacksburg, Virginia. In 1974, she received the first of numerous honorary doctorate degrees, this one from Wilberforce University. At age thirty-one, she was the youngest recipient of such a prestigious honor. Among numerous other honors, she has been the YWCA Woman of the Year in Cincinnati, named to the Ohio Women's Hall of Fame, and named Outstanding Woman of Tennessee. PBS produced a film about her life in 1987 titled *Spirit to Spirit: The Poetry of Nikki Giovanni*.

POETRY

Black Feeling, Black Talk. Detroit: Broadside Press, 1968. (Out of Print)
Black Judgement. Detroit: Broadside Press, 1968. (Out of Print)
Black Feeling, Black Talk/Black Judgement. New York: Morrow/Avon, 1970.
Re: Creation. Detroit: Broadside Press, 1970. (Out of Print)
My House. New York: Harper Trade, 1972.
The Women and the Men. New York: Morrow/Avon, 1975.
Cotton Candy on a Rainy Day. New York: Writers & Readers, 1978.
Those Who Ride the Night Winds. New York: Harper Trade, 1983.
The Selected Poems of Nikki Giovanni. New York: Morrow/Avon, 1996.
Love Poems. New York: Morrow/Avon, 1997.
Blues: For All the Changes: New Poems. New York: Morrow/Avon, 1999.
Grand Fathers: Reminiscences, Poems, Recipes, and Photos of the Keepers of Our Tradition. New York: Henry Holt & Company, 2000.

NONFICTION

Night Comes Softly: Anthology of Black Female Voices. Newark: Medic Press, 1970.
Gemini: An Extended Autobiographical Statement on My First Twenty-five Years of Being a Black Poet. Indianapolis: Bobbs-Merrill, 1971. Rpt., Penguin Books, 1980.
A Dialogue: James Baldwin and Nikki Giovanni. New York: Lippincott, 1973.
A Poetic Equation: Conversations between Nikki Giovanni and Margaret Walker. Washington: Howard University Press, 1974.

RECORDINGS

Truth Is on Its Way. With The New York Community Choir, Benny Diggs, director. Right On Records, 1971.
Like a Ripple on a Pond. With The New York Community Choir, Benny Diggs, director. Niktom Records. Distributed by Atlantic Recording Corporation 1973.
The Way I Feel. With Music Composed by Arif Mardin. Niktom Records. Distributed by Atlantic Recording Corporation, 1975.
Legacies. Folkways Records FL 9798, 1976.
The Reason I Like Chocolate. Folkways Records FC 7775, 1976.
Cotton Candy on a Rainy Day. Folkways Records FL 9756, 1978.
Spirit to Spirit. Directed by Mirra Banks. Produced by Perrin Ireland. PBS Television, 1987. Videocassette.

REFERENCES

Cook, Martha. "Nikki Giovanni: Place and Sense of Place in Her Poetry." In *Southern Women Writers: The New Generation*. Ed. Tonnette Bond Inge. Tuscaloosa: University of Alabama Press, 1990. 279–300.

Fowler, Virginia C. *Nikki Giovanni*. New York: Twayne, 1992.

Fowler, Virginia C., ed. *Conversations with Nikki Giovanni*. Jackson: University Press of Mississippi, 1992.

Gaffke, Carol. T., ed. *Poetry Criticism*. Vol. 19. New York: Gail Research, 1997.

Giddings, Paula. "Nikki Giovanni: Taking a Chance on Feeling." In *Black Women Writers (1950–1980): A Critical Evaluation*. Ed. Mari Evans. New York: Doubleday, 1984. 211–17.

Giovanni, Nikki. "An Answer to Some Questions on How I Write: In Three Parts." In *Black Women Writers (1950–1980): A Critical Evaluation*. Ed. Mari Evans. New York: Doubleday, 1984. 205–210.

Harris, William J. "Sweet Soft Essence of Possibility: The Poetry of Nikki Giovanni." In *Black Women Writers (1950–1980): A Critical Evaluation*. Ed. Mari Evans. New York: Doubleday, 1984. 218–28.

Noble, Jeanne. "Speak the Truth to the People." In *Beautiful Also Are the Souls of My Black Sisters: A History of the Black Woman in America*. Englewood Cliffs, NJ: Prentice-Hall, 1978. 146–208.

Palmer, Roderick. "The Poetry of Three Revolutionists: Don L. Lee, Sonia Sanchez, and Nikki Giovanni." In *Modern Black Poets*. Ed. Donald B. Gibson. Englewood Cliffs, NJ: Prentice-Hall, 1973. 135–46.

Reynolds, Barbara. "Inquiry." *USA Today*, September 19, 1985.

Tate, Claudia. *Black Women Writers at Work*. New York: Continuum, 1983. 60–78.

JUPITER HAMMON

(1711–1806)

"An Evening Thought: Salvation by Christ, with Penetential Cries," published on December 25, 1760, marked the first appearance in print of writing by a person of African descent in the American colonies. This accomplishment is even more laudable when it is known that Hammon was enslaved and living in the eighteenth century.

Hammon was fifty years old when the poem was published and was the property of the Lloyd family, whose business ventures, including slave trading, evolved into the Lloyds of London. Hammon had been born at their plantation in Oyster Bay, Long Island, New York. The Lloyd family papers confirm that Hammon was a slave all of his life.

Much about Hammon's life has been pieced together through information found in and suggested by the records of the Lloyd family as well as historically informed conclusions about slave existence in the Northeast in the eighteenth century. The source of Hammon's literacy, for example, has been a subject of speculation. It has been assumed that he might have been exposed to formal education along with John Lloyd, the second son born to the Lloyd family who shared the same birth year as Hammon. The speculation also includes the suggestion that Hammon was taught through the Society for the Propagation of the Gospel, an organization of the Church of England whose mission was teaching slaves in America, Native Americans, and white colonists without religion. The organization reached Oyster Bay when Hammon was a teenager. The Lloyd family belonged to the Church of England.

Although Hammon himself mentioned a few personal details in his essays, still few facts are known through direct information about his personal existence. Historians believe they have detected the presence of the Quaker religion in Hammon's work, and they point out that in order for a slave to be published during Hammon's era, he would have needed the political and financial support of Quakers. Visits by John Woolman, the well-known eighteenth-century Quaker abolitionist, to Oyster Bay coincided with Hammon's time of living there, and the small town was recognized for the presence of feverent Quaker abolition work. Finally, the Quakers in Philadelphia published Hammon's last prose after his death and in the dedication suggested an association with the author. No record or anecdote mentions Hammon's having married or having had children, but official records verify that black women were scarce in the northern colonies with the male-to-female ratio being ten to one. Hammon worked as a clerk in the Lloyd family business, so his educational level was obviously sufficient for these purposes.

During the Revolutionary War, the Lloyds moved to Hartford, Connecticut. Records reveal that Hammond published five works there. In addition to essays, he published three poems in addition to his first, "An Evening Thought": "An Address to Miss Phillis Wheatly [sic], Ethiopian Poetess," "A Poem for Children with Thoughts of Death," and "A Dialogue Entitled The Kind Master and the Dutiful Servant." Other works by Hammon mentioned in papers or journals of the period have not been found. Historian Jacqueline Overton has said that Hammon was a folk poet whose work was well known in his surroundings.

His first poem, "An Evening Thought," is considered his most significant contribution to African American literary history because it is the beginning of the tradition of printed verse. It reflects the religious fevor of the era in its content and its structure. Hammon used the meter familiar to the Great Awakening. Like Phillis Wheatley, any reference to or criticism of the institution of slavery is so muted as to be virtually undetectable by modern readers. Also like Wheatley, Hammon was criticized for the omission. His subtlety, however, was essential if the writer wished the work to be printed. The eighty-eight lines of the poem repeatedly exhort the acceptance of Christ, for it is through Him that "redemption [comes] now to every one." Obviously, Hammon makes the case that black people will be included among the saved.

POETRY

America's First Negro Poet: The Complete Works of Jupiter Hammon. Ed. Stanley Ransom Jr. New York: Associated Faculty Press, 1970.

REFERENCE

Brawley, Benjamin. *Early Negro American Writers*. 1935. Rpt., Mineola, NY: Dover, 1992.

Kaplan, Sidney, and Emma Nogrady Kaplan. *The Black Presence in the Era of the American Revolution: 1770–1800*. Washington, DC: Smithsonian Institution Press, 1973.

O'Neale, Sondra. *Jupiter Hammon and the Biblical Beginnings of African-American Literature*. Lanham, MD: Scarecrow Press, 1993.

Robinson, William H., Jr. *Early Black American Poets: Selections with Biographical and Critical Introductions*. Dubuque, IA: W.C. Brown, 1969.

Wegelin, Oscar. *Jupiter Hammon: American Negro Poet, Selections from His Writings and a Bibliography*. 1915. Rpt., Freeport, NY: Books for Libraries Press, 1970.

FRANCES ELLEN WATKINS HARPER

(1824–1911)

Frances Ellen Watkins Harper
Credit: Photographs and Prints Division, Schomburg Center for Research in
Black Culture, The New York Public Library, Astor, Lenox and Tilden
Foundations

Frances Harper heads a long list of black poets whose poetry was motivated by their social activism. She shaped her poems to the abolitionist cause as she traveled the Northern states in the nineteenth century, establishing a reputation as a committed orator and writer. Referred to as the "bronze muse," Harper was the most widely known black poet writing between Phillis Wheatley and Paul Laurence Dunbar. Harper also had the distinction of being the first black woman to publish a short story, "The Two Offers," and was the second black woman to publish a nineteenth-century popular novel, *Iola Leroy* (1892). Before scholarship unearthed a novel preceding that date, *Our Nig; Or Sketches From the Life of a Free Black* by Harriet E. Wilson, Harper's novel was considered the first one by a black woman. Her poetry, however, sustains her presence in literary tradition.

The poet, an only child, was born in Baltimore to free parents. Her mother died in 1828, and Harper was sent to live with Mr. and Mrs. William Watkins, her aunt and uncle. Her uncle operated the William Watkins Academy for Negro Youth, where Harper was educated through reading the Bible and composition. Her uncle, a self-educated minister as well as a shoemaker, William J. Watkins, was a passionate abolitionist, and his zeal for slaves' liberation was a contributing influence on his young niece. When she completed her studies at age fourteen, in 1838, she became a residential housekeeper and seamstress, the work ordinarily available to free black women. Fortunately, Harper continued to study at the local library and to write poems and articles that a local newspaper published in the 1840s. Also during this time, she is said to have published *Forest Leaves*, her earliest volume of poems, but no copies of it have been found.

Between 1850 and 1852, Harper attended Union Seminary, a new vocational school for free blacks near Columbus, Ohio, founded by the African Methodist Episcopal Church. She also taught there, the first female teacher hired, to instruct students in embroidery and sewing, then known as the domestic arts. The school later became part of Wilberforce University, founded in 1856, where many black people received an undergraduate education before slavery ended. Harper then returned to Little York, Pennsylvania, for a year and taught small children. In this town, she met William Grant Still, head of the local Underground Railroad station, who became her longtime correspondent and friend. Harper also came into contact with fugitives from slavery using the Underground escape routes, a series of protective stops along a defined path to the free states. Deeply affected by their condition, and the power of the Fugitive Slave Act being enforced in her home state of Maryland, Harper committed herself to working for slaves' freedom. She moved to an Underground Railroad station in Philadelphia, most likely Still's home, where she lived off and on with Still's family for twenty years.

Harper's commitment shaped the rest of her life. Her work, and that of many other black and white people, helped slavery to its death. Between 1854 and 1860, Harper spoke against slavery and read her poetry, sometimes twice a day, in more than eight states, including the New England states, Ohio, New York, Pennsylvania, and New Jersey. From 1854 to 1865, Harper was hired as a lecturer and poet for the Maine Antislavery Society. She took on the same work for the Pennsylvania Anti-Slavery Society from 1857 to 1858. Her friend William Grant Still described Harper's dramatic recitations and speeches as extremely audience effective. She continued until nearly eighty years of age to crusade for social reform in many nineteenth-century movements, including affiliation with the American Women's Suffrage Association.

Her best-known volume of poems, *Poems on Miscellaneous Subjects*, published in Boston in 1854, became part of Harper's strategy for persuading audiences to support abolition. William Lloyd Garrison, perhaps the best known abolitionist, wrote the preface for Harper's *Poems*. The book sold 50,000 copies and went through twenty editions. The second enlargement of *Poems* in 1871, called the 20th edition, had twenty-six poems and three prose essays. Her verse was direct in its intent and conventional in form and poetic technique like that of other popular poets of the period including Henry Wadsworth Longfellow and John Greenleaf Whittier. Harper's pieces depended on regular rhyme since much of its power was transmitted through her oral presentations. In fact, because Harper's poetry tapped the oral tradition recognized in African American culture, she has been labeled an "orator poet" along with earlier black poets Lucy Terry, Jupiter Hammon, George Moses Horton, James Whitfield, and James Madison Bell, whose work had strong qualities of orality.

From the 1854 volume until 1901, Harper's thematic concerns encompassed religion, race, and social reform; love and death; and antislavery sentiments. Many poems such as "That Blessed Hope" and "Saved by Faith" drew from the Old and New Testaments. She invoked the God of the Israelites in "Ethiopia" for his ability to bring about freedom. "The Bible Defense of Slavery" was among a similar group of poems in which Harper decried "prophets of evil" who fed the outrage against miscegenation and used it against the slaves. Race and the plea for social reform often overlap in Harper's work as in "The Slave Auction" and "The Slave Mother," two of her most anthologized pieces. "The Slave Auction" drew its strength from the powerful image of the auction block and the separation of families. The powerful, emotional images of cruel familial separation argued the case for immediate reform without Harper's articulating it. "The Slave Mother" also emphasized separation but focused narrowly on the severed bond of mother and child and the mother's helplessness in protecting her child. "Bury Me in a Free Land" argues for the reform that would make everyone free since the speaker will not rest even in death if slaves still walk the land. Often considered her best antislavery poem, the stanzas of "Bury" build in dramatic intensity. They subtly communicate the idea that slavery is a form of death analogous to the real death that the poem's speaker anticipates when she demands burial in a land of freedom.

Harper's activism brought her into contact with other major activists of the day including Frederick Douglass. In 1858, Harper lived in William Still's home along with Mrs. John Brown a few weeks before John Brown's execution for his violent strike against slavery at Harpers Ferry, Virginia. Harper donated money to Brown's followers who remained imprisoned.

Harper married Fenton Harper, a widower with three children, in 1860 and withdrew from public life for a few years. Little is known about her life at that time, but the Harpers made their home near Columbus, Ohio, and had one daughter, Mary. Local newspapers did report some lectures that Frances Harper gave and printed a few new poems. When Fenton died in 1864, debtors are said to have claimed virtually all of the Harpers' household belongings. Frances Harper was thus obligated to financially support herself and her daughter. She returned to the lecture circuit, again immersing herself in combating slavery through traveling and speaking against it. Harper's daughter Mary did not marry and died about two years before her mother.

After the Civil War, between 1867 and 1871, Harper traveled the Southern states for the first time, financing herself. Her meeting places were plantations, schools, churches, and courthouses, and she lived among the people she addressed. She was thus in a pivotal position to know the educational, social, and economical needs of a recently freed population, particularly its women. Harper publications continued with the publication of *Moses*, later enlarged to *Idylls of the Bible* (1901); the enlarged edition of *Poems* (1871); and *Sketches of Southern Life* (1872).

Moses is considered by some scholars to be Harper's best book. Instead of the conventional rhyming couplets and stanzas characteristic of her earlier work, Harper wrote a forty-page blank verse poem that is a dramatic biblical allegory. Possibly inspired by Lincoln's role in the emancipation of black people, the poem prophesies the coming of a racial leader like Moses. The speaker narrates the biblical story of Moses to symbolize the hope of the black population and emphasizes spiritual and physical liberty along with morals. The poem cautions avoiding the fate of the Israelites, who wandered forty years in the wilderness. This lengthy poem perhaps places Harper in the front ranks of other black writers who have written analogies between the fate of the black population and the Israelites and Moses as their spiritual leader.

Sketches of Southern Life seems clearly inspired by Harper's extended contact with black Southern folk life, as Jean Toomer was inspired to write *Cane* (1923) after a few months in Georgia. *Sketches* consist of connected verse narratives written to approximate the speech that Harper heard. However, she did not write dialect. Avoiding the limitations of that style, Harper fashioned narrators, Aunt Chloe and Uncle Jack, who were judicious and politically informed. They discuss the contemporary concerns of blacks, including politics and education. They also emphasize the role of religion in racial uplift. Overall, the two narrators offer a portrait of slave and rural life.

Harper remained committed to her vision to eradicate slavery and, after that, to lending her energy and talent to other reform measures. She took to the stage as an outspoken woman when it was an unpopular and unexpected role for black women. She remains a significant figure in the tradition of black poetry for the volume of work she produced in the nineteenth century and for her ability to execute a poetry of protest.

POETRY

Poems on Miscellaneous Subjects. Boston: J.B. Yerrinton & Son, Printers. 1854. Nendeln [Liechtenstein] Kraus Reprint, 1971. (Out of Print)

Moses: A Story of the Nile. 2nd ed. Philadelphia: Merrihew, 1869. (Out of Print)

Poems. 1871. Rpt., New York: Books for Libraries Press, 1970. (Out of Print)

Sketches of Southern Life. Philadelphia: Merrihew, 1872. (Out of Print)

The Sparrow's Fall and Other Poems. N.p., 1890 (?). (Out of Print)

Atlanta Offering. Philadelphia: George S. Ferguson, 1895. Rpt., Manchester: Ayer, 1977. (Out of Print)

Poems. 1896. Rpt., Nashville: Post Oak Publications, 1998.

Idylls of the Bible. Philadelphia: n.p., 1901. (Out of Print)

Complete Poems of Frances E.W. Harper. New York: Oxford University Press, 1988.

A Brighter Coming Day: A Frances Ellen Watkins Harper Reader. Ed. Frances Smith Foster. New York: Feminist Press, 1990. (Out of Print)

Light beyond the Darkness. N.p., n.d. (Out of Print)

REFERENCES

Foster, Frances. "Frances Ellen Watkins Harper." *In African American Writers*. Ed. Lea Baechler and A. Walton Litz. New York: Charles Scribner's Sons, 1991. 159–76.

Gloster, Hugh. *Negro Voices in American Fiction*. Chapel Hill: University of North Carolina Press, 1948.

Graham, Maryemma. "Frances Ellen Watkins Harper." *In Dictionary of Literary Biography*. Vol. 50 Ed. Trudier Harris and Thadious M. Davis. Detroit: Gale Research, 1986. 164–73.

Hill, Patricia Liggins. "Let Me Make the Songs for the People." *Black American Literature Forum* 15 (Summer 1981): 60–65.

Loewenberg, Bert James, and Ruth Bogin. *Black Women in Nineteenth Century American Life, Their Words, Their Thoughts, Their Feelings*. University Park: Pennsylvania State University Press, 1976. 243–51.

Sherman, Joan. *Invisible Poets*. Urbana: University of Illinois Press. 62–74.

Still, William Grant. *The Underground Railroad*. Philadelphia: Porter & Coates, 1872. 755–80.

Michael S. Harper

(1938–)

Michael S. Harper
Credit: Brown University
Photo credit: John Foraste

M usic, history, art, and family are among the themes that Michael Harper explores in a distinctive and fresh voice and style. Harper's first book, *Dear John, Dear Coltrane* (1970), though published on the hem of the Black Arts Movement, does not look backward to that era but forward. Harper's work builds on that of numerous predecessors in the subjects that reoccur in his numerous volumes, but his methods are original. The esteem with which Harper is regarded is suggested through his award-winning work. His first book of poetry, *Dear John*, was nominated for a National Book Award. The Poetry Award of the Black Academy of Arts and Letters in 1971 was awarded to *History Is Your Own Heartbeat*. Moreover, Harper has won the National Institute of Arts and Letters Creative Writing Award, a Guggenheim Fellowship, a National Endowment for the Arts grant, and a Massachusetts Council Creative Writing Award. *Images of Kin* was awarded the Melville-Cane Award and was nominated for the 1978 National Book Award.

Harper was born in Brooklyn, New York, to Walter Warren, a postal worker and supervisor, and Katherine Johnson Harper, a medical stenographer. Mrs. Harper was Episcopal and her husband was Catholic. In 1951 the family moved to West Los Angeles to a predominantly white community primarily to remove their children from the presence of gangs. Some black homes in their new area were bombed in the early 1950s. Young Harper was in the eighth grade, and the resettlement was traumatic for him. Michael has credited Brooklyn with his substantial development rather than Los Angeles. His parents had a large collection of records, so Michael grew up with the music of Charlie Parker, Charles Mingus, and Dexter Gordon.

In the first of three instances where his academic ability would be doubted, Harper was placed in industrial arts when he attended Susan Miller Dorsey High School. His father's intervention resulted in Harper's being placed on an academic tract, and he graduated in 1955. In 1956 he enrolled at Los Angeles State College. He seemed destined for medicine since two of his grandfathers were doctors. Roland Johnson, his maternal grandfather, had delivered Harper at birth, and his great-grandfather, Dr. John Albert Johnson, was a physician as well as a bishop in the AME Church and a missionary to the dioceses of South Africa from 1907 to 1916. Harper's enrollment in a formal premed course, however, resulted in a zoology professor advising him to drop the program. For a second time, someone in academe had viewed race as incompatible with success in academics.

During his undergraduate years, Harper worked the graveyard shift at a post office where many of his companionable coworkers were black men with advanced degrees who could not get work commensurate with their educational preparation. His education was thus continued at his work.

Upon graduation, perhaps on the advice of two undergraduate mentors who were alumni of the Iowa Writers Workshop of the University of Iowa, Harper enrolled in the Workshop in 1961. He had begun writing poems in high school but in college had switched to short fiction and short dramatic forms. At Iowa, where he was the only black student in his poetry and fiction classes, he began seriously writing poetry and worked mostly in isolation. Similar to Sterling Brown's experience at Williams College many years earlier, black students at Iowa were restricted to living in segregated housing. Harper's friends were foreign students, one from Ghana, West Africa, who taught Harper the Anansi stories, African-based folktales that have survived predominantly in the Caribbean.

When Harper returned to Los Angeles in 1962, he began his college teaching career. His first job at Pasadena City College gave way between 1964 and 1968 to a position at Contra Costa College, San Pablo, California. In 1968–1969, he was visiting professor at Reed College and at Lewis and Clark College, and in 1969–1970 at California State College.

In San Francisco, Harper married Shirley Ann Buffington in 1965 and began his family, which grew to three children—Roland Stephen, Patrice Cuchulain, and Rachael Maria. Tragedy touched his life, however, when two sons died in infancy. The second son has been memorialized in the poems of his name, "Reuben, Reuben" and "We Assume: On the Death of Our Son, Reuben Masai Harper," both in *Dear John*.

Since 1970 Harper has been professor at Brown University in Providence, Rhode Island, where he has moved up the ranks to become Israel J. Kapstein Professor of English. Several of his students have become nationally known novelists and poets including Gayl Jones, Sherley Anne Williams, Melvin Dixon, and the scholars Claudia Tate and Herman Beavers. Harper has also been a visiting professor at Harvard, Yale, Carleton College in Northfield, Minnesota, and an Elliston Poet, Distinguished Professor, at the University of Cincinnati.

Harper traveled extensively in the 1970s. He visited Ghana, South Africa, Zaire, Senegal, Gambia, Botswana, Zambia, and Tanzania on an American specialist grant in 1977. Other locations included Germany, Egypt, Scandinavia, and Mexico.

Numerous majority and black poets have influenced Harper's work.

Like any good poet, he has read voraciously the work of other poets. The result is a solid grounding in the traditions of American poetry, a feat evident in Harper's poems. His influences are numerous, including Walt Whitman, the modernist poets William Carlos Williams, T.S. Eliot, Robert Lowell, and Theodore Roethke, and African Americans Paul Laurence Dunbar, Langston Hughes, Robert Hayden, Gwendolyn Brooks, and Sterling Brown. Harper shares with Brown a deep appreciation of the black oral tradition and succeeds in joining black idioms and cultural motifs with experiences that define all humanity. Harper has been called a narrative poet, and he almost always uses free verse. His poems are densely constructed, and his is a poetry of ideas that demands the reader's attentiveness.

Dear John, Dear Coltrane, Harper's first book, contained ten years of poems, though they are not all specifically about the famed jazz musician John Coltrane, as the title implies. In fact, initially the book had a different name, but since his original title was already in use, Harper selected the present one. Musicians, music, and John Coltrane, as a major jazz stylist, are important to the conception of the book and to the techniques of many of the poems. Specifically, jazz with its distinctive rhythms, its open-ended forms, and its energy informs the major concept of this book and is indispensable in Harper's shaping of poems throughout his work. His poems are seldom in traditional forms like the sonnet or villanelle; they are modeled around music. Jazz and blues often function as inspiration, metaphor, or rhythm. Harper is unabashedly a devotee of music and a preserver of the black oral tradition and of the memory and talent of John Coltrane.

John Coltrane, with whom Harper was friends until the musician's death in 1967, has perhaps exercised as much influence on modern black poets as he has on other musicians, judging from the number of poets who have written poems about him. The title poem of the volume, "Dear John, Dear Coltrane," is subtitled with the name of Coltrane's signature song, "A Love Supreme." The phrase also is used doubly as a refrain and as a line of ironic punctuation that is strategically placed in the poem. Human regeneration is at the heart of the poem "Dear John." Out of the violence perpetrated against potent southern black men, a force crystallizes and spirals in an unanticipated form. John Coltrane is this force, negating violence and death through his inimitable music and answering hate with *a love supreme* through which he enables the survival of others more than himself. The poem's middle section, printed in italics, evokes the black oral tradition, black vernacular speech, and blues, all of which are reflected in Coltrane's jazz styling. The musician's style of living is ultimately his downfall, and Harper refers to Coltrane's sickness and his diseased liver in the last stanza of the poem. Nevertheless, the influential and regenerative force of his music, particularly "A Love Supreme," will remain. Harper suggests this permanence through his technique of balancing the end of the poem with four repetitions of the phrase "a love supreme," in an anchoring gesture of finality. In "Dirge for Trane," the poet's voice agonizes over being in Mexico since Coltrane had been dead for ten days before Harper heard the news. Other poems to musicians in *Dear John* include "Effendi" for jazz pianist McCoy Tyner, "For Bud" for Bud Powell, and "To James Brown," but poems about music and musicians occur throughout Harper's published volumes.

Similarly, poems that evoke history occur throughout Harper's work. He often creates situations where the contradictions between oral and written versions of history emerge. Thematically, Harper layers the historical with the personal so that the personal may be undistinguishable from the historical. However, *History Is Your Own Heartbeat* is distinguished by Harper's combining of myth and history with the poet's personal history. It is a more tightly conceived book than *Dear John*. Part One begins with "Ruth's Blues," a poem in twenty parts. This poem anchors the book's concern with history and myth, it introduces the blues that is indicative of the black experience, and it offers a family that is both literal and symbolic. The hospital in the work symbolizes America and its sickness, but the poem is also about Ruth as a woman. Harper has admitted to the poem's complexity.

Part Two of *History Is Your Own Heartbeat* offers twenty-eight poems, most dedicated to persons who have assisted Harper's intellectual growth in various ways. Notable is "Madimba," the poem for Gwendolyn Brooks, who read and praised Harper's work since his first manuscript. Music informs the poem, since its composition is indebted to a song played by McCoy Tyner and since the madimba is an African instrument that has no middle parts. It is a highly symbolic and allusive poem, referencing music, including "a love supreme" but also the famous explanation of double consciousness from W.E.B. Du Bois.

In Part Three, Harper brings together the concerns that dictate the volume, emphasizing myth and history, the black past in American history, and Africa as the spiritual homeland. The meaning of the title is apparent: All Americans have had a role in the history of the country and must claim their responsibility to the past, present, and future. Several poems in *Dear John* also concern Mexico, where Harper spent a summer with his wife and oldest son. The beauty there helped him understand how to write about painting as indicated in "High Modes," "Apollo Vision," and "Zeus Muse."

By the time Harper publishes *Images of Kin* (1977), which offers mostly poems selected from previous volumes along with fourteen new ones, his patterning of kinship with historical figures and others, his emphasis on traditions concerning race and the consequence on contemporary black life and his attraction to jazz and blues forms have become recurrent and identifiable features of his poetry. In the new poems in *Images of Kin*, identified in the section "Healing Songs," Harper seems to be entering a period of resolution in the conflicts that race and history have previously engendered in his work.

Honorable Amendments (1995) also continues the tradition of interests and style now familiar to readers of Harper. Consistently, his work has received praise for its creativity and originality but acknowledgment, too, of its complexity, even to seasoned readers. Perhaps *Honorable Amendments* links most obviously with earlier work through Harper's references to history and black music hero John Coltrane, who in this volume is joined with a pantheon of others including Dexter Gordon, Sarah Vaughan, Romare Bearden, and Willie Mays.

Harper continues to improve on his prolific output and to enhance the study of African American poetry through his involvement in editing anthologies that make a wide variety of poetry available to a large audience. His prodigious work is continually acknowledged, including his appointment as the first Poet Laureate of the state of Rhode Island between 1988 and 1993.

POETRY

Dear John, Dear Coltrane. Pittsburgh: University of Pittsburgh Press, 1970. Rpt., Champaign: University of Illinois Press, 1985.

History Is Your Own Heartbeat: Poems. Urbana: University of Illinois Press, 1971. (Out of Print)

Photographs: Negatives: History as Apple Tree. San Francisco: Scarab Press, 1972. (Out of Print)

Song: I Want a Witness. Pittsburgh: University of Pittsburgh Press, 1972. (Out of Print)

Debridement. New York: Doubleday, 1973.

Nightmare Begins Responsibility. Urbana: University of Illinois Press, 1975.

Images of Kin: New and Selected Poems. Urbana: University of Illinois Press, 1977.

Rhode Island: Eight Poems. Roslindale, MA: Pym-Randall Press, 1981.

Healing Song for the Inner Ear: Poems. Urbana: University of Illinois Press, 1985.

Songlines: Mosaics. Providence, RI: Brown/Ziggurat Press, 1991.

Honorable Amendments. Urbana: University of Illinois Press, 1995.

Songlines in Michaeltree: New and Collected Poems. Urbana: University of Illinois Press, 2000.

EDITED ANTHOLOGIES

(With Robert Stepto). *Chant of Saints: A Gathering of Afro-American Literature, Art, and Scholarship*. Urbana: University of Illinois Press, 1979.
Every Shut Eye Ain't Asleep: An Anthology of Poetry by African Americans since 1945. Boston: Little, Brown, 1994.
(With Anthony Walton). *The Vintage Book of African American Poetry*. New York: Vintage Books, 2000.

RECORDINGS

Hear Where Coltrane Is. Washington, DC.: Watershed Tapes, 1984. Cassette.
The Heart of Things. New York: David Grubin Productions, 1995. Videorecording

REFERENCES

Clark, Norris B. "Michael Harper." In *Dictionary of Literary Biography*. Vol. 41. Ed. Trudier Harris and Thadious Davis. Detroit: Gale Research, 1985. 152–66.
Cooke, Michael G. *Afro-American Literature in the Twentieth Century*. New Haven, CT: Yale University Press, 1985.
Gabbin, Joanne V. "Conversation: Michael S. Harper and Aldon Lynn Nielsen." In *The Furious Flowering of African American Poetry*. Ed. Joanne V. Gabbin. Charlottesville: University of Virginia Press, 1999. 77–90.
O'Brien, John, ed. *Interviews with Black Writers*. New York: Liverwright, 1973. 95–108.
Ramazani, Jahan. *Poetry of Mourning*. Chicago: University of Chicago Press, 1994. 254–61.
Stepto, Robert B. "After Modernism, After Hibernation: Michael Harper, Robert Hayden, and Jay Wright." In *Chant of Saints*. Ed. Michael Harper and Robert B. Stepto. Chicago: University of Chicago Press, 1979. 470–86.

ROBERT HAYDEN

(1913–1980)

Robert Hayden
Credit: Photographs and Prints Division, Schomburg Center
for Research in Black Culture, The New York Public Library,
Astor, Lenox and Tilden Foundations
Photo credit: Timothy D. Franklin

Like many African American writers, Robert Hayden sandwiched his poetry writing between a university teaching career and his family life. He matured as a writer before the poetic fervor of the 1960s and taught in the South at Fisk University in Nashville, Tennessee. Hayden's poetry was applauded by scholars and critics before his reputation was well established. Unfortunately, he is still not well known outside of academic circles. He has consistently been praised for his polished crafting of poems, the unique perspectives in his work, his exact language usage, and his absolute command of traditional poetic techniques and structures. Events and figures in African American history are significant in his work, but he also writes about many other subjects. His themes have been described as embracing struggle in various permutations.

Born in Detroit, Michigan, to Asa and Ruth Sheffey, Hayden was originally named for his father Asa. However, with the breakup of his family, he lived with Sue Ellen Westerfield and William Hayden, who renamed him Robert Earl Hayden. His mother remained a part of his life, and the Haydens never officially adopted Robert Earl, though he was led to believe that they had. He accidently discovered this information when he was forty years old. Hayden grew up in a Detroit neighborhood that was racially diverse until white flight left it mostly African American. He remembers it in his poem "Elegies for Paradise Valley." William Hayden was a stern man and preferred athletics for his adopted son. Robert Earl was plagued with poor eyesight, however, and was introverted and studious. The poems "Names," "Those Winter Sundays," and "The Ballad of Sue Ellen Westerfield" reflect Hayden's memories of his neighborhood and his adoptive parents.

Hayden attended Detroit City College (now Wayne State University) between 1932 and 1936, majoring in Spanish and minoring in English. For his master's degree he studied at the University of Michigan from 1941 to 1946 with the poet W.H. Auden, whom Hayden has credited with enabling him to identify his strengths and weaknesses as a poet. As a young college writer, Hayden was attracted to the poetry of Harlem Renaissance writers, especially Countee Cullen, Jean Toomer, and Langston Hughes, though he read widely and indiscriminately all the poetry he could find. He also admired the poems of Elinor Wylie, Edna St. Vincent Millay, Sara Teasdale, Carl Sandburg, Hart Crane, and W.B. Yeats, whose poetic response to the problems of the Irish was particularly compelling to Hayden. Like the young Gwendolyn Brooks, Hayden also sent some of his early work to Hughes for the mature poet's assessment. Hughes counseled that he should find his own voice. Hayden stayed on at the University of Michigan for two years as a teaching fellow and was the first African American teacher in the English Department. He won the university's Hopwood Award for poetry for two years.

During the economic depression Hayden worked with the Works Progress Administration (WPA) Federal Writer's Project from 1936 to 1938 on two projects that were important to the content of some of his later poetry. In the first project Hayden researched the history of abolition movements and Underground Railroad activity in Michigan. Much of this knowledge undoubtedly fueled interest in his African American heritage and became part of the large body of history poems he wrote over the years. Hayden had a strong sense of the past and its continuing influence on present time, which invades many of his poems.

The decade of the 1940s proved very significant in other ways in Hayden's life and career. His first book of poetry, *Heart-Shape in the Dust* (1940), appeared but was considered an apprentice work, as can often happen with first books. He had not yet found the distinctive voice that would mark his work. In 1941 Hayden and Erma Inez Morris married. One daughter, Maia, was born to them. Initially, the couple lived in New York while Erma studied at the Julliard School of Music. While there, they met and visited with Countee Cullen, one of the writers whose work Hayden had admired. Hayden also changed his religion from Baptist to the Baha'i Faith. He alludes to his faith in "From the Corpse Woodpiles, from the Ashes," and in "Words in the Mourning Time."

In addition to marriage, in 1946 he began teaching full-time at Fisk University, where he remained for twenty years. Among his students who became well-known writers were Myron O'Higgins and William Demby. Although it was nearly impossible to find the unbroken spaces of time required for writing books, Hayden juggled university and personal responsibilities and managed to publish four of the nine volumes of his career output, including *Selected Poems* (1966). That collection marked a turning point, for it led to Hayden's being awarded the Grand Prize for Poetry at the First World Festival of Negro Arts in Dakar, Senegal, in the same year. In 1969, after a series of visiting appointments at universities, Hayden returned to the University of Michigan where he taught until his death from cancer.

By the 1960s and the Black Aesthetics or Black Arts Movement, when a younger generation of African American poets wrote politically and emotionally charged protest poetry predominantly directed to a black audience, Hayden's philosophy about the function of poetry and the way he defined himself as a writer were well established. His refusal to remake himself according to the images of the 1960s earned him criticism from some writers and commentators. Hayden remained true to his concept of poetry as an artistic form rather than a polemical act and to his conviction that poetry should, among other things, address the qualities shared by humankind, including social injustice. Hayden's reputation and the esteem with which he is regarded have outlasted that of many of the poets of that decade.

Perhaps Hayden's beliefs about the relationship of the poet to his poems also played a part in his refusal to write emotionally driven protest poems. Hayden's practice is to create distance between the speaker and the activity of the poem. He thus objectifies the experience through the use of a persona. This method is very successful in a poem like "Those Winter Sundays" but would not succeed in a poem whose purpose is to arouse mental or physical action in a reader. This three-stanza poem is written from the perspective of memory, an older person remembering acts that went unappreciated during youth. In winter, the father rose early and made the fire to warm the house and polished the son's shoes as well, but he was not thanked and was spoken to carelessly. The reader understands that the lack of appreciation was possibly connected to a less-than-loving atmosphere that filled the house along with the cold. Nevertheless, as an adult, the persona questions and seems saddened by his lack of understanding about adult responsibility and the manifestations of love. Other poems that address personal experiences but also spiral outward away from the poet include "The Whipping," "Electrical Storm," and "The Night-Blooming Cereus."

In 1946, "Middle Passage," one of Hayden's most respected and reprinted history poems, appeared. Along with "Runagate Runagate," the two works recreate the epic voyage of the Middle Passage and the perils of escaping slavery. "Middle Passage" is a long poem and is divided into three parts. The poem is structured like a collage; it has a variety of speakers, lines from hymns, a prayer for the safe passage of the slave vessel, verbatim text from the captain's log, a slave trader's personal narrative, an account of the slave-led mutiny onboard the *Amistad*, and an objective narrator. These various components are indicated by the print's placement, indention, or italicizing on the page. The poem begins with italicized words that, like *Amistad*, are names of Spanish slave vessels. The first part recreates the atmosphere and workings of a slave-bearing vessel and the crew's fears of illness, storms, and being lost at sea. An account of another doomed vessel, *The Bella J*, foreshadows what will happen on this voyage. Part three of the poem focuses on the *Amistad* mutiny and the case for their freedom argued in the Supreme Court by John Quincy Adams. The three parts of the poem are unified by the refrain that the Middle Passage is a "voyage through death to life upon these shores." Given the struggle of Cinque and his countrymen for their liberation, the poem underscores the irrepressible human urge for freedom, whatever the cost.

The companion poem to "Middle Passage," "Runagate Runagate," whose title someone has called a deliberate corruption of "renegade," is also similarly structured to create the effect of a collage, but it has only two lengthy sections. It has a complex perspective, an objective observer/commentator, a slave owner advertising for runaways, and the slave's voice deciding to escape and narrating as one of Harriet Tubman's escaping group. Stanza one of the poem is particularly noteworthy because of Hayden's recreation of an escaping slave running in the dark, being pursued by hounds, being fearful but running nevertheless. He achieves the feel of flight and the fear of the unknown by his word choices and by totally omitting punctuation in that stanza.

"Crispus Attucks" is another example of Hayden's history poems. In this ironic four-line poem Hayden conveys the image of Attucks covered by the flags of Betsy Ross and Marcus Garvey and propped up by bayonets. The image reinforces the ironic position of Attucks as an American hero slain in the first battle of the Revolutionary War but invisible in mainstream history except when his name appears in a footnote. Moreover, his death did not extend the protection of the American flag to his people, and his action was incompatible with that of Marcus Garvey, who in the 1920s developed a back-to-Africa plan for black nationhood.

Other noteworthy poems referencing African American history include "Night, Death, Mississippi," from the perspective of an elderly Klan member, "The Ballad of Nat Turner," and numerous poems named for other historical figures such as "Frederick Douglass," "El-Hajj Malik El-Shabazz" (Malcolm X), and "John Brown."

Hayden's career as a poet was perhaps crowned by his two appointments as poetry consultant to the Library of Congress between 1976 and 1978. By that time, he had also enjoyed other significant affirmations of his work, including a nomination for a National Book Award for the volume *Words in the Mourning Time* (1970). All but two of his books had been published (the 1982 volume of *American Journal* was a posthumous collection of his last years). He had become a "poet's poet" for some emerging writers like Michael Harper. Perhaps most important, he had retained the artistic integrity by which he had fashioned his life and his work.

POETRY

Heart-Shape in the Dust. Detroit: Falcon Press, 1940.
(With Myron O'Higgins). *The Lion and the Archer*. Nashville, TN: Hemphill Press, 1948.
Figure of Time: Poems. Nashville TN: Hemphill Press, 1955.
A Ballad of Remembrance. London: Paul Breman, 1962.
Selected Poems. New York: October House, 1966.
Words in the Mourning Time. New York: October House, 1970.
The Night-Blooming Cereus. London: Paul Breman Ltd., 1972.
Angle of Ascent. New York: Liveright, 1975. (Out of Print)
American Journal. Taunton, MA: Effendi Press, 1978. Rpt., New York: Liveright, 1982.
The Collected Poems of Robert Hayden Ed. Frederick Glaysher. New York: Liveright, 1996.

ANTHOLOGIES

Kaleidoscope: Poems by American Negro Poets. New York: Harcourt Brace & World, 1967.
(With David J. Burrows and Frederick R. Lapides). *Afro-American Literature: an Introduction*. New York: Harcourt Brace Jovanovich, 1971. (Out of Print)

REFERENCES

Blount, Marcellus. "Robert Hayden." In *Encyclopedia of African-American Culture and History*. Vol. 3. Ed. Jack Salzman, David Lionel Smith, and Cornel West. New York: Macmillan Library Reference, 1996. 1241–42.

Davis, Charles T. "The Structure of the Afro-American Literary Tradition: Robert Hayden's Use of History." In *Black Is the Color of the Cosmos: Essays on Afro-American Literature and Culture, 1942–1981*. Ed. Henry Louis Gates Jr. New York: Garland, 1982. 253–68.

Fetrow, Fred M. "Portraits and Personae: Characterization in the Poetry of Robert Hayden." In *Black American Poets between Worlds, 1940–1960*. Ed. R. Baxter Miller. Knoxville: University of Tennessee Press, 1986. 43–76.

———. *Robert Hayden*. Boston: Twayne, 1984.

Hatcher, John. *From the Auroral Darkness: The Life and Poetry of Robert Hayden*. Oxford, England: George Ronald, 1984.

Hirsch. Edward. "Mean to Be Free." *The Nation* 241. 21 (December 21, 1985): 685–86.

Jones, Norma R. "Robert Hayden." In *Dictionary of Literary Biography*. Vol. 76. Ed. Trudier Harris and Thadious Davis. Detroit: Gale Research, 1988. 75–88.

Kalasky, Drew, ed. *Poetry Criticism*. Vol. 6. Detroit: Gale Research, 1993. 175–202.

Mann, James. "Robert Hayden." In *Dictionary of Literary Biography*. Vol. 5. Ed. Donald Greiner. Detroit: Gale Research, 1980. 310–17.

O'Brien, John. *Interviews with Black Writers*. New York: Liveright, 1973. 108–23.
Post, Constance J. "Image and Idea in the Poetry of Robert Hayden." *CLA Journal* 22.2 (1976): 164–75.
Rev. of *American Journal*. *Virginia Quarterly Review* 58.4 (1982): 134.
Williams, Pontheolla T. *Robert Hayden: A Critical Analysis of His Poetry*. Urbana: University of Illinois Press, 1987.

GEORGE MOSES HORTON

(1797?–1883?)

The distinction of being the first slave to publish a book while living in the South belongs to George Moses Horton. *Hope of Liberty*, the first of Horton's three books, appeared in 1829 while he was in bondage in central North Carolina. His natural talent for poetry and his acquiring literacy are an intriguing part of his story. Although not all of his story is known, a good amount has been revealed through the introductions to his books and through scholarly research.

The sixth of ten children, Horton was born in Northhampton County, North Carolina, located in a small northeastern section of the state. His owner, William Horton, having acquired a larger farm, moved to Chatham County, North Carolina, adjacent to Orange County where the University of North Carolina was located. By 1806, William Horton owned over 400 acres planted in corn and wheat. During this period, George Moses began to like music and to determine that he wanted to read and write. Having acquired an old spelling book, he studied it on Sundays and learned to spell and to read the Bible and hymns. As important, he found he could construct poems in his head.

Ownership of George Moses changed in 1814 when William Horton divided some of his property among his sons, one of whom acquired George Moses. About 1817, George Moses began the innocent practice that would catapult him to fame. He began walking about eight miles to the University of North Carolina campus in Chapel Hill to sell fruit to the students. Shortly thereafter, he began to show his facility with verse by composing love poems that spelled the first name of a male student's girlfriend by beginning a line with each letter in the girl's name. A poem for "Alice," for example, would have five lines, and the poems were called acrostics. During the week, Horton composed the poems for oral delivery on Saturdays and earned between twenty-five and seventy-five cents, depending on their level of difficulty.

During the 1820s Horton was an anomaly in the campus community since a prevalent belief of that era accepted slaves' intellectual deficiency. Horton's ability came to the attention of two influential people, the university president, Joseph D. Caldwell, and Caroline Lee Hentz, a novelist and the wife of a university professor. Since Horton did not learn to write until about 1832, Hentz wrote down his poems and submitted some of them to a Northern publication, the *Lancaster Gazette*, in Massachusetts. It accepted "Liberty and Slavery" and "On Poetry and Music" for publication.

At the university, Caldwell, Hentz, and several others initiated a series of efforts to gain Horton's freedom. Their efforts caused the *Raleigh Register* to print an article about Horton that included some of his poems. The Manumission Society was interested in his case, and the *Freedom's Journal*, a Northern black newspaper, issued an appeal to New York black Northerners to contribute money for Horton's liberty. All of these efforts failed, and Horton remained a slave until the Union army marched through the South. When *Hope of Liberty* was published, efforts to free Horton intensified but were nevertheless futile.

Hope of Liberty appeared when its author was about age thirty-two. Its preface revealed that Horton's owner did not know about his poetry and that Horton was learning to write. This revelation means that Horton held in memory and dictated the twenty-one poems in the volume. He included some of the love poems written for the girlfriends of Chapel Hill male students, but most of his concerns in the volume were religion, nature, writing poetry, and liberty. Religion does not dominate his work, though several poems reference Bible stories and Christian virtues. Several of Horton's nature poems reveal a fine sensibility to the rural countryside where he lived. The poems about slavery, however, have proven of major interest to readers because Horton was self-engaged in the cause of his own freedom. However, he lived in a slave state and was dependent on whites for getting his poems into print. The conflict is obvious, and Horton's dilemma between direct, critical expressiveness and the reward of seeing his work printed must certainly have induced self-censoring.

"On Liberty and Slavery," Horton's most anthologized poem, has been analyzed for the intensity of its desire for the poet's liberty and for his cleverness in veiling that desire. In the poem's ten stanzas, the first three address the consequences of bondage. A slave is deprived of joy through the seemingly everlasting labor and pain of the institution. Is there no relief this side of the grave to eliminate the anguish, the poem asks? The remaining stanzas of the poem address freedom. It is welcomed as a joyful sound that can drown grief and fear and end oppression. Horton engages elaborate metaphors for the concept of freedom, visualizing liberty soaring on the wings of a dove that "breathed her notes from Afric's grove." Liberty is the golden prize, the natural gift of God, while slavery is barbarian. Liberty, bringing comfort, is visualized as a natural mother upon whose breast the poet can rest and smile and as an asylum. Given the constraints on Horton as a slave poet, it is reasonable that his verse would not rant and rail against the institution. Horton proved himself a survivalist as well as a poet.

Horton's second most referenced poem, "The Slave's Complaint," is distinguished by its structural form as much as its content. Repetition and questioning are the poem's major rhetorical devices as stanzas end with the question "forever?" Making this single word its own line places the weight of the entire stanza on it, a weight that becomes cumulative and therefore powerful through its repetition in seven stanzas. Couched in metaphor, the speaker's questions are whether his condition will earn ridicule forever; whether he must remain in the darkness of slavery; and if he must live without hope and cheer. But there is hope, which the speaker hopes will burn forever. He appeals to heaven as his only confidant. When earthly life ends, then a "kind and eternal friend" might summon him to ascend from slavery "forever."

Horton's verses range from elaborately conventional eighteenth-century poetics to the clear, direct language he uses in "The Slave's Complaint." His rhythm tends to be of regular meter, and he employs a predictable rhyme scheme.

Horton's *Hope of Liberty* was reprinted twice during his lifetime. Two more volumes appeared, *The Poetical Works of George Moses Horton, the Colored Bard of North Carolina* in 1845 and *Naked Genius* in 1865. Individual poems appeared in the *Southern Literary Messenger* in 1843, and the *Raleigh Register* printed a letter from the poet in defense of an American literature. In 1843 Horton appealed to the famous abolitionist William Lloyd Garrison for assistance in getting a manuscript titled *The Museum* printed. His letter indicates the poet's awareness of what his literacy and talent meant in the milieu of the time. However, Garrison never received the letter, which Horton asked the new university president, David Swain, to mail. A second time later in his life, in soliciting aid for his personal liberation, Horton wrote Horace Greeley, journalist and abolitionist, and a second time entrusted the letter to David Swain, who never mailed it. Also in 1843, with the death of Horton's owner, he passed to another Horton family member named Hall, who raised Horton's hire fee to fifty cents daily. In 1852 Hall proposed to sell Horton for $250 to David Swain. Hall's plan, which included a phrase about Horton's obligatory lifetime service to Swain, was rejected.

Horton apparently married a slave woman in Chatham County in the 1830s. Scholar Joan Sherman has written that Horton had a son named Free Snipes who died in Durham in 1896 and a daughter Rhody who married and was living in Raleigh in 1897.

Finally, when the Union army occupied the region, Horton gained his freedom and found a patron in a young army captain, H.S. Banks. Horton's new poems plus forty-four from his second volume, *Poetical Works*, and a "Sketch of the Author" appeared in a new volume, *Naked Genius*, in 1865. Other volumes were supposedly forthcoming, but if they were published, none are extant. Without his new patron, Horton relocated to Philadelphia. What happened to him is uncertain, though there is a report of Horton in a letter that says he died around 1883.

POETRY

Hope of Liberty. Raleigh, NC, 1829. (Out of Print)
The Poetical Works of George Moses Horton, the Colored Bard of North Carolina. Hillsboro, 1845. (Out of Print)
Naked Genius. Raleigh, NC, 1865. Rpt., Chapel Hill, NC: Greensboro Printing Co., 1982.

REFERENCES

Richmond, Merle A. *Bid the Vassal Soar: Interpretive Essays on the Life and Poetry of Phillis Wheatley and George Moses Horton*. Washington, DC: Howard University Press, 1974.
Sherman, Joan, ed. *The Black Bard of North Carolina: George Moses Horton and His Poetry*. Chapel Hill: University of North Carolina Press, 1997.
Walser, Richard. *The Black Poet*. New York: Philosophical Library, 1966.

LANGSTON HUGHES

(1902–1968)

Langston Hughes
Credit: The National Portrait Gallery, Smithsonian Institution

Langston Hughes published and enjoyed success in virtually all genres of creative writing, but poetry established his reputation during the heyday of the Harlem Renaissance, a period of creativity in the arts most often dated between 1920 and 1930. His work includes essays, short stories, plays, juvenile poetry and fiction, the Jesse B. Semple dialogues (syndicated in newspapers), and autobiography. He authored and edited more than forty books.

In his autobiography *The Big Sea*, Hughes broadly details his background. He was born in Joplin, Missouri, but grew up in Lawrence, Kansas, cared for by his elderly grandmother, Mary Leary. His grandmother's first husband, Lewis Sheridan Leary, was killed in John Brown's raid on Harpers Ferry, and her second husband, Charles Howard Langston, was also a strong-willed abolitionist. Hughes's mother, Carolina Mercer Lanston (called Carrie), was born to this union. She was given the middle name of her father's famous brother, John Mercer Langston, a graduate of Oberlin College, a professor of law, and acting president of Howard University, among other noteworthy honors. Although Charles Howard Langston and his family had been socially prominent, his move to Lawrence, Kansas, where racial hostility was severe, did not improve their prosperity. When Langston died, the family was left almost destitute, though Carrie graduated from high school and finished a course in teaching. Despite this practical training, she wanted to be an actress. She met and married Hughes's father, James Nathaniel Hughes, after she left Lawrence and settled in Guthrie, Oklahoma. Langston Hughes declared that his father hated Negroes and hated himself for being one. The marriage was short-lived, and Hughes's father relocated to Mexico. Hughes lived with either his grandmother until she died in 1915 or his mother who, over the years, lived in Topeka or Kansas City and sometimes spent the summer elsewhere. She enjoyed traveling and theater and took Hughes with her, but these pleasures were limited by finances. When Carrie Mercer remarried, she did not take Hughes to live with her. He was left, briefly, with friends of his grandmother's. Hughes's life was marked by the loneliness of living with an elderly relative who could not assimilate to changing times, by the rancor of his father toward African American people, and by his parents' near abandonment.

Hughes's school experiences were not always positive, either. In school in Lawrence, Kansas, he was a good student, but he experienced racial hostility from several teachers. These feelings would eventually find their way into his poetry just as the lyrics and rhythms of the blues that he once heard on a visit to Kansas. According to Arnold Rampersad's biography of the poet, in his eighth-grade year, Hughes's mother finally took him to live in Lincoln, Illinois, with her new husband and his child. Once again, the family relocated, and Hughes completed eighth grade from Central High School in Cleveland, Ohio. The program listed him as class poet, a position he acknowledged as beginning his writing interest. Unfortunately, Hughes's stepfather left Cleveland and his mother soon followed, but Hughes was left in the city to fend for himself. He rented an attic room and knew only how to make rice and hot dogs. He was on his own and active in his school, including writing verse for the school magazine and running track and field.

In June of 1919, Hughes's father abruptly reentered his life and took the boy to his residence in Toluca, Mexico. Hughes discovered his father, though financially successful, was tightfisted and bitter and hated poor people and blacks. Hughes quickly came to hate him. The event that crystallized this revelation threw Hughes into a psychosomatic illness that required hospitalization. Disguised as a Mexican, he returned by train in September to the United States. His senior year at Central High School was very successful, particularly in his growing interest in poetry. He composed one of his very popular and distinctive love poems, "When Susanna Jones Wears Red," that year.

At graduation, when his friends were preparing to attend Columbia University in New York, Hughes thought he would go there, too. He decided to enlist his father's financial support and to visit him in Toluca, Mexico, again. Reflecting on the great Mississippi River out of the train window as he crossed into Missouri, Hughes composed his signature poem "I've Known Rivers," writing on an envelope in his pocket. It is perhaps his most renowned poem. In it, a collective voice identifies with the heritage of Africa through references to rivers—the Euphrates, the Congo, and the Nile—as sustainers of life and to the continuity of that ancient heritage, displaced but resumed along the Mississippi River in North America. "I've Known Rivers" is a poem of maturity and insight, although Hughes was not yet twenty years old. The poem was published in *The Crisis*, the journal of the National Association for the Advancement of Colored People (NAACP), in June 1921.

To the young Hughes's dismay, James Hughes's plan for his son was studying engineering abroad in Germany or Switzerland, followed by a career in Mexico. Neither James nor Carrie Hughes supported their son's desire to be a writer, even after he was being published. The elder Hughes's plan was calculated to prevent his son's living among poor black people in the United States. Ironically, James Hughes's hatred of the poor endeared them to Langston. During the summer of 1920, besides studying Spanish, Hughes wrote "Aunt Sue's Stories" and "Mother to Son," among his best-known poems. Both poems are brief but are remarkable for their maturity and for the image of elder women passing their stories and experiences on to a new generation. Other pieces that Hughes sent to *The Crisis* magazine were also accepted and published. James Hughes was more interested in his son's payment than in the fact of Langston's work appearing in print. However, he was sufficiently impressed and agreed to finance Langston's study at Columbia for a year. Hughes had been in Mexico a year when he boarded the train in 1921 for New York, little suspecting how auspicious this timing was for his future as a writer. He and his father did not see each other again. Hughes left Columbia University after a year, but he later graduated from Lincoln University in Pennsylvania in 1929.

If Hughes could have read his future, the promise of Harlem for his writing and for his social integration in numerous communities would have astounded him. Before the 1920s ended, he had become a commanding figure in the creative epoch called the Harlem Renaissance. He had published groundbreaking criticism in voicing his position on the responsibility of the black artist to embrace all of African American culture in the essay "The Negro Artist and the Racial Mountain," published in *The Nation* in 1926. Finally, he had written two books of poetry, *The Weary Blues* (1926) and *Fine Clothes to the Jew* (1927).

In the 1930s when the power of the Renaissance was dissipated by the Great Depression, Hughes's radicalism found pronounced expression. Some of the poetry earned the dubious label of most radical poetry by an American. Religious and conservative groups used "Goodbye Christ," an irreverent rejection of the Christian's God, as proof of his communist ideology. Eventually, Hughes suppressed his radical socialist poems. He traveled extensively in the 1930s, spending time in Cuba, Haiti, Soviet Asia, Japan, Mexico, and Paris. In the Soviet Union in 1932, along with twenty-two other African Americans, Hughes was scheduled to participate in a Soviet film about race relations in the United States, but the project was abandoned. In Spain in 1937, he covered the Spanish Civil War for black newspapers.

In the 1950s, McCarthyism touched Hughes as it did many other Americans. Hughes testified for an hour before the McCarthy Committee on March 26, 1953, about his communist beliefs. An arrangement had preceded the public testimony where Hughes would not be asked to "name" others but to admit his own pro-communist inclinations. "Good-

bye, Christ" was included in the record as evidence of Hughes's thinking. He experienced repercussions, including being dropped from his
lecture bureau, criticism for not adopting the stand of Paul Robeson, and
over the years, the public accusation of being communist. Nevertheless,
he was able to salvage his literary career.

The most distinctive qualities of Hughes's poetry are its colloquial language or black vernacular, blues and jazz rhythms, and ironic humor.
The speech of the ordinary person, the use of popular culture, and situations common to working-class people made his poetry appealing to
the masses in the 1920s. During an era when black leaders and writers
held conflicting opinions about the function of art produced by African
Americans, Hughes's deliberate appeal to the working class through language and music was controversial and often earned him criticism. Like
several of his contemporaries, including Sterling Brown, Zora Neale Hurston, and James Weldon Johnson, Hughes did not view the written arts
as forms restricted by the level of one's education. Thus diction, syntax,
rhythm, cultural references, and urban idioms were primary tools of accessibility that made his poetry popular and appealing.

Hughes's diction and syntax cast in the natural rhythm of the speaking
voice thus established the oral qualities of his work. Poems such as "Day-
break in Alabama," "Mother to Son," or the series of Madam poems
written in the voice of Madam Alberta K. offer examples of Hughes's
use of accessible language. Moreover, in his ability to evoke the oral
traditions of a folk culture, Hughes effectively portrays their collective
sound in such poems as "Feet of Jesus" and "Sunday Morning Prophecy."

As important, the blues and jazz poems in Hughes's first two published volumes distinguished him as an innovative voice. In perhaps his
most famous blues piece, the title poem of his first volume, the blues
singer accompanies his song, "The Weary Blues," on piano in a Harlem
club, but the performer is afflicted with the blues as well. The poem
contains blues lyrics depicting loneliness and dissatisfaction with life.
Performing the blues, however, has the same cathartic effect on the
singer as a blues performance has on the audience. Temporarily, the
condition is purged from them all, and the blues singer can sleep like a
dead man. In Hughes's poems as in blues music, the blues became a
metaphor for addressing life's shortcomings such as economic woes,
thwarted romance, or individual isolation. Similarly, in adapting the
rhythms and dissonance of jazz to poems, Hughes sought to make the
printed word reproduce the jarring undercurrent of upbeat jazz music.
His success is evident in "Negro Dancers" and "The Cat and the Saxo-

phone" in *The Weary Blues* and later in "Dream Boogie" in his *Montage of a Dream Deferred*.

Hughes's ability to blur the lines between music and poetry is also evident in *Montage of a Dream Deferred* (1951) through yet another new poetic form. He adapted his verse to the structural qualities of bebop music, as performed in jam sessions by jazz musicians, and to jazz, ragtime, swing, blues, and boogie-woogie in a sort of evolutionary nod to the unfolding of popular black music. *Montage*, a book-length poem on contemporary Harlem, is separated into short poems and phrases and unified by the notion of the dream deferred. It is divided into six parts— "Boogie Segue to Bop," "Dig and Be Dug," "Early Bright," "Vice Versa to Back," "Dream Deferred," and "Lenox Avenue Mural." The volume is characterized by fragmentation in numerous forms, for example, in its changes of diction, arresting interjections, and passages that recall jam sessions. The poems communicate that black people have been hindered from full participation in the American Dream. Specifically, the denial includes poor housing, substandard living generally, and lack of access to profitable employment. "Theme for English B" and "Harlem" are two frequently anthologized poems excerpted from *Montage*. The twenty-two-year-old "colored" speaker in "Theme" investigates his identity. He concludes that, although he had much in common with ethnically different people, he is a separate identity. Thus, the theme he writes will be distinctly flavored by all that he is. In "Harlem," using cumulative and intense images of loss, rot, and decay, Hughes succinctly questions the potentials for a dream continually deferred. Does it shrink and wrinkle like a raisin in the sun, or does it explode? Lorraine Hansbury borrowed a line of "Harlem" in her explosive drama of a family's dream deferred titled *A Raisin in the Sun*. Hughes's panoramic examination of his beloved adopted community of Harlem through the rhythms of bebop reaffirms his commitment to music as a major source of expression in his work.

Hughes's commitment to depicting the total experience of his African American community is readily apparent in the variety of his work. More than his contemporaries and more than his predecessors, he adeptly blended poetic form with content and serious and humorous moods, often in the same poem. A poem like "Minstrel Man," for example, offers the culturally denigrated image of grotesquely painted lips to emphasize the irony of pain and laughter existing simultaneously. "The Jester" offers the frowning mask of tragedy and the laughing mask of comedy to make the ironic point that for the black jester laughter and pain are indistinguishable. However, a significant number of poems may be characterized as straightforward serious pieces. Among these are those that celebrate the beauty of blackness and the African heritage as in "Dream Variations," "Afro-American Fragment," "I, Too," and "The Negro Speaks of Rivers."

When Hughes died, he was the Dean of African American letters. His influence and mentoring of other writers included names as diverse as the Cuban writer Nicolás Guillén, Aimé Césaire, Gwendolyn Brooks, and Margaret Walker, to name only a few of the writers who credit Hughes's work as a major model. He had earned innumerable awards, including the Harmon Foundation Medal and a prize of $400 in 1930; in 1941, a Rosenwald Fund fellowship to write plays; in 1943, his undergraduate school, Lincoln University, gave him an honorary doctorate; Western Reserve University in Cleveland, Ohio, gave another in 1963; in 1946, an award of $1,000 from the American Academy of Arts and Letters for distinguished service as a writer; and in 1960 the Spingarn Award, established in 1914 by Joel Spingarm of the NAACP to recognize the "highest or noblest achievement by an American Negro during the preceding year." Hughes had earlier been denied the prize because of the controversy surrounding "Christ in Alabama." In 1961, he was inducted into the National Institute of Arts and Letters and attended a presidential luncheon given at the White House by John Kennedy for Léopold Sédar Senghor, poet and President of Senegal.

POETRY

The Weary Blues. New York: Knopf, 1926. (Out of Print)
Fine Clothes to the Jew. New York: Knopf, 1927. (Out of Print)
The Dream Keeper & Other Poems. New York: Knopf, 1932. Rpt., Madison: Turtleback Books, 1996.
Shakespeare in Harlem. New York: Knopf, 1942. (Out of Print)
Fields of Wonder. New York: Knopf, 1947. (Out of Print)
One Way Ticket. New York: Knopf, 1949. (Out of Print)
Montage of a Dream Deferred. New York: Holt, 1951. (Out of Print)
Selected Poems of Langston Hughes. New York: Knopf, 1959.
Ask Your Mam: 12 Moods for Jazz. New York: Knopf, 1961. (Out of Print)
The Panther and the Lash: Poems of Our Time. New York: Knopf, 1967. Rpt., New York: Vintage, 1992.

AUTOBIOGRAPHY

The Big Sea. New York: Knopf, 1950. Rpt., New York: Hill & Wang, 1993.
I Wonder as I Wander: An Autobiographical Journey. New York: Rinehart, 1956. (Out of Print)

SELECTED ANTHOLOGIES

(With Arna Bontemps). *The Poetry of the Negro, 1746–1949.* New York: Doubleday, 1949.

(With Arna Bontemps). *The Book of Negro Folklore*. New York: Dodd, Mead, 1958.
(With Arna Bontemps). *The Poetry of the Negro, 1746–1970*. Rev. and updated ed.
New York: Anchor Press, Doubleday, 1970.

REFERENCES

Baxter, Ronald Miller. "Langston Hughes." In *Dictionary of Literary Biography*. Vol.
48. Ed. Peter Quartermain Detroit: Gale Research, 1986. 218–35.
Berry, Faith. *Langston Hughes: Before and Beyond Harlem*. Westport, CT: Lawrence
Hill, 1983.
Dace, Tish. *Langston Hughes: The Contemporary Reviews*. New York: Cambridge
University Press, 1997.
Emmanuel, James. *Langston Hughes*. New York: Twayne, 1967.
Huggins, Nathan. *Harlem Renaissance*. New York: Oxford University Press, 1971.
Lewis, David Levering. *When Harlem Was in Vogue*. New York: Knopf, 1981.
Rampersad, Arnold. *The Life of Langston Hughes I: 1902–1941*. New York: Oxford
University Press, 1986.
Rampersad, Arnold, and David Roessel, eds. *The Collected Poems of Langston
Hughes*. New York: Knopf, 1995.
Smethurst, James Edward. " 'Adventures of a Social Poet': Langston Hughes in
the 1930s." In *The New Red Negro: The Literary Left and African American
Poetry, 1930–1946*. New York: Oxford University Press, 1999. 93–115.
Wagner, Jean. "Langston Hughes." In *Black Poets of the United States*. Trans. Ken-
neth Douglas. Urbana: University of Illinois Press, 1973. 385–474.

GEORGIA DOUGLAS JOHNSON

(1886–1966)

Georgia Douglas Johnson
Credit: Photographs and Prints Division, Schomburg Center for
Research in Black Culture, The New York Public Library, Astor,
Lenox and Tilden Foundations

Georgia Douglas Johnson is a poet and playwright who has deserved more attention than has been forthcoming to her, although she was a prominent writer during the Harlem Renaissance. During the recent period of African American scholars and others resurrecting neglected writers, Johnson has not yet become a frequently studied poet like her male 1920s peers, although she published three books of poetry between 1918 and 1928. Three volumes in the 1920s by any measure was a notable feat for the times. One explanation for the critical neglect of women poets whose work was at its zenith in the 1920s has been that they only published in magazines and journals, thus denying critics access to a significant body of their work for its evaluation. However, such is not the case for Johnson who did publish books. Moreover, the span of her works anchors her in significant periods in African American literary tradition, the Renaissance of the 1920s and the era of protest writing in the 1940s, though that era was dominated by the novel. Johnson's last volume *Share My World: A Book of Poems* in 1962 makes her a significant bridge between generations of poets. Nevertheless, Johnson has been primarily relegated to minor status, though her work, when evaluated, has earned praise and scholars have conceded that her work occupies an important place in the progress of the African American literary tradition.

Johnson was born in Atlanta, Georgia, to George and Laura Jackson Camp. Following her education in the public schools, she attended Atlanta University, Howard University, and the Oberlin Conservatory of Music in Ohio. She once wrote that although her career had followed words rather than music, she never lost her first love of music.

Georgia Douglas married Henry Lincoln Johnson, a prominent Washington lawyer and politician, and they had two sons, Henry Lincoln Jr. and Peter Douglas. Henry Johnson Sr. was appointed under President Taft to Recorder of Deeds, a position that increased the social prominence of the Johnsons in Washington. Johnson involved herself in civic and social activities in the city, particularly those of concern to black women. She also worked in government during some of her years in Washington, including tenure in the Department of Labor as Commissioner of Conciliation under Calvin Coolidge. Henry Lincoln Johnson died in 1925 after a third stroke. Their sons were enrolled at Dartmouth College at the time.

Johnson did not share many details about her life; subsequently, much of its detail remains unknown or depends on the anecdotes of friends and acquaintances. Although she lived in Washington, D.C., when the heartbeat of literary production in the 1920s was New York's Harlem, her home was nevertheless a beloved meeting place for writer friends, including Langston Hughes; Countee Cullen; Jessie Fauset, the novelist and essayist; Alain Locke, Howard University professor and Harlem Renaissance mentor to younger writers; and others. These so-called Saturday Soirees at the Johnson home reached their zenith matching the pitch of literary activity in Harlem. Johnson provided a significant connection for Washington and Harlem literary figures.

In the introduction to her poems in Countee Cullen's anthology *Caroling Dusk*, Johnson briefly explained how her love for poetry began. She recalled reading a poem before she left Atlanta about a child's efforts to keep a struggling rose alive in a window in New York. The child's life was bound up in the struggle. When Johnson learned that the author was William Stanley Braithwaite and that he was a man of color, her commitment to write was born at that moment. Johnson kept her resolution, producing over 200 poems in her four collections as well as other poems that appeared in magazines. Ironically, Johnson was directed to send some of her early poems for evaluation to her inspiration, to Braithwaite, the well-known poet and critic in Boston. Jessie Fauset, novelist and essayist, assisted Johnson in selecting poems for her first published volume, *The Heart of a Woman*. Maya Angelou has paid homage to Johnson by borrowing this title for one of her autobiographies.

Somewhat like James Weldon Johnson, Johnson inherited the conventional poetic style that characterized nineteenth-century poetry. Her work was described as genteel and compared to the prominent white poet Sara Teasdale. Johnson's work was romantic; her lyrical poems usually ranged from four to eight to fourteen lines; and her verses were thoughtful meditations that did not concern themselves with the political world. They did, however, communicate the poet's awareness of racial inequality.

Like most of her contemporaries in the 1920s, Johnson published in *The Crisis* magazine with a poem appearing in 1916, but she had published in *Voice of the Negro* in 1905. Her first volume, *Heart of a Woman* (1918), contained sixty-two short lyrics on contemplative subjects like "Sympathy" and "Fantasy." The signature poem in the collection, "Heart of a Woman," introspectively examines a woman's heart through images of exploration. It expresses some alienation and dissatisfaction and it returns to an "alien cage" to break on its bars. The early 1920s woman, the poem suggests, found the larger world an unattractive site of exploration for women, yet the private domain offered stultifying enclosure. More generally, the poems in the volume also address nature, love, and romantic feelings. The poet writes objectively, however, maintaining a formal distance between herself and the abstract ideas in the poems.

With her second volume, *Bronze* (1922), Johnson had altered the tone of many of her poems so that she was more aligned with the pronounced racial consciousness of her fellow writers. The history of black Americans is also more evident in the subjects of poems, for example, in "Sorrow Singers," "The Passing of the Ex-Slave," and "The Octoroon." The particular problems that beleaguered slave mothers are recognized in the section of *Bronze* titled "Motherhood." Finally, in the last section of the volume, the focus on racial history is capped by tributes to those whose work has addressed the difficult social, economic, and educational issues of black life such as W.E.B. Du Bois, Mary Church Terrell, and Abraham Lincoln.

By the time Johnson's third volume, *An Autumn Love Cycle* (1928), was published, her husband had died, and her life was altered. Perhaps a reflective mood attributable to her changed status derailed the consciousness of history and racial issues that had informed *Bronze*. In any event, the poems in the third book look backward to her first one. As its title suggests, love is the subject. "I Want to Die While You Love Me," perhaps Johnson's most well-known poem, appears in the third section of the book. It is an extravagant piece, convincing in its declaration of the power of love.

Like many other 1920s writers, Johnson readjusted her objectives in response to the limitations on publishing caused by the Great Depression of the 1930s. Having written plays during the 1920s, including a first-place recognition in *Opportunity*'s drama contest in 1927, Johnson believed her plays might find an audience through President Roosevelt's New Deal and the Works Progress Federal Theatre Project (FTP). Johnson submitted five plays between the years of the FTP's inception, 1935, and 1939, when its existence ended, but she had no luck in having them accepted. Thus, she continued to write poetry and to be published in journals, including *Opportunity*. In the 1940s and until her death, Johnson's work continued to appear in black publications such as *Phylon* and the *Journal of Negro History*, both publications of Atlanta University, and in edited anthologies of black writing.

Atlanta University awarded Johnson an honorary degree of Doctor of Literature in 1965. She died at her home on S Street, a home she refused to sell when the neighborhood began to deteriorate.

POETRY

The Heart of a Woman and Other Poems. Boston: Cornhill Co., 1918. Rpt., New
York: AMS Press, 1975.
Bronze: A Book of Verse. Boston: B.J. Brimmer Co., 1922. (Out of Print)
An Autumn Love Cycle. New York: H. Vinal, 1928. (Out of Print)
Share My World: A Book of Poems. Privately printed in Washington, DC, 1962. (Out
of Print)

REFERENCES

Dover, Cedric. "The Importance of Georgia Douglas Johnson." *Crisis* 59 (1952):
633–36, 674.
Fletcher, Winona L. "From Genteel Poet to Revolutionary Playwright: Georgia
Douglas Johnson as a Symbol of Black Success, Failure, and Fortitude."
Theatre Annual 40 (February 1985): 40–64.
———. "Georgia Douglas Johnson." In *Dictionary of Literary Biography: Afro-
American Writers from the Harlem Renaissance to 1940.* Vol. 51. Ed. Trudier
Harris and Thadious Davis. Detroit: Gale Research, 1987. 153–164.
Hull, Gloria. *Color, Sex, and Poetry: Three Women Writers of the Harlem Renaissance.*
Bloomington: Indiana University Press, 1987.
Redding, J. Saunders. *To Make a Poet Black.* College Park, MD: McGrath, 1939.

JAMES WELDON JOHNSON

(1871–1938)

James Weldon Johnson
Credit: Fisk University Archives and the Van Vechten Trust
Photo credit: Carl Van Vechten

J ohnson's many talents and accomplishments earned him the title of Renaissance Man. Along with writing poems, song lyrics, a novel, an autobiography, and a history of black New York and editing significant collections of poetry and spirituals, he was a principal, teacher, professor, lawyer, diplomat, and secretary of the National Association for the Advancement of Colored People (NAACP). In addition to his literary pursuits, he was a significant figure during the creative decade known as the Harlem Renaissance for his efforts at ensuring the literary prominence of other writers. He dedicated himself to informing the nation about the capable art of the Negro through articles, reviews, and groundbreaking anthologies such as *The Book of American Negro Poetry*. He also linked black literary traditions between the nineteenth and twentieth centuries.

Johnson was born in Jacksonville, Florida, to middle-class parents, both of whom were freeborn. His father, James Johnson, born in Virginia, had lived in New York before the Civil War; and his mother, Helen Dillet, born in Nassau, Bahamas, had also lived in New York. During Johnson's growing-up years, and those of his younger brother Rosamond, his father was a headwaiter at a major Jacksonville resort, and his mother a teacher at Stanton School. Both boys grew up in a culturally enriched home of music and books. James Johnson was self-educated, including teaching himself Spanish to increase his value at his resort job, but had attended and enjoyed theater when he lived in New York. Helen Dillet wrote poetry for herself and was an artist and pianist. The parents transmitted their artistic values to their two sons.

James Weldon attended Stanton School, completing his eighth-grade year in 1887. During that time, many schools in black communities did not have high schools, but black colleges provided high school preparatory classes in anticipation of college enrollment. Johnson chose to attend high school prep classes at Atlanta University, a leading black college of the day. Also typical of higher education for black people of the time, the preparatory classes were staffed by white New England teachers. Black students were indoctrinated with the concept of "service." Education was intended as preparation for service to the community and not for individual gain.

Johnson successfully completed the preparation classes, placed in the freshman class of 1890, and completed his undergraduate work in 1894. His four years were filled with activity, as his adult life would prove to be. In addition to classic studies, he worked four years in the university printing office, where he learned the practical information that he later used in journalism and editing. Additionally, he spent two of his undergraduate summers teaching in black rural schools in Hampton, Georgia, an invaluable experience with a version of black life different from his middle-class experiences. He continued writing poetry.

After graduation in 1894, Johnson became the principal of the 1,000 students and twenty-five faculty members at Stanton School in Jacksonville. Immediately tapping his multiple talents, he inaugurated a black weekly newspaper, the *Daily American*, that survived for eight months. In 1896, Johnson began eighteen months of studying law in the office of a white attorney, after which time he took and passed the oral examination for certification by the bar. He practiced law while retaining his principalship, but his partner performed the work in court.

In 1897 Johnson began a productive and lucrative seven-year collaboration with his brother John Rosamond that would take both of them to New York and to London with James Weldon as lyricist, Rosamond as musician, and performer Bob Cole in a vaudeville act. It is important to remember that at the end of the nineteenth century, the era of Paul Laurence Dunbar's popularity, dialect poetry and the minstrel show were the forms of popular entertainment for the black audience. Black performers on stage were mostly limited to exaggerated buffoonish comedy in burnt-cork makeup and overdrawn red lips. Like his friend Paul Laurence Dunbar, Johnson initially wrote, in the vernacular of the times, "coon show" songs, and he wrote several poems in dialect. One of his best efforts, "Sence You Went Away," appeared in *Century* magazine and was set to music by Rosamond. It is a poem of lamentation about the loss of the speaker's loved one. Nature seems to conspire in the speaker's sorrow by the stars shining less bright and the moon losing its light, thus adding to the lover's misery. But also during this period, for Jacksonville's 1900 celebration of Lincoln's birthday, Johnson wrote "Lift Every Voice." Also set to music by Rosamond, it was sung by 500 Stanton School students. The poem is intended to energize a jaded or tired people's spirit by infusing it with hope. It reminds the reader (or singer) of the faith that has permeated the past and acted as a wedge against hopelessness and despair. The poem acknowledges a painful African American history but counsels perseverance until victory is assured.

Johnson resigned his job as principal in 1902 to move to New York City, once he was assured by the royalty checks that he could make a living as a lyricist. This move exposed him to numerous opportunities for advancement and involvement in public life, both of which he seized. In addition to the successful music business, for example, Johnson enrolled at Columbia University where he studied for three years with an emphasis on English literature and drama. His professor, Brander Matthews, helped him place poems in national publications. After working for the election of Teddy Roosevelt to the presidency, including writing two campaign songs, a contact Johnson had made suggested he apply for a post in the Consular Service. From 1906 to 1914, he served first in Puerto Cabello, Venezuela, and three years later in Corinto, Nicaragua. In 1910, Johnson married Grace Nail, reared in a wealthy New York home, and she joined him in Corinto. Since he had a vice consular, Johnson still had time for writing and publishing poems.

"Fifty Years," written in recognition of the fiftieth anniversary of the Emancipation Proclamation, recalled how far black people had come since the Emancipation and since their arrival on American soil. It pointed out that black people should share equal rights with all other Americans because that right had been earned through their work. "Fifty Years" appeared in the *New York Times* on January 1, 1913, as a formal poem written in conventional meter and rhyme, a style typical of Johnson except when he wrote *God's Trombones*.

With a change in the country's administration, Johnson resigned from the Consular Service to accept a contributing editor position with the *New York Age*, a weekly black newspaper, in 1914. He founded "Poetry Corner" in 1915 and sometimes printed his own poetry, but mostly he printed new poets and wrote reviews of poetry. Johnson used his public forum to stress his philosophy that great literature secures the reputation of a great race. In 1916, the NAACP asked him to become field secretary, a position that included keeping track of lynchings and riots and creating new branches of the organization across the country. Four years later, Johnson became secretary of the organization and was the first African American to hold that position. This prominent post offered excellent visibility for the literary projects that would occupy the last third of Johnson's life and career.

On the eve of the Harlem Renaissance, in 1917 when his *Fifty Years and Other Poems* was published, Johnson had already lived two-thirds of his life, much of it involved in working with words and publishing in mainstream journals. However, he had written mostly conventional poetry in verse form, meter, and rhyme. Sixteen of the poems in the collection were "Jingles & Croons," his designation for the dialect poems he included. Johnson's interest in and appreciation for the folkways of black Americans were perhaps suggested in his dialect poems, but "O Black and Unknown Bards," in standard English, celebrates folk poets as composers of the spirituals, the sacred songs composed by blacks for worship and communication during slavery. The first stanza questions how the initial conception of the spirituals came to be from those held in dark bondage. Who was inspired to sing out "Steal Away to Jesus," "Jordan Roll," "Swing Low Sweet Chariot," or "Nobody Knows de Trouble I See," all mentioned in the poem. The speaker believes that no German master composer ever dreamed better harmonies than the spiritual "Go Down Moses." Johnson succeeds in communicating the speaker's awe at the power of these songs whose authors remain unknown for their accomplishments.

In 1922, Johnson published a pioneering anthology of the work of thirty-two black poets, *The Book of Negro American Poetry*. The book introduced the voice of Anne Spencer through five of her poems. Spencer, like Emily Dickinson, saw only a few of her poems in print during her lifetime. Johnson often stayed overnight at the residence of Spencer and her husband in Lynchburg, Virginia, in work-related travel when hotels were segregated. The book also introduced poems by the young Claude McKay, destined to become a major voice of the Harlem Renaissance, but some of the other major poets had not yet made their mark. The work of Langston Hughes, Arna Bontemps, and Countee Cullen thus appeared in the expanded edition of the anthology published in 1931. The preface to the anthology is significant in Johnson's discussion of black nineteenth-century poets and for his careful explanation of the limitations of dialect poetry.

Johnson's major poetic accomplishment, *God's Trombones*, appeared at the height of the Harlem Renaissance. Choosing the word *trombone* came about when Johnson, in 1918, attended a church service in Kansas City. Although the minister began speaking formally, as the sermon progressed, he descended the ladder of formality until his impassioned voice suggested to the poet the throaty sound of the trombone. Seeing the audience mesmerized by this folk style, Johnson hurriedly copied down the title "The Creation," which became the first of *God's Trombones* seven poetic sermons conceived in the bygone style of a black country preacher. The sermons reflect Johnson's ear for folk speech and black vernacular stylistics in the way the poems convert biblical stories and poems to black folk rhetoric. These individually titled sermons include "The Prodigal Son," "Noah Built the Ark," and "The Judgment Day." "Go Down Death—A Funeral Sermon," "The Crucifixion," and "Let My People Go" are less dependent on stories of the Bible. The poet also added a prayer similar to one that might open a religious service.

Because Johnson's work with the NAACP required so much of his time, the entire book did not appear until 1927. Johnson thus had two significant works in one year, the anonymously published novel *The Autobiography of an Ex-Colored Man* (1912), now credited to Johnson, and the poems. *God's Trombones* represent Johnson's foray into an unconventional poetic form since he wrote the sermons in free verse. He believed that this form closely approximated the shifts in passion and pace that a preacher illustrated during verbal delivery. Johnson also made a conscious decision that he would not use dialect, as it was too limited for the emotional range he wished to achieve in the sermons. Thus he is free to engage creative metaphors and black idioms and to work a wide emotional range.

The most anthologized and the first of the sermons, "The Creation," was published in the *Freeman* in 1920. As its title suggests, it is the story told in Genesis of the world and man's creation. However, Johnson's preacher personalizes the story, rendering God with the human characteristic of loneliness, which is his motivation for creating man. Narrating the world's creation, the preacher's images of the earth's wonders are strong and highly visual, but when man is created, the imagery is specifically black. God is compared to a mammy kneeling in the dust to shape clay in his image. "The Creation" and several other sermons have become popular pieces in church and school programming. The performer enhances the poems through the physical styling and voicing of a folk preacher. Repertory groups also perform *God's Trombones* in its entirety, often interspersing spirituals with the poems.

Johnson's last collection of original poems, *St. Peter Relates an Incident: Selected Poems*, appeared in 1935, just three years before his death in an automobile accident. The title poem, "St. Peter Relates an Incident of the Resurrection Day," had originally appeared in 1930, the same year Johnson resigned from the NAACP. It was a satire inspired by white and black mothers who traveled to France to visit the graves of their sons killed in World War I. The mothers were separated by race and the black ones were sent on a second-class vessel. In Johnson's poem, on Resurrection Day, the Klan was charged with escorting the Unknown Soldier to heaven but was taken aback upon discovering he was black. As they bickered about how to proceed, the soldier maneuvered his own route to heaven as he sang "Deep River," and St. Peter admitted him.

By the time he died, Johnson's reputation as a diplomat, political and cultural activist, and writer was highly respected. The reception of *God's Trombones* through its reviews had sealed his reputation as a significant producer of black poetry. It was especially important because its author had used the black idiom to achieve an elevated and dignified tone, a feat that was not possible in dialect poetry. Johnson thus elevated the folk sermon to the heights of art and pointed the way for future writers to work with flexiblity of language and form within black folk culture.

POETRY

God's Trombones. New York: Viking Press, 1927. Rpt., New York: Viking Penguin, 1990.

St. Peter Relates an Incident of the Resurrection Day. New York: Viking, 1930.

St. Peter Relates an Incident: Selected Poems. New York: Viking, 1935. Rpt., New York: AMS Press, 1974. (Out of Print)

AUTOBIOGRAPHY

Along This Way: The Autobiography of James Weldon Johnson. New York: Viking, 1933. Rpt., New York: Capo, 1973.

EDITED ANTHOLOGIES

Fifty Years and Other Poems. Boston: Cornhill Co., 1917. Rpt., New York: AMS Press, 1975.

The Book of American Negro Poetry. New York: Harcourt, Brace, 1922. Rpt., San Diego: Harcourt Trade Publishers, 1969.

REFERENCES

Fleming, Robert E. *James Weldon Johnson*. Boston: Twayne, 1987.

———. *James Weldon Johnson and Arna Wendell Bontemps: A Reference Guide*. Boston: G.K. Hall, 1978. 3–67.

Jackson, Blyden, and Louis D. Rubin. *Black Poetry in America: Two Essays in Interpretation*. Baton Rouge: Louisiana State University Press, 1974.

Kinnamon, Keneth. *Dictionary of Literary Biography*. Vol. 51: *Afro-American Writers from the Harlem Renaissance to 1940*. Detroit: Gale Research, 1987. 168–82.

Levy, Eugene. *James Weldon Johnson: Black Leader, Black Voice*. Chicago: University of Chicago Press, 1973.

Redding, J. Saunders. *To Make a Poet Black*. Chapel Hill: University of North Carolina Press, 1939.

Wagner, Jean. *Black Poets of the United States*. Trans. Kenneth Douglas. Urbana: University of Illinois Press, 1973.

JUNE JORDAN

(1936–   )

June Jordan
Credit: June Jordan

As a child, June Jordan was seduced by the written word and was writing poetry as early as age seven. Along with poetry, she has collected her essays into five books since 1981; been a freelance journalist for newspapers and periodicals including *New Republic*, *Times Magazine*, and *Essence*; served as a contributing editor to periodicals, including the feminist *Chrysalis*; been a regular political columnist for *Progressive* magazine; written plays; compiled an anthology of African American poetry, and produced poetry and novels for young readers. In fact, *His Own Where*, written in black English, was nominated for a National Book Award. Across genres, Jordan has published twenty-five books. Her work is shaped by her activist political orientation, her intimacy with the African American community's experience, her humanitarian spirit, and her commitment to truth.

Jordan was born to Jamaican immigrant parents, Granville and Mildred Jordan, and grew up in the Bedford Stuyvesant community of Brooklyn, New York. Her parents were working class. Both Jordans worked night shifts in order to increase their salaries, her father as a postal worker and her mother as a private duty nurse. June Jordan was exposed to religious training primarily through her mother by their visits to the Universal Truth Center on 125th Street. Jordan also took piano and voice lessons and went to camp outside the city during summer. Her uncle, who lived upstairs in their brownstone, taught her self-defense maneuvers against community bullies.

At age twelve or thirteen, Jordan entered the prestigious prep school Northfield in Massachusetts. The disparity and cultural separatism of the communities represented by Harlem and Northfield were a shock to her. The shock continued during her undergraduate experience at Barnard College, where she enrolled in 1953. She dropped out of Barnard, but while there, she had met her future husband, Michael Meyer, an anthropology student at Columbia University. Their interracial marriage took place in 1955, and they had one son, Christopher David, in 1958. Jordan's marriage ended in 1965.

The career that would include poetry and the numerous other genres in which Jordan is expert began in the 1960s, as did the crystallizing of her political activism during the Harlem Riot of 1964. Jordan was among the mourners planning to attend the funeral of the young man slain by a policeman when, by her account, the churchgoing assembly was retained by squads of police in riot gear with guns drawn. In "Letter to Michael," published as an essay in *Civil Wars* (1981), Jordan describes the chaos, fear, anger, and wounded in a letter to her husband, who was in Chicago in graduate school at the time. Jordan's activism on behalf of children also took root in the 1960s when she worked on a film about Harlem youth called *The Cool World*. This experience resulted in a non-traditional essay consisting of interviews, narrative, and overheard conversation on the set. Her interest in enhancing the education and lives of children has spanned her career. It includes conducting workshops and reading poetry throughout the New York City school system in a program sponsored by the Academy of American Poets and writing novels for young people.

Also in the 1960s, Jordan's interest in urban design resulted in her collaborating with R. Buckminster Fuller on a redesign project for 250,000 inhabitants in Harlem. Fuller subsequently nominated her for the Prix de Rome in Environmental Design, which she won in 1969. The award financed Jordan for a year at the American Academy in Rome. Several poems in the collection *Things That I Do in the Dark* (1977) reflect this international experience. One of her projects for the year was the juvenile novel *His Own Where*. The work created a community controversy and was banned from the libraries because of its black vernacular language and parents' fear that it would negate their insistence on standard English for their children. Jordan's goal for the novel had been to provoke a response in young people to their environment and to urban design.

Like many poets, Jordan teaches at the college level and is a nationally sought-after lecturer and reader of her poetry. Her first teaching job at City College in New York in 1967 included Audre Lorde among her accomplished colleagues. Jordan's academic vitae also includes visiting positions at Connecticut College, Sarah Lawrence College, Yale, and Barnard College, where she shared The Reed Lectureship with novelist, poet, and essayist Alice Walker. Since 1989, she has been a professor of African American Studies and Women's Studies at the University of California, Berkeley. Jordan has been especially successful in promoting the writing and reading of poetry across her ethnically diverse campus community through a program she conceived and executed called *Poetry for the People*. Students read their work alongside published poets and produce an anthology. Jordan's conception and shaping of this successful program as well as her poetry teaching strategies are recognized in the publication *June Jordan's Poetry for the People*, edited by Lauren Muller and the Poetry for the People Collective.

Jordan's work has also been recognized through numerous awards and grants. Among them are the Rockefeller grant for creative writing in 1969, a Yaddo fellowship in 1979, and a fellowship in poetry from the

National Endowment for the Arts in 1982. More recently, she received the Lila Wallace-Reader's Digest Writer's Award for 1995–1998 and the PEN West Freedom to Write Award.

Although Jordan's fascination with the written word is manifested through her many interests and abilities, poetry is her first love. From childhood, she seized on the idea of wanting to be a "great poet." She later discarded the "great" part of the equation but never the idea of being as good as she could be. Before she was ten years old, her father had exposed her to poets of the Bible, Shakespeare, Edgar Allan Poe, and Paul Laurence Dunbar. In the decade of her twenties, she read all African American poetry that affirmed her cultural experiences, including Margaret Walker, Robert Hayden, and Langston Hughes. In later years she included Emily Dickinson, Jane Cooper, Adrienne Rich, Audre Lorde, Marge Piercy, Alice Walker, and Honor Moore. British romantic Percy Shelley has been a constant influence.

Jordan writes most of her poetry using free verse, that is, lines free of prescribed meter and rhyme. The music and rhythm of her lines, then, are dependent on the grace with which she uses language and numerous other poetic strategies. Jordan's poetry has been applauded for its rhythmic qualities and for her technique of breaking lines in specific ways that promote strong rhythm. That several of her poems have been set to music by Bernice Reagon, the founder of the well-known black women's a capella group Sweet Honey in the Rock, is testament to the lyrical rhythms of Jordan's poetry. Reagon used "Alla Tha's All Right, But" and "A Song of Sojourner Truth." Structurally, the lyric predominates among Jordan's work, but a few dramatic monologues can be found in her cannon as well as a few sonnets. Her work also illustrates careful crafting. Jordan has admitted to a self-apprenticeship during the early years of her writing, when she disciplined herself to write in the styles of different highly regarded poets, not in order to imitate them but to expose herself fully to the techniques of her chosen craft. Another quality that persists throughout her poetry is its orality, the manner of Jordan's inscribing the sound of a speaking voice. This quality is particularly pronounced when the speaker uses black vernacular or urban black English.

Like most poets, Jordan's themes are expansive and include love, grief, loss, sexuality, women, and the political. Her poems can be classified by a variety of subjects including family, love, politics, and humor. References to her parents, immediate family, and friends are sprinkled throughout her many books of poems. In *Things That I Do in the Dark*, which contains twenty years of Jordan's poetry, "Who Look at Me," a long poem dedicated to her son Christopher, addresses the apparent invisibility of black people by European Americans and the layers of history and experience that should be visible. There is an elegiac "Poem for Granville Ivanhoe Jordan" as well as several poems for her mother, who committed suicide in 1966, that allude to the complexity and pain of her existence. These include "For My Mother," "On the Spirit of Mildred Jordan," "Getting Down to Get Over," and the prose poem "Ah, Momma."

Poems with love as their focus are numerous in Jordan's work. In *Haruko/Love Poems* (1993) the selections in the first half of the book are written to Haruko using the style of the Chilean poet Pablo Neruda's love poems. Jordan also uses the directness and brevity of haiku poetry, a Japanese stanza form of three lines, each with a designated number of syllables. Beyond this basic form, the poems reflect Jordan's distinct originality. The second section of the volume consists of select love poems from over twenty-two years of the poet's writing. Particularly romantic are "Poem for Haruka" and "Mendocino Memory," and "It's About You on the Beach," a poem of economy, color, and motion ending with the image of a body running on the beach like "a long black wing." Jordan's love poems are not limited to romantic interests, and readers will find no hint of sentimental clichés.

Although "Ghazal at Full Moon" is included in *Haruko/Love Poems*, it is also an example of Jordan's personal politics, her outrage at how different people of the earth are discarded by those who presume themselves superior. In "Ghazal at Full Moon" the profile of a Native American on a buffalo nickel initiates a meditation on indigenous peoples outside the United States including those in Guatemala, Jamaica, Nicaragua, Pakistan, Bangladesh, Bombay, and other locales. As in the United States, the survival of indigenous people has been in peril. "Poem about My Rights," in *Passion* (1980), combines the personal and the political through the speaker's litany of perceived wrongs—gender identity, a woman alone in the evening, age, sex, and skin color. If she were victimized by rape, under certain conditions she would still be wrong. Jordan uses the rape metaphor to critique the aggressive tactics of South Africa on smaller countries. This is a fast-paced poem of pronounced orality and a razor-sharp intellect.

Jordan's lengthy preface to *Passion* reaffirms her ongoing conflict with the politics of poetry as it is practiced and controlled in America via the publishing establishment. Evoking Walt Whitman as a poet of ordinary people with a vision that encompassed dispossessed people and a poet who initially self-published and promoted his own work, Jordan names herself and other New World poets of color as Whitman's descendants.

Her interest in the display of power is consistent—whether invested in the police, wealthy companies, or heads of state—and is communicated throughout her poetry. In *Passion*, "Poem for Nana," the enviromental damage of an oil spill, the absence of native people for whom the earth was sacred and the finding of a Native American girl's ice-preserved corpse are set against a South African government official's fear of a breakdown in political order. The speaker prays he is correct. These poems are representative of the passion and range of Jordan's interests in humanitarian rights and forces that deny them.

Given her passionate seriousness, readers may be pleasantly surprised to discover Jordan's rollicking sense of humor. In the poem "Notes on the Peanut" in *Passion*, for example, the persona George Washington Carver speaks about some of the 30,117 uses of the peanut such as a Renoir masterpiece reproduction from peanut chips and shoelaces from biodegradable peanut plant leaves. The humor rests in the combination of hyperbole or extreme exaggeration and verbal irony set within a strong narrative frame.

The title poem of the volume *Kissing God Goodbye* also illustrates Jordan's ability to combine humor with other values. "Kissing God Goodbye" is witty, politically tinged, and irreverent. It is a poem of backlash against the concept of an omnipotent masculine God whose inscrutable, mysterious ways are accepted. But not in Jordan's poem, as the speaker holds heterosexual men accountable for misogyny, the pestilence of earth, man's inhumanity to man, and death, along with all the other categories of wrong or evil. The promises of the Bible constitute the evidence for the accusations. The coup of the poem is in the self-identified speaker, an embracing "female" who claims the autonomy of her own breath.

Many of Jordan's poems combine her strong narrative ability with other qualities. In *Living Room* (1985), whose poems are dedicated to the children of Atlanta and Lebanon, "Des Moines Iowa Rap" is a ballad that critiques welfare inequity through the example of a navy veteran who tries suicide so that his wife and daughters can qualify for economic aid. "47,000 Windows" in *Things That I Do* offers a dense narrative critique of the consequences of overpopulation and basic human needs in New York's Lower East Side in the nineteenth century.

The writer Alice Walker has called Jordan a "universal" poet. This apt description captures the expansiveness of Jordan's work. Her positions and opinions are highly respected as evidenced by the numerous organizations who invite her to speak and by the awards she continues to garner.

POETRY

Some Changes. New York: Dutton/Plume, 1971. (Out of Print)
New Days: Poems of Exile and Return. New York: Emerson Hall, 1974. (Out of Print)
Things That I Do in the Dark: Selected Poems. New York: Random House, 1977. (Out of Print)
Passion: New Poems 1977–80. Boston: Beacon Press, 1980. (Out of Print)
Living Room 1980–84. New York: Avalon, 1985.
Lyrical Campaigns: Selected Poems. London: Virago, 1989. (Out of Print)
Naming Our Destiny: New and Selected Poems. New York: Avalon, 1989.
Haruko/Love Poems. New York: Little, Brown, 1993.
Kissing God Goodbye: Poems 1991–1996. New York: Doubleday, 1997.

EDITED POETRY ANTHOLOGY

SoulScript: AfroAmerican Poetry. New York: Doubleday, 1970. (Out of Print)

REFERENCES

Bloom, Harold, ed. *Black American Women Poets and Dramatists*. New York: Chelsea House, 1995. 135–49.
De Veaux, Alexis. "Creating Soul Food: June Jordan." *Essence* (April 1981): 82, 138–50.
Erickson, Peter. "June Jordan." In *Dictionary of Literary Biography*. Vol. 38. Ed. Thadious Davis and Trudier Harris Detroit: Gale Research, 1985. 146–62.
———. "The Love Poetry of June Jordan." *Callaloo* 9.1 (1986): 221–34.
Freccero, Carla. "June Jordan." In *African American Writers*. Ed. Lea Baechler and A. Walton Litz. New York: Charles Scribner's Sons, 1991. 245–62.
Hunter, Jeffrey W., and Jerry Moore, eds. "June Jordan." In *Black Literature Criticism: Supplement*. Detroit: Gale Research. 200–213.
Johnson, Ronna C. "June Jordan." In *The Oxford Companion to African American Writers*. Ed. Trudier Harris, Frances Smith Foster, and William Andrews. New York: Oxford University Press, 1997. 409–10.

ETHERIDGE KNIGHT

(1931–1991)

Etheridge Knight
Credit: Eunice Knight-Bowens
Photo credit: Robert Turney

Knight's first collection of poems, titled *Poems from Prison* (1968), was literally named, for he was an inmate at Indiana State Prison at the time the poems were written. The date of publication is also significant because it places the author among an outpouring of poetry from the period known as the Black Arts Movement. Dudley Randall's Broadside Press, so instrumental to black writers during this period, published Knight's work. Gwendolyn Brooks wrote the preface and singled out Knight's poems as having controlled softness, robust warmth, music, and "blackness, inclusive, possessed, and given; freed and terrible and beautiful." Randall's and Brooks's stamps of approval and recognition constituted major endorsements for an emerging writer, and Knight's work quickly became well regarded. Knight knew the European tradition from prison reading. Eventually he numbered among his long list of supporters the mainstream poets Galway Kinnell, Donald Hall, and James Wright, among others.

Knight was born in Corinth, Mississippi, to Bushie Knight and Belzora Cozard Knight, but he grew up in Paducah, Kentucky, with six siblings. His father gave up farming to become a laborer in 1939 on the construction of the Kentucky Dam, thus necessitating the family's move to Paducah. When he was ages eleven through fourteen, Knight and his siblings were sent back to Mississippi to live during the summers to keep them out of trouble. However, Knight had already begun running away from home.

He left school and home after the eighth grade and located himself in male street environments where another kind of education occurred. He joined the army at age seventeen in 1947, forging his parents' signature in his attempt to escape the streets. Knight was in the service twice; the first time he was too young and was kicked out. He rejoined at age eighteen, but then had served only eleven months when the Korean War began. He trained as a medical technician and was on active duty in Korea. He also became addicted to drugs during his service stint. In a style characteristic of his ability to cut to the root of the matter, Knight wrote of this experience in *Poems from Prison* (1968) that he "died in Korea from a shrapnel wound, and narcotics resurrected me. I died in 1960 from a prison sentence and poetry brought me back to life" (quoted on the back cover of *Poems from Prison*).

Knight had spent his twenties on the street as an addict engaged in crime until his sentence for an armed robbery that he committed to acquire money for drugs. He was transferred from the Indiana State Reformatory (his parents had moved to Indianapolis while he was in the army) to the Indiana State Prison in Michigan City, because of his initial rage during incarceration. He was released from prison in 1968.

Knight was married three times. His first marriage to fellow poet Sonia Sanchez ended in divorce, as did the second to Mary Ann McAnnally. In a third relationship with Charlene Blackburn, Knight had a son, Isaac "Bushie" Knight, the middle name given in memory of his paternal grandfather's nickname.

Knight began writing in prison in 1963, "poeting," as he aptly called his work. His first poem was published in 1965, a tribute to the singer Dinah Washington. His art emerged from the tradition of oral art in African American culture, the sermon and particularly the toast, a lengthy narrative recitation that boasts extraordinary human feats through verse that is rhymed and rhythmic. Knight heard sermons from Southern Baptist preachers. He was exposed to the toast in poolrooms when he was seven or eight years old and also from "Hound Mouth," a local man whom he referred to as the village poet. Hound Mouth sat in the park and recited toasts from memory about numerous subjects including the sinking of the *Titantic* and the signifying monkey. When Knight began fashioning his own toasts, he sang of expressively male, urban, and often violent feats. The prison culture at Indiana State Prison provided him male culture and a receptive audience for the content of his toasts. During his prison experience, Knight refined the toasts but also defined himself as a poet. He also wrote poems other than toasts and submitted them. Randall and Brooks visited him in prison in Michigan City.

Knight's attitudes about the relationship between the poet, the poem, and the community were perhaps shaped by his encounters with and observations of Hound Mouth. Knight accepted the poet and poem as songs being truthfully given back from the community from which they had originated. Poets for him were singers, preachers, and prophets addressing life's big questions and problems not through everyday speech but through myth and symbol.

The toasts that Knight recited in prison were symptomatic of the rich oral culture that would eventually infuse his work. This culture also gave him the blues forms that had infused the work of numerous African American poets such as Langston Hughes and would shape some of the poet Yusef Komunyakaa's work in the 1980s and 1990s as well. Komunyakaa, in particular, has commented on the tradition of the blues that he considers himself to share with Knight. In correspondence with Komunyakaa, in fact, Knight wrote that jazz, blues, and gospel were natural occurrences in his work, a "physicality," in fact. Knight believes the "speech patterns—the intonations, inflections, nuances—are to a larger degree determined by the music of our lives" (quoted in Clytus 127). In an interview with Charles Rowell, Knight refined his beliefs about blues as culture, distinguishing between blues culture and revolutionary culture. The blues allowed catharsis but did not incite action in order to change the conditions that produced the blues, while revolutionary culture is dynamic in a way that brings change.

The poem "While Watching B.B. King on T.V. While Locked in No. 8 Cell, No. 5 Cage of the Bridgeport, Conn., State Jail" does not seem to reflect the distinction referred to above. Instead, it suggests that the song the legendary blues performer B.B. King is singing makes a failed attempt to satisfy a definition of the cultural arts that would alienate it from the black culture that produced it. The sound is different, the poem says, but the pain on the singer's face is the same. The poem concludes: *"Blues ain't culture"*—blues are a testament to oppression. The B.B. King poem is not written in a blues format, but "A Poem for Myself" employs a traditional blues structure and a prototypical blues situation. A black boy from Mississippi leaves his mother and father at age twelve to escape the rural South. He travels predictably north, to Chicago, Detroit, and New York, but his blues go along with him. Thus in the last stanza, the boy is returning home, resolved to either be free in Mississippi "[o]r dead in the Mississippi mud," a choice often typical of blues verses and songs.

The influence of jazz on Knight's poetry is as significant as the blues. Jazz blends joy and despair for Knight, as it does for many other poets, and he directly references it in many poems. "For Eric Dolphy" celebrates a major jazz figure whose primary instruments were clarinet, oboe, and flute. The poem's speaker understands the music on a visceral level: It's love that he hears in the music, and he understands it as an expression of love in the way he understood his sister's love. She cried when he received a whipping. Structurally, the appearance of the poem on the page is designed to reflect Dolphy's style of flute playing. The extra spaces between the words in Knight's poem correspond to the breath between phrases in Dolphy's playing. The numerous one-word lines in the poem perhaps reflect Dolphy's staccato phrasing. Establishing a correlation between jazz poems and jazz music is difficult since music is aural and poetry can be seen on the page. Thus some jazz poems incorporate very strong visual images in order to approximate sound. Knight's poem in celebration of the innovative drummer Max Roach, titled "Jazz Drummer," achieves its force through such concrete images as the drummer having steel in his hand and being compared to a Makabele warrior.

Knight came out of a southern tradition that perists beneath his urban street diction and style. Based on the poetry, his southern experience did not leave him angry and bitter as it left, for example, the novelist Richard Wright, born and reared near Natchez, Mississippi, though Wright's birth and times preceded Knight's. Perhaps Knight's lack of bitterness may be attributed to his internalization of the blues with its built-in provision for cartharis even if it didn't move him to revolutionary fevor.

The poems in Knight's first volume, *Poems from Prison*, are characterized by a determined, thinking voice who understands political oppression and loss but who also remembers family. "The Idea of Ancestry," one of Knight's better-known poems, details his persona's sense of belonging and his efforts to retain familial links during incarceration. The prisoner compares himself to a salmon swimming upstream to get home last year, though he traveled with a "monkey on my back." The demands of the monkey drove him away after a while, in search of a fix, and he ultimately lands in prison. However, prisoner and family remain connected, although the contact now is principally through their pictures in the prison cell. Knight has said that this poem resulted from his having spent thirty or forty days in solitary confinement. After ten days, he said, he started remembering his early life and the taking away of identity that comes with the assigned prison number. To retain himself, he needed to place himself in a real context, which was his family. "To Make a Poem in Prison" says that what poets need for poems is unavailable in prison. In the direct way that characterizes his style, the poem begins by describing how difficult it is to make a poem in prison. The violence of prison life is not absent in this volume. In "Hard Rock Returns to Prison from the Hospital for the Criminal Insane," the prisoner named Hard Rock was a character/prisoner of legend, the kind that toasts are sung about. He was *hard*, a model of resistance and daring for the others. But having returned, he has been lobotomized, as the rumors declared, his resistance reduced to stupid grinning regardless of what anyone said to him. He describes the scars of fear, as if inflicted by a whip: "had cut grooves too deeply across our backs." The concluding imagery creates an immediate vision of the whips used during slavery, but the context is greater than that: It is the entire context of fear, physical oppression, and reductiveness used in the victimizing of African American men. Appropriately, "Hard Rock" is followed by "He Sees Through Stone," where the prisoner is elderly, unnamed, and silent but all knowing. He instinctively understands the structures of oppression.

Knight's poetry, in tremendous competition with much that was published in the late 1960s and early 1970s, nevertheless has an enduring quality that some other published poetry did not have. Paradoxically, his work is gentle and lyrical at the same time that it is raw and streetwise. The result is an intriguing and sustaining tension. In addition to the support that his work received from Gwendolyn Brooks and Dudley Randall, Haki Madhubuti in *Dynamite Voices* (1971) praises Knight for the qualities that others have recognized, including his music, carved images, and folk voices. Madhubuti quibbles in a few lines only with Greek allusions in the poem "To Gwendolyn Brooks." Those references seem only an indication of the high regard with which Knight held his mentor. Kumunyakaa, however, writing more recently, recognizes qualities that would have placed Knight's poetry on the "sidelines" of the Black Arts Movement in comparison to the style and diction of those who were in its central current (Clytus 131). He finds Knight's poems more grounded than other voices of the movement. He does not find them reactionary or confrontational; rather, they seek a level of truth that defines Knight's essence, his coming to his own voice and technique within the traditions that he learned from reading in prison in addition to his own cultural experiences.

Knight's work includes editing a book of writings by other prisoners at Michigan City, along with some of his own work, which was published as *Voci Dal Caracere* (*Black Voices from Prison*) in Bari, Italy, in 1968 and in English in 1970. *Born of a Woman: New and Selected Poems* (1980) and *The Essential Etheridge Knight* (1986) were brought out by Houghton Mifflin and the University of Pittsburgh Press, respectively.

As a well-regarded poet, Knight served as poet-in-residence at several universities during his career, including the University of Pittsburgh in Pennsylvania, Lincoln University in Jefferson City, Missouri, and the University of Hartford in Connecticut.

Knight's honors include a Guggenheim Foundation and a National Endowment for the Arts awards. He received the Shelley Memorial Award for achievement in 1985 from the Poetry Society of America. He also won the Before Columbus Foundation American Book Award in poetry for his last book in 1986. Martin University in Indianapolis gave Knight an honorary Bachelor of Arts degree and named him its Poet Laureate in 1990.

Despite his awards and his commitment to writing, over the years Knight continued to return to his addiction. Knight died of inoperable lung cancer six weeks prior to his sixtieth birthday.

POETRY

Poems from Prison. Detroit: Broadside Press, 1968.
(With others). *Black Voices from Prison*. 1968. Rpt., New York: Pathfinder Press, 1970. (Out of Print)
Belly Song and Other Poems. Detroit: Broadside Press, 1973.
Born of a Woman: New and Selected Poems. Boston: Houghton Mifflin, 1980. (Out of Print)
The Essential Etheridge Knight. Pittsburgh: University of Pittsburgh Press, 1986.

REFERENCES

Anaporte-Easton, Jean, ed. "Etheridge Knight: A Special Section." *Callaloo* 19.4 (Fall 1996): 939–81.

Clytus, Radiclani, ed. "Yusef Komunyakaa on Etheridge Knight." In *Blues Notes: Essays, Interviews, and Commentaries*. Ann Arbor: University of Michigan Press, 2000. 126–34.

Franklin, H. Bruce. "The Literature of the American Prison." *Massachusetts Review* 18 (1977): 51–78.

Hill, Patricia Liggins. "Blues for a Mississippi Black Boy: Etheridge Knight's Craft in the Black Oral Tradition." *Mississippi Quarterly* 36 (1982): 21–33.

Lee, Don L. (Haki Madhubuti). *Dynamite Voices: Black Poets of the 1960s*. Detroit: Broadside Press, 1971.

Lumpkin, Shirley. "Etheridge Knight." In *Dictionary of Literary Biography*. Vol 41. Ed. Trudier Harris and Thadious Davis. Detroit: Gale Research, 1985. 202–211.

McCullough, Ken. "Communication and Excommunication: An Interview with Etheridge Knight." *Callaloo* 5 (1982): 2–10.

Rowell, Charles H. "An Interview with Etheridge Knight." *Callaloo* 19.4 (1996): 967–980.

Yusef Komunyakaa

(1947–   )

Yusef Komunyakaa
Photo credit: Joyce Pettis

K omunyakaa has distinguished himself as a prolific and prize-winning poet, having produced thirteen books of poetry (including an early chapbook, *Toys in a Field* [1987]) since 1987. Numerous prestigious prizes testify to the esteem given his work. His volume *Neon Vernacular* won the Pulitzer Prize for Poetry in 1994 and the Kingsley-Tufts Poetry Award from the Claremont Graduate School in California, a cash award of $50,000. In 1993, Komunyakaa was also nominated for the *Los Angeles Times* Book Prize in Poetry, and in 1997 he was awarded the Hanes Poetry Prize. *I Apologize for the Eyes in My Head* won the San Francisco Poetry Center Award, and in 1991 he won the Thomas Forcade Award. *Thieves of Paradise* (1998) was a finalist for the 1999 National Book Critics Circle Award. Moreover, Komunyakaa's poetry has been compared to the quality of Ralph Ellison's and James Baldwin's, two of the most revered among male African American writers. Although Komunyakaa's reputation is based on his poetry, he also has written songs and prose performance pieces. His work illustrates reverence for the oral and musical traditions of African American culture, among other traditions.

Komunyakaa, née James Willie Brown, was reared in Bogalusa, Louisiana, an impoverished area about seventy miles from New Orleans, the oldest of four brothers and one sister. Komunyakaa assumed his distinctive surname not as a symbolic rite of personal liberation but rather as an assertion of kinship ties. The name belonged to Komunyakaa's great-grandparents who, entering the United States in Florida shortly after 1900, self-protectively took on an American name. In Komunyakaa's youth, the name was like a family secret, and he never learned the full story surrounding the immigration. However, he learned that when his great-grandmother brought her three children into the United States, the one destined to become his grandfather had to wear mismatched shoes, a male and a female one. Komunyakaa's poem "Mismatched Shoes" builds on the core of this incident.

Komunyakaa's parents were working-class rural people. His father was a carpenter, his mother was in the home, and he had access to his grandparents when he was growing up. Komunyakaa attended Central High School and graduated in 1965.

After high school, he enrolled in the army and was sent to Vietnam in 1969. As an information specialist, or army news reporter, when there was an engagement, he was taken to its center by helicopter. Vietnam would have profound consequences for him as he reveals in *Dien Cai Dau* (1988), a reflective volume of poetry inspired by his Vietnam experience. Komunyakaa earned his B.A. degree from the University of Colorado in 1975 as an English and sociology major; an M.A. degree from Colorado State in 1979; and the M.F.A. degree in creative writing from the University of California at Irvine in 1980.

From 1984 to 1985, Komunyakaa was poet-in-residence in the schools in New Orleans. He also held a visiting professorship at the University of New Orleans, where in 1989–1990 he held the Ruth Lilly Professorship, an endowed chair. He taught at Indiana University and subsequently became Holloway Lecturer at the University of California, Berkeley, in 1992. He is presently professor in the Council of Humanities and Creative Writing at Princeton University.

In 1985, Komunyakaa married the Australian novelist and short story writer Mandy Jane Sayer, and they have a daughter. He has traveled to Australia four times, the first in 1986 when he stayed a year. Komunyakaa returned to Vietnam in 1990 in the company of five other veterans.

While growing up in Bogalusa did not provide Komunyakaa with an abundance of material assets, that environment is significant in fashioning his approach to poetry. For example, as early as age seven or eight, Komunyakaa was aware of the prominence of blues music to his environment and was listening to blues and jazz on the radio. His continued listening as a young adult functioned as a musical connection to his younger years. Komunyakaa's father's occupation as a carpenter was part of his environment, and he often had to assist with the work. As an adult composing poetry, Komunyakaa has found himself meditating about his father's carpentry work. Ironically, the symmetry and precision of the occupation is reflected in the shape and sharpness of diction that he employs in the construction of poems. "Songs for My Father" is based on an incident between the poet and his father. The young narrator has a complex relationship with his father who never approved of poetry as a vocation, but the sick father asks for a poem for his birthday. The poet couldn't produce it, however, and the father died within the year. Generally in his poems, Komunyakaa also recalls in detail the terrain that surrounded his parents' house. During his youthful years, he had an active imaginative life as he roamed in the woods near his house and projected himself to other mysterious but grand places. The violence of natural predators in the landscape also exposed him to violence as a part of life.

Komunyakaa traces his attraction to poetry to its inclusion in his elementary and high school curriculums where he read Shakespeare, Edgar Allan Poe, Emily Dickinson, and Alfred Lord Tennyson. African American literature was limited to "Negro History Week" in February. Nevertheless, he enjoyed Melvin Tolson, Langston Hughes, Gwendolyn Brooks, and Phillis Wheatley. He also was intrigued by the Bible and voluntarily read it twice before completing high school. Its rhythms and graceful language have been noted as influential in Komunyakaa's work. He admits to numerous influences, including Margaret Walker, Walt Whitman, the Argentine writer Jorges Luis Borges, Gabriel Garcia Marquez, and the work of Harlem Renaissance poets, among others.

Komunyakaa began seriously writing poetry as an undergraduate at Colorado State in the early 1970s, and his first brief volumes of poetry were published in that decade. *Copacetic*, a longer volume completed in 1981 in Bogalusa, includes many of the first poems and covers Komunyakaa's years in Panama, Puerto Rico, Japan, and Colorado Springs. Many of the poems also focus on South Africa. The term *copacetic* is connected in the poet's mind with the feelings and emotions of jazzy-blues. Thus the environment for many speakers in the poems is a blues one, and blues as structure or mood or music can be found throughout Komunyakaa's work. His blues tendencies, in fact, link him with the blues traditions forged by Langston Hughes and, later, Amiri Baraki. "Blackmail Blues" and "Mojo" are typical blues poems. The central themes of the volume are carried in "Fake Leads," "The Way the Cards Fall," "Jumping Bad Blues," and "Blues Chant Hoodoo Revival." The images conveyed in many of these poems point to Komunyakaa's southern background and suggest numerous manifestations of how blues has characterized black living in the South.

Both *Magic City* (1992) and *Dien Cai Dau* (1988) are written from loose autobiographical perspectives. In *Magic City* gardening, preserving the harvest, youthful sexual experiments, racial violence, community entertainment, family separation, and a fecund southern terrain are among the scenes that form the context for the poet's coming of age. "Immolatus," for example, a narrative of a hog killing, has as its companion "The Smokehouse," which details smoking the pork of the slain hog. Johnson's strong facility with narrative is apparent in poems such as "The Cooling Board," "Yellowjackets," and "The Steel Plate." Notable for their emphasis on coming-of-age experiences are "Nude Tango," "Sex, Magnolias, & Speed," and "History Lessons."

The poems in *Dien Cai Dau* offer a probing exploration of the Vietnam experience. The speaker's remarkably detached voice details the violence, fear, and absurdity of men living and dying in war. Nonessential verbiage is peeled away, leaving strong images and content that reveal helplessness, outrage, fear, and even curiosity. In the ironically titled "You and I Are Disappearing" for example, the speaker-soldier's memory is dominated by an image of a "girl still burning" in his memory. Except for the soldier's terse statement that he helplessly watches, the poem consists of cumulative similes that carry the vivid, rapid nature of the flagration. Whether the victim is self-immolated or her burning somehow the result of battle is inconsequential. "We Never Knew" depicts violent death lyrically through the image of a bullet-pierced dying man dancing and swaying before he falls. When a fellow soldier reaches the body, he returns a clutched photograph to the soldier's wallet, returns the wallet to the soldier's pocket, and in a thoughtful gesture, turns the body over so the lips will not be on the dirt. Johnson seems to suggest through this act that although the soldier's life cannot be reclaimed, some ritual acknowledging life's end must be performed by the living. "To Do Street," however, depicts racial division among soldiers and the inequity that black soldiers sometime experienced in Vietnamese clubs. Johnson underscores the absurdity and irony of these acts through the image and double entendre of tunnels. In the clubs, the men seek Vietnamese women, the female kin of those men killed by all the American soldiers. The prostitutes, however, give preference to the whites. Nevertheless, when black soldiers receive the sexual services they enter the same bodily passageways that the white soldiers have recently exited, just as both black and white soldiers have occupied the same tunnels for physical survival in the alien terrain of Vietnam. The poem thus illustrates the absurdity of preferences based on race when all of the men are united by the struggle for life.

Komunyakaa also uses the Vietnamese terrain in his poems. "A Greenness Taller Than Gods" and "Somewhere Near Phu Bai," where terrifying facets of nature are examined. In an interview, the poet observed that urban soldiers were often more terrified by the terrain than by the enemy. Nature became part of the disguise in guerrilla warfare. In "Hanoi Hannah," however, images of nature are integrated as the backdrop against which the technology of war—its artillery shells and Howitzers with their colors and sounds—can be illustrated.

"Facing It," composed in 1984, juxtaposes the backward reflective focus of the volume's poems with the present. Physically, the speaker is looking at the Vietnam Veterans Memorial. The poem's content is composed of numerous concrete images rendered surreally by the eye's perception of light and the objects reflected off of, but simultaneously pulled back into, the shiny hard surface of the monument, the dead men's names. This looking inward but seeing outward suggests the speaker's precarious balance between surviving the grief of war and being emotionally sucked in by it. The poem ends with the surprise image of a woman brushing a boy's hair, an image that implies the ability to move on with normal activities of life.

Komunyakaa's identity as an African American is a quiet feature of his poems rather than a loud, intrusive one. Often, racial subtleties are tucked away in references that echo reflectively to past historical incidence and practices as in the title poem of *I Apologize*. The focus on "eyes" (as noun) in the title and the repetition of "I" (as pronoun) in the body of the poem, both with the same pronunciation, places emphasis on man "seeing" or looking. Yet the speaker's dramatic monologue denies his having seen anything as he tries to convince an unidentified listener. The speaker is the archetypal black man whose eyeballing of white women has brought undue attention to him. The poem is his ingenious denial, a dissembling through self-effacement even as he declares his humanity in the line "I'm just like the rest of the world." His use of "Sir" as a term of address identifies his inquisitor as a white man. Having to plead innocence and detachment when he has "eyed" whatever would have compelled any human's attention has historically been a plight in which black men have found themselves. "I Apologize" is also representative of Komunyakaa's talent for subtly recalling and reproducing experiences that force the reader's insights into play. He integrates a similar kind of examination into strong narrative poems that are based on real-life situations, as in "Jeanne Duval's Confession," or in poems based on fictional events such as "Trueblood's Blues." Jeanne Duval was French writer Charles Baudelaire's inspiration, and Komunyakaa writes the poem from her perspective. Trueblood, a disgraced farmer in Ralph Ellison's novel *Invisible Man*, has committed an unspeakable act of incest but can't stop recounting it for white listeners, including the philanthropist northerner Mr. Norton. Trueblood's listeners participate vicariously in the despicable act even as he confirms their opinions of his baseness. His tale is his own blues, the human weakness of being unable to stop himself when he realizes that he is no longer engaged in a dream and that the listeners are using him against himself. "Tobe's Blues" is based on the silent servant in William Faulkner's "A Rose for Emily," and "Homage to a Bellboy" is based on the incident in Richard Wright's *Black Boy* when a young Wright had to serve a room where the white woman is nude. Conventions of the era demanded that the server ignore the obvious nudity, a convention that Komunyakaa explores ironically in the title poem of his volume *I Apologize for the Eyes in My Head*.

Komunyakaa's work and the awards it has earned continue to bring him to the attention of an ever-widening audience. He seems positioned, indeed, to occupy a place of respect in the tradition of African American literary history.

POETRY

Dedications and Other Darkhorses. Laramie, WY: R.M.C.A.J. Books. 1977. (Out of Print)

Lost in the Bonewheel Factory. Spokane, WA: Lynx House Press, 1979.

Copacetic. Middletown, CT: Wesleyan University Press, 1984. (Out of Print)

I Apologize for the Eyes in My Head. Middletown, CT: Wesleyan University Press, 1986. (Out of Print)

Dien Cai Dau. Middletown, CT: Wesleyan University Press, 1988. Hanover, NH: University Press of New England, 2000.

Magic City. Hanover, NH: Wesleyan University Press, 1992.

Neon Vernacular: New and Selected Poems. Hanover, NH: Wesleyan University Press, 1993.

Thieves of Paradise. Hanover, NH: Wesleyan University Press, 1998.

(With Alpay Ulku). *Meteorology.* Rochester: BOA Editions, Ltd., 1999.

Talking Dirty to the Gods: Poems. New York: Farrar, Straus, and Giroux, 2000.

Pleasure Dome: New and Collected Poems. Hanover, NH: University Press of New England, 2001.

EDITED POETRY ANTHOLOGY

(With Sascha Feinstein). *The Jazz Poetry Anthology.* Bloomington: Indiana University Press, 1991.

(With Sascha Feinstein). *The Second Set: The Jazz Poetry Anthology.* Vol. 2. Bloomington: Indiana University Press, 1996.

OTHER

Blues Notes: Essays, Interviews, and Commentaries. Ed. Radiclani Clytus. Ann Arbor: University of Michigan Press, 2000.

REFERENCES

Aubert, Alvin. Rev. of *Neon Vernacular. African American Review* 28 (1994): 671–72.

Gotera, Vicente F. "Lives of Tempered Steel: An Interview with Yusef Komunyakaa." *Callaloo* 13.2 (1990): 215–29.

Hunter, Jeffrey W., and Jerry Moore, eds. "Yusef Komunyakaa." In *Black Literature Criticism: Supplement.* Detroit: Gale Research, 1999. 214–35.

Jones, Kirkland. "Yusef Komunyakaa." In *Dictionary of Literary Biography.* Vol. 120. Ed. R.S. Gwynn. Detroit: Gale Research, 1992. 176–79.

Kelly, Robert. "Jazz and Poetry: A Conversation." *Georgia Review* 46.4 (1992): 645–61.

Salas, Angela M. "Flashbacks through the Heart": Yusef Komunyakaa and the Poetry of Assertion." In *The Furious Flowering of African American Poetry.* Ed. Joanne V. Gabbin. Charlottesville: University of Virginia, 1999. 298–308.

AUDRE LORDE

(1934–1992)

Audre Lorde
Credit: W.W. Norton
Photo credit: Dagmar Schullz

One of the astounding facts about Audre Lorde is that, according to her account, her first language was poetry. As a young child who stuttered, she thought and responded in poems rather than sentences. If asked a simple question, she was more likely to offer a brief poem that contained the answer in a line or an image to avoid the responses from adults if she stuttered. Perhaps, then, Lorde's career in the form of language that she originally thought in, or poetry, was not a surprise to anyone who knew her from childhood. Lorde had become a respected poet by the middle 1970s, less than ten years after her first book. Although it appeared in 1968 during the Black Arts Movement, it reflected that era neither in style, temperament, nor poetic technique. Lorde thus initially communicated her distinctive voice. She would not be part of any status quo, although her politically conscious work would be committed to addressing inequities, women, and Third World situations. Lorde's work has proven that she is a poet for all time and not for an era.

With poetry having been so integral to her personal experience, it follows that Lorde would believe that poems grow out of "the poet's experience in a particular place and a particular time, and the genius of the poem is to use the textures of that place and time without becoming bound by them" (Rowell 55). When that happens, as Lorde stated in an interview with Charles Rowell, the poem can create its own world and function for others who have not had that particular experience. Lorde's numerous volumes therefore invite readers into poems that offer vastly different experiences between 1968 and 1992, the years of her productivity. Having never experienced the world as pretty and charming, Lorde's poetry is never romantic in an easy way. Writing from the intersecting identities of being a black, lesbian, feminist, warrior, poet mother, as she terms herself, her writing is filtered through these multiple prisms that are neither static nor easy. Minimally, then, her poetry requires the reader to engage his or her conscience, to read with a politically tuned mind, and to be jolted out of simple or false assumptions.

Lorde was born in Harlem, New York, the youngest daughter of Frederick Byron and Linda Belmar Lorde. The Lordes had been married a year when they arrived in New York in 1924, Frederick from Barbados and Linda from Grenada. Frederick initially worked as a laborer at the Waldorf Astoria and his wife as a maid, but he attended night school and eventually opened a real estate business, and his wife worked with him there. The Lordes, like numerous other black Caribbeans, assumed they would return "home" one day. They raised their three daughters to believe that home was their islands rather than their New York apartment. Therefore, when Audre left New York in 1987 to live in St. Croix, U.S. Virgin Islands, she felt very much at home with the people, their culture, and their problems.

The Lordes also raised their daughters in a household that was West Indian in the language the parents used, the foods they ate, and the discipline administered, in spite of its physical location in Harlem. Audre recalled her childhood and adolescence as lonely periods defined by exact expectations from her parents. Her parents also protected their daughters from racial slights and insults, so successfully, in fact, that when Lorde was in elementary and high school, she had no descriptive terms for the attitudes that set her apart from her white classmates. Lorde was born nearsighted, legally blind, and did not speak until she was four or five. A short story read by a librarian thrilled her to the extent that she spoke.

With the exception of one year spent as a student at National University of Mexico in 1954, Lorde's formal education took place in New York City. She attended a Catholic elementary school and high school there, where she published her first poem. A revelation for Lorde during high school was that people normally thought in sequential, linear steps or sentences rather than what she called "bubbles up from chaos that you had to anchor with words" (Lorde, *Sister* 83). By age nineteen, Lorde had finally begun to speak and write in full sentences, although sustained thought in this linear mode rather than in poems was difficult for her. Understandably, then, she wrote very little prose, publishing only a short story under a pseudonym. She wrote poems during high school and had a poem published in *Seventeen* magazine at age fifteen, a poem that her English teachers said was too romantic. After high school, she attended Hunter College and received her undergraduate degree in library science in 1959, and a master's degree from Columbia University in 1961. During college, Lorde supported herself by working as a medical clerk, x-ray technician, and factory worker. With her degrees, however, she began working in her field of preparation, first at Mount Vernon Public Library (1961–1963) and then as head librarian at the Town School Library in New York (1966–1968). She was known as the librarian who wrote. In 1962, Lorde married Edwin A. Rollins, an attorney. A son, Johnathan, and a daughter, Elizabeth, were born to them. The couple divorced in 1970. "And What about Children," one of Lorde's early poems, references the negative expectations that some people voiced about her interracial marriage and any resulting children.

A pivotal year in the poet's career development was 1968 when Lorde was granted a National Endowment for the Arts grant; published her first book of poetry, *The First Cities*, and became poet-in-residence at Tougaloo College, a historically black college in Tougaloo, Mississippi. In Lorde's first trip to the Deep South, the teaching experience brought her to the realization that teaching and writing would be her life's valuable work. In her first book, Lorde focused on feelings and relationships and made her commitment to blackness implicit. *Cities* was noted by reviewers and received positive comments, especially for its fresh phrasing.

Following her stay at Tougaloo College, Lorde combined college-level teaching with a noteworthy publishing record. She became an instructor at City College in New York (1968–1970) with contiguous work at Lehman College (1969–1970). At John Jay College of Criminal Justice in New York, she worked her way to full professor during the years 1970–1981. She returned to her undergraduate alma mater, Hunter College, as a full professor in 1981. Although Lorde continued prolific writing and publishing, during this period, Lorde was battling breast cancer. It was diagnosed in 1970, and she underwent a radical mastectomy. Lorde's directly titled essays, *The Cancer Journals*, (1980) chronicle her experience with the disease and with the male-dominated medical profession.

In the late 1980s, the cancer metastasized to Lorde's liver, and in 1987, she underwent a second surgery. She chose an unorthodox treatment for the disease in these years, electing a holistic treatment of homeopathy, meditation, and self-hypnosis. She went annually to Berlin, Germany, for experimental cancer treatments that were successful for a time. Always the activist and writer, regardless of physical conditions, in Germany Lorde involved herself with the Afro-German population, especially women poets, who were bringing their African linguistic heritage to bear on their German language and poetic forms. In 1987, Lorde relocated to St. Croix, having decided that her weakened state unfitted her for the physically compelling logistics of life in New York City.

By 1987, Lorde was a seasoned poet and activist and had addressed a significant problem in the publishing industry for nontraditional writers. Her eight volumes of poems included such recurrent themes as the search for identification, black women's capability to survive, childhood, patriarchal power, the past, global injustice, oppression, social activism, and the feminist drive for power. In fact, her passion for feminism and women's activism on all fronts contributed to her assistance in founding Kitchen Table Press, along with Barbara Smith and Gloria Hull, fellow black women writers and critics. Kitchen Table Press, the first of its kind, met a need unrecognized at the time by large, mainstream presses. It published and distributed works of feminist vision by women of color from different communities.

Her second volume, *Cables to Rage* (1970), published in London and distributed by Dudley Randall's Broadside Press, included the themes of temporal human love, human betrayal, birth, and love. "Martha" in this volume is frequently cited because it is Lorde's first poetic statement of her homosexuality. *From a Land Where Other People Live* (1973), also from Broadside Press, is concerned with identity as an African American and as a woman, though relationships are prominent. Lorde writes about mother and daughter relationships and about women as lovers and sisters. This volume is also significant in its inclusion of Lorde's activist positions, for she speaks out about political struggles in so-called Third World countries. *From a Land* was nominated for the National Book Award. *The New York Head Shop and Museum* (1974), from Broadside Press, used the language of the 1960s in proffering its grim vision of the city. After three books issued by Dudley Randall, a black publisher, *Coal* (1976), a compilation of Lorde's first two volumes, was the writer's first book from the mainstream publisher W.W. Norton. The major advantage was to make her work easily available to large mainstream audiences.

Critics consider Lorde's next two volumes, *Between Our Selves* (1976) and *The Black Unicorn* (1978), as the poet's most accomplished volumes, particularly the latter. *Unicorn* embraces and reclaims Africa through mythology and history, specifically using Dahomean Amazons, the maternal goddesses Seboulisa and Yemanjà, and supporting the idea of woman's mythic and primal significance. Lorde had received critical respect with the previously published volumes, but with *Unicorn*, she was applauded for incorporating the spiritual presence of Africa.

Lorde's collected edition *Chosen Poems—Old and New* appeared from W.W. Norton in 1982, and *Our Dead Behind Us* in 1986. *Our Dead* contained easier language and references than either *Coal* or *Unicorn*; thus, the poems are more accessible to many readers.

Lorde's *The Marvelous Arithmetics of Distance*, contains poems written between 1987, the year she moved to St. Croix, and 1992, the year she died there. Characteristic of Lorde's style in language, each word in the poems has the effect of being chiseled from granite to stand solitary with its meaning subsumed within. This quality forces the reader to focus on each word, not only because of meaning but also because Lorde's work includes no excessive words. Thus, each word and the spaces between them matter. In fact, she frequently makes one word perform the function of "linking"; that is, the same word ends one thought but also begins the next thought on the next line. This linking method controls reading pace as does Lorde's tendency to dictate the reader's pause before words by inserting a space in the line before a word. The reader is thus forced to pause and perhaps to reflect as well. The minimal use of internal punctuation in stanzas works in concert with the way one has to read Lorde's poems.

While no single theme or idea dominates the poems in *The Marvelous Arithmetics of Distance*, its scope of subjects includes poems that refer to Lorde's family, the Caribbean, her cancer, and her companion Gloria. The abstraction of the opening poem, "Smelling the Wind," which incorporates the book's creative title in one of its lines, invites speculation that the poet views a phase of her life as a voyage toward death. The brief poem uses the metaphor of travel, a familiar face on the horizon, dreams anchored, and one season to make another voyage. No calculation, presumably of the new voyage, is permitted, as the distance is incalculable. Distance, in fact, is a motif in the volume. "Legacy—Hers" suggests that lessons have been gleamed from Lorde's mother Linda, who is named in the poem, but the lessons are unclear and leave the daughter "still seeking," except that she learned how to die from the mother's examples. "Inheritance—His," the longest in the volume, names Lorde's father. It questions secrets and behaviors of a father who remained silent about much of his Caribbean experiences. In "Restoration: A Memorial—9/18/91," the date about a year before her death, Lorde is in Berlin, having undergone chemotherapy. However, she is remembering another life, one nearly destroyed by the hurricane Hugo when its destructive force decimated many Caribbean islands as well as parts of the mainland. The poem asks a question that remains unanswered—whether the speaker would give up the protection of exile "for the muddy hand-drawn water" that resulted from the destruction. Death is likened in this poem to a star sitting on a teacup flaming drops of honey. That Lorde has no illusions about the death she faces is clearly expressed in the last two poignant poems of the book. "Today Is Not the Day," dated April 22, 1992, expresses the poet's knowing that fact and refusing to look the other way. In alluding to slipping anchor and uncoiling into the water, this poem connects with the imagery of sea travel and distance in "Smelling the Wind." The last poem in the volume, "The Electric Slide Boogie," is a celebration of normal life activities on New Year's Day. Although Lorde admits that her body is weary, she nevertheless responds to a celebration in the house. The ending lines "How hard it is to sleep" are an ambiguous but clear reference to her coming death in the prime of her life.

POETRY

The First Cities. New York: Poets Press, 1968.
Cables to Rage. Detroit: Broadside Press, 1970.
From a Land Where Other People Live. Detroit: Broadside Press, 1973.
The New York Head Shop and Museum. Detroit: Broadside Press, 1974.
Between Our Selves. Point Reyes, CA: Eidolon Editions, 1976.
Coal. New York: W.W. Norton, 1976.
The Black Unicorn. W.W. Norton, 1978.
Chosen Poems—Old and New. New York: W.W. Norton, 1982: Rev. ed, 1992.
Our Dead Behind Us. W.W. Norton, 1986.
The Marvelous Arithmetics of Distance. New York: W.W. Norton, 1993.
The Collected Poems of Audre Lorde. New York: W.W. Norton, 1997.

OTHER

Zami: A New Spelling of My Name (A Biomythography). London: Pandora, 1982.

REFERENCES

Breman, Paul. "Poetry into the 'Sixties." In *The Black American Writer*. Vol. 2. Ed.
    C.W. E. Bigsby. Deland, FL: Everett Edwards, 1969.
Brooks, Jerome. "In the Name of the Father: The Poetry of Audre Lorde." In *Black
    Women Writers (1950–1980): A Critical Evaluation*. Ed. Mari Evans. New
    York: Anchor Books, 1984. 269–76.
Hull, Gloria T. "Living on the Line: Audre Lorde and *Our Dead Behind Us*." In
    *Changing Our Own Words: Essays on Criticism, Theory, and Writing by Black
    Women*. Ed. Cheryl A. Wall. New Brunswick, NJ: Rutgers University Press,
    1989. 150–72.
Keating, AnaLouise. *Women Reading Women Writing: Self Invention in Paula Gunn
    Allen, Gloria Anzaldùa and Audre Lorde*. Philadelphia: Temple University
    Press, 1996.
Lorde, Audre. "My Words Will Be There." In *Black Women Writers (1950–1980):
    A Critical Evaluation*. Ed. Mari Evans. New York: Anchor Books, 1984. 261–
    68.
———. *Sister Outsider*. Freedom, CA: The Crossing Press, 1984.
Martin, Joan. "The Unicorn is Black: Audre Lorde in Retrospect." In *Black Women
    Writers (1950–1980): A Critical Evaluation*. Ed. Mari Evans. New York: An-
    chor Books, 1984. 278–91.
McLauren-Allen, Irma. *Dictionary of Literary Biography*. Vol. 4. Ed. Trudier Harris
    and Thadious Davis. Detroit: Gale Research, 1985.
Rowell, Charles H. "Above the Wind: An Interview with Audre Lorde." *Callaloo*
    23.1 (2000): 52–63.
Tate, Claudia, ed. "Interview with Audre Lorde." In *Black Women Writers at Work*.
    New York: Continuum, 1983. 100–116.
Vinson, James, ed. *Contemporary Poets*. London: St. James Press, 1975.

NATHANIEL MACKEY

(1947–   )

Nathaniel Mackey
Credit: University of California—Santa Cruz

Mackey has published widely in numerous genres, including fiction, poetry, and cultural and literary criticism. All of his work has been commended for its innovative departures from conventional form and content. Mackey's activity as an editor includes an anthology of jazz-related poetry, a special issue of *Callaloo* on the Caribbean novelist Wilson Harris, and the literary magazine *Hambone*. In 1982 Mackey became its editor and publisher, rechristened it *Hambone*, and broadened its scope to include contributors of various racial and ethnic backgrounds. Mackey juggles his writing and editing with university teaching.

Mackey was born in Miami, Florida, to Sadie Jane Wilcox and Alexander Obadiah Mackey, the youngest of three siblings. His mother was from Georgia and his father was born in the Panama Canal Zone to Bahamian parents. The children moved with their mother to northern California when their parents separated, then later to Santa Ana in southern California. Mackey completed high school in Santa Ana and enrolled at Princeton University for his undergraduate degree. After graduation in 1969, he taught mathematics to eighth graders in Pasadena and then enrolled at Stanford University for Ph.D. work in English and American literature. He was awarded the degree in 1975. Mackey has taught at the University of Wisconsin at Madison, the University of Southern California, and the University of California, Santa Cruz, where he has been a member of the faculty since 1979. Mackey married Pascale Gaitet in 1991; he has a stepson, Joe, and a daughter, Naima.

Mackey was intrigued with music by age eight or nine and at that time was hearing it in the Baptist church, but he was not interested in writing. In his early teens, he began listening to the jazz of Miles Davis, John Coltrane, and Ornette Coleman and reading poetry. In high school, Mackey stumbled upon *Pictures from Brueghel* by the modernist physician poet William Carlos Williams and became intrigued by it. Mackey also discovered Amiri Baraka during this time and was attracted to Baraka's focus on music in his writing and to the liner notes that Baraka wrote for a jazz album by John Coltrane. Williams and Baraka have since been joined by numerous other writers whose techniques or emphases appeal to Mackey's wide-ranging interests. At Princeton Mackey began writing and decided that if he were good enough, he might want to continue it as a career.

Mackey's first full-length book of poetry, *Eroding Witness*, was chosen for publication by the board of The National Poetry Series in 1984 as one of its annual five collections. Selected by poet and board member Michael S. Harper, Harper's brief comment to the book explains a direction for Mackey's poems that is useful for the first volume as well as for the poet's subsequent ones. "These poems are about prophecy and initiation; the uncompromising narratives that sing but *don't explain* are the sounds of a mythmaker-griot in the midst of ceremonial talk, the totems of incantation, the way to the source, the origins of power" (Harper's italics). As this sentence suggests, the content of Mackey's poems includes liberal cross-cultural borrowings and incorporates different African and Caribbean religions, cultures, and literatures.

Mackey has candidly talked about his allusions and use of African and Caribbean cultures in creating the context for his poetry with editor and interviewer Charles Rowell. Like Jay Wright, in particular, Mackey weaves together references and cultural and mythological traditions from numerous geographical sites, including Spain, the Caribbean, Africa, America, and the Arabic and Iberian worlds, but there is little in the poem to suggest those sources to the uninitiated reader. Mark Scroggins has written that Mackey's works are "complex and initially bewildering," that they have a "dense web of intertextual references . . . to other texts, to musical compositions (especially jazz), and to his own previous writings" (179). Ideologically, Mackey is committed to his poetry's difference from conventional poetry. For example, he writes poems that are not developed as structured narratives. The poems do not offer necessarily unified stories, and the voice is not always easily identifiable. Thus when a reader has finished one of Mackey's poems, the feeling may not be that a story, message, or theme has been communicated and that an identifiable, first-person voice has been the guide. In yet another way, Mackey's poems are different because he writes them to be in conversation with themselves, that is, for the individual poem to be incomplete and always part of a larger picture. Therefore, his poems may not have the resolution that readers have come to expect. From poem to poem or from one book of his poetry to the next, Mackey's poems may connect with each other, each one expanding the larger work. This conversation from text to text also means that Mackey orchestrates repetition in his work, including between the poetry and his prose publications.

Mackey's concern with the appearance of the poem on the page is connected to his knowing that it will be read. "The page and the ear coexist," he has said (quoted in Rowell 713); thus he designs the words on the page with their performance potential and capability in mind. He writes consciously, led by the rhythms of words and music and the interplay of what is pleasing to the ear and to the eye. He finds uniformity in stanza arrangement in many conventional poems jarring to the natural way the poem will be read and thus works to avoid that practice in his work.

Mackey points to literary predecessors such as T.S. Eliot, who also wrote poems outside of the convention of the fixed voice and easily accessible narrative structure. Additionally, the early experimental work of Amiri Baraka, both in form and in its use of music, and the nonconventional work of major poets Robert Duncan and William Carlos Williams are influences on or predecessors for Mackey's work. His writing also shows some affiliation with the cross-cultural leanings of Henry Dumas, a black poet who died young. Mackey's experimentation in form and his cross-cultural borrowings or intertextual kinships motivate critics to classify his work as modernist or postmodernist. Some consider his position in contemporary poetry somewhat problematic, and his work often occurs in anthologies of experimental poetry.

Mackey's first volume, *Eroding Witness*, incorporates his two chapbooks (first, short books of poetry often privately published with minimal circulation) *Four for Trane* and *Septet for the End of Time*, as section four of the book. The reader is introduced to a serial poem titled "Song of the Andoumboulou" that will reappear in numbered sections in subsequent volumes. Drawing on his cross-cultural studies, Mackey defines the Andoumboulou as a failed, early form of human being in Dogon cosmology. He uses the figure as representative of our present and our past condition. Loosely, it functions as the rough draft of a human being. Mackey began writing his serial poem in the 1970s, and the first publication of it occurred in 1974. The first seven "Andoumboulou" sections appear in *Eroding Witness* as section two of the book. Eight more sections of "Andoumboulou" appear in his second book, *School of Udhra*, and the third book, *Whatsaid Serif*, consists completely of the "Andoumboulou," ending with the number 111. True to Mackey's objectives, several sections relate backwards to poems in *Eroding Witness* and *School of Udhra*.

In *Eroding Witness* Mackey's task for the section containing *Four for Trane* and *Septet for the End of Time* is to trace cultural and mythological origins located in the traditions of Vodun, Dogon cosmology, Santería, and African American music from Coltrane's jazz to the rock era of Jimi Hendrix. This task represents in minuscule fashion what Mackey attempts large scale across the canvas of his work. He is motivated by trace elements present from one culture to another, particularly when conventional anthropological or historical intellectual thought fails to recognize their presence. The religions of Vodun and Santería from the Caribbean, South America, and Cuba, for example, represent syncretism, the bringing together and mixing of disparate ritual and religious elements from Africa with elements of European Catholicism. On one level *Eroding Witness* explores how these forces interact altogether.

Thus a major thematic strand in the volume is the past. "Kitchie Manitou," for example, evokes the voyaging of the peoples of the Americas from Asia. "Passing Thru" similarly tells of voyaging, but of Africans. Since a people's culture is not abandoned during their physical sojourning, the poem mentions transporting an endangered culture along lines similar to the work of Ivan Van Sertima in *They Came Before Columbus*. Van Sertima sought to prove the presence of others who predated Columbus in the New World. "Passing Thru" is about the carrying of ritual objects, in this case the sacred stones of religious ritual that became Santería in the New World. This poem's concern with traces and glimpses of a culture that evolved in the Americas and the Caribbean through the African diaspora is merely indicative of the kinds of cultural connections that appear in the body of Mackey's work. "Song of the Andoumboulou: 4" similarly reflects Mackey's intrigue with syncretism and schism. It refers to symbols and artifacts of Catholicism and Vodoun at shrines in Cuba. The Catholic saints displayed at Santería shrines are inconsequential in comparison to the powerful icons, the stones, behind the curtain. These are the artifacts that crossed the Middle Passage concealed in slaves' stomachs. While it appears that the two cultures are united, a powerful schism is clearly at work, and the dichotomy between dominant and marginal is still present.

Cultural theories, speculative histories, the literary work of international writers, and music all interest Mackey, and he references some part of it—a work, an idea, a phrase, a character, a score, or a musician and more—in his work. "The Sleeping Rocks" in *Eroding Witness*, for example, is dedicated to Wilson Harris, a formidably complex Caribbean writer whose work Mackey finds compelling. The poems in this first volume are an excellent indication of Mackey's interest in modes of knowledge that work outside of the Western prescription of reason. To some extent, the sequence of eight poems at the end of the volume, "Septet for the End of Time," offers one way of viewing Mackey's probing of difference and overlap. They grew out of "Capricorn Rising," dedicated to Pharoah Sanders, a tenor saxophone player with John Coltrane's group. The poem offers imagery that later poems revisit and expand. It is concerned with music, its ideas, and its dangers, as well. Each poem begins with the phrase "I wake up," a repetition that carries special meaning, as Mackey explained to Charles Rowell in an interview.

"These three words are important to the whole book, because the book, from the first poem on, signals a task which the poetry has set for itself or which I have set for it or which poetry has set for me, which is the task of trying to enter a realm which it imagines as a submerged realm. This could be the realm of sleep or the realm of dream, as it comes to be in section four, or it can be the realm of the underwater" (Rowell 709). There are also several epigraphs taken from three different types of texts—the French anthropologist Marcel Griaule's *Conversations with the Ogotemmeli*, *The Koran*, and the *Pyramid Texts of Unas*. Mackey's interest is why these disparate works each position the number seven as so significant in these very different cultures.

Mackey's interest in disparate cultures and his engagement of them across his works are reminiscent of the work of Jay Wright. Mackey's literary kinship with Wright is perhaps most directly expressed in his second work, *School of Udhra*. As a result of rereading Wright's work, in fact, the poem "Tonu Soy" emerged for Mackey, which he dedicated to him. The phrase means "seven" in the language of the Dogon of Mali, a group of African people whose cosmology interests both Mackey and Jay Wright. Both *School of Udhra* and *Whatsaid Serif* continue the serial poem "Song of the Andoumboulou," work with the movement of time, and contain thematically significant allusions to music in different cultures. However, the latter volume has a few differences. In *Whatsaid Serif* the poetry is more inclined to narrative and is concerned with the explicit sense of a journey through its use of trains, buses, and boats. It also references Gnosticism. The travel elicits the atmosphere of separation and reassembly that gave rise to Gnosticism, a syncretic religion already anticipated in Vodoun and similar impulses generated by dislocation.

The beginning poems of *Serif* suggest the African diaspora as "the same cry" is heard in many different locations. It creates an intriguing tension and a sense of unity and disparateness. The locations are not all part of the African diaspora, however, but include locations in Spain, Egypt, Ethiopia, and Bahrain, and Mackey is achieving another kind of cultural syncretism. The poem "Tonu Soy" seems to anticipate this subject in the line "syncretist wish to be beyond schism." Moreover, the conversational mode between volumes continues as well between *Serif* and *School of Udhra*, particularly in the references to musical and cultural motifs.

A student or reader of Mackey's work will benefit from tracking down many of the allusions that are made within a poem, but also reading his interviews will prove invaluable. He is forthcoming about his objectives, his methodology, and the impressive number of texts across time and cultures that he reads, synthesizes, and integrates into his prose and poetry.

POETRY

Eroding Witness. Chicago: University of Illinois Press, 1985.
School of Udhra. San Francisco: City Lights Books, 1993.
Whatsaid Serif. San Francisco: City Lights Books, 1998.

RECORDING

Strick: Song of the Andoumboulou 16–25. (With percussionist Royal Hartigan and reed player Hafex Modirzadeh). Memphis: Spoken Engine Company, 1995. (These poems make up the first half of *Whatsaid Serif*.)

REFERENCES

Funkhouser, Christopher. "An Interview with Nathaniel Mackey." *Callaloo* 18.2 (1995): 321–34.
Habell-Pallàn, Michelle. "Nathaniel Mackey." In *The Oxford Companion to African-American Literature*. Ed. William Andrews, Frances Smith Foster and Trudier Harris New York: Oxford University Press, 1997. 468.
Naylor, Paul, guest editor. "Nathaniel Mackey: A Special Issue." *Callaloo* 23.2 (Spring 2000): 669–807.
Nielsen, Aldon L. " 'Gassire's Lute.' " *Talisman: A Journal of Contemporary Poetry and Poetics* 9 (Fall 1992): 66–68.
Rowell, Charles H. "An Interview with Nathaniel Mackey." *Callaloo* 23.2 (Spring 2000): 703–15.
Savery, Pancho. "The Third Plane at the Change of the Century: The Shape of African-American Literature to Come." *Left Politics and the Literature Profession*. New York: Columbia University Press, 1990. 236–53.
Scroggins, Mark. "Nathaniel Mackey." In *Dictionary of Literary Biography: American Poets since World War II*. Vol. 169. Ed. Joseph Conte. Detroit: Gale Research, 1996. 179–91.

Haki Madhubuti

(1942–)

Haki Madhubuti
Credit: Haki Madhubuti and Third World Press
Photo credit: Linda Koolish

P oet, essayist, publisher, social activist, teacher, and speaker, the person known until 1973 as Don Luther Lee took on a Swahili name that means justice, awakening, and strong. In the tradition of Amiri Baraka and other black writers and revolutionaries who were cultural nationalists, Madhubuti sought to align the name by which he was identified with his interior identity. Madhubuti became a major spokesperson of the Black Arts Movement of the 1960s primarily through his poetry and through his efforts to activate the philosophy of the movement within the community through independent institution building. To that end, he cofounded the Third World Press in 1967 with Carolyn Rodgers and Johari Amini, and he has continued to operate it and an accompanying bookstore, The African American Book Center. Consistent with the philosophy of community building and enrichment originating from within, Madhubuti also founded and edited *Black Books Bulletin,* a journal of reviews and articles on black books, and cofounded the Institute of Positive Education, an African heritage–centered school in 1969. All are based in Chicago where the author lives and teaches. Through national and international lecturing, and his involvement in education, Madhubuti has continued to revitalize the transforming ideas of black arts from the 1960s and to engage issues of art and survival in the black community in the succeeding decades.

Madhubuti's role in black arts, in education, and in perpetuating poetry by black writers is widely acknowledged. He is a professor of English and founder and director emeritus of the Gwendolyn Brooks Center at Chicago State University. He initiated the Annual Gwendolyn Brooks Writers' Conference on Black Literature and Creative Writing in 1990, the longest-running annual black writers' convention in the country. Moreover, he is a founder and board member of the National Association of Black Book Publishers and a founder and chairman of the board of The National Literary Hall of Fame for Writers of African Descent. The extensive list of awards he has received includes the National Endowment for the Arts, National Endowment for the Humanities fellowships, the National Council of Teachers of English Black Caucus Award, an American Book Award in 1991, and the Gwendolyn Brooks/Alain Locke Literary Excellence Award from the US Organization of Los Angeles.

Madhubuti was born in Little Rock, Arkansas, but the family moved to Detroit when he was young. He moved to Chicago from Detroit at age sixteen to live with his aunt after his mother, Maxine Graves Lee, died. His father, James Lee, had left the family. He attended Dunbar

Vocational High School, served in the U.S. Army from 1960 to 1963, received an associate degree from Chicago City College in 1966, attended Roosevelt University in Chicago (1966–1967), and earned his Master's in Fine Arts degree in 1984. He was awarded the Doctor of Humane Letters from DePaul University of Chicago and Sojourner-Douglass College in Baltimore in 1996.

Before he began writing poetry full-time, Madhubuti was employed in numerous positions in the 1960s including apprentice curator of Chicago's DuSable Museum of African History, a post office clerk, a stock clerk for the retailer Montgomery Ward, and a junior executive for the mail order and retail business Spiegel.

He has credited his years in the army with learning discipline and with allowing him the time to immerse himself in reading black history and literature. When he began writing poetry in the 1960s, his philosophy about black art was already in place. It was that black art should benefit the community through a definitive political stance and be produced within and controlled by that community. Thus, Madhubuti self-published his first poetry collection, ordering a thousand copies, and sold them himself from various places in the community such as barbershops and at the el stop. Later, the black publisher and poet Dudley Randall in Michigan issued his work. Until 1973, his work was published under the name Don L. Lee.

Madhubuti admires several white writers, among them Robert Bly and Henry Miller, but his models are predominantly black poets. They include Amiri Baraka, Robert Hayden, Sterling Brown, Langston Hughes, Claude McKay, Jean Toomer, Margaret Walker, and Gwendolyn Brooks. In fact, Madhubuti's enrollment in a workshop with Brooks in Chicago in 1967 was the beginning of a sustained, reciprocal relationship of friendship, respect, and support. Madhubuti credits her with instructing him and other members of the street group, the Blackstone Rangers, with the rigorous demands of language in poetry. Madhubuti's graditude to Brooks includes several individual poems of tribute to her and the edited anthologies in her honor, *Say That the River Turns: The Impact of Gwendolyn Brooks* and *To Gwen, With Love* (coedited with Pat Brown and Francis Ward).

The titles of his first three volumes of poetry—*Think Black, Black Pride,* and *Don't Cry, Scream*—manage to capture his response to the community spirit of the times. Like Langston Hughes, his work immediately cast him as a poet of his people in its motivational political stance and its blunt urban idioms, rhythms, and metaphors. The content of Madhubuti's early volumes advocated a physical and spiritual survival of the black community. It invested the word *black* with deep meaning through referencing the African heritage. Its language was vibrant and animated and meant to legitimize the distinctiveness of black culture and its verbal expressiveness. Thus, his lines were at their best when read aloud and meant to be integrated into the oral tradition. In fashioning his poetry to capture the sound of the black urban community, like many other poets of the 1960s, Madhubuti collapsed words, for example, "yr/self," and invigorated his lines with musical qualities. He moved from the personal to an inclusive community as he urged collective responses to oppression and advocated black unity.

Several poems directly call for embracing a new unity. In "The New Integrationist," its simple form underlies the depth of its call. Beginning with the small "i," the eight lines consisting of one word each call for "negroes" to integrate with black people. Thus the poem advocates a transition in attitude from mentally accepting second-class citizenship and all that the word "negro" traditionally meant to embracing a self-defined, politically astute image. "A Message All Blackpeople Can Dig (& a few negroes too)," which appeared in Madhubuti's third volume, continues to recognize that not all black people have undergone a mental transformation. Nevertheless, the poem's speaker is positive that change is forthcoming; through unity a "takeovertakeover overtakeovertakeovertake over" for placing earth into the hands of human beings is possible. "A Poem to Complement Other Poems" uses the word "change" repeatedly to convey the theme of self-transformation. In his poems, Madhubuti equates "negroes" and "niggers" as those who are not yet "Black" in their self-concept or in their relation to community. Blackness is thus more than skin color indicative of ancestral heritage; it is also a distinctive state of mind as Madhubuti employs it.

Music also plays a pivotal role in Madhubuti's poems, both in its rhythms and through direct reference. "On Seeing Diana Go Maddddddddd" uses subtle humor to criticize Diana Ross's forgetting the Detroit roots of her working-class origin and becoming a symbol that many people no longer admire. The poem's refrain, "Stop! in the name of love, before you break my heart" from a Supremes' hit, is cleverly used to call Diana Ross back to her community. Perhaps Madhubuti's best-known use of music occurs in "Don't Cry, Scream," the title poem from his third volume. The poem represents the wailing and screaming sounds of John Coltrane's saxophone. To visually reproduce the fragmented nature of a jazz composition, its many stanzas are aligned variously at left, at extreme right, or off center, thus spreading over the page to suggest the sound of music. Most innovative, however, is the stretching out of various words by multiplying their vowels so that the scream of the horn lies on the page. As Coltrane's jazz style was a way of articulating the discordant elements of black life and of displacing the pain of inequality, at least for a while, Madhubuti wants to achieve the same feat with words. He wants his poetry to sing at the range where it will be heard and will make a difference. Throughout Madhubuti's poetry, music is given the dominance that it has traditionally played in African American existence.

Like other poets of the 1960s, Madhubuti's work was evaluated as racist and propagandistic by mainstream critics. The evaluation proved ineffective, however, in curbing the style of poetry that characterized a decade of high productivity, fueled the Black Arts or Black Aesthetics Movement, and was the literary complement of the civil rights movement. In the introduction to *Don't Cry, Scream*, Gwendolyn Brooks answers such criticism by affirming that Madhubuti, whom she called a pioneer and a prophet, achieved his goal of reaching a black audience. His intended audience finds their experiences in his poetry rather than in the elegant verse of Ivy League published journals.

Madhubuti's collected poems, *Directionscore* in 1971, brought together his work from the previous decade and gave him the opportunity to refine the vision expressed in his earlier work. His decision to retain the chronology of his earlier work resulted in a coherent presentation of the philosophy that had brought him to the forefront of his 1960s peers. His emphasis on black unity remains a cornerstone of his ideology. However, his volume *HeartLove: Wedding and Love Poems* (1998) removes the emphasis on black unity from the political arena and places it on matters of the heart.

The three sections of *HeartLove* (with artwork by Jon Onye Lockard)— "Wedding Poems," "Quality of Love," and "Extended Families"—contain poems that Madhubuti has crafted for specific occasions, especially for weddings. Although love is the primary motivation, as the volume's title indicates, the poems are not the gushing, superficially romantic lyrics that one might expect from a novice poet. Rather, they reflect the thoughts and experience of a seasoned poet, husband, and father. In "Love Gets Too Much Credit Until It Finds You" the speaker uses the concept of "credit" to emphasize the abstract nature and random presence of love. Love is not attained like material things; it is not charged on cards, "bartered with food stamps," or "redeemed with cashier checks or money orders." "She Never Grew Up" addresses the confusion and pain that results when a woman equates her beauty with the love of shallow men. The thematic thread running throughout the poems is that love is a precious gift, and those chosen to receive it must guard its presence solemnly and seriously.

Madhubuti has continued publishing poetry but also has written several collections of essays that are focused by the continuation of racial, social, and economic problems affecting the family unit and the African American community. He also continues to spread his ideology through an extensive lecturing schedule at colleges and universities around the country.

POETRY

Think Black! Detroit: Broadside Press, 1967. (Out of Print)

Black Pride. Detroit: Broadside Press, 1968. (Out of Print)

Don't Cry, Scream. Detroit: Broadside Press, 1969. Chicago: Third World Press, 1992.

We Walk the Way of the New World. Detroit: Broadside Press, 1970. (Out of Print)

Directionscore: Selected and New Poems. Detroit: Broadside Press, 1971. (Out of Print)

Book of Life. Detroit: Broadside Press, 1975. Chicago: Third World Press, 1992. (Out of Print)

Earthquakes and Sunrise Missions: Poetry and Essays. Chicago: Third World Press, 1984. (Out of Print)

Killing Memory, Seeking Ancestors. Detroit: Lotus Press, 1987.

GroundWork: New and Selected Poems of Don L. Lee/Haki Madhubuti from 1966–1996. Chicago: Third World Press, 1996.

HeartLove: Wedding and Love Poems. Chicago: Third World Press, 1998.

REFERENCES

Hill, Patricia Liggins, Bernard Bell, Trudier Harris, William J. Harris, R. Baxter Miller, and Sondra O'Neale. *Call & Response: The Riverside Anthology of the African American Literary Tradition.* New York: Houghton Mifflin, 1998. 1536–1546.

Hurst, Catherine Daniels. "Haki R. Madhubuti." *In Dictionary of Literary Biography.* Vol. 41. Ed. Trudier Harris and Thadious Davis. Detroit: Gale Research, 1985. 222–32.

Malkoff, Karl. *Crowell's Handbook of Contemporary American Poetry.* New York: Crowell, 1973.

Melhem, D.H. *Heroism in the New Black Poetry: Introductions and Interviews.* Lexington: University Press of Kentucky, 1990.

Young, Robyn, ed. *Poetry Criticism.* Vol. 5. Detroit: Gale Research, 1992. 319–47.

COLLEEN J. MCELROY

(1936–   )

Colleen J. McElroy
Credit: Colleen J. McElroy
Photo credit: Eleanor Hamilton

Colleen McElroy has been a speech therapist and a talk show host, but her loves are writing and traveling. She has authored two travel memoirs and television scripts, collaborated on the choreopoem (a poem with the elements of drama and intended for group performance), *The Wild Gardens of the Loup Garou* with novelist and poet Ishmael Reed, written a play about Harriet Tubman titled *Follow the Drinking Gourd*, and published two books of short stories, *Jesus and Fat Tuesday*, and *Driving Under the Cardboard Pines*. However, poetry has been her sustaining genre.

McElroy was born to Ruth Celeste and Purcia Purcell Rawls, who divorced in 1938. In the 1940s McElroy lived with her mother and a younger brother in St. Louis. Her mother remarried in 1943 to an army sergeant, Jesse Dalton Johnson, who was stationed in numerous cities at home and abroad. Thus by the time McElroy was twenty-one, she had called St. Louis, Wyoming, Kansas City, and Munich, Germany, home. As a child, however, McElroy's inclination for travel was fed by a legacy of travel stories from her grandma, Anna Belle Long, whose tales were not grounded by personal experience. Anna Belle Long never traveled farther north than her own St. Louis community and only went south as far as Texas, where she had relatives.

McElroy credits two facts with shaping her preference for traveling and writing: her grandmother's dressing-room mirror and the fabled interstate highway, Route 66. In the attic in front of the full-length mirrow, McElroy played dress-up in old clothes and listened to a collection of 78 rpm recordings of all types of music. She danced by herself in her grandmother's attic to her reflection in the full-length mirror. By perfecting the current popular dances with her two cousins, when she was older she had become sufficiently proficient to teach dance at an Arthur Murray studio.

In her grandmother's attic, McElroy also expressed her creativity in another way. She played out stories in both spoken and imagined language to the lyrics of Ethel Waters, Valaida Snow, and Florence Mills, popular singers and actresses of the time. These women, who defied other people's ideas of what they were supposed to be, became the young girl's heroines. She fell in love with the rhythm of language and with its words and the images conveyed through them. McElroy's early effort at practicing this language herself is connected to a memorable and rare car trip from St. Louis to California, a trip she relates in her memoir *A Long Way from St. Louie*. Since segregation policies prevented a traveling black family sleeping in a hotel, the family stayed with relatives or friends of friends until those connections ended as McElroy's family drove farther westward. In Arizona, her uncle, who was the driver, suggested they sleep in the car at the Grand Canyon. McElroy awoke at dawn to find herself face to face with a mountain lion looking in at them from the warm hood of the car. She woke her uncle to look. When the big cat was distracted by noises outside, her uncle gunned the motor and backed down the mountain at thirty miles per hour. The majesty and beauty of the animal, however, inspired McElroy's earliest remembered attempt to capture feeling in language through imagery.

McElroy attended college in Munich, Germany, but received her B.A. degree in Kansas City. She studied in the speech and hearing program at the University of Pittsburgh but returned to Kansas City for graduate work in neurological and language learning patterns. She became director of Speech and Hearing Services at Western Washington University. She studied ethnolingistic patterns of dialect differences and oral traditions at the University of Washington and received her Ph.D. degree there. Divorced in 1975, McElroy and her children, Kevin and Vanessa, lived in Bellingham, Washington, until she moved to Seattle, where she joined the faculty at the University of Washington. She became the first black woman to earn the rank of full professor at the university in 1983.

Bellingham, Washington, proved to be a nurturing community for McElroy's efforts at writing when she was in her thirties. The community boasted numerous supportive writers. Moreover, McElroy was reading the work of black poets including Langston Hughes, Gwendolyn Brooks, Anne Spencer, Robert Hayden, and Margaret Walker. Denise Levertov, the poet, also encouraged her work. In the 1970s McElroy brought out two chapbooks of her poems.

McElroy's work has been recognized by significant prizes and fellowships. *Queen of the Ebony Isles* (1984) was selected for the Wesleyan University Press Poetry Series and also received the American Book Award in 1985. She has received two National Endowment for the Arts Fellowships, two Fulbright Fellowships, a Dupont Visiting Scholars Fellowship, and a Rockefeller Fellowship.

Tightly woven poems brimming with wisdom, emotion, remarkable language, precise detail, and energetic, unifying imagery often drawn from nature and geography characterize McElroy's work. Her love of travel extensively informs her poems, primarily through metaphor and allusion. Thus one finds references to people, art, food, or just the arduous nature of travel in Europe, South America, Japan, Majorca, Africa,

Southeast Asia, and the small towns and villages within these places. Along with travel, family and music are McElroy's most recurring subjects as the titles *Music from Home* and *Travelling Music* may suggest.

McElroy's most effective poems of family are those that begin with a memory—a story, an event, or a family character—that she has refashioned for use in the service of poetry. In *Music from Home* (1976), an early volume, the section of family poems suggests McElroy's comfort with exploring personal events and incidents for hidden insights. In "Under the Oak Table," for example, a young girl sits under the table gathering family history and life lessons by listening to her heavy-legged aunts. In "For My Children" an adult speaker searches for a heritage beyond St. Louis and finds a "link between the Mississippi and the Congo." "Webs and Weeds," one of McElroy's few rhyming poems, names her first adolescent love, the ironically named George Darlington Love. The speaker and her cousins are on the brink between childhood and adolescence, coming of age against any odds and in a setting that was anything but nurturing for a girl's coming out. These poems are peppered with allusions to popular culture outside the black community, such as to movie figures Hopalong Cassidy, Black Bart, and Brenda Starr.

Numerous poems in her volumes, in fact, are centered on girls' experiences, and McElroy is very adept at capturing a stunted girlhood or the wispy dividing line between a girl's and a woman's behavior. The social and cultural context, anchored primarily through the distinctiveness of place, is established by allusions. The card game 21 played in the house by male family members, the Fifth Dimension singing group, girls playing the boasting verbal jousting game the Dirty Dozens, or jumping Double Dutch are just a few of the familiar images that fleck the family and girls' poems. McElroy's poems offer juxtapositions between the familiar and the historic as well as between personal history and cultural inheritance.

McElroy's growth as a poet is apparent in a comparison between the family-centered poems of *Music from Home* and the same type of poems in *Queen of the Ebony Isles* (1984). The travel metaphor employed in "Monologue for Saint Louis" functions dually to encompass literal distance as well as the maturity that the poet has attained. The poems in the award-winning *Queen*, focused by memories and events from childhood, are very tightly constructed units, but their sparse images nevertheless have to carry considerable weight in the poems. For example, the traveler in "Monologue" has returned home but is stifled by "clusters of words" that remind the traveler of the blue-black grapes that grew thickly on the neighbor's vine. This image of tight, compacted grapes conveys the sense of resistance that the traveler encounters, a resistance aimed at her difference from the ordinary women who stay at home and lack the imagination even to understand her travel activity.

McElroy's extensive travel seems not to have shown her too much of the ugly side of life. However, in "A Little Travelling Music," the speaker says that earth is not a planet she would choose for her own "[w]ith its inventory of mountainous sorrows." She wants something more than bad memories. McElroy writes her awareness of the inequities that bring fire and destruction to American cities in "Atmospheric Pressure" and "The Verdict: Los Angeles 1992." Rather than the large political intrigue and conflict, however, McElroy focuses on the small detail and on people. "Trompe L'oeil Slovenia," its title using the French term meaning "to fool the eye," reveals, ironically, a traditional patriarchal culture where the weight of work rests on the shoulders of women, as a handsome cabbie drives the speaker to see the eastern side of the Alps.

Home and travel operate in opposing spheres. A traveler can return home, but home's inevitable changes erase its old comforts, leaving it an alien place. On the other hand, recurrent images, physical motions, or music can conjure home in the most different of places, which is the theme in "While Poets Are Watching" in *Queen* as well as in "Hooking Up with Ray Charles and the Great Percy Sledge in Madagascar" in *Travelling Music*.

McElroy is more conventional than not in the poetic structures that she uses. She uses free verse, mainly writes the lyric, includes a few sonnets, as in "Sprung Sonnet for Dorothy Dandridge" a verse of sixteen lines rather than fourteen. There is reasonable variety in the appearance of her poems on the page; that is, the poet does not indulge needlessly in a visual aerobics of words on the page, though the poems in *Travelling Music* offer more stanzaic variation than McElroy's earlier volumes. In diction, she mixes black vernacular with standard usage as the poem's needs dictate. In "Bo Jangles Visits the Studio" in *Travelling*, for example, and other poems that are focused by music, the diction reflects the mood and subject of the work. The opening line of "Bo Jangles, "hip hop ain't no hoola hoop," simultaneously signals its contemporary musical focus expressed through fitting diction.

McElroy's increasing number of books of poetry is testament to her reverence for what language can accomplish in the imagination of a skilled writer. Her work is increasingly included in anthologies, a good sign that she is reaching a wide audience.

POETRY

Music from Home: Selected Poems. Carbondale: Southern Illinois University Press, 1976. (Out of Print)
Winters without Snow. Berkeley: Reed & Cannon, 1979.
Lie and Say You Love Me. Tacoma, WA: Circinatum Press, 1981. (Out of Print)
Queen of the Ebony Isles. Middletown, CT: Wesleyan University, 1984.
Bone Flames. Hanover, NH: University Press of New England, 1987. (Out of Print)
What Madness Brought Me Here: New and Selected Poems, 1968–1988. Hanover, NH: University Press of New England, 1990.
Travelling Music Poems. Ashland, OR: Story Line Press, 1998.

CHAPBOOKS

The Mules Done Long Since Gone. Seattle, WA: Harrison-Madrona Center, 1972. (Out of Print)
Looking for a Country Under Its Original Name. 1979. Yakima, WA: Blue Begonia Press, 1984. (Out of Print)

MEMOIRS

A Long Way from St. Louie. Minneapolis, MN: Coffee House Press, 1997.
Over the Lip of the World: Among the Storytellers of Madagascar. Seattle: University of Washington Press, 1999.

REFERENCES

Margulis, Jennifer. "Colleen McElroy." *The Oxford Companion to African American Literature*. Eds. William Andrews, Frances Smith Foster, and Trudier Harris. New York: Oxford, 1997. 488.
McElroy, Colleen. *A Long Way from St. Louie*. Minneapolis, MN: Coffee House Press, 1997.

CLAUDE MCKAY

(1889–1948)

Claude McKay
Credit: Van Vechten Trust and Atlanta University Center, Robert W. Woodruff Library

Like many of the poets of the 1920s who migrated to New York, Claude McKay brought the distinctive experience of having grown up in another locale. His native Jamaica shaped his values and attitudes in a particular way. Older than many of the New Negro Movement poets and having published two books in Jamaica before arriving in New York, McKay nevertheless became a revered writer of that decade when work by African American writers reached unprecedented levels of artistic merit and mainstream attention. Many qualities in the content and structure of his work melded well with the decade. He wrote lovely lyrics but also angry sonnets that called attention to white patriarchal dominance and class issues. Like many of his contemporaries, McKay was not only a poet but also an essayist, journalist, autobiographer, short story writer, and novelist. In fact, he had the distinction of having written the first black novel to reach the bestseller lists, his controversial *Home to Harlem* (1928).

McKay was born Festus Claudius in Jamaica, West Indies, to Thomas Francis and Ann Elisabeth McKay. He was the youngest of eight children. McKay's parents instilled racial pride in their son primarily through Thomas Francis's storytelling about his African born father, a member of the West African Ashanti nation. McKay's education was also enhanced when he was sent to live with his oldest brother Uriah Theophilious, a schoolteacher, amateur journalism correspondent for the city newspaper, and an agnostic in his religious belief. Uriah shared his views with his younger brother and allowed him full perusal of his library, which included the British classic writers and histories. McKay prepared to take the examination to become a teacher as well, but he passed the test for a Government Trade Scholarship in 1906 and won a stipend to attend a trade school in Kingston, Jamaica.

McKay was in the city in 1907 when a horrendous earthquake occurred. The city with its mixed populations showed the impressionable boy a caste system where peasant blacks were subordinated to the lowest level. As a result of this recognition, McKay kept his allegiance aligned with the working class during his adult years. He left for the village of Browns Town to learn the skill of being a wheelwright but gave that up. Eventually, he returned to Kingston and became a constable. Initially, that experience was positive, although it also showed him an underside of the human experience that left a lasting impression.

McKay began writing poetry during his early years. He wrote in the conventions of traditional British poetry, but during his stay in Browns

Town, he had written a few pieces in the Jamaican vernacular. He received encouragement to continue writing in that vein from a British folk story collector living on the island, Walter Jekyll, who exerted a lasting impression on McKay throughout the writer's adult life. He stimulated McKay's creativity and intellectualism and assisted him in getting his writing published. One of McKay's biographers has written that Jekyll's influence was apparent in McKay's choice of friends in the United States. He aligned himself with white, well-to-do men who lived bohemian lives.

The year 1912 proved pivotal for McKay. He published *Songs of Jamaica* and *Constab Ballads*, both of which contain poems in Jamaican vernacular. *Constab Ballads* offered poems set in the city that suggested McKay's increasing sensibility to social protest. Additionally, in 1912, the young poet left Jamaica for life in the United States. He spent only six months at Tuskegee Institute, the well-known vocational school founded by Booker T. Washington in Alabama, before McKay's disenchantment motivated him to enroll at Kansas State College in Manhattan, Kansas. As a black West Indian in both these settings, McKay was something of a cultural outsider among both southern blacks and midwesterners.

In 1914 McKay moved to New York, the literary and cultural center of the United States, and to Harlem, the cultural mecca for black people. He also married Imelda Edwards, his childhood sweetheart. Theirs was a short-lived marriage because she did not like New York and returned to Jamaica. The couple had a daughter, Eulalie Ruth Hope, but McKay reportedly never had a relationship with her. To support himself, McKay worked various jobs that were available to black men. At various times, he was a porter, houseman, janitor, butler, and waiter. These jobs gave him an intimate view of the perils of the black working class in America.

McKay's opinions about economics and the black working class were fashioned by his cultural and political experiences as a West Indian. He believed capitalism and economics were the problems rather than racism. He was a British citizen who had been conditioned by a British colonial system to think in terms of class. His ideas about solutions to the race problem differed from the major leaders in Harlem such as James Weldon Johnson and W.E.B. Du Bois. McKay was not allied with the National Association for the Advancement of Colored People (NAACP) but with radical organizations whose views were socialist. He denied having joined the Communist Party, but he openly admired the Bolsheviks.

After his arrival in New York, McKay began trying to publish his poems and to read the radical journals that fascinated him. He was dismayed to discover that editors of mainstream journals seemed to want poems with racial themes. Even the *Liberator* rejected most of his submissions. McKay chafed under and rejected recognition based solely on racial themes. He preferred that his art be judged for whatever merits it offered regardless of its subject matter.

It is ironic, therefore, that McKay's most famous and militant poem, "If We Must Die," which immediately targeted him as a radical new spokesperson for black people, contains no specific words of racial identification. It has universal application to oppression, violence, and self-respect as its selection by British Prime Minister Winston Churchill illustrated when he read it to the House of Commons during World War II in response to Nazi Germany's aggression. However, the poem's origin was in response to racial situations in post–World War I America, specifically the race riots in Chicago. Numerous cities in 1919, including East St. Louis, Missouri, experienced an increasingly intolerant atmosphere, much of it in reaction to the returning black soldier's expectation that having fought abroad for the preservation of democracy, he was entitled to expect it in his homeland. So much bloodshed occurred, in fact, that the summer of 1919 was dubbed the "red summer." During this period, McKay also experienced the threat of bodily violence. Working as a train waiter for the Pennsylvania Railroad between New York and Washington, he and other service workers went about in groups and carried revolvers for protection. The speaker in "If We Must Die" counsels his listeners, besieged like himself by a "murderous, cowardly pack," not to behave as if they are confined within a pen like hogs who offer no resistance to aggression. Rather, they must fight back, regardless of the odds. If death is the result, it will be a noble death met in spite of a unified counterattack. As he does in several poems, McKay's chose the Italian sonnet as structure for "If We Must Die." The restricted fourteen lines of the sonnet and its prescribed rhyme and metric qualities create remarkable tension between a tight structure and the freewheeling rage in the poem's content. The poem appeared in the *Liberator*, a major coup for McKay. "If We Must Die" also attracted attention from the committee in the U.S. Justice Department investigating African American radicalism and sedition; they thought McKay was inciting black people to communist ideology.

In 1919, McKay left the United States to visit England, which he considered his spiritual homeland. However, race tensions speedily dispelled his illusions about the British. He worked there briefly for a radical journal, the *Worker's Dreadnought*.

Although McKay is regarded as a trendsetting poet of the Harlem Renaissance, he was physically absent from Harlem during most of the

1920s. After the journal assignment in 1919, he returned to New York and worked for the *Liberator* until late in 1922, when he resigned as coeditor. He left for Moscow to attend a conference and stayed on there. The FBI maintained a file on his activities. Diagnosed with syphilis while in Russia, and believing Germany offered better medical treatment, he left Russia early in 1923 and stayed three months in Germany. He went briefly to Paris, then to Toulon, France, in 1924, but returned to Paris where he lived mostly hand to mouth until 1930. Between 1930 and 1933, when he began negotiating to reenter the United States, he lived in Tangiers, Morocco.

McKay was thus self-exiled from the United States when most of his poetry and fiction were published. *Spring in New Hampshire* (1920) was published in England. *Harlem Shadows* (1922), published on the cusp of the Harlem Renaissance and in the midst of American modernist poetry as practiced by the mainstream writers T.S. Eliot and Ezra Pound, merely expanded the first volume and included his best work since 1912. The publication greatly enhanced McKay's reputation. Yet McKay was neither a modernist in embracing radical new poetic structures nor adventuresome in constructing his own.

Given the subjects of many of the lyrical poems and his affection for the sonnet of the Elizabethan era, he has been called a traditionalist in his poetics. McKay also did not embrace the philosophy of art for art's sake, believing that art must serve a political purpose. Many of his poems in theme and content convey his disenchantment with the economic plight and politics of black lives. "Tiger," for example, is a politically aware poem critical of the status quo that President Roosevelt's New Deal would perpetuate in spite of promises to the contrary. The white man, representative of capitalism in the poem, is visualized as a tiger ripping at the throat of blacks even as they die. Europe, Africa, and Asia depend on the New Deal, but like the old system, the new one will rest on race and command of the dollar, and the tiger will continue to rip black throats through economic exploitation. McKay's poems in this vein are precursors of the anger conveyed through poetry that Black Arts writers communicated. "America," a sonnet like "Tiger," is structured through paradox, or contradictory emotions. "America" contains a reference to the tiger's teeth in the black throat stealing life as well. However, the speaker loves this place America, for its energy offers him the strength to be vigorous against her hate. The speaker, without terror or maliciousness, looks into the future and sees the grandeur of America, but the image is negative. America's wonders appear to sink in sand. "The White House," yet another piece similar to the above two, is perhaps more direct in its disease with the state of affairs. The white house of the title is not in reference to the American president's home but is used symbolically, as McKay clarified in his autobiography, *A Long Way from Home* (1937). Whereas a tiger (or capitalism) had sucked the blood and life of black people in the above poems, doors are closed against the speaker in "The White House," and he is "sharp as steel with discontent." Nevertheless, he will continue courageously and gracefully, even though his emotion threatens to rent him asunder, beholding the closed door. He must, then, seek wisdom and find there a suprahuman ability to protect his heart from the flux of hate around him. "Lynching" offered a graphic visualization of the festive occasion in which many mob hangings of black men occurred in the South. McKay's poems established him as a champion of the black and exploited underclass.

In contrast to McKay's poems calling the country to account for its own shortcomings, he wrote lyrical pieces of great beauty and sensitivity. "The Tropics in New York," for example, as the title might suggest, offers images of lush tropical fruit—bananas, mangos, ginger-root, tangerines, grapefruit—in a New York display window. To the speaker of the poem, presumably a displaced Caribbean, the fruit produces a hunger so intense for the beautiful topography of the island that the observer turns aside and weeps. "Spring in New Hampshire" offers equally strong images of nature. "Harlem Shadows" uses genteel terms such as "lass" and "half-clad girls" to describe prostitutes working the streets of Harlem on "sacred brown feet," but it offers no moral condemnation. Through tone and diction, the speaker empathizes with the victimization visited upon the women through a world of poverty and dishonor. Similarly, the subject of "The Harlem Dancer," also a young prostitute, participates in the merriment of the occasion, singing, dancing, and smiling. Her description is romantically soft, and the speaker sees her through the organic image of a palm that has passed through a storm and is lovelier for it. The point of the poem is smartly delivered in the closing couplet: The prostitute is physically present but emotionally she has absolved herself of the attention.

When McKay finally returned to America in February 1934, through the assistance of James Weldon Johnson and Max Eastman, the acclaim for his most recent work, the fiction, had been displaced by the rigors of an economic depression. He could not find work and was reduced to working in a camp for a dollar a day. Again, Johnson and Eastman came to his aid, and McKay received a grant to write his autobiography, *A Long Way from Home*. He also worked with the Federal Writers Project as did many black writers during the depression. Except for the publication of his autobiography and a few prose articles, McKay was unable to interest publishers in new work for the remainder of the 1930s. His health declined in the early 1940s, and he died of heart failure in a Chicago hospital on May 22, 1948.

POETRY

Constab Ballads. 1912. Manchester: Ayer, n.d.
Songs of Jamaica, 1912. Miami, FL: Mnemosyne, 1969.
Spring in New Hampshire, and Other Poems. London: Grant Richards, 1920. (Out of Print)
Harlem Shadows. New York: Harcourt, Brace, 1922. (Out of Print)
Selected Poems. New York: Harcourt, Brace, & World, 1953. Mineola, NY: Dover Publications, 1999.
The Dialect Poetry of Claude McKay. Freeport, NY: Books of Libraries Press, 1972.

AUTOBIOGRAPHY

A Long Way from Home. New York: L. Furman, 1937. Temecula, CA: Reprint Services Corporation, 1991.

REFERENCES

Bronze, Stephen H. "Claude McKay." In *Roots of Negro Racial Consciousness: The 1920s: Three Renaissance Authors*. New York: Libra Publishers, 1964. 66–89.
Collier, Eugenia W. "The Four-Way Dilemma of Claude McKay." *CLA Journal* 15.3 (1972): 345–53.
Cooper, Wayne F. *Claude McKay: Rebel Sojourner in the Harlem Renaissance*. Baton Rouge: Louisiana State University Press, 1987.
Elimimian, Isaac I. "Theme and Technique in Claude McKay's Poetry." *CLA Journal* 25.2 (1981): 203–11.
Giles, James R. *Claude McKay*. Boston: Twayne, 1976.
Kent, George E. "The Soulful Way of Claude McKay." In *Blackness and the Adventure of Western Culture*. Chicago: Third World Press, 1972. 36–52.
Lee, Robert A. "On Claude McKay's 'If We Must Die.' " *CLA Journal* 28.2 (1974): 216–21.
Redding, J. Saunders. "Emergence of the New Negro." In *To Make a Poet Black*. College Park, MD: McGrath, 1939. 93–125.
Tillery, Tyrone. *Claude McKay: A Black Poet's Struggle for Identity*. Amherst: University of Massachusetts Press, 1992.

E. ETHELBERT MILLER

(1950–   )

E. Ethelbert Miller
Credit: St. Martin's Press
Photo credit: Mark Cohen

A career as a poet, editor, and director of the African American Studies Resource Center at Howard University is far from the career in law that Miller once vaguely imagined as an undergraduate. His fascination with poetry deterred him from that goal, and he has since worked as a tireless advocate for and practitioner of the art since the 1970s. Alongside his volumes of poetry, Miller has edited several poetry anthologies and served on numerous boards and councils important in granting fellowships to black poets.

Miller was born in the Bronx, New York, to West Indian working-class immigrant parents, Egberto Miller, a postal worker, and Enid Miller, a seamstress. Egberto Miller's family, who came to New York from Panama, changed their last name and severed their connections with family left behind. E. Ethelbert, christened Eugene but called Gene, was the youngest of the Miller's three children, Richard and Marie. The Millers were protective of their offspring and kept them sheltered from the harsh experieces of the urban streets.

Miller began his education at P.S. 39 and attended a middle school named for Paul Laurence Dunbar and a high school named for Christopher Columbus. Writing poetry was not a pastime during these years, but Miller was an effective baseball player. Years later when poetry became his obsession, he incorporated his love of baseball into his art. In 1968 he left the Bronx by train—on his own for the first time and the first family member to attend college—for Howard University. It was Miller's first extensive interaction with a "black" community, and his arrival coincided with the fervor of campus unrest and an aggressive Black Arts Movement. While both factors proved influential on Miller in his search for self-definition and a career to commit to, the emphasis on art and community espoused by the arts movement proved irresistible. His plan to study political science in preparation for law school was interrupted by the force of African American poetry and his attraction to it. Miller completed requirements for the B.A. degree in African American Studies in 1972.

Howard University, the city of Washington, and the emphasis on Afrocentricity proved to be supportive environments for Miller as he tentatively began writing poetry and educating himself in black culture. During his sophomore year, Miller changed his name, dropping the "Gene" that his parents had used, to become E. Ethelbert as part of his self-invention. In the initial years of fashioning himself into a writer, Miller names poets and editors Stephen Henderson and Ahmos Zu-

Bolton alongside Bob Stokes, a lover of poetry, as those with whom he might share a developing poem. He also attended a class at the university taught by Don L. Lee (Haki Madhubuti), a visiting professor at the time. Sterling Brown, the renowned poet, editor, professor, and unmatchable resource, returned to Howard University during this formative period of Miller's development as a writer. Early in his development Miller once appeared at All Souls Church in Washington, D.C., to read his poetry with Sonia Sanchez, Askia Toure, Carolyn Rodgers, and others. During the heady years of the 1970s, Washington was to Miller what Harlem had been to Langston Hughes.

Shortly after his graduation, Miller became director of the African American Studies Resource Center where, since 1974, he has influenced and shaped an important collection of African American literary and historical resources. The position also offered the opportunity for Miller to meet and maintain contact with leading writers and poets. During this time, Miller married his first wife, Michelle, a student at the university. The union ended in divorce. Miller married a second time to Denise King, a management counselor and ordained minister. They have two children, Jasmine-Simone and Nyere-Gibran.

In addition to his work at Howard University, Miller has been an associate faculty member at Bennington College, Bennington, Vermont; a visiting professor at the University of Nevada, Las Vegas; scholar-in-residence at George Mason University; a member of the board of the National Writers Union and Associated Writing Programs; a senior editor of the *Washington Review*: and an advisory editor for both *African American Review* and *Callaloo*. Miller regularly serves on various grant-awarding boards in the Washington, D.C., area. His commitment to promoting African American poetry and poets is thus extensive, and in his metropolitan area, he has been referred to as "an aesthetic entrepreneur." He founded and directed the Ascension Poetry Series (1974–2000), a forum for emerging poets, some reading publicly for the first time. The longevity of this series is perhaps sufficient testament to its importance in the Washington arts community. However, Miller's single-handed tenacity in assisting the writing and identity of emerging poets for twenty-six years and keeping black poetry vital in the community is evidence of his profound generosity and soul. He also attempted to establish creative writing programs at historically black colleges through the Associated Writing Programs. Miller's insight and resourcefulness reflect his commitment to community and education.

Since the beginning of his interest in African American poetry during his second year at Howard, Miller has rarely, if ever, taken a sabbatical from his craft. *First Light: New and Selected Poems* (1994) offers the best of his work from numerous books, but unlike most volumes of "selected" poems, Miller grouped his poems without indicating the original volume of their appearance. Stylistically, Miller's work is fashioned for consumption by the mildly interested reader as well as the poetry enthusiast. In length the poems range from a few lines to medium length, and long poems are almost rare. The diction is succinct, and the metaphors are subtle. The poems convey a reflective quietness even when the subject does not lend itself to that tone. A reader aware of Miller's experience growing up in a New York borough might expect to discern a gritty urban speech or to read work burdened by urban experiences, but his poetry is seldom setting-specific in that way. His work exhibits an excellent command of voice; whether the speaker is a dejected woman or two truck drivers discussing a promising baseball player, their voices ring convincingly true. Overall, Miller's work is engaging, and the second and third reading of a particular poem can be surprisingly rewarding for its unexpected insights about the complexities of being human.

First Light also conveys the wide range of issues that have informed Miller's work during his career. One finds the solitary nature of experience, politics, baseball, relationships (familial and romantic), the disappointment of love, and poems about writing poetry. "Marathon," "A Walk in the Daytime Is Just as Dangerous as a Walk in the Night," "Baptism," and "Path," for example, all address different forms of isolation and their consequences. In "Marathon" the speaker reflects on the decade of his twenties having passed and implies that the emptiness of those years has resulted in his lack of focus for the next decade of life. Thus, "Marathon," a long course, collapses a modern life with the fugitive slave existence of the past and the conclusion suggests that at this point present existence may be less purposeful than it was in the past. Similar evocative descriptions and phrases occur in "A Walk in the Daytime," where the solitary speaker walks in upstate New York and dismisses specific fears of the South. The dismissal of fear is premature, however, for when the solitary walker is accosted with the epithet "nigger" from a passing car, the man feels the vunerability of a woman subject to attack. The walk thus symbolizes every other solitary stroll characterized by isolation and fear. Through selected images and symbols, these poems also illustrate the way the present may be disrupted by the past. They confirm that what we remember, even when we think we have forgotten, has a way of unsettling calm moments in the present. In "Baptism," the speaker is spiritually isolated when he is among a group of believers. However, in "Path," a seven-line poem featuring one

word per line, being alone is "holy." Those thematically focused by loneliness roughly balance other poems offering some redemption from the
potentially devastating state of loneliness.

Many of Miller's poems also address the experiences and pain of other
ethnic groups. In particular, in a section titled "El Salvador," he incorporates problematic political activities in South America, the Caribbean,
and South Africa. Overall, these poems, like "San Salvador," "Nicaragua," "Chile," "Soldier," and "She Wore a Red Dress," convey the consequences of repressive regimes on the psyche of the people who suffer
under them. Characteristic of Miller's work, these poems are not bellig-
erent and loud, as armed conflict is. Rather, they chronicle the individual
will in its counter offense to survive the fray of war. In "El Salvador"
flowing red blood covering everything is indicative of the death of war.
"She Wore a Red Dress," whose title suggests an appreciative poem
about a woman in a red dress, has no such woman. The unidentified
speaker, even in the middle of seeming normal activity, is always looking
over his or her shoulder, trying to outstep death. The El Salvador section
of *First Light*, containing thirty-one poems, ends with those that celebrate
the survival of the human spirit. Through the imagery of a new day,
music, dancing, and freedom after imprisonment, "The Door" details the
jubilance that, after a national election, anticipates the satisfactory consequence that signals an end to the armed conflict. Nature celebrates,
too, as the imagery conveys in the line: "the sky cleared and the sun
found its guitar."

A significant number of poems in *First Light* primarily focus on different types of relationships. These works illustrate Miller's deft handling
of emotions whether in male, familial, or romantic relationships. For example, nine poems in a brief section titled "Bill Mazeroski Returns Home
from the World Series," true to the implication in the title, are united
through baseball. Using baseball as a creative and insightful metaphor,
Miller explores several contradictory experiences including loss, disappointment, indecision, and accomplishment. These poems also illustrate
the poet's mastery of the narrative form. "The Trade," for example, is a
player's narrative of devaluing, of being traded to a different team after
ten years and of his wife's leaving him. While the two events are not
simultaneous, playing for a new team triggers memories of the failed
marriage. The language of baseball to describe the player's love for his
wife suggests he loves them equally, but the poem offers no condemnation of that possibility. The player's understanding that the marriage
cannot be salvaged is also communicated through a baseball reference:
The wife stands before him as "helpless as the rookie." In contrast to the

loss of "The Trade," "Bill Mazeroski Returns Home from the World Series" suggests the pleasure of accomplishment that Mazeroski desired and achieved. Miller perhaps expects readers to know that Mazeroski, a second baseman in the 1960 World Series that had reached the seventh game between the Yankees and the Pittsburgh Pirates, hit the game-winning home run at the end of the ninth inning. The poem, told from the player's perspective, reinterates a promise to his dad that his name would be important. Seeking to displace the nation's memory of its president, Eisenhower, Mazeroski wants them to recall him instead swinging his bat, rounding the bases, and heading "home to every fan in the world."

Many of Miller's poems are focused by deteriorated relationships. "Playoffs," "Helen," and "Helen & Martha," all among the baseball poems, are also poems where the male or female partner is in the process of exiting the relationship. "Family Pictures" is ironically named because the image of the couple succintly offered in the poem depicts a couple going their separate ways. Miller makes the language do the work of illustrating the man's and woman's isolation through mundane details—showering separately, one partner having coffee, the other one tea—thus communicating the division that exists in the household. "Hotel" is an equally ironic poem, beginning with the husband's assertion that he last made love to his wife on their wedding night ten years ago. The marriage is faulty at the promise of its birth since in the new wife's brief absence, the groom talks to an old lover who called. When the wife returns, she sees the look on her new husband's face. Presumably, she understands that it is not she who has inspired that look.

Miller's body of work illustrates in part a philosophy that he has articulated. His belief is that poetry should move the poet beyond race alone, that it should internationalize and widen his preoccupation with black issues. Miller's range of interests and subjects coincide fittingly with this philosophy. Readers of his work can see that while it is anchored by the experience of black Americans, it is not limited; rather, it also embraces the ever-altering manifestations of being human and finding one's way through love, joy, pain, alienation, misunderstanding, and acceptance. Miller's commitment to poetry as a means of documenting the complexity of experience reaches far and wide to touch readers as well as writers.

Miller's ongoing commitment to poetry and his value as a mover and a shaker in the academic and arts community in the Washington area has been recognized through numerous positions and awards. He is a commissioner for the District of Columbia Commission on the Arts and

Humanities. He won the Mayor's Art Award for Literature in 1982, the Public Humanities Award from the D.C. Community Council in 1988, the Columbia Merit Award in 1993, and the O.B. Hardison Jr. Award for art and creativity in teaching in 1995. His anthology *In Search of Color Everywhere* won the Pen Oakland Josephine Miles Award in 1994 and was a Book-of-the-Month Club Selection. Lastly, Emory & Henry College in Emory, Virginia, has awarded Miller an honorary doctorate degree.

POETRY

Andromeda. Boulder Creek, CA: Chiva Publications, 1974. (Out of Print)
The Migrant Worker. Washington, DC: Washington Writer's Publishing House, 1978. (Out of Print)
Season of Hunger/Cry of Rain: Poems 1975–1980. Detroit: Lotus Press, 1982. (Out of Print)
Where Are the Love Poems for Dictators? Washington DC: Open Hand Publishing, 1986.
First Light: New and Selected Poems. Baltimore: Black Classic Press, 1994.
Whispers, Secrets, and Promises. Baltimore: Black Classic Press, 1998.

MEMOIR

Fathering Words: The Making of an African American Writer. New York: St. Martin's Press, 2000.

EDITED ANTHOLOGIES

Synergy: An Anthology of Washington, DC Black Poetry. Washington, DC: Black-South Press, 1975.
Women Surviving Massacres and Men: Nine Women Poets: An Anthology. Washington, DC: Anemone, 1977.
In Search of Color Everywhere. A Collection of African American Poetry. New York: Stewart, Tabori and Chang, 1994.

REFERENCES

Haywood, Elanna N. "E. Ethelbert Miller." In *The Oxford Companion to African American Literature.* Ed. William L. Andrews, Frances Smith Foster, and Trudier Harris. New York: Oxford University Press, 1997. 499–500.
Ramsey, Pricilla R. "E. Ethelbert Miller." In *Dictionary of Literary Biography.* Vol. 41. Ed. Trudier Harris and Thadious M. Davis. Detroit: Gale Research, 1985. 233–40.

Thylias Moss

(1954–   )

Thylias Moss
Credit: University of Michigan Photo Services

The poems of Thylias Moss have been described as stunning, riveting, powerful, witty, dense, lush, encyclopedic, and able to inhabit the real and surreal world simultaneously. Moss is a prolific writer whose excellent work has been recognized nationally. She enjoys reading and performing her poetry because she finds the rhythms and cadences of language thrilling. She has said that she is dissatisfied with her work unless it is reaching forward and occupied with its own reaching. Perhaps this objective explains the stunning variety of descriptions that her poems have earned.

Moss was born Thylias Rebecca Brasier to Calvin Theodore and Florida Missouri Gaiter Brasier in Cleveland, Ohio. Wishing to give his daughter an unused name, Calvin Brasier originated Thylias. The Brasiers had both come from the South, her father from Tennessee and her mother from Valhermosa Springs, Alabama. Her father was employed as a mechanic, and her mother was a maid, a position that becomes the subject of several of Moss's poems. The Brasiers supported their young daughter's interest in reading and writing, and Thylias wrote her first poem at age eight on the back of a church bulletin. She is the couple's only child.

The Brasiers lived with their daughter in an attic apartment in the home of a Jewish couple. Moss was accepted as the Jewish couple's granddaughter and was introduced to and participated in their special holidays. Moss's carefree childhood that had lasted for five years abruptly ended when her mother employed a thirteen-year-old babysitter, the daughter of their new landlords. The babysitter, Lytta, figures prominently in Moss's memory as an abuser and tormentor from the time Moss was five until she was nine, and Lytta's parents moved away. Moss has written a memoir titled *Tale of a Sky-Blue Dress* (1998) whose title recalls the garment the baby-sitter often wore. Moss never revealed this abuse to anyone, but she contemplates its consequence in the memoir and explores it in her poetry.

Moss completed Alexander Hamilton Junior High School and John Adams High School and attended Syracuse University between 1971 and 1973. She withdrew, however, returned to Cleveland, and married John Lewis Moss, whom she knew from her church and who was then in the military. Moss found employment as an accounts payable clerk with a Cleveland business. By the time she resigned, she was a junior executive. Moss resumed her college education at Oberlin in 1979, where she earned her undergraduate degree in creative writing in 1981, graduating with the highest grade-point average in her class. She completed requirements for the M.A. degree in 1983 from the University of New Hampshire. She taught at Phillips Andover Academy in Massachusetts in the 1980s but relocated to the University of Michigan at Ann Arbor, where she became professor of English.

Moss and her husband have two young sons, Dennis and Ansted, and John Lewis Moss is an administrator at the University of Michigan.

Hosiery Seams on a Bowlegged Woman, Moss's first book of poems, was published in 1983, the same year she completed her M.A. degree. The Cleveland State University Poetry Center had encouraged Moss to complete a volume of poems after she won the prestigious Academy of American Poets College Prize in 1982 for her poem "Coming of Age in Sanduski."

Moss has continued to receive numerous awards and grants, including the Kenan Charitable Trust and the National Endowment for the Arts and a fellowship from the Artists' Foundation of Massachusetts. Her books have also won prestigious recognition. *Pyramid of Bone* (1989) was first runner-up for the National Book Critics Circle Award; *Rainbow Remnants* (1991) won the Witter Bynner Prize, an annual recognition by the American Academy and Institute of Arts and Letters for a "distinguished younger poet." *Rainbow Remnants* was also chosen by Charles Simic as one of the five annual choices for the National Poetry Series, a prestigious recognition that positions the chosen volume as one of the best five in the country for the year. Moss has also received the Dewar's Profiles Performance Artist Award in 1991, a cash award of $10,000, a Guggenheim Fellowship, and a 1996 MacArthur Fellowship.

Hosiery Seams on a Bowlegged Woman introduced many of the themes that Moss has continued to explore such as emotional attachments between fathers and daughters, marriage, mothering, rape, and abortion. Her autobiography often becomes the backdrop from which she draws subject matter for poems. Her autobiography includes her distinctive ethnic composition consisting of Cherokee, Choctaw, and African ancestry. For example, during childhood she traveled with her parents to Tennessee and Alabama to visit relatives and encountered the public signs of segregation. Poems like "Lunchcounter Freedom," "The Lynching," and "*Nigger* for the First Time" reference those childhood memories. However, Moss does not shape her poems around the identity of herself as a black woman struggling because of race. She has said that identity is not her only subject, and when it enters her poems, it is a supportive force behind the work rather than in front of it.

Pyramid of Bones had the distinction of being a solicited book by

Charles Rowell for the Callaloo Series at the University Press of Virginia. The title became a point of some contention, but *Pyramid* was finally chosen from five potential titles submitted by the author. Moss's focal subjects in the volume are motherhood, heritage, and God.

Moss writes prose poems whose paragraph-like structures permit fuller exploration of some of the themes and ideas that are more concisely offered in her traditional lyrics. "The Warmth of Hot Chocolate," for example, offers a provocative, almost tongue-in-cheek meditation on the presence of angels, God, and evil. The speaker, an angel, says that someone told her she defied logic as an angel who didn't believe in God. Her wings grow out of her heavy hair, she says. Demons can't fly because their abode is too hot to allow the necessary hair. God forgot to create wings for himself when he was "forging himself out of pure thoughts," the speaker says. God is personalized through the speaker's comparison of him to being like the feel of chocolate being swallowed, but God is also decentered in the speaker's references to him in the evolutionary process of earth. Another prose poem, "Renegade Angels," can be read in part as a companion piece to "The Warmth of Hot Chocolate" in its balancing of the sacred and the profane. From what appears a common observation in the first line of the poem, "Every night women in love gather outside the window and it is nothing special," Moss elevates women for their ability to produce and contain the eggs that produce children, then to care for them. The lines of the gospel tune "all day, all night, angels watching over me," through adult retrospection, designate mothers rather than the angels traditionally envisioned on high.

Children are a crucial subject in Moss' *Last Chance for the Tarzan Holler* (1998), but they serve as catalysts for a more profound meditation rather than as the focus of the poem. Children as well as a proselike line or an incident also become catalysts for drawing the reader into the maelstrom of the poem, though the reader may be left there in circuitous motion, floundering to seize the meaning. The theme of mutilation on an incomprehensible level as the universe remains incomprehensible is evident in the first section of poems grouped together under the title "Fire Work." In "A Way of Breathing" perhaps it is merely by chance that the child playing jacks was not born a "child of Thalidomide" and, in macabre humor, can say, *"Look Ma, no hands, no cavities."*

As easily as the speaker can suction up jacks into her cleaner, a "rebel" can shoot out "bang-bang." Mutilation or violence, a reader seems led to conclude, is as easy as breathing for some people. In "Beginning the Rock at Abbot School," the setting is identified as the 1960s, and a thrown rock strikes the speaker on his forehead *"like my grandmother's hand*: blunt love." The thrown rock, subject to gravity, is merely the device by which Moss compels the reader to enter into certain memories. For the poem's speaker, it is the memory of dancing to the radio and disturbing the household. At the end of the poem a reference to Galileo's brain and the allusion to gravity are unexpected. The speaker holds the memory of the rock that was like her grandmother's hand (blunt love) when too much dancing upset expectation and a normal household. Her grandmother's hand communicated love. But what is the speaker destined to feel when she is drawn to the memory of hate?

"Juniper Tree of Knowledge," a ballad structured by a myth, brutality, death, and mutilation, is a horror tale. A new mother dies at the birth of her magnificent baby. The father remarries, but the new wife, jealous of the memory of the deceased wife, epitomized by the surviving stepson, kills him through decapitation as he retrieves a coveted apple from her apple chest. She sticks his head back on, and when her own young daughter comes home, she encourages her to slap her stepbrother. In macabre humor, the head flies off, and the evil new wife has falsely shifted the guilt for his death to her daughter. The daughter is made coconspirator when the mother makes soup from the boy's bones and serves it to his unsuspecting father, who eats heaping bowls of it. The stepdaughter salvages the boy's sweet bones and buries them outside, next to the tree where his mother is buried. That night, a bird sings this horrible event. Eventually, the bird and its listeners go to the house where the stepmother tries to flee; but the bird drops a millstone on her, and she becomes food for condors and vultures. Miraculously John is resurrected, and Marie, the innocent coconspirator, will become the woman of the house.

Bones figure prominently in "Juniper Tree," as they do in "Those Who Love Bones," which is anchored by a woman's excessive love of eating and feeling bones. However, the poem references the bones of Joseph Merrick, the British patient whose story was told in the movie *The Elephant Man*, and the bones of the victims of the regime of Vietnam's Pol Pot. These poems illustrate several of Moss's effective techniques in structuring content. She subjects a theme such as mutilation and its consequences to examination across a spectrum of possibilities. In "Beginning the Rock at Abbott School" the potential mutilation is of the spirit; in "Juniper Tree of Knowledge," the mutilation is physical and the known guilty party is punished with death; in "Those Who Love Bones," the subjects are genetic, natural, abnormal, and unnecessary mutilation, all exposed in the same poem by various allusions. But by far, the most extensive reference is to a woman who enjoys eating and sucking bones from her food. Given the emphasis on ingested bones in "Juniper Tree of Knowledge," Moss seems to be suggesting that various forms of mutilation may indeed be equal, although the consequences may differ. It is a complex assertion, and the book consists of equally complex poems.

Moss's poems have increasingly grown more difficult and more dense since *Rainbow Remnants in Rock Bottom Ghetto Sky*. But like most literature that is at first seemingly unyielding, persistence in rereading her work proves fruitful. Based on the prestigious awards her work has won, many readers have been justly rewarded.

POETRY

Hosiery Seams on a Bowlegged Woman. Cleveland, OH: Cleveland State University Poetry Center, 1983. Cleveland, OH: League Books Publisher, n.d. (Out of Print)
Pyramid of Bone. Charlottesville: University Press of Virginia, 1989. (Out of Print)
At Redbones. Cleveland, OH: Cleveland State University Press, 1990. (Out of Print)
Rainbow Remnants in Rock Bottom Ghetto Sky. New York: Persea Books, 1991. (Out of Print)
Last Chance for the Tarzan Holler. New York: Persea Books, 1998.
Small Congregations: New and Selected Poems. New York: HarperCollins, 1999.

MEMOIR

Tale of a Sky-Blue Dress. New York: Bard, 1998.

REFERENCES

Bates, Gerri. "Thylias Moss." In *Dictionary of Literary Biography*. Vol. 120. Ed. R.S. Gwynn. Detroit: Gale Research, 1992. 220–222.
Bloom, Harold, ed. *Black American Women Poets and Dramatists*. New York: Chelsea House, 1996.

MARILYN NELSON

(1946–)

Marilyn Nelson
Credit: Fran Funk

L ike many African American poets, Marilyn Nelson's numerous talents are manifested in a career that combines teaching and writing. A prize-winning poet, her first book for an adult audience, *For the Body*, appeared in 1978, and other volumes have followed. Nelson's first four poetry volumes were published under the name Marilyn Waniek. In addition to writing and teaching creative writing at the university level, Nelson has also served as a lay associate in the National Lutheran Campus Ministry program at Lane Community College in Eugene, Oregon.

Nelson was born in Cleveland, Ohio, to Melvin M. and Johnnie Mitchell Nelson. Her father, a member of the last class of aviators graduated from Tuskegee Institute, was an aviator and officer in the air force. Her mother was a graduate of Kentucky State University and had perfect music pitch. The couple had two daughters and sons; one son was diagnosed with Down's syndrome and died in early childhood. Nelson's father's affiliation with the air force meant that the family frequently relocated. Thus she grew up on military bases in Texas, Kansas, California, Colorado, Oklahoma, New Hampshire, and Maine. She was often either one of a few or the solitary African American student in her classes. Nelson was studious and began to love books and poetry early.

Nelson graduated from the University of California at Davis with a B.A. degree in English, where she was one of five African Americans in a student body of approximately 12,000. She earned the M.A. degree from the University of Pennsylvania in 1970, and the Ph.D. degree from the University of Minnesota. Nelson became an assistant professor of English at Lane Community College in Eugene, Oregon, between 1970 and 1972, and at Norre Nissum Seminarium Fellowship in Denmark the following year. Between 1973 and 1978 she taught literature in the English Department at Saint Olaf, a small Lutheran college in Northfield, Minnesota, and taught one semester in Germany at the University of Hamburg. Since 1978, Nelson has been teaching at the University of Connecticut in Storrs.

Divorced from German husband Erdmann Waniek, Nelson married Roger Wilkenfield, also a university professor, in 1979. The couple has a son, Jacob and daughter, Dora.

Nelson began writing seriously during her undergraduate years when she enrolled in a poetry writing workshop at Davis. However, the civil rights movement was also under way, and Nelson worked through the Southern Christian Leadership Conference in Chicago the summer of 1965 and in activist roles at Davis as well. Busy with a married life, work, travel, and courses in a Ph.D. program, Nelson temporarily gave up writing. During her last year of coursework at the University of Minnesota, however, she enrolled in two poetry workshops, one offered privately by Etheridge Knight. Consistent with Knight's emphasis on poetry and its relationship to community, his class gave regular unannounced group readings at bars or restaurants. During Nelson's travel in Europe the semester she taught at the University of Hamsburg, she began to write poetry at a steady pace, and her commitment to writing intensified. Upon returning to Minnesota, she translated (with Pamela Espeland) children's poems by the Danish poet Halfdan Rasmussen, which were published as a chapbook called *Hundreds of Hens and Other Poems* (1982). The poems she had been writing became her first adult book of poetry and appeared in print in 1978.

Nelson's poetry is refreshing in its engaging candor and subtle humor. It is characterized by direct language and draws liberally from images of nature and domesticity. Her ability to anchor her ideas in ordinary experience points her and the poems to a promontory that is profoundly revelatory about life. Nelson's poems offer thoughtfully chosen details that create immediacy and liveliness, and her subjects are numerous. She prominently centers women in her poems as she examines history, memory, and death. The family is central to her poetic vision, but by anchoring the family to its history or to contemporary social issues, she transforms what might be a personal history into startling poems of profound interest. Thus, the history of African Americans is almost always a subtext in the work. Most of her poems are of medium length, occupying one page, but several are longer. In structure, she uses free verse in inventive stanzas but also uses the traditional forms of the sonnet, villanelle, and the ballad. At least one long narrative poem, "I Dream the Book of Jonah," contains some blues-structured stanzas. Nelson's Jonah, she has said, is Mississippi John Hurt, a legendary bluesman.

For the Body introduces most of the concerns that resurface in Nelson's later books. The body, a metaphor for human beings, for family, for neighbors, and for people generally, secures the poet's interest in the messages humans fail to heed, in human pain and pleasure, and in the death that surrounds life, all expressed in the first poem in the book, "Dedication." These interests prevail, but specific concerns exist within them. Human misconceptions ("Other Women's Children"), unattainable human desires ("The Fish Weeps"), questions of identity ("The American Dream," "Home"), and the importance of family and home ("I Imagine Driving Across Country") are among the important secondary concerns.

With each volume, however, Nelson seems determined to explore her subjects differently. The poems in the second volume, *Mama's Promises* (1985), are less elliptical than those in the first, and the poet's voice seems more comfortable with itself. Identity, rebirth, regeneration, motherhood, and being a child are the apparent themes in this volume. Often, themes are presented from two perspectives, since the daughter has become a mother and a wife, reliving the work of previous generations. The speaker (daughter) can often look backward and forward to her own experiences. The significance of this book of twenty-three poems for Nelson is suggested when she includes most of them in *The Fields of Praise: New and Selected Poems* (1997).

A sequence of poems in *The Homeplace* (1990) illustrates Nelson's interest in connecting family history with national history and her ability to draw the past into the present through memory. In "The House on Moscow Street," for example, the speaker's memory summons great-grandfather Pomp and his wife Annie who lived in the house. Aunt Jane, a laundress, had bought the house in 1872 and had the first indoor plumbing in town installed on a corner of the back porch. Aunt Jane willed the house to Annie, the daughter of a woman Aunt Jane had known in slavery, so that Annie and Pomp could move from Shelby Hill into town. The "Shelby Hill" reference, the site where Annie had borne their "high-yellow brood," is often on Annie's mind. That name permits Nelson to generate several related poems in the sequence and accounts for the poet's constructing an intergenerational story that is the author's own history. Pomp and Annie sent all their children to college, except for Geneva. One of their daughters was destined to become Nelson's grandmother. "The House on Moscow Street" ends with a reference to "generations lost to be found." For the present generation, "much underlined Bibles" and legal documents such as deeds, wills, or manumission papers comprise the bridges to those lost generations. The speaker in "Diverne's House," though three generations removed from the era of slavery, examines documents in a country courthouse to confirm or to refute the myth of a woman named Diverne, who was enslaved for nineteeen years. The documents record a marital history for Diverne but stop short of confirming the myths that exist in the family's oral history. "Diverne's Waltz" offers additional history on this ancestor. As a slave, Diverne is cook and servant for a party at her owner's house when she catches the attention of Henry Tyler, who, apparently, has just enlisted in the Civil War. He twirls her in a waltz at the festivity. Nelson joins Tyler to a legion of similar acts involving unequal fraternization between powerful white men and powerless black women through an image of silent, grinning, white male spectators that evokes their past behavior.

Mr. Tyler "sees men grin. His father shakes his head." Diverne's inter-action with her owner continues in "Balance," a poem that implies Div-erne's weighty knowledge balanced against waiting for the inevitable encounter. Diverne "honed [Tyler's] body's." Tyler's sexual conquest of her, told in "Chosen," was not rape, although Diverne was terrified and he had his whip. Pomp resulted from this union. Pomp's history and that of his family, begun in "The House on Moscow Street," also contin-ues in "Daughers, 1900," "Chopin," "Hurrah, Hurrah," "The Ballad of Aunt Geneva," "High and Haughty," "Juneteenth," "Armed Men," and "Aunt Annie's Last Prayer." In a note to the poems, Nelson says that the family history is indebted to her mother's stories, a gift the poet reciprocates by rendering the stories into poems.

Also reflecting Nelson's conflating of African American history with her own personal history, *Homeplace* includes poems indebted to stories of the Tuskegee Airmen, the fraternity of African American aviators. These were the history-making pilots from Tuskegee Institute trained for service in World War II. Although most of her poems confirm her facility with realistic dialogue, the voices in this group of poems are among her most effective for conveying the nuanced voice raised in storytelling. Poems in the group include "Tuskegee Airfield," Freeman Field," "Lonely Eagles," "Star Fix," and "Porter."

Nelson's use of history, particularily the reconstruction of her family's history, is reminiscent of both Lucille Clifton's and Rita's Dove's inter-generational poetry. In *Mama's Promises*, Nelson, like Clifton, writes spe-cifically about her mother. Nelson suggests the cyclic nature of experience in "Mama's Murders" when, leaning into a mirror, she looks like her mother but, upon closer inspection, sees many generations of dead women, "all of them Mama." Several poems grow out of the poet's experiences as a mother, a wife, and her mother's daughter. Motherhood is the giving of life, but paradoxically, it is also the giving of death. It is fulfillment and frustration, as in "The Dangerous Carnival"; it is also fear, as in "The Lost Daughter," Nelson's memory of getting lost when she was four or five years old during a shopping trip with her mother. And motherhood is a responsibility that threatens to inundate the mother in "Bali Hai Calls Mama."

Magnificat, Nelson's subsequent volume, differs in its emphasis and in the poetic structures employed. *Magnificat* is the prayer of Mary, Jesus' mother, when she acknowledges God's honor in her selection as the Sav-iour's mother. The emphasis in the poems reflects the religious tenor of the title. It includes a group of "Abba Jacob" poems that Nelson says were inspired by one of her friends who is a monk-priest. Moreover, the poems follow the format of apothegms, proverbs or pointed sayings of the Desert Fathers, the earliest Christian monks. Patience, renunciation, and gratefulness are recurrent themes in this book. When Nelson writes about a mother in "The Dream's Wisdom," for example, a dream restores the speaker's dead mother for a day, but she must be given up again. Nelson's humor lies on the surface of the poem in "Gloria," where the first-person speaker is grateful for "postal efficiency," for mail forwarded "to the correct local address," and in "Dusting," where the gratefulness is "for dust."

The fourteen "Abba Jacob" poems appear in the third section of *Magnificat*. Nelson reprints many of them and composes a few new ones for *Fields of Praise*, the collected and new poems. The "Abba Jacob" poems are pithy, mostly short in length, and have the tenor of a tight lesson of life about them, a lesson that mostly ensues from logical thought and mundane experiences. In "Abba Jacob at Bat," for example, a young visitor wearing an Angels baseball cap inspires a memory in the mind of a man who died in the monk's arms. Putting on the young visitor's cap himself, Abba Jacob proclaims that it reminds us to live. However, it isn't only the cap that reminds but the inevitability of death that is the catalyst for embracing life.

Nelson's volumes to date align her with the important work of other African American poets in significant ways. She has shown herself to be an original thinker, and she has written poetry that appeals to a wide audience.

The recognition extended to Nelson's work attests to its standing in the literary community. She has won two creative writing fellowships from the National Endowment for the Arts, a Fulbright Teaching Fellowship, and the 1990 Connecticut Arts Award. *The Homeplace* was a finalist for the National Book Award in 1991 and winner of the Annisfield-Wolf Award in 1992. Similarily, *The Fields of Praise* was a finalist for the National Book Award in 1997, the PEN Winship Award, and the Lenore Marshall Prise. It won the 1998 Poets' Prize.

POETRY

For the Body. Baton Rouge: Louisiana State University Press, 1978.
Mama's Promises. Baton Rouge: Louisiana State University Press, 1985.
The Homeplace. Baton Rouge: Louisiana State University Press, 1990.
Magnificat. Baton Rouge: Louisiana State University Press, 1994.
The Fields of Praise: New and Selected Poems. Baton Rouge: Louisiana State University Press, 1997.

REFERENCES

Andrews, Shelly, ed. "Marilyn Nelson." *Contemporary Authors Autobiography Series*. Vol. 23. Detroit, MI: Gale Research, 1996. 247–67.

Boelcskevy, Mary Anne Stewart. "Waniek, Marilyn Nelson." *In The Oxford Companion to African American Literature*. Ed. William L. Andrews, Frances Smith Foster, and Trudier Harris. New York: Oxford University Press, 1997. 756.

Jones, Kirkland. "Marilyn Nelson Waniek." In *Dictionary of Literary Biography*. Vol. 120. Ed. R.S. Gwynn. Detroit: Gale Research, 1992. 311–15.

DUDLEY RANDALL

(1914–   )

Dudley Randall
Credit: Walter P. Reuther Library, Wayne State University

As owner and founder of Broadside Press who published first-time poets in the 1960s, Randall became a major player in the aggressiveness of the Black Arts Movement in the late 1960s and early 1970s, publishing the first-time books of numerous writers who emerged as major voices of that decade. He identified an essential need in African American letters and was well positioned from his Detroit, Michigan, location to expose the vigorous voices of a new breed of writers. He was also an accomplished poet.

Randall was born to Arthur George Clyde and Ada Viola Bradley Randall in the District of Columbia. The young Randall's early interest in writing motivated his father to increase opportunities for his son to hear African American poets and intellectuals read their work or lecture. Thus, Dudley Randall was taken to hear James Weldon Johnson and W.E.B. Du Bois. As early as age nine, he was writing, and the local newspapers, the *Detroit Free Press* and *Detroit News*, published his first work during early adolescence.

As a young man, Randall was employed at the foundry of the Ford Motor Company, from 1932 to 1937. He served in the army in the South Pacific between 1943 and 1946. Following that tenure, he attended Wayne State University where he majored in English and was awarded a degree in 1949 when he was thirty-five years of age. He also satisfied the requirements for an M.A. degree in the humanities, except for completing the thesis. However, he earned an M.A. degree in Library Science from the University of Michigan in 1951. With this degree, Randall became librarian at Lincoln University (1951–1954), at Morgan State University (1954–1956), and at the Wayne County Fellowship Library System (1956–1969). He founded Broadside Press in Detroit, Michigan, during those years, in 1965. Randall also taught English at the University of Michigan in 1969. Between 1969 and 1976, he was poet-in-residence at the University of Detroit, from which he retired. Between 1970 and 1976, he served on the advisory panel of the Michigan Council for the Arts. Amid his professional activity, Randall married Vivian Barnett Spencer in 1957. The couple had one daughter, Phyllis.

Randall's career combines involvement in the arts on numerous levels, teaching in the university, writing poetry, being a publisher of poets, and translating Russian poets. After World War II, having learned to read Russian, Randall subsequently translated poems by K.M. Siminov and Alexander Pushkin.

His publishing and writing, however, are his most significant achievements in African American literary tradition. The founding of Broadside Press proved significant to the publishing of black poetry particularly during the era of black nationalism when it was deemed crucial that black art production be controlled within the black community.

Broadside Press, as its name may suggest, was conceptualized to circulate famous poems for easy accessibility by printing them on single large sheets. Randall's first group of Broadsides was titled "Poems of the Negro Revolt." In the 1960s, however, Randall encountered established poets such as Margaret Walker and Gwendolyn Brooks. He reprinted Brooks's "We Real Cool" and subsequently published her *Riot I* (1969), *Family Pictures* (1971), *Aloneness* (1971), and *Report from Part One* (1972), which was the first book of her autobiography. Randall also began budding friendships and acquaintances with new writers of the era such as Sonia Sanchez, Haki Madhubuti, Nikki Giovanni, and Audre Lorde. Subsequently, Broadside Press brought out both Haki Madhubuti's second and third books of poetry, *Black Pride* (1968) and *Don't Cry, Scream* (1969), the latter the first cloth edition that Broadside had produced. It also published Audre Lorde's third book of poetry, *From a Land Where Other People Live* (1973), which was nominated for a National Book Award. Broadside also published *Black Feeling, Black Talk* and *Black Judgement* by Nikki Giovanni, *We a BaddDDD People* by Sonia Sanchez, and *Poems from Prison* by Etheridge Knight. Randall's press was thus instrumental in promoting, or at least making available to the public, the cohesive mood of protest and righteous anger that characterized the new black voices of the 1960s.

The first collection that Randall's press brought out was his coauthored book with poet Margaret Danner where each of them wrote ten poems on facing pages. Randall and Danner had read together at the cultural facility in Detroit known as Boone House, and over time, they amassed a group of poems on the same subjects but from different perspectives. This group became the ten poems of *Point, Counterpoem* and included some of Randall's best-known poems. "The Ballad of Birmingham" and "Booker T. and W.E.B." are both based on historical incident "Ballad," initially printed as the first in a series of broadsides in 1965, is based on the deaths of four little girls in the bombing of the 16th Street Baptist Church in Birmingham, Alabama. The poem focuses on dialogue between one girl and her mother and highlights the irony of the mother's wanting the child to be safe and thus permitting only her church attendance. Its dramatic irony and its lack of sentimentalism achieve its effectiveness. "Booker T. and W.E.B.," initially published in *Midwest Journal* in 1952, recalls the philosophical controversy between those two men over the best route to parity for black people. The brief poem succinctly captures their disagreement, its rhyme generates light humor, and the poem conveys the impression that the two would never achieve consensus. "Southern Road" and "Souvenirs," also from his first volume, earned critical praise as well.

Broadside also brought out its first full-scale book, the anthology *For Malcolm: Poems on the Life and Death of Malcolm X* (1967), edited with poet and visual artist Margaret G. Burroughs. Randall continued, meanwhile, to write and to engage in some travel. He visited Paris, Prague, and the Soviet Union with other black artists in 1966 and the West Africa nations of Ghana, Togo, and Dahomey in 1970.

Randall brought out brief collections of his poems between 1968 and 1981. *Cities Burning*, his first collection of twelve poems, appeared after the 1967 riot in Detroit. Overall, the poems address an era in disarray. "Roses and Revolutions," "Primitives," and "A Different Image" are among the highly regarded poems in this volume. *Love You* (1971), as the title implies, was composed of fourteen brief love lyrics. The most distinctive of the group is the often anthologized. "The Profile on the Pillow," is a poem distinguished by its contrasting shapes—the profile "dark against the white [pillow]"—and the imagery of the holocaust of either fire or ice through which the memory of the profile will persist. *More to Remember: Poems of Four Decades* (1971) collected fifty poems over a thirty-year period from the 1930s through the 1960s. *After the Killing* (1973) offers fifteen new poems on topics contemporary to the issues of the early 1970s. *A Litany of Friends: New and Selected Poems* (1981) followed Randall's emergence from suicidal depression, a condition that had frozen his productivity. The work offered thirty new poems written during his recovery. The title poem with its ceremonial tone and forty lines names and recognizes the friends who helped Randall through his mid-1970s depression. In "My Muse," Randall writes of "Zasha," his African muse, his counterpart to "Catullus's Lesbia," and to the muses of Shakespeare, Dante, and Poe. In "A Poet Is Not a Jukebox," Randall seems to speak retrospectively on a personal and collective level to those who wish to dictate subjects for black poets. Thus, a poet is not like a jukebox where a quarter put in elicits the tune the payer desires.

Randall's poetic style—his structures, diction, syntax, subjects, and the appearance of the printed page—is traditional. His work includes a few sonnets, for example, and his best poems have a deeply reflective quality unlike the brash spontaneity that marked many of the young 1960s writers. Much of his imagery is from nature, but some evokes an urban milieu and some the Bible. A subtle sense of humor is apparent, too, perhaps more revealed in selections in *More to Remember*.

Randall's role in the tradition of African American poetry is inestimable, particularly for the new poetic voices of the 1960s. Given their anger and poetic form that was deemed radical by the establishment, mainstream publishers predictably would have been slow or would have refused to publish them. Randall's philosophy for the press, to publicize single poems and simultaneously to make them easily and inexpensively available, needed little alteration to fit the small volumes of protest poetry that he subsequently began to publish. As others have recognized, he was indeed a bridge of salvation between generations of poets from the 1940s to the 1960s.

Randall's contributions to African American poetry and the arts were acknowledged throughout his career. He received the Wayne State University's Thompkins Award for Poetry and Fiction in 1962 and 1966 and the Michigan Council for the Arts Individual Artists Award in 1981. Also in 1981, Mayor Coleman A. Young named Randall poet laureate of Detroit. Moreover, he received the Life Achievement Award from the National Endowment for the Arts and an Honorary Doctor of Letters from Wayne State University. In 1987 Randall received the Distinguished Alumni Award from the University of Michigan. A documentary film, *To a Black Unicorn: Dudley Randall and the Broadside Press*, was screened at the Detroit Institute of Arts in 1996 on his eighty-second birthday. In recognition of Randall's lifetime achievements the Chrysler Corporation Fund arranged an endowed scholarship in his honor in the Department of Africana Studies at Wayne State University in 1997. And in 1998, he was inducted into the National Hall of Fame for Writers of African Descent in Chicago.

POETRY

(With Margaret Danner). *Poem, Counterpoem*. Detroit: Broadside Press, 1966. (Out of Print)
Cities Burning. Detroit: Broadside Press, 1968. (Out of Print)
Love You. Broadside Press, 1970. (Out of Print)
More to Remember: Poems of Four Decades. Chicago: Third World Press, 1971. (Out of Print)
After the Killing. Chicago: Third World Press, 1973.
Broadside Memories: Poets I Have Known. Detroit: Broadside Press, 1975.
A Litany of Friends: New and Selected Poems. Detroit: Lotus Press, 1981.

EDITED ANTHOLOGIES

(With Margaret G. Burroughs). *For Malcolm: Poems on the Life and the Death of Malcolm X* Detroit: Broadside Press, 1967.

Black Poetry: A Supplement to Anthologies Which Exclude Black Poets. Detroit: Broadside Press, 1969.
The Black Poets. 1971. Rpt., New York: Bantam, 1985.

OTHER

Broadside Memories: Poets I Have Known. Detroit: Broadside Press, 1975.

REFERENCES

Boyd, Melba Joyce. " 'Roses and Revolutions' Dudley Randall: Poet, Publisher, Critic, and Champion of African American Literature Leaves a Legacy of Immeasurable Value." *The Black Scholar* 31.1 (2001): 55–57.
Miller, R. Baxter "Dudley Randall." *In Dictionary of Literary Biography.* Vol. 41. Ed. Trudier Harris and Thadious Davis Detroit: Gale Research, 1985. 265–73.
———. "Endowing the World and Time: Life and Work of Dudley Randall." In *Black American Poets between Worlds, 1940–1960.* Ed. A. Baxter Miller. Knoxville: University of Tennessee Press, 1986. 77–92.
Rowell, Charles H. "In Conversation with Dudley Randall." *Obsidian* 2.1 (1976): 32–44.
Thompson, Julius E. *Dudley Randall, Broadside Press, and the Black Arts Movement in Detroit, 1960–1995.* Jefferson, NC: McFarland, 1999.
Waniek, Marilyn Nelson. "Black Silence, Black Songs." *Callaloo* 6.1 (1983): 156–65.

ISHMAEL REED

(1938–   )

Ishmael Reed
Credit: Perseus Basic Books
Photo credit: Richard Nagler

As a novelist, essayist, editor, founder of journals, and poet, Reed has chiseled out an important niche for himself in African American letters. Particularly in fiction, his innovative subjects and experimental forms have set his work apart from that of other novelists. Also distinguished by his use of satire, parody, and his cross-cultural borrowings that complicate the fiction for some readers but enrich it for others, Reed's work is widely considered to be complex. Both the fiction and its author are also considered controversial; Reed's fiction challenges the status quo as it overturns conventional structures of the novel. Calvin Hernton suggests the power of Reed's work in saying that Reed has "taken the American language out on a limb and whipped it to within an inch of its life. In so doing, he has revitalized the American language with the nitty-gritty idioms of black people's conceptualization of what it means to live in dese new-nited states of merica" (Hernton 221). In addition to fiction and essays, Reed has published four books of poetry.

Reed was born in Chattanooga, Tennessee, to Henry Lenoir, a fundraiser for the YMCA, and Thelma Coleman, a homemaker and salesperson. His stepfather was Bennie Stephen Reed, an autoworker. However, Reed grew up in Buffalo, New York, and attended the University of Buffalo between 1956 and 1960. He began his studies in the night school division but moved to day school on the strength of an early short story titled "Something Pure," which captured the attention of his English teacher. In 1962, he moved to Lower East Side New York and began writing as a journalist. In 1967, Reed published his first novel and relocated to the culturally diverse San Francisco Bay area in California. He has taught at numerous universities since his first stint at the University of California at Berkeley in 1968, including the University of Washington, State University of New York at Buffalo, Yale University, Dartmouth College, University of Arkansas at Fayetteville, Columbia University, and Harvard University.

Reed is married to Carla Blank, a choreographer, his second wife. From two marriages, he has two daughters, Tennessee and Timothy Brett.

Reed names his influences as paintings, music, and architecture across cultures but refuses to name people as influences. He had always been fascinated by history as well. He calls himself a classicist, but he is usually grouped with the avant-garde due to his experimental fictional forms. He confesses to writing poetry and fiction when inspired to work on it, anywhere from five minutes to twenty-four hours at a time. He has learned what poetry is by writing it, and he reads poetry extensively when writing fiction. Some of his poetry, like the fiction, is based on merely listening to people and organizing what he hears. He believes the African American poet is at his or her best as a humorous poet rather than as a singer of spirituals.

Reed's work has been widely recognized through prestigious awards and honors. He has been nominated for the National Book Award in fiction and in poetry for *Conjure: Selected Poems, 1963–1970* (1972). He won the Poetry in Public Places award in New York City in 1976 for his poem "From the Files of Agent 22," and he has won the National Endowment for the Arts publishing grants for merit.

In addition to writing across numerous genres, Reed's work includes the founding of publications, instituting literary awards, and serving in numerous organizations for the purpose of increasing the visibility of African American writing and acknowledging underrecognized writers. To this end in 1973 he cofounded the Before Columbus Foundation to produce and distribute the work of unknown ethnic writers. With poet Al Young, he also founded *Quilt* magazine in 1980. With Kathryn Trueblood and Shawn Wong, Reed also edited *The Before Columbus Foundation Fiction Anthology: Selections from the American Book Awards, 1980–1990* (1992).

Unfortunately, Reed's poetry has received far less commentary than has his fiction. But like his fiction, the poetry illustrates Reed's irrepressible cleverness and energetic style with language, a broad sense of ironic humor, and a novel incorporation of folk culture through adapting the phenomenon of "hoodoo" for a literary aesthetic. Reed advances the idea of his literary aesthetic, "hoodoo," in poetic form in his first brief volume *Catechism of D Neoamerican Hooodoo Church* (1970). Hoodoo, thought to be an alteration of the word "voodoo," flourished in southern black folk culture as the form of West African religious belief and practice that survived the transplanting of Africans to the Americas. Numerous synonyms, such as "conjure" and "root working," have mildly nuanced differences in meaning and may vary among geographic regions, but they identify the phenomenon. However, "hoodoo" in the United States and "obeah" on some Caribbean islands are the words that parallel "voodoo" to convey an established religion. Hoodoo's adherents sanction its powers of intercession and transformation. They believe that practicing it can alter circumstances graciously or grievously and that it links black Americans with their cultural ancestry. Hoodoo is resilient and all encompassing, having been stretched to accommodate the varying demands of an African diaspora. It is reasonable therefore, even genius, for Ishmael Reed to seize hoodoo, to which he adds the prefix "neo" as a signal of its contemporaneity, as the framework for a black literary aesthetic. Reed puts his theory to work in his novels *Yellow Back Radio Broke-Down* (1969), *Mumbo Jumbo* (1972), and *Flight to Canada* (1976).

In a group of related poems, Reed centers his new black literary aesthetic as a countercultural force and the source of black power. "Black Power Poem" is short but significant because it situates neo-hoodooism in opposition to the aggregrate power structure in white America. In fact, neo-hoodooism is fought against by an alliance of American culture made up of the arts, medicine, politics, technology, religion, and the multimedia, respectively, represented in "Black Power Poem." The last line of the poem sarcastically suggests that what is represented by the poet Allen Ginsberg, the physician Timothy Leary, the politician Richard Nixon, the scientist Edward Teller, the preacher Billy Graham, and the media, taken together, is tantamount to a powerful religion. However, neo-hoodooism has parallel power. Using an appropriate metaphor for conflict, the metaphor of boxing, the poem concludes with the idea that the powers will combat each other. The six-page prose poem "Neo-Hoodoo Manifesto" sets out Reed's concept of what hoodoo is. It is an all-encompassing religion, a "Lost American Church" synonymous with the distinctive characteristics that comprise African American culture; it is a quality of being, a style, music, and art. It is the dances of the African diaspora revisioned in popular African American dances. It "borrows from Haiti Africa and South America." Reed's structural style in the poem is the collage, a style that effectively communicates the syncretism of the phenomenon he has adapted to literary function. For example, the poem includes a song stanza, an article from The *New York Times* (credited in the poem) about the pope's outlawing jazz in Catholic services, and an excerpt from Edmund Stillman and William Pfaff's *The Politics of Hysteria*, which shows conflict between cultures.

Following his manifesto, Reed positions "The Neo-HooDoo Aesthetic," a poem structured as a gumbo recipe, a classic dish as evocative of New Orleans as New Orleans is of the cultural practice of hoodoo. Reed includes the key to the poem in its content when he explains that the label "Neo-HooDoo Aesthetic" means that "the proportions of ingredients used depend upon the cook!" Inclusiveness, in other words, is a key concept of the artistic and cultural aesthetic of neo-hoodooism. Its practictioners, like Reed himself, may exercise the liberty of blending, exchanging, or creating anew in their artistic expression. They are neither required nor expected to follow literary conventions as set forth in mainstream artistic tradition. In making gumbo, each cook has his or her secret ingredient to assure individual uniqueness within the concept of the whole. In other words, art will not be prescriptive.

In "Catechism of d Neoamerican Hoodoo Church" Reed illustrates his considerable satiric ability and more directly articulates his position for artistic freedom and flexibility, pointing out that poets' pens "do not move by decree," and art will not be controlled. Artistic freedom has its price, however. The artist and his work are criticized, lampooned, and rejected by those who are conventional and have self-identified as the arbiters of taste or the stylemakers of the moment. Reed refers to the Beat Generation poets, a group of influential white American poets including Robert Creeley and Allen Ginsberg. In another section of the poem Reed refers to another rejection, his lecture being canceled at Delaware State after a background check suggested to the status quo that his ideas were too unconventional.

Reed's response is to take refuge in neo-hoodooism, that is, to conjure his attackers. Therefore, he calls into service the conventional devices of this mysterious cultural practice—a black cat, a root, a picture of the grave of the infamous New Orleans voodoo queen Marie Laveau, and his grandfather, a "nigro-mancer from chattanooga" from whom he has acquired power. Connecting himself to his grandfather and trading on the word "necromancer," Reed inducts the tradition of a master conjurer who traditionally passed his knowledge down to a family member or chose a worthwhile apprentice to whom the knowledge would be taught. In any event, neo-hoodoo power will effect change. This is the message of its prophet "ishmael." How, Reed asks, "did [the goodhomefolks] know he was d'afflicted one?" The prophet is rejected, of course, and persecuted by the public. The poem's lengthy conclusion reiterates the enabling power of neo-hoodooism so that its adherents might reject the artistic constrictions of the majority who narrowly define what can be written, painted, danced, or loved. The new "houngans," voodoo priests, have the power to make their art the way they want to. They can ignore the dictates of the false prophets.

Reed's satiric humor, apparent in the poems that detail his position about a new black aesthetic called neo-hoodooism, is manifested throughout his poetry. In "What You Mean I Can't Irony?" for example, the poem details advice given to the poem's speaker from a woman lawyer at a cocktail party with mostly African Americans. With a portrait of Andrew Carnegie beaming down on the assembly, she advises the speaker to go to Europe to increase his cultural perspective. The discrepancies in this seven-line poem create the irony as the poem's title creates humor: Go to Europe where the perspective will be obviously European rather than African is the advice at a cocktail party, a social function unrelated to African derivation, where a magnate of industrialism looks down on a function that is billed as "black black" to emphasize its immersion in African and black American culture. As a satiric humorist Reed is a legend.

The diction in his poetry also mirrors the informality of everyday speech, but Reed is a wizard with the language. For example, in "Untitled III," in *Conjure*, the four-line poem uses ordinary spoken language to satirize social pretention. In "Untitled III" the people in Columbia Heights speak French and attending a party there "bore[s] you to tears." Reed is also adept at conveying black vernacular language through spellings such as "wd" for "would," "yr" for "your," "tho" for "though," or "d" for "the," a device that occurs frequently in black poetry in the 1960s and effectively evokes the spoken sound of the language. Reed's ability to reproduce a strong aural resonance from the folk tradition is also demonstrated in "Railroad Bill, a Conjure Man," subtitled "A Hoodoo Suite," a long poem of twenty-five stanzas. Railroad Bill, fashioned in the tradition of Sterling Brown's and Margaret Walker's folk heroes, is a first-rate conjure man with shapeshifting talents. In other words, he can change himself to nonhuman things such as a tree, a lake, an animal, or a song. His escapades, legend in his own community, are preserved in folk songs, but he is under pursuit by the authorities. Reed structures the poem around attempts at circumventing Railroad Bill and his shapeshifting evasions. Cowards finally ambush Railroad Bill by shooting him in the back, but the community refuses to accept his death and insists that Railroad Bill can be seen all around them as different objects. Another poet might have ended the poem with Bill's presumed death, but in Reed's hands, the folk hero becomes a means for satirizing Hollywood and its treatment of black heroes like Nat Turner, the Virginia slave preacher insurrectionist, and Jack Johnson, the boxer. Hollywood hires a teacher from Yale to edit the script and to modernize it. In the conclusion, the last laugh is on Hollywood, because Bill the conjure man changes himself into a production assistant and edits the film himself.

Reed's poetry reflects its creator's rich love of the infinite possibilities of language and his intolerance of restrictions, particularly on black art. He uses his poetry, as he uses his fiction, to lamblast critics and promoters of the status quo. Reed has a catholic mind, integrating references to history, to American popular culture, and to world culture with apparent ease, sophistication, and brashness.

POETRY

Catechism of D Neoamerican Hoodoo Church. London: Paul Breman, 1970. Highland Park, MI: Broadside Press, 1971.
Conjure: Selected Poems, 1963–1970. Amherst: University of Massachusetts Press, 1972.
Chattanooga: Poems. New York: Random House, 1973.
A Secretary to the Spirits. New York: NOK Publishers, 1977.
New and Collected Poems. New York: Atheneum, 1988.

REFERENCES

Dear, Pamela S., ed. "Ishmael Reed." *Contemporary Authors. New Revision Series*. Vol. 74. Detroit: Gale Research, 1995. 313–19.
Fox, Robert Elliot. "Ishmael Reed." In *The Oxford Companion to African American Literature*. Ed. William L. Andrews, Frances Smith Foster, and Trudier Harris. New York: Oxford University Press, 1997. 624–26.
Hernton, Calvin. "Blood of the Lamb." in *Amistad 1: Writings on Black History and Culture*. Ed. John A. Williams and Charles F. Harris. New York: Vintage, 1970. 183–225.
Martin, Reginald. *Ishmael Reed and the New Black Aesthetic Critics*. New York: St. Martin's Press, 1988.
Settle, Elizabeth A., and Thomas A. Settle. *Ishmael Reed: A Primary and Secondary Bibliography*. Boston: G.K. Hall, 1982.
Wordworks, Manitou, ed. *Modern Black Writers*. 2nd. ed. Detroit: St. James Press, 1999.

CAROLYN RODGERS

(1945–   )

Carolyn Rodgers emerged as a prominent poet during the 1960s during the era that has come to be known as the Black Arts Movement. Like the poets of her era, Rodgers addressed contemporary issues in the language of everyday, predominantly urban discourse. She also used the style—disrupted print, collapsed words (yr for your), lowercase letters—that marked the 1960s poets as anticonventional and innovative in some circles and propagandistic sloganeers in other circles. Rodgers was thus instrumental in helping to create the distinctive poetry that, despite its naysayers, has helped to transform African American poetic tradition.

Rodgers was born to Clarence and Bazella Colding Rodgers and attended the public schools in Chicago. Both her parents were lovers of music and required their children to learn music. Rodgers became very adept at playing guitar. In 1960 she enrolled at the University of Illinois and began experimenting with writing at that time. Rodgers has said that writing allowed her to vent certain frustrations. She transferred to Chicago's Roosevelt University in 1961 and received her undergraduate degree there. She earned the M.A. degree in English from the University of Chicago. Perhaps predictably, Rodgers began work as a social worker because in the early 1960s that occupation alongside teaching was one of the few open to black women even in urban areas. Rodgers worked at the YMCA (1963–1966) and some years later in the poverty program.

Like many poets, Rodgers has used her talent for the instruction of others. She has taught at Columbia College (1968–1969); the University of Washington (1970), Malcolm X Community College (1972), Albany State College (1972), and Indiana University (summer 1973). She worked in English remediation at Chicago State University in 1981, was an instructor at Columbia College from 1989 to 1991, and since 1998 has been a faculty adviser to the student newspaper and instructor at the Harold Washington College in Chicago. Among her several language-related occupations, Rodgers has also been a book reviewer and a columnist for a newspaper in Milwaukee.

During the mid 1960s period, Rodgers met writers such as Haki Madhubuti, Johari Amini, Sterling Plumpp, and Hoyt Fuller, when she began attending the Organization of Black African Culture (OBAC) Writer's Workshop meetings and the Gwendolyn Brooks's Writers Workshop. Both Brooks and Fuller, a poet, journalist, and editor of the cultural magazine *Black World*, became Rodgers's mentors, encouraging her to continue writing and to pull her poems together into her first book.

Rodgers had cofounded Third World Press with Madhubuti and Amini also in 1968, and the press brought out her first book, *Paper Soul*, in 1968. Although the work placed her within the ideology of the Black Arts Movement, it also signaled her distinctiveness. Her poems suggested a woman who knew conflict and who recognized the tension between conventional black life and the tug of the new ways of thinking and behaving. It questioned the Vietnam conflict and decried the impact of cities on the black population. The first book also included themes of identity, love, woman's quest for love, revolution, and religion. One of the most anthologized poems from *Paper Soul*, "Now Ain't That Love," depicts an identity that seems dependent on the man in the speaker's life. "Testimony," however, is more representative of the spirit of cultural revolution in the first volume. Here Rodgers takes traditional religion to task along with other institutions that do not promote an activist spirit. Like Sonia Sanchez and Madhubuti, Rodgers committed herself to truth telling in her work.

After the first volume of poetry, Rodgers won the first Conrad Kent Rivers Memorial Fund Award, and following the second book, she was awarded the Poet Laureate Award of the Society of Midland Authors and an award from the National Endowment for the Arts. These recognitions confirm Rodgers's potential and growth, qualities that Gwendolyn Brooks and Hoyt Fuller must have recognized. In fact, her first three volumes from Third World Press garnered enough attention that for the next two books, Rodgers signed with a mainstream press. She also severed her relationship with the OBAC.

Rodgers encountered some resistance to the excesses of style in her work, although she was incorporating language and stylistic techniques that were part and parcel of that verbally aggressive era in poetry. Although she used obscenities and black street talk, as did her peers, she was singled out for criticism. In an article on Rodgers's poetry, Bettye J. Parker-Smith suspects that the conventional belief that respectful women did not use profanity was, in part, responsible for the condemnation. Aside from profanity, Rodgers's poetry was also criticized for its inconsistent use of black street language. In some instances, she mixed standard English with street talk in the same poem. Rodgers responded to her critics' admonitions in a poem titled "The Last M.F." The poem ironically engages the paradox of being a woman, stereotypically soft and feminine, and being a revolutionary as the rhetoric of the times demanded. Since the criticism against Rodgers had included her language use and, by extension, her voice, she structured "The Last M.F." by alternating arguments about women speaking. The poem ironically and subversively acknowledges the admonishments with phrases like "so i say" and "whether i say it or not," where she deliberately uses the uncapitalized "i." When she then uses the capital "I," it effectively shouts at the reader.

Rodgers's second book, *Songs of a Blackbird* (1969), illustrated her concern with women's issues through themes of identity, mother-daughter conflict, love, and survival. Some of the poems, such as "Breakthrough," address Rodgers's awareness of her own evolving self with an identity that is in transition. Being a writer who can communicate "self" through poetry is also important in expressing that identity. Rodgers's emerging identity includes the classic issue of autonomy apart from her mother. The poet brings this issue to her work in "Jesus Was Crucified" and "It Is Deep." Belonging to another generation the mother does not understand this different daughter in a different time. Rodgers writes from the mother's perspective. The mother questions the value of the college education she labored to provide for her daughter at considerable expense, thinking it is to blame for her daughter "actin not like decent folks" and rejecting Christianity. In "It is Deep" the mother visits her daughter and sees a physical sight strange to her with its symbols of revolution and revolutionary poets. Nevertheless, she leaves her daughter cash for some immediate needs. Significantly, the rhetoric of the Black Arts Movement proves useless in Rodgers's movement toward self-definition.

In her third volume, *How I Got Ovah: New and Selected Poems* (1975), Rodgers's search for an elusive identity expressed in the second book is over. The largely autobiographical poems here illustrate that she has abandoned her militancy in favor of a woman responsive to love, family, community, and religion. In "Some of Me Beauty" the speaker rejects hate in favor of self-definition as a black woman. The poems about her mother are particularly compelling and have been widely anthologized and referenced. These include "for muh'dear," "It Must Be Deep," "It Is Deep," "how I got ovah II," and "It Is Deep II," where the mother-daughter conflict must be resolved. The resolution includes the daughter's recognition of the mother's trials and the mother's reliance on religion. "[F]or muh' dear," the initial poem in the volume, contains no psychological conflict with the mother. The latter poem offers an account of the speaker's conversion to the Christianity of her mother. Through referencing poems from the second book and her search for identity, Rodgers effectively illustrates her change or "getting over." "Living Water" suggests the poet's realization that some of her earlier rhetoric amounted to emptiness. "For Women" recognizes women as the "fruit of the earth." "It is Deep" contains the famous line of recognition that the mother is "a sturdy Black bridge" that supported the daughter's journey. The first scholarly text for African American women's studies, edited by Beverly Guy Sheftall and others, borrows the phrase *Sturdy Black Bridges* for its title, and the phrase became a much-referenced term to recognize the intergenerational debts black women owe their female ancestors.

How I Got Ovah (1975) marked a turning point in Rodgers's career for the maturity that she brings to her work and for the potential she has realized since the first book less than ten years earlier. The feminist themes of the book, Rodgers's perceptiveness about mother and daughter relationships, the astute realizations about black women in their relationships with husbands or boyfriends, and the language that adeptly communicated the emotion in the poems all mark Rodgers's distinctiveness.

The Heart as Ever Green appeared in 1978. Rodgers does not stray very far from the concerns that have occupied her poetry previously—Christianity, feminism, love, and an awareness of blackness. However, the imagery drawn from nature that Rodgers uses is a distinguishing facet of this volume. She has continued writing, including a novel, *A Little Lower Than Angels*, in 1984. However, her later work has not garnered the national attention that the 1970s work elicited. Thus Rodgers's reputation and her honors and awards are tied to that era. Her honors include a National Endowment for the Arts Award in 1970, the Poet Laureate Award, Society of Midland Authors in 1970, the National Book Award nomination in 1976 for *How I Got Ovah*, the Carnegie Award in 1979, and a Gwendolyn Brooks fellowship.

POETRY

Paper Soul. Chicago: Third World Press, 1968. (Out of Print)
Songs of a Blackbird. Chicago: Third World Press, 1969.
How I Got Ovah: New and Selected Poems. New York: Doubleday, 1975. (Out of Print)
The Heart as Ever Green. New York: Doubleday, 1978. (Out of Print)
Translation: Poems. Chicago: Eden Press, 1980.
Finite Form: Poems. Chicago: Eden Press, 1985.
Morning Glory. Chicago: Eden Press, 1989.
We're Only Human. Chicago: Eden Press, 1994.
The Girl with Blue Hair. Chicago: Eden Press, 1996.
A Train Called Judah. Chicago: Eden Press, 1996.
Salt. Chicago: Eden Press, 1998.

REFERENCES

Dictionary of Literary Biography. Vol 41. Ed. Trudier Harris and Thadious Davis. Detroit: Gale Research, 1985. 287–95.

Ford, Karen. *Gender and the Poetics of Excess: Moments of Brocade*. Oxford: University Press of Mississippi, 1997.

Jamison, Angelene. "Imagery in the Women Poems: The Art of Carolyn Rodgers." In *Black Women Writers (1950–1980): A Critical Evaluation*. Ed. Mari Evans. Garden City, Anchor Doubleday, 1984. 377–92.

Parker-Smith, Bettye J. "Running Wild in Her Soul: The Poetry of Carolyn Rodgers." In *Black Women Writers (1950–1980): A Critical Evaluation*. Ed. Marie Evans. New York: Anchor Books, 1984. 393–410.

Rodgers, Carolyn. "An Amen Arena" (Interview). In *Black Women Writers (1950–1980): A Critical Evaluation*. Ed. Marie Evans. New York: Anchor Books, 1984. 373–76.

SONIA SANCHEZ

(1934–   )

Sonia Sanchez
Credit: Temple University

P oet, playwright, activist, children's fiction author, and mother, Sonia Sanchez's first published book of poetry, *Homecoming* (1969), established her as a major proponent of the Black Arts Movement along with Amiri Baraka, Haki Madhubuti, Mari Evans, and others. One of the distinguishing elements of Sanchez's initial work that has persisted is its oral quality. Many poets of the 1960s relied on language rhythms and melodies that evoked visceral responses from their audience. Sanchez, a distinctive performance poet who uses chants, singing, and strong language as systemic in her work, has intensified the orality of her poems until it is, arguably, her most recognizable quality. The orality, along with other features of her work, makes Sanchez a sought-after poet at colleges and universities. Perhaps it is also this quality, along with her acceptance of difference, that makes her a mentor and model for contemporary young poets who, drawing from the strong poetic tradition among African Americans, are further enhancing it through the creativity of hip-hop and rap. Sanchez, in fact, has performed with the rapper Rakim. She has also recorded records and compact discs of her work.

Sanchez was born in Birmingham, Alabama, to Wilson L. and Lena Driver, who named their daughter Wilsonia. The mother died when Sonia was about a year old, and Sonia and her sister lived with various relatives until the family moved to Harlem when she was nine years old. Sonia was a shy child who stuttered. She got into the habit of writing what was difficult for her to verbalize, and family members began to comment that her writing rhymed and that she was writing poetry. Sanchez outgrew the stuttering, but she kept it as a technique in her poetry.

In New York, Sanchez studied political science at Hunter College and graduated in 1955. Her graduate work included studying poetry with Louise Bogan at New York University. Her teaching career, beginning in the 1960s, included San Francisco State College, the University of Pittsburgh, Rutgers University (1970–1971), and Amherst College (1972–1975). At San Francisco State College, Sanchez was instrumental in orchestrating black studies as a part of the curriculum during a period marked by student unrest. In fact, she and the psychologist Nathan Hare were major players in setting up the first black studies program. Sanchez joined the faculty at Temple University in 1977, where she is Laura Carnell Professor of English and Women's Studies. She has been poet-in-residence at numerous institutions including Spelman College in Atlanta and Tulane University in New Orleans.

The name Sanchez is from her first marriage to Albert Sanchez, a

Puerto Rican, to whom she was married for four years. Sanchez's marriage to poet Etheridge Knight in 1968 also ended in divorce. She has three children, Anita, Morani Neusi, and Mungu Neusi.

Sanchez joined the Nation of Islam in 1972 and was a member until 1975. The Nation's emphasis on morality, nationhood, and a community that is financially self-determined were important to her and reflective of her personal ideology. However, Sanchez's distaste at the parochialism of the organization's orthodoxy and its sexism finally motivated her departure, though her work during this period reflects some of the Nation's principles.

Sanchez's poetic voice was a preeminent, catalytic presence in the Black Arts Movement. Like several of her contemporaries she understood the function of the poet as a seer, teacher, and transmitter of values and truth for the benefit of his or her community. "I write to tell the truth about the Black condition as I see it," Sanchez says in a personal essay in *Black Women Writers (1950–1980)*. "So when I decide to tell the truth about an event/happening, it must be clear and understandable for those who need to understand the lie/lies being told" (Sanchez 415). Since the 1960s Sanchez's poetry has continued to promote unity, self-worth, love, self-respect, and community among black people. Her work advocates a self-revolution that is as important as the political one.

Like the work of most poets, Sanchez's books over a thirty-year period of creativity reveal her development as a mature writer. *Homecoming* as her first volume sets out the poet's ideological positions. In her study of Sanchez's work, Joyce Ann Joyce explains this first book as "stylistically unintellectual, unacademic, and anti-middle-class, for [Sanchez's] idioms come straight from the mouths of Black people who intuitively understand that vulgarities cut deeper and closer to our real feelings than do the niceties of standard middle-class English" (65). Sanchez thus makes her poetic language an expression of her politics. *We a BaddDDD People* (1970) was also Sanchez's necessary experimentation with language, tone, and humor. The haiku pieces of *Love Poems* (1973), however, mark a transition. Although relationships continue to be a focus, the tone is modulated, unlike the tone in the earlier books. Sanchez conceptualized *A Blues Book for Blue Black Magical Women* (1974) as a necessary revelation about struggling through layers of misinformation, marginalization, isolation, and sexual quicksand in the process of becoming a woman. It emphasizes the roles of African American women as wives, lovers, sisters, mothers, laborers, and warriors. *A Blues Book*, an autobiographical sojourn as well, also charts the poet's movement into full womanhood.

The work in *I've Been a Woman: New and Selected Poems* (1979) firmly establishes Sanchez as a warrior poetic force entrenched and immovable in American letters. *Under a Soprano Sky* (1987) offers numerous poems in tribute to mentors and supporters. As the lyricism of the title implies, lyrics and strong imagery characterize the poems. *Shake Loose My Skin* (1999), a collection of new and collected poems, offers work from six previous collections. Perhaps its greatest value is its compact illustration of Sanchez's ability to swing gracefully between prose poems and lyrics and between the gritty language of urban residents and the jazzy-blues articulations of the black community.

Initially, Sanchez used the popular styles of 1960s black protest poetry. These included representing the sound of language through spelling, suggesting, and emphasizing a word's pronunciation through its visualization as in the word "BaddDDD," and liberally employing the slash mark as in "sat/ur/day," again for emphasis and perceived pronunciation. Having committed herself to writing for a black audience, she used the idiom, dialect, and street language of the group. Sanchez also experimented with the physical placement of the poem on the page as a strike against conventional expectation of how a poem "looks." She referred to her early poetry as a "call to arms." As the poet activist, she wanted her work to motivate readers to perceive the nature and extent of their oppression and to turn it back against their oppressors, the idea expressed in "For Unborn Malcolms" and "There Are Black Puritans." "So This Is Our Revolution" laments that self-defeating behavior persists among black people. "Let Us Begin the Real Work" says the work begins with reclaiming and teaching children for nationhood. The idea is superior to image or metaphor, but these devices are certainly present. In her early work Sanchez keeps the poems brief and the language economical and sharp.

In addition to brief lyrics, Sanchez is also adept at the condensed image-driven Japanese form of haiku. The conciseness required in this form requiring five, seven, five syllables in its three lines, respectively, has proven appealing to a wordsmith of flexibility like Sanchez. She uses this form in *Homegirls and Handgrenades* (1984) to write about numerous subjects. One haiku employs the image of a boat slip at the marine as comparison to a man's one-night involvement with a woman; a love poem uses the image of stars exploding in blue black skin; and still another about the different ways men and women express emotion suggests that a man may not cry "til he knocked all over." At the other end of the spectrum, she also writes long prose poems like those that also appear in *Homegirls and Handgrenades*. These poems read like condensed short stories or sketches, but their compelling images and metaphors mark them as poems.

Throughout Sanchez's numerous books, music persists as a significant structural and stylistic quality. One of her highly regarded poems, "a/coltrane/poem," is inspired by the jazz saxophonist John Coltrane, whose influence on the 1960s protest poets is profound and unparalleled by any other jazz figure. Purportedly, Sanchez has said that she wrote the poem out loud, sang it out in order to write its visuals, its oral quality, and its images. Sanchez riffs off Coltrane's well-known recordings "A Love Supreme" and "My Favorite Things," transposing his sounds to the printed page in a poem that attacks capitalism and the failed promises of the American dream for African Americans and then asks black people to "RISE. & BE. What u can."

Sanchez also employs the form and mood of blues music in her work. *Homegirls*, for example, offers a section titled "Blues Is Bullets," suggesting that blues is a physical and spiritual force. The prose poem "After Saturday Night Comes Sunday" tells a blues story of a wife's disappointment and loss in love due to her husband's drug addiction. Sanchez writes a blues poem in "Norma." In this biographical account of Sanchez's fellow high school classmate, a girl's academic potential is lost to drugs and premature motherhood. The blues is the realization of Norma's squandered talent, along with Sanchez's regret at such a senseless loss.

Even as her poetry advocated political struggle during the 1960s and 1970s, Sanchez's themes have persistently addressed love, family, male/female relationships, children, and black women. Love, as a multitextured phenomenon, is illustrated in her work in its application to oneself and one's community as well as in romantic relationships. Sanchez is never sentimental about this subject, however. The first section in *Homegirls and Handgrenades* consists of lyrical love poems. It ends with a prose poem, an elderly woman on a park bench who tells a young mother about how she once loved. *Like the Singing Coming Off the Drums* (1998) is a book of love poems dedicated to Tupac Shakur, the rap artist who was murdered, and it includes tributes to others including the black intellectual Cornel West. From the perspective of a political activist, Sanchez's work also recognizes black women's oppressions both from the men in their lives and from their social and economic positions in American society. Sanchez also champions the irrepressible spirit of black womanhood as in the exuberant poem "I've Been a Woman," even as she recognizes the contradictory impulses in a black woman's life.

Through a celebratory outpouring of lush images, Sanchez captures the agelessness, beauty, and sensuality of the black woman. This woman is also a regenerative force, anchored in the past but also searching and moving forward. Her source of identification is with "the ancient/black/woman." Finally, the poem's subject is fully alive through the senses that make her a part of all that is around her.

Sanchez has retained the personal introspection that marked her early writing, but she has also expanded her range and creativity with each new book. For example, her activism encompasses numerous oppressed groups as illustrated in the "Poem for July 4, 1994," where she speaks to gays, Asians, Jews, Native Americans, lesbians, and Muslims. In "Elegy (For MOVE and Philadelphia)," in *Under a Soprano Sky*, she writes about the tragic assault in 1985 on the black political group when their dwelling was assaulted by the police department and about the tragic deaths that included children. She calls Philadelphia a "disguised southern city." In so doing, Sanchez evokes the atmosphere of a lynching to illustrate the insistent, murderous power exercised by those who possess it. The poem does not end with reconciliation but with the idea that somewhere beyond the city's ordinary façade of activity, honor and peace lie in wait. The short poem placed next to "Elegy," dominated by an image of burned South African children, resonates with the unspoken: Apartheid is also alive and well in Philadelphia.

Placing children at the center of her outrage about Philadelphia's debacle is not a new emphasis for Sanchez. The abuse of children and their well-being has been a significant focus of her work from the beginning and is perhaps most strikingly indicated through her works composed for them, including *Un Huh, But How Do It Free Us* (1973) and *Adventures of Small Head, Square Head and Fat Head* (1973). Sanchez's outrage at violent deaths and other outrages committed against children is apparent in poems such as "A Poem of Praise," written for a young man who died early. The sense of progression to an early death is indicated in the poem by the ironic refrain, "And to live seventeen years is good in the sight of God."

Does Your House Have Lions? articulates a different but nonetheless equally painful experience. A book-length epic poem using four voices, the volume simultaneously combines the intensively personal and public in chronicling Sanchez's brother's physical and spiritual demise. *Does Your House* charts his migration from the South to the North, his experience in the homosexual culture of New York, the family alienation that followed, and his illness and death from AIDS in 1981. The book is Sanchez's most formally structured. According to fellow poet June Jordan, writing in *Feminist Bookstore News* that Sanchez marries her poetry with intimate emotion even as she works within the difficult and strict three-line Italian stanza form called *terza rima*. This conventional form is atypical of Sanchez's work.

Sanchez's reputation for performance poetry is almost as well known as the poems themselves. In her ability to fuse herself with the emotion of the poem and to transmit that emotion whole to the listener, she is matchless. Sanchez's voice becomes her instrument of transmittal as John Coltrane's tenor saxophone or Buddy Guy's guitar transmit their messages. Sanchez alters her voice by octaves; she cries, moans, shouts, stutters, screeches, or laughs, as the emotion of the poem scans her face. A Sanchez performance is exhilarating and cathartic. It's the African tradition of interaction between speaker and audience—call and response—at its most vital.

Sanchez's work has garnered numerous awards, including an honorary Ph.D. in the fine arts from Wilberforce University, a 1998 nomination for the National Book Critics Circle Award for *Under a Soprano Sky*, and the NAACP (National Association for the Advancement of Colored People) Image Award. Moreover, she was awarded the Peace and Freedom Award from the Women's International League for Peace and Freedom in 1988 and the American Book Award from the Before Columbus Foundation for *Homegirls* in 1985.

POETRY

Homecoming. Detroit: Broadside Press, 1969 (Out of Print)
We a BaddDDD People. Detroit: Broadside Press, 1970. (Out of Print)
It's a New Day. Detroit: Broadside Press, 1971. (Out of Print)
Love Poems. New Rochelle, NY: Okpaku Communications Corporation, 1973.
A Blues Book for Blue Black Magical Women. Detroit: Broadside Press, 1974. (Out of Print)
I've Been a Woman: New and Selected Poems. Oakland: Black Scholar Press, 1979. (Out of Print) Rpt. Chicago, IL: Third World Press, 1985.
Homegirls and Handgrenades. New York: Avalon, 1984.
Under a Soprano Sky. Trenton, NJ: Africa World Press, 1987.
Wounded in the House of a Friend. Boston: Beacon Press, 1997.
Does Your House Have Lions? Boston: Beacon Press, 1998.
Like the Singing Coming Off the Drums: Love Poems. Boston: Beacon Press, 1998.
Shake Loose My Skin: New and Collected Poems. Boston: Beacon Press, 1999.
(With Derrick I. Gilbert). *Henna Man: Poems*. New York: Berkley, 2000.

RECORDING

(With Sweet Honey in the Rock, performance group). *Sacred Ground*. Redway, CA: EarthBeat Records, 1995.

REFERENCES

Baker, Houston A., Jr. "Our Lady: Sonia Sanchez and Writing of a Black Renaissance." In *Studies in Black American Literature*. Vol. 3. Ed. Joe Weixlman and Houston Baker Jr. Greenwood, FL: Penkeville Publishing, 1988. 167–202.

Gabbin, Joanne Veal. "The Southern Imagination of Sonia Sanchez." In *Southern Women Writers: The New Generation*. Ed. Tonette Bond Inge. Tuscaloosa: University of Alabama Press, 1990. 180–203.

Joyce, Joyce Ann. *Ijala: Sonia Sanchez and the African Poetic Tradition*. Chicago: Third World Press, 1996.

Palmer, R. Roderick. "The Poetry of Three Revolutionists: Don L. Lee, Sonia Sanchez, and Nikki Giovanni." *CLA Journal* 15.1 (1971): 25–36.

Sanchez, Sonia. "Ruminations/Reflections." In *Black Women Writers (1950–1980): A Critical Evaluation*. Ed. Mari Evans. New York: Anchor Books, 1984. 415–18.

Sanders, James Robert. "Sonia Sanchez's *Homegirls and Handgrenades*: Recalling Toomer's *Cane*." *MELUS* 15.1 (1988): 73–82.

Tate, Claudia. "Sonia Sanchez." In *Black Women Writers at Work*. New York: Continuum, 1983. 132–48.

Williams, David. "The Poetry of Sonia Sanchez." In *Black Women Writers (1950–1980): A Critical Evaluation*. Ed. Mari Evans. New York: Anchor Books, 1984. 433–48.

MELVIN B. TOLSON

(1900–1966)

Melvin B. Tolson
Credit: Melvin B. Tolson, Jr.

Tolson was a playwright, novelist, renowned speaker, college professor of English, and poet who published three books of poems and wrote several others. He was one of those rare people who excelled in numerous tasks with equally stunning results. In the 1920s when the Harlem Renaissance was under way, Tolson was completing college and taking a teaching job in Texas. His long career as a university professor at two historically black colleges was executed simultaneously with his many writing projects. Tolson's years of productivity thus spanned from the Renaissance to the Black Arts Movement, though he is not aesthetically aligned with either movement. For Tolson creativity was not tied to a contemporary literary style.

Melvin Beaunorus Tolson, the eldest of four children, was born in Moberly, Missouri, to the Reverend Alonzo Tolson and Lera Hurt Tolson. Neither his father nor his mother enjoyed the privilege of a formal education. However, Reverend Tolson taught himself Greek, Latin, and Hebrew; and Mrs. Tolson was an excellent seamstress and a singer. All the siblings sang and played instruments. Reverend Tolson's ministry necessitated frequently moving the family between Missouri and Iowa.

Tolson was quiet, artistic, studious, and an avid reader as he grew up. He began writing verses as a child, published his first poem at age twelve in an Oskaloosa, Iowa, newspaper, and recited the poems of Paul Laurence Dunbar in public speaking in eighth grade. At this young age, Tolson tried to imitate Dunbar's dialect poems.

In 1919 Tolson enrolled in Fisk University and in 1920 transferred to Lincoln University in Pennsylvania. Majoring in journalism and theology, he graduated with honors in 1923. During college he met his wife, Ruth, with whom he enjoyed a forty-four year union. The couple had four children, all born in the 1920s. Upon graduation, Tolson settled in Marshall, Texas, and in 1924 he began teaching at Wiley College, an institution established by the Methodist Church. He taught there for twenty-four years, where his teaching, directing drama, and coaching the debate team for ten years won him rave reviews. Alongside these time-consuming activities, Tolson wrote poetry and drama.

Thus in the middle years of the Harlem Renaissance though Tolson was interested in writing, he was not a part of that movement. However, his thesis for the M.A. degree from Columbia University, earned in 1940, was titled "The Harlem Group of Negro Writers." His research focus suggests that he was in touch with the literary happenings of black America. Tolson studied for the degree at Columbia in 1931–1932 and lived near Harlem. The demands on him from Wiley College consumed his time so that it was 1940 before he completed all requirements for the degree.

By 1939, Tolson had completed *A Gallery of Harlem Portraits* and submitted the manuscript for consideration to Maxwell Perkins at Charles Scribner's Sons and to Bennett Cerf, editor at Random House. Both rejected it. Their apologetic explanation that it was not the quality of the work but the reception of poetry in general from the American reading public did little to brighten Tolson's spirits. Nevertheless, the late 1930s and early 1940s were very productive for him. In 1937, for example, his column "Caviar and Cabbage" began to appear in the *Washington Tribune* and was published until June 1944. He had written two plays that, unfortunately, have been lost, but he signed with the William Morris agency to represent him in motion picture and stage rights to the plays. Additionally, poems that were not part of the *A Gallery* were published.

Tolson's first national attention as a poet came in 1940. He was invited to compete in the National Poetry Contest in Chicago, sponsored by the American Negro Exposition. His submission "Dark Symphony" won and has become one of the poet's most quoted and anthologized poems. The poem was exhibited in the Hall of Literature at the Exposition and printed in the *Atlantic Monthly* in September 1941. As its title suggests, "Dark Symphony" prominently incorporates music in its structure. Divided into six movements, the divisions are subtitled with phrases such as "Allegro Moderato" and "Lento Grave." "Dark Symphony" is strongly historic as the poem's divisions follow from slavery and its spirituals to the New Negro of the 1920s who strides in "seven-league boots" looking toward the new tomorrow.

In 1944, Tolson's first book, *Rendezvous with America*, was published to positive and enthusiastic reviews. As with many first books, particularly when they are published years after the poet has been writing, *Rendezvous* offers valuable insight into the poet's development. For example, Tolson had mastered the classic poetic structures in evidence in his book by rigorously putting himself through training exercises in various techniques practiced by writers acknowledged as masters of the craft. His control of and versatility with traditional forms are readily apparent in *Rendezvous*. Tolson's lifelong passion for art and music are also evident in his first book in the way he uses image, allusion, and meter.

Rendezvous is notable for its four long poems "Rendevous with America," "Dark Symphony," "The Idols of the Tribe," and "Tapestries of Time." The title poem is set during World War II but includes American history from the pilgrims through Pearl Harbor. "Rendezvous" emphasizes and celebrates America's strength as a result of its racial diversity. "Idols" recognizes the damage done to humanity's desires as a result of its prejudices and praising of idol gods. "Tapestries" redeems faith in the progress of humanity despite a history of mistakes and violence.

In 1947, Tolson left Wiley College for another small black college, Langston University, in Langston, Oklahoma, where he was professor of English and drama and drama director until his retirement in 1964. That same year, Tolson was named poet laureate of Liberia and began composing a poem of tribute, *Libretto for the Republic of Liberia*. Liberia in West Africa had been organized under the auspices of the American Colonization Society for the purpose of using freed slaves as missionaries. Congress approved support funds, and the initial group of eighty-six former slaves sailed for Liberia in 1820. The colony struggled against land claims from England and France and hostility from neighboring Africans but survived and became a constitutional government in 1847.

Tolson's *Libretto* was not immediately accepted for publication; in fact, it took six years before its appearance in 1953. The years were nevertheless significant to Tolson's evolution as a modern poet whose work reflected contemporary philosophy about poetry. He revised the *Libretto*, and Alan Tate, an esteemed mainstream poet, agreed to write a preface for it. *Libretto*, a lengthy ode of 770 lines designed to reflect the musical scale, features sections named "Do," "Re," "Mi," "Fa," "So," "La," "Ti," and "Do." The poet's design and originality permeate the poem. Each section begins with the question "Liberia?" followed by lines of negation, that is, what the small country is not. Lines that affirm what Liberia is then follow these lines. As much modern poetry does, the poem contains allusions and references that may evade the ordinary reader. Tolson wrote a seventeen-page section of notes for explanatory purposes. The poet has said that he did not deliberately write an obscure poem. His approach in writing a poem, however, was to approach it with the same precision a mathematician uses in solving a problem. Thus each section of the poem is distinctive, and the lines are enriched by symbolism, alliteration, assonance, onomatopoeia, or allusions. For example, the section "Fa" has three symbols representative of attacks on the young republic of Liberia. "So" contains thirty African proverbs. "Ti," often considered the most difficult section because of its allusions to numerous sources in several languages, references the "Calendar of the Century" to call attention to the birth of the Republic and to its need for protection. The final section, "Do," is visually obscure: Foreign phrases are used in every stanza, and the punctuation is irregular. The lack of form symbolizes the disorder and hopelessness of Liberia at one period of its existence. However, the last section of "Do" predicts an Africa that will be self-governing, a vision that scholars have declared as in advance of its time in 1953.

After *Libretto*, the mainstream poet John Ciardi nominated Tolson for a Bread Loaf Fellowship, calling him "the most rocket-driven poet we have published." The recognition that *Libretto* received was nevertheless insufficient honor for the original concept of the poem and the way it broadened the possibilities of poetry. Alan Shapiro, a mainstream poet who wrote an introduction for *Harlem Gallery*, suggests that the response to Tolson's work was part of the trend of ignoring African American poets at the time. He believes that part of the widespread disregard for the poet by establishment writers was Tolson's distinctively African American sensitivity. The *Libretto*, he writes, "pulls the rug out from under the poetry of the Academy; on the stylistic level, outpounding [Ezra] Pound, it shocks the learned into a recognition of their own ignorance" (12). In 1954 the Liberian government honored Tolson and his poem by sponsoring a literary tea for him in Washington, D.C., at the Liberian embassy. Among other awards associated with the poem, in 1956, Tolson was invited to attend the presidential inauguration in Liberia at the expense of the Liberian government.

One of several poems that Tolson worked on between 1948 and 1952 along with *Libretto*, "E. & O.E," a long psychological poem, won the Bess Hokim Award by *Poetry* magazine in 1951. Unlike the public and historical nature of *Libretto*, "E. & O.E" was a personal statement of doubt linked to psychological awareness and looked forward to *Harlem Gallery*, Tolson's revised manuscript from 1939.

Harlem Gallery: Book I, The Curator is the first part of a projected five-part poem designed to depict the significant historical eras of the black man's sojourn in America. The concept was epic in its vision; however, Tolson was unable to complete it before his untimely death. In *The Curator*, however, he examines the black artist through the narrator, a Curator of the Harlem Gallery. From this position, the curator is privy to different classes of black people and to the problems of the black artist. The Curator, a black intellectual and former professor of art, is the key to the highbrows, middlebrows, and lowbrows in the Harlem Gallery. The Curator's friend, Dr. Nkomo, functions as his counterpart or alter ego. The numerous engaging characters in the poem are imaginary, though a few recall certain characteristics of people whom Tolson knew.

Although Tolson's embracing of modernist trends in American poetry earned him comparison to leading mainstream modernists such as T.S. Eliot, Ezra Pound, and Hart Crane, scholars have consistently recognized his emphasis on African American culture and history in his work. Before he could complete his epic vision, however, Tolson died of stomach cancer in 1966. That year he was awarded the annual poetry award by the American Academy of Arts and Letters.

POETRY

Rendezvous with America. New York: Dodd, Mead, 1944. (Out of Print)
Libretto for the Republic of Liberia. New York: Twayne, 1953. (Out of Print)
Harlem Gallery: Book I, The Curator. New York: Twayne, 1965. Rpt., Charlottesville: University of Virginia Press, 1999.
A Gallery of Harlem Portraits. Columbia: University of Missouri Press, 1979. (Out of Print)

OTHER

Caviar and Cabbage: Selected Columns by Melvin B. Tolson from the "Washington Tribune," 1937–1944. Ed. Robert M. Farnsworth. Columbia: University of Missouri Press, 1982. (Out of Print)

REFERENCES

Farnsworth, Robert. *Melvin B. Tolson* 1898–1966: *Plain Talk and Poetic Prophecy.* Columbia: University of Missouri Press, 1984.
Flasch, Joy. *Melvin B. Tolson.* New York: Twayne, 1972.
Randall, Dudley. "The Black Aesthetic in the Thirties, Forties, and Fifties." In *Modern Black Poets.* Ed. Donald B. Gibson. Englewood Cliffs, NJ: Prentice-Hall, 1973. 34–42.
Redmond, Eugene B. *Drumvoices.* Garden City, NY: Doubleday, 1976.
Russell, Mariann. *Melvin B. Tolson's "Harlem Gallery": A Literary Analysis.* Columbia: University of Missouri Press, 1980.
Shapiro, Karl. "Introduction," *Harlem Gallery.* London: Collier-Macmillan, 1969. 11–14.

Jean Toomer

(1894–1967)

J ean Toomer's literary prominence was swift and sure as his best-
known book, *Cane*, came to critical attention in 1923. Its innovative
blend of poems, prose vignettes, and a drama, with its hauntingly rich
poetic prose, signaled for many observers a dawning day in African
American letters. In *Black Poetry in America*, Louis Rubin wrote that in
"mastery of technique, richness of language and imagery, and passionate
imagination," Toomer superceded all black poets before Langston
Hughes (33). Although Toomer lived almost until the 1970s and continued to write dramas, poems, short fiction, and autobiography during
those years, most of his work was not destined for publication during
his lifetime. He was never again to experience the critical acclaim lav-
ished on *Cane*.

Toomer was born in Washington, D.C., to Nathan and Nina Pinchback
Toomer, where he grew up in the home of his maternal grandfather,
P.B.S. Pinchback. Pinchback was a strong figure in the young writer's
life, the patriarch in the home, and a public figure of reckoning. During
the Civil War Pinchback had mustered a company for the Federal army
and become its captain. During Reconstruction, self-identifying as Negro,
Pinchback rose rapidly through several high-ranking political positions
including lieutenant governor, state senator, and governor of Louisiana.
He was also sent to Washington as a state senator, but the position was
contested and he was refused. Nevertheless, Pinchback had established
himself as a politician and adventurer who vigorously embraced a good
life and raised his children in upper-middle-class environments. His
three sons attended the University of Pennsylvania, Yale, and Andover,
respectively, and were trained to become professional men, while his
daughter Nina, who became Jean Toomer's mother, was sent to a finish-
ing school to acquire the graces available to young ladies of her class.
When the political tide changed, Pinchback left Louisiana for Washington where his home would also become Jean Toomer's home.

Although his famous grandfather dominated Toomer's memory, he
was biologically the son of Nathan Toomer, who won out over Nina
Pinchback's numerous other suitors. They married and lived in the house
Pinchback bought for them. Jean Toomer was initially named for his
father, who deserted his wife and son by leaving on business and never
returning. Financial straits forced Nina to return to her parents' home.
She reinstated her maiden name, and Jean Toomer was known as Eugene
Pinchback and "Pinchy" to his neighborhood boyfriends. He later took
on the name "Jean" and remembered seeing his father only once as a

young boy. His mother remarried, however, and between 1906 and 1909, Toomer lived with her and his new stepfather in New Rochelle and Brooklyn, New York. His mother died after what was thought to be a successful appendectomy in 1909, and Toomer, aged fifteen, returned to Washington with his grandparents.

Toomer attended M Street High School, where he was not a model student. Following the educational tradition in the family, he was sent away to college through his grandfather's financial support, but the goal of completing a college degree eluded Toomer. He studied numerous subjects, however, at a variety of universities: the University of Wisconsin at Madison in 1914, Massachusetts College of Agriculture in 1915, American College of Physical Training in 1916, University of Chicago in 1916, New York University in 1917, and City College of New York (now the City University of New York) in 1917. Perhaps most important for his personal philosophy and his writing, however, he attended Gurdjieff Institute in France in 1924, where he became a follower of Armenian mystic George Gurdjieff. Margaret Naumberg, wife of the writer Waldo Frank, had introduced Toomer to the mystic's principles of religion, Freudianism, and mysticism.

Toomer was a voracious reader, reading American writers Sinclair Lewis, Theodore Dreiser, and Waldo Frank, who was to become his mentor and friend; the Russians Tolstoy and Dostoevsky; the French Flaubert and Baudelaire; and Samuel Taylor Coleridge and William Black among the British. Toomer also read books about race and its problems in America. Like his grandfather, Toomer privileged his black ancestry before *Cane* was published, but he had experienced living among both whites and blacks when he grew up in Washington. Toomer was purportedly a blend of Scotch, Welsh, German, English, French, Dutch, Spanish, and African. The insistence during Toomer's era of a strict racial identity rather than a multicultural one perhaps fueled the writer to proclaim himself neither black nor white but of the American race.

Toomer's growing desire to become a writer took him to New York in 1919 after his elusive search for a formal college degree and after numerous small jobs. Some of his earliest writing experience was gained in Greenwich Village, where he met writers Edwin Arlington Robinson and Waldo Frank. However, in 1920, Toomer returned to Washington, D.C., to be caretaker for his aging grandparents. A year later, exhausted from the job, he relinquished their care to a nurse and accepted the temporary position of principal at Georgia Normal and Industrial Institution in Sparta. Living and working alongside southern black people proved a life-transforming experience for Toomer. The subject matter for *Cane* awaited him as its chronicler, although he lived in Georgia only six months. It was his first experience with rural black people, and he found their earthiness and spirituality different from urban black people in Washington, D.C. Additionally, Toomer toured the South with his white writer friend and mentor Waldo Frank in 1922. Both of them assumed a black identity during the trip.

Shortly after *Cane* was published in 1923, Toomer became associated with the philosophy of George Gurdjieff. Gurdjieff's philosophy was aspiration toward the "objective consciousness." It placed emphasis on becoming aware of the individual's status as part of a larger, universal being. This philosophy was particularly attractive for Toomer in the post–World War I atmosphere of alienation and in his personal seeking for wholeness. He accepted that individuals had indeed become separate from each other and from their environment. After his tenure at the Gurdjieff Institute in Fontainebleau, France, during the summer of 1924, Toomer devoted his energy to spreading the mystic's philosophy. Toomer's work also illustrated his adherence to Gurdieffian principles rather than reflecting the concerns of the black community that animated the work of black writers throughout the 1920s. Thus Toomer's contribution to the Harlem Renaissance was essentially *Cane*, for after his immersion in Gurdjieff, publishers resisted his work. They also resisted it because Toomer had transcended being black to embrace a multiethnic heritage. Publishing companies, having stumbled upon the commercial value of touting their authors as Negro, also were disinterested in anyone designating himself of the "American race." Many people forgot about him, though he continued to write. Along with many books by African Americans that had been out of print, *Cane* was rediscovered during the heady literature fever days of the 1960s and was republished in 1969.

In 1924 Toomer started a Harlem group that included the elite of the Harlem Renaissance—the writers Wallace Thurman, Arna Bontemps, and Nella Larsen, the visual artist Aaron Douglass, and the model Harold Jackman—to study Gurdjieff's principles. Langston Hughes says in his autobiography *The Big Sea* that earning a life in Harlem took precedence over the time required for meditation and reflection, and the group quickly dissolved. In the fall of 1926, Toomer traveled again to Gurdjieff's French establishment. Gurdjieff's philosophy became the motivating force in Toomer's life. Toomer moved to Chicago, began a group of disciples there, and remained in the city the rest of the decade. His grandfather died in 1928. In 1931, Toomer married Margery Latimer, a white writer known for her psychic abilities and her interest in the mystical and occult. She died during childbirth complications, but their daughter, Margery Latimer Toomer, survived and was reared by Toomer's friends in Chicago until he remarried in 1934. His second wife, Marjorie Content, a photographer and the daughter of a well-known New York stockbroker, moved with Toomer to a farm outside Doylestown, Pennsylvania.

Toomer's interest in writing poetry was consonant with the move toward modernism in American poetry in the post–World War I years. It is perhaps predictable that he was influenced by Orientalism, French and American Symbolism, and Imagism. His model in French Symbolism, Charles Baudelaire, influenced many of the compact poems in *Cane*. From the American Imagists, he responded to their emphasis on the dominance of imagery and to their economical lines.

Several scholars have divided Toomer's career into phases, including the aesthetic period; the African American period; the Gurdjieffian or "objective consciousness" period; and the conversion to Quakerism period. Others recognize that his writing of poetry can also be classified into categories: the poems in *Cane*; the poems separately published; and a large group of poems that remained unpublished during Toomer's lifetime.

Cane was composed between September 1921 and December 1922, its thirteen poems interspersed among the prose vignettes and thematically resonant with them. *Cane* is divided into three sections, the first set in the South, the second in the North, and the third, the drama "Kabnis" returns to the South. Several of the poems, including "Reapers," "November Cotton Flower," "Cotton Song," "Song of the Son," "Georgia Dusk," "Nullo," "Conversion," and "Portrait in Georgia," convey awareness of the link between the present generation and their ancestral heritage. Ten poems, included among the prose pieces in Part I, share images with them and thematically convey or support similar ideas. For example, "Reapers," the first compact, eight-lined poem, follows the vignette "Karintha," and lyrically tells the story of a girl ripened too soon in life's mysteries and of the death of her newborn baby. The principal image in reapers, as the title may suggest, is the grim reaper, or death, but Toomer uses the image ambiguously, as both death and as the harvester, moving through a field gathering but also killing small animals with his scythe. "November Cotton Flower" both reflects the uniqueness of Karintha in her environment and also foreshadows the story "Becky," the tale of the white woman who "had two Negro sons." The mood of death is initially dominant, as the season of winter symbolizes, and the cotton, made nonproductive by the drought, is vanishing. However, the unforeseen and marvelous occurs: A cotton plant blooms in November to produce beauty in the middle of decay. The poems "Face" and "Cotton Song" appear follow "Becky." "Face," like the best efforts of the Imagists, offers a starkly drawn visual portrait. Through Toomer's sensibilities, it is the face of a black peasant woman whose eyes are "mist of tears" and whose face is like "cluster grapes of sorrow." "Cotton Song" blends the work songs and spirituals of the black folk tradition.

"Song of the Son," perhaps the most frequently anthologized of the poems, conveys the central idea that inspired *Cane.* Toomer arrived in the South during a period of intense transition, when folk communities were being dismantled through migration and the integrity of southern folk enclaves was endangered. Thus "Song of the Son" is a lyric of that leaving, told through images of the physical beauty of the land, the setting sun, and planting and regeneration. The poet Toomer has arrived in time to salvage the fruit of the passing era, and one seed in his hands becomes "an everlasting song" or *Cane.* He is the son returned to tell their story. Toomer's images of the dusk, night, darkness, and the setting sun, used throughout the poems and prose vignettes, are visually arresting, but their starkness also conveys the realities of the southern black experience. It is a land of violence against black men and women, and they are likely to be consumed by its cycle. Other poems in Part I of *Cane* include "Georgia Dusk," "Nullo," "Evening Song," "Conversion," and "Portrait in Georgia." The poems in Part II, "Beehive," "Prayer," and "My Throat Is Dry," like the prose, offer images of the harsh life found in the North, as do the prose vignettes in that section.

Toomer continued to write as he practiced and taught Gurdjieff's principles, but critics agree that the innovation and creation that distinguished *Cane* had disappeared. The only poem of note, "The Blue Meridian," was a long narrative poem that appeared in *The New American Caravan* in 1936.

"The Blue Meridian," considered by some scholars a minor classic in American literature, appears to be a synthesis of Toomer's ideas and a recognition of Americans' heritage, but one in which the African American experience is overlooked. Toomer believed that the various mixed ethnic strains in America of which he was a product gave him a special vision of America. Moreover, he believed that he was the first one conscious of this new race that he called the "American race." In "The Blue Meridian," Toomer projected these ideas. The poem has also been called Whitmanesque because of its affinity with the ideals of Walt Whitman. Like Whitman, Toomer believed in a mystical selfhood, individual freedom, and democracy for their expression.

In 1939, Toomer's father-in-law financed a nine-month sojourn in India for the writer and his family, a trip Toomer insisted he needed for internal self-revitalization. However, he apparently returned without it. He had kidney surgery in 1940 and remained ill for some time. Toomer and Marjorie joined the Society of Friends in 1940, and perhaps he found the revitalization that he had traveled around the world looking for, at least temporarily.

POETRY

Cane. New York: Boni and Liveright, 1923. Rpt., New York: W.W. Norton, 1987.
The Collected Poems of Jean Toomer. Ed. Robert B. Jones and Margery Toomer Latimer. Chapel Hill: University of North Carolina Press, 1988.

OTHER

The Wayward and the Seeking: A Collection of Writing by Jean Toomer. Ed. Darwin Turner. Washington, DC: Howard University Press, 1980.

REFERENCES

Byrd, Rudolph P. *Jean Toomer's Years with Gurdjieff*. Athens: University of Georgia Press, 1990.

Draper, James P., ed. *Black Literature Criticism*. Vol 3. Detroit: Gale Research, 1992. 1748–68.

Hughes, Langston. *The Big Sea*. New York: Alfred A. Knopf, 1940.

Jackson, Blyden. "Jean Toomer's *Cane*: An Issue of Genre." In *The Waiting Years*. Baton Rouge: Louisiana State University Press, 1976. 189–97.

Jackson, Blyden and Louis D. Rubin Jr. *Black Poetry in America*. Baton Rouge: Louisiana State University Press, 1974.

Kerman, Cynthia Earl, and Richard Eldridge. *The Lives of Jean Toomer: A Hunger for Wholeness*. Baton Rouge: Louisiana State University Press, 1987.

Larson, Charles R. *Jean Toomer & Nella Larsen: Invisible Darkness*. Iowa City: University of Iowa Press, 1993.

McKay, Nellie Y. *Jean Toomer, Artist: A Study of His Literary Life and Work*. Chapel Hill: University of North Carolina Press, 1984.

Scruggs, Charles. "Jean Toomer: Fugitive." *American Literature* 47. 1 (March 1975): 84–96.

Thompson, Larry E. "Jean Toomer: As Modern Man." In *The Harlem Renaissance Remembered*. Ed. Arna Bontemps. New York: Dodd, Mead, 1972. 51–62.

QUINCY TROUPE

(1943–)

Quincy Troupe
Credit: Coffee House Press
Photo credit: John Corteze, Jr.

A writer of nonfiction and poetry, Troupe's creativity is apparent in numerous genres. He has founded magazines, notably *American Rag*, a magazine for publishing Third World writers, and *Confrontation: A Journal of Third World Literature*. His edited anthology *Giant Talk* (1975, with Rainer Schulte) with work by black Americans, Native Americans, Latino Americans, black Africans, and Central and South Americans is representative of Troupe's commitment to exposing underexposed writers. Troupe's *The Inside Story of TV's Roots* in 1978 (with David L. Wolper) sold over a million copies. His collection *James Baldwin: The Legacy* (1989) was well received, and his two books on the famous jazz musician, Miles Davis, *Miles and Me* and *Miles: The Autobiography* (coedited 1990), winner of an American Book Award, have revealed his talents to a more extensive audience.

Troupe was born in New York, son of Quincy Troupe Sr., a baseball player in the Negro leagues, and Dorothy Marshall Smith Troupe. He was raised, however, in St. Louis, Missouri. Troupe Jr. studied political science as an undergraduate at Grambling College, now Grambling State University, in Louisiana, and earned his A.A. degree in journalism in 1967 from Los Angeles City College. He played on the basketball team in the army until a knee injury sidelined him. During his recovery he began writing poetry. In the late 1960s in Los Angeles, Troupe involved himself in community affairs, first with creative writing for the Watts Writers' Movement (1966–1968). He edited *Watts Poets: A Book of New Poetry and Essays* as a result of this work. Later Troupe served as director of the Malcolm X Center in Los Angeles between 1969 and 1970. During the summers he also directed the John Coltrane Summer Festivals in the city.

Troupe has taught at numerous universities, including the University of California at Los Angeles, University of Southern California, Ohio University, Richmond College, University of California at Berkeley, California State at Sacramento, University of Ghana at Legon, College of Staten Island, the City University of New York, and the University of California at San Diego, where he currently teaches literature and writing classes. Troup is in high demand as a visiting poet. In interactions with creative writing students and general audiences, he is described as dynamic and energetic, a performer of his work rather than a reader of it.

Troupe is married to Margaret Porter and has four children—Antoinette, Tymme, Quincy, and Porter.

Troupe's work has been recognized by numerous significant awards.

In 1972 the International Institute of Education awarded him a travel grant for $10,000 with which Troupe toured the West African nations of Senegal, Ivory Coast, Guinea, Ghana, and Nigeria. He was awarded the National Endowment for the Arts award in poetry in 1978, and a $6,000 award from the New York State Council of the Arts in 1979. His volume of poems *Snake-Back Solos* won an American Book Award in 1980.

The poets who have influenced Troupe perhaps reflect his openness to their visions and techniques. They include poets Pablo Neruda of Chili, Aimé Césaire of Martinique, and César Vallejo of Peru, who have most probably helped shape Troupe's use of dreamlike progressions of words, phrases, and images in many of his stanzas. The African Americans Sterling Brown and Jean Toomer have been influential as well. Particularly Brown's precedent can be observed when Troupe uses the folk ballad, folk heroes, and a bluesy style of expression.

Music and musicians and the oral folk arts are other recognizable influences in Troupe's poems. The title poem "Snake-Back Solo," for example, dedicated to musicians Louis Armstrong, Steve Cannon, Miles Davis, and poet Eugene Redmond, blends music and poetry in its tribute to music's creators. The poem's speaker describes his solo—the creative, innovative music of the solitary player offered against but also within the music of the group. Troupe evokes the broad sound of a jazz line to describe the set: "boogalooin bass down way way low." This line also illustrates Troupe's technique of referencing and mixing music with black vernacular language and culture. "Boogalooin" is a way of saying that the bass player's sound is dancing low, beneath the other instruments, because the "boogaloo" was a dance in the 1960s. A "riff" is a short repeated phrase in jazz that is played over changing chords or harmonies or used as a background to a solo improvisation. The soloist's music enters almost undetected, that nuance communicated by the term "mojoin" from "mojo," a synonym for conjure, a phenomenon in black folk culture suggesting magic. The poem's speaker plays a deep blues that affirms what has been known about the mixing of this emotion and its representation through art. Using images of windows, rivers, and light, the speaker affirms the power of music to transport one to a place of ease and serenity. The Mississippi River, variously known as "snakeback" or "big muddy," is a venue and a metaphor for linking the blues sounds of Louis Armstrong and Miles Davis. The river is also a conduit for bring one *on* home, *up* home, or *down* home, as the poem's speaker "riffs" or signifies on familiar use of black vernacular language. On another level the speaker signifies on the place of the Mississippi River in the forced or unforced migrations of black Americans.

Music and its referents are constant in Troupe's work. "Time Line of Breath and Music" in *Choruses* (1999), for example, effectively illustrates another way that Troupe links music and poetry. He matches the progression of meaning in "Time Line" to the abstract quality of music. In contrast, "Can You Chain Your Voice to a River" has nothing of the abstract but is a blues narrative that might be sung or recited. In either case, Troupe focuses on creating the tone of black vernacular language so that the blues quality is linked to the source of its origin. In "Tempus Fugit/C.T.A," dedicated to jazz musicians Miles Davis, Bud Powell, and Jimmy Heath, the subject is the birth of new music sounds that are nevertheless based on the forms and sounds that preceded them. A poem like "One for Charlie Mingus" in *Avalanche* (1996) attempts to describe the sound of music, an impossible feat except through the use of figurative language. The bass player Mingus creates "jambalaya rhythms," a phrase that evokes the spiciness and textural mix of foods in "jambalaya," a dish of rice, chicken, sausage, shrimp, and tomatoes, that presumably originated in New Orleans, as some say jazz originated. We hear "voices springing from tongues of mingus riding sweet bass strings." The rich blending of forms within African American culture that is apparent in Troupe's work illustrates what he discovered about poetry as early as his years working with the Watts workshop: Amazing poetry can come out of black vernacular language and black culture.

In addition to his focus on music and musicians, Troupe's work illustrates its author's broad concerns about the nature of the world we live in. In *Choruses*, for example, "Looking Out Between Thinking" is a reflective poem about the private and "cosmic suffering" we feel but cannot always describe. There is optimism, however, a recurring theme in Troupe's work, a space beyond one's suffering where one can see that "colors of rainbows come from someplace deep." "America's Business: A Simple Prayer" lacks optimism and instead is sharply critical of contemporary society's shallowness. America's business in this poem is entertainment and greed, each feeding the other. The speaker offers numerous entertainment images in popular culture such as Donald Duck and Mickey Mouse, and "marilyn monroe manson as cross-dresser." The speaker also focuses on the media and the "disinformation" that is taken seriously. The end of the poem is a prayer for deliverance from being consumed by the purveyors of greed. The final image evokes these purveyors as the hungry lions, waiting daily to feed on the people being thrown to them.

"Signs and Demarcations" extends Troupe's concern to the world arena where the destructiveness and maiming of hate seem constant. Hate can be invisible, concealed behind "apple-pie american flesh & blood images," but it attains an undeniable visibility in Oklahoma City, at the World Trade Center in Manhattan, and in reincarnated Nazis who take the streets and perversely use certain symbols. "Gray Day in January in La Jolla," dedicated to Troupe's son, Porter Sylvanus, contemplatively uses the focus in the nation on William Jefferson Clinton's second inaugural ceremony. Troupe's effective visual and aural images— eyes "boring into the back of clinton's head like cold barrels of shotguns"—create a tension-filled and dangerous atmosphere. Judging by the physical visuals, the dignitaries gathered, and flags flying, the day is solemnly patriotic, but Troupe's images undermine the display to show that the patriotism is superficial. In relation to his young black son just entering adolescence and the periphery of adult comprehension about his world, Troupe is reflecting about the recent, senseless death of Ennis Cosby, the son of entertainer Bill Cosby who was killed along the ramp to a California freeway as he changed the tire on his automobile. Troupe thinks of the hidden dangers that his son also will face. The poem thus very effectively brings together disparities and illustrates their interdependency—the national state with the personal, the superficial with the real, and Washington, D.C. with La Jolla, California.

Many of Troupe's poems also illustrate his art of creating an individual but representative portrait, usually in an urban setting, that results in a stinging social commentary that is more likely to be implied than stated. In *Snake-Back Solos*, for example, "New York Streetwalker," "On a New York Street Corner," and "New York City Beggar" detail a prostitute, a blind man playing music, and a beggar, respectively, all reduced to eking out a living on a city street. The content in each poem is dependent on a technique over which Troupe illustrates mastery, that is, exhaustive units of creative and often astounding images. In the poems above, the accumulated images work to illustrate the hollowness of the prostitute's, the blind musician's, and the beggar's existence. However, the weight of the social commentary shifts to the reader rather than becoming a didactic appendage to the poem. In "New York City Beggar," for example, perhaps the most effective of the trio, when the speaker keeps his requested dime, the beggar says "thank you" and adds "boss." The beggar holds up a "V" for victory or peace, curses softly, and walks away. The beggar's response is ironic since the speaker is thanked for absolutely nothing. More important, if one assumes that the keeper of the dime, like the author, is also African American, then by thanking him in such a fashion the beggar dismissively classes the man who refused to give a down-and-out beggar a coin with the oppressor. The retort is a classic one of nondeserved and empty gratitude to a white man.

Troupe's work is also characterized by an engaging variety. In *Choruses*, for example, he includes poems recognizing Michael Jordan's superior game playing in "Forty-One Seconds on a Sunday in June, in Salt Lake City, Utah" and the record-breaking batting of Mark McGuire and Sammy Sosa in "Swinging for Glory." "A Poem for 'Magic' " in *Avalanche* (1996) recognizes the wizardry of Earvin Johnson on the basketball court. Several poems are dedicated to members of his family or are written about them. These include "Mother" in *Choruses*, "The Old People Speak of Death," "Old Black Ladies Standing on Bus Stop Corners #2," both written to the poet's grandmother, and "Poem for My Father" (Quincy T. Troupe Sr.) in *Avalanche* (1996). Often, Troupe inundates the reader with the words and images of a poem. However, it is clear that the technique is being used to illustrate the author's sense of humor, as in "Slippin' & Slidin' Over Syllables for Fun" in *Avalanche*. Some short poems are lyrical surprises, such as "Firestorm," "San Juan Island Image," and "Taos, New Mexico, Image & Myth," all in *Avalanche*; and "Your Lover's Eyes Speak," "Just Beneath the Promontory," and "Come Closer" in *Choruses*.

Troupe has been a persistent presence in African American letters since the 1960s. His first volume set him apart as a distinctive voice, and his award-winning second volume *Snake-Back Solos* established his admirable versatility in poetic structure and style. His subsequent volumes have enhanced his reputation for poetry in a busy career that includes writing nonfiction, university teaching, and an activist community presence in the arts. The poems in *Avalanche* reflect the presence and concept of a literal avalanche in the arrangement of its new and previously published poems. As Troupe explains at the outset, an avalanche initially is a wrenching apart that is communicated through loud, dissonant sound. Second, what has broken away settles and tries to accommodate itself to a different place. Third, what has settled becomes a new landscape and retains none of the violence of its origination. Through language and form the three sections of poems in the volume thus mimic the three stages of an avalanche. It is an innovative and daring concept that Troupe achieves, possibly because from the beginning his work has included liberal recognition of the natural world.

Choruses illustrates Troupe's ongoing involvement with the role of the arts in our modern-day physical world. The Point Loma Poems in section three of the volume were written as part of a project for The Point Loma

Wastewater Treatment Plant in San Diego, California, that brought together engineers, architects, painters, a composer, a musician, and a poet to develop a plan for the development of the wastewater facility. Some of Troupe's poems will be sandblasted into granite throughout the facility, and others will be inscribed underground where workers may have access to art in the absence of sunlight and air. Troupe found his own voice and structures early in his poetic career. His example illustrates that he continues to find novel ways to keep his art vibrant and relevant to a constantly changing world and literary scene. In any case, Troupe's increasing body of poetry illustrates his unflagging and imaginative commitment to the craft.

POETRY

Embryo Poems, 1967–1971. New York: Barlenmir House, 1972.
Snake-Back Solos: Selected Poems. 1969–1977. Berkeley and New York: I. Reed Books, 1978.
Skulls along the River. Berkeley and New York: Reed and Cannon, 1984. (Out-of-Print)
Weather Reports: New and Selected Poems. New York: Writers and Reading Publishing, 1991.
Avalanche. Minneapolis: Coffee House Press, 1996.
Choruses. Minneapolis: Coffee House Press, 1999.

REFERENCES

Coleman, Horace. "Quincy Thomas Troupe, Jr." In *Dictionary of Literary Biography.* Vol. 41, *Afro-American Poets since 1955.* Ed. Trudier Harris and Thadious Davis. Detroit: Gale Research, 1985. 334–48.
Metzger, Linda, ed. *Black Writers.* Detroit: Gale Research, 1988.

Margaret Abigail Walker

(1915–1998)

Margaret Abigail Walker
Credit: University of Georgia
Photo credit: Rachel Griffith

The heritage of being a black southerner is arguably Margaret Walker's major asset in her vision as a writer. Her poetry draws from the rhythms, speech, folkways, joys, and pains of black Americans predominantly in the South. She uses a variety of poetic forms including the lyric and the sonnet as she examines heritage, decries persistent racial inequity, employs folklore, and applauds human survival.

Walker grew up in a home environment where the rich heritage of black culture was evident in the community and in the lives of her parents the Reverend Sigismund C. Walker and Marion Dozier Walker. The family moved from Birmingham, Alabama, to New Orleans, Louisiana, when Walker was a young child. Mr. Walker, a Jamaican, was a scholar and preacher, and Mrs. Walker, a pianist and teacher who loved literature and initiated her daughter's interest in poetry and literary classics at an early age. In addition to playing the piano in the home, Mrs. Walker read various poets to her daughter, including Paul Laurence Dunbar, John Greenleaf Whittier, and Shakespeare. As early as age eleven, Margaret Walker was reading the poems of Langston Hughes and Countee Cullen for herself. The budding young poet was also privileged to have in their home her maternal grandmother who told the youngster stories about her female ancestor, Walker's great-grandmother, who had survived the Civil War. This survivor became the model for Walker's protagonist in her only novel, *Jubilee* (1966), originally written as her Ph.D. dissertation for creative writing.

Walker graduated from Northwestern University, Evanston, Illinois, in 1934 with an undergraduate degree in English. She worked on Chicago's North Side for the Works Progress Administration recreation project, developed a friendship with the emerging writer Richard Wright, and worked on her poetry. During those depression years Walker honed her writing skills and published in magazines and journals, including the prestigious *Poetry*. In 1939 she enrolled at the University of Iowa Writers' Workshop for an M.A. degree where she completed the manuscript of poems that became *For My People* (1942). She began university teaching, the vocation that she was destined to share along with writing, in 1941 at Livingstone College in Salisbury, North Carolina, and at West Virginia State College in 1942.

The year 1943 became important in Walker's life for professional and personal reasons. She was invited by the teacher and critic Arthur P. Davis to come to Virginia Union where he taught to read her award-winning poem "For My People," and Walker married Firnist James Alexander in 1943. The first of the couple's four children was born in 1944, and Walker returned to teaching. In 1949 Walker, her husband, and their growing family relocated to Mississippi and Jackson State University, where she taught until her retirement in 1979. The demands of college teaching, raising a family, research spanning thirty years for her novel, earning a Ph.D., publishing scholarly essays, and being an activist in her community seized the time that Walker might have claimed to write more poetry or novels.

Walker's first published book, *For My People* (1942), won the Yale Younger Poet's Award and established her reputation as a significant literary voice. She was the first American black woman honored in such a prestigious national literary competition. Other awards over her long career include a Rosenwald Fellowship, Ford Foundation Fellowship, the Houghton Mifflin Literary Fellowship award for her novel *Jubilee*, the National Endowment for the Humanities senior fellowship for independent study, the National Endowment for the Arts senior fellowship for lifetime achievement and contribution to American literature, the National Book Award for Lifetime Achievement, the W.E.B. Du Bois Award, and numerous honorary doctorate degrees.

For My People, responsive to a depressed economy and to the second-class citizenship of black people, has become a classic in African American literature. Some of its poems voice dissatisfaction at the apathy of the population as the depression wrecks hope for black America in the 1930s. Others, including "Southern Song," "Sorrow Home," and "Delta," criticize the racial violence of the South even as they recognize the psychological bond between the region and the poem's speaker. Historical lineage and the ancestral homeland of West Africa are incorporated in the volume in "Dark Blood." The compact poem "Lineage" celebrates the strength of grandmothers who performed backbreaking farm labor, and its speaker is dismayed that as a modern woman she is less strong than were her foremothers.

The ten poems in the middle section of *For My People* constitute a tribute to the oral tradition in black culture. Acknowledging such a tradition is important for several reasons. Many Harlem Renaissance writers of the 1920s, for example, in embracing modernism and its forms and linguistic practices saw little value in promoting forms or characters from folk culture. However, the poets of the 1930s in Walker's era were in part reactionary to the ideologies of the 1920s writers. Another rationale for Walker's celebration of folk heroes is the immersion in southern folk culture that was hers by her birthright and by personal interest. Therefore, Walker celebrates folk heroes "Bad-Man Stagolee" and "Big

John Henry" but also "Poppa Chicken," "Kissie Lee," and "Mollie Means," the only supernatural figure. Written in ballad rhythm and style, the poems offer different kinds of characters whose deeds have been lifted to heroic stature in the black community through its oral tradition. All of the characters violate convention in some way, and their reputations elevate them, paradoxically, to a respectful infamy preserved through songs, poems, and stories. The characters in their respective behaviors are bigger than life in their daring assertiveness. Big John Henry's extraordinary physical strength and commitment to his work are his distinguishing characteristics. Poppa Chicken's reputation has been earned by his exploits with the ladies. Walker's choices suggest the complex social fabric of the black community.

The title poem "For My People" has become Walker's best known and most frequently anthologized poem. Although she has asserted that it was typewritten in only fifteen minutes and underwent little, if any, revision, it is an encompassing work that conveys a panoramic history of black America. The speaker in each stanza focuses on scenes from the rural or urban black experience. The identified images coalesce to suggest a multidimensional mosaic. In the third stanza, for example, children in rural Alabama backyards are enacting adult occupations through playing preacher and doctor. The sixth stanza spins the reader to overpopulated streets in urban black communities and captures the mix of hope and hopelessness in Chicago, New York, and New Orleans. Structurally, the nine stanzas of "For My People," written in free verse, are each dependent on the final stanza for their completed idea. Using almost no internal punctuation, Walker assembles a rushing tumble of verbs and gerunds designed to convey an urgent call to her people in all places. In a stylistic voice that echoes the cadence of black southern preachers through tight parallel structure and the repetitive phrase of "for my people," Walker demands in the final stanza the presence of another world that might have to be acquired through a bloody peace.

The bloody peace anticipated in *For My People* became the literal context for Walker's second volume, *Prophets for a New Day* (1970), poems that grew out of the civil rights decade. Only "Elegy" and "Ballad of the Hoppy Toad" are unrelated to the 1960s racial strife. Drawing on biblical prophecy, Walker uses analogy to bring together biblical sages with contemporary, life-sacrificing activists of the decade. Predictably, the southern preacher's diction familiar from her childhood and reprised in the rhetorical flourishes of orators like Martin Luther King Jr., Jessie Jackson, and Malcolm X appropriately informs these poems. Although the volume focuses on 1960s leaders, Walker also evokes the presence of earlier revolutionaries such as Nat Turner, Gabriel Prosser, Denmark Vesey, and others who had resisted oppression but whose names are often forgotten. In "At the Lincoln Monument in Washington August 28, 1963," the legendary Moses leading his people to the Promised Land represents Dr. King, but his name is not mentioned. Andy Goodman, Michael Schwerner, and James Chaney, the three young civil rights workers murdered in Mississippi, are identified in a poem named for them. Other leaders named or obliquely referenced include Malcolm X, Medgar Evers, Reverend Ralph Abernathy, and Dr. Benjamin Mays. As she had done in *For My People*, Walker recognizes the love and reverence for the South as one's spiritual homeland but also its presence as a site of physical and spiritual oppressiveness.

Walker's next significant volume was the collected edition of her previously published work and thirty new poems titled *This Is My Century: New and Collected Poems* (1989). Walker's knowledge, respect, and reverence for history predominate in the new poems. She taps mythology and ancient history as background for the history of black existence in the new world, and she recognizes other figures whose ideas have had world impact. The poems are both introspective and retrospective meditations as the poet takes personal authority to reflect on the past several hundred years.

The title poem, "This Is My Century/Black Synthesis of Time," consists of five parts. Walker purports that black mankind has the spirit of the ancient gods of Africa. Cinque, the captured African whose leadership directed the mutiny aboard the *Amistad*, and whose freedom was secured in the Supreme Court by the defense of former President John Quincy Adams, is singled out in part five as a magnificent man endowed by the gods to rule. "Giants of My Century" recognizes world-class transformers of knowledge including Albert Einstein, Sigmund Freud, Karl Marx, Søren Kierkegaard, and W.E.B. Du Bois. "Five Black Men . . . And Ten Will Save the City" cast Frederick Douglass, Du Bois, Marcus Garvey, and Malcolm X as brothers of freedom across the spectrum of history. In "On Youth and Age II," less formal in diction and tone than the above poems, Walker criticizes the destructive forces in American culture—poor parenting and housing, drugs, violent cartoons—and concludes that her century needs intensive care. Most of the remaining poems in the volume, especially "Old Age," "I Hear a Rumbling," "Dies Irae," and "The Telly Boob-Tube on the Idiot Box," are clarion calls to arouse consciousness of the culture's deterioration. The volume overall is not suffused with a hopeless vision as "Solace" makes clear, but Walker's observations and experiences in her world speak to her of the dire necessity for its change.

By the time of her death, Walker's fiction, nonfiction, and poetry had made her a legend in her own time. Among many notable recognitions extended to her are these: Jackson State University has acknowledged Walker's decades of service on its campus with the Margaret Walker Alexander National Research Center. Her work has become the subject of scholarly conferences, book chapters, dissertations, and books. An educational video, *For My People: The Life and Writing of Margaret Walker* (1998), produced and directed by Judith McCray, Juneteenth Productions, documents Walker's literary significance. Moreover, before her death, the city had renamed the street of her residence in her honor, and the governor of Mississippi had proclaimed "Margaret Walker Alexander Day" in the state.

POETRY

For My People. New Haven, CT: Yale University Press, 1942.
Prophets for a New Day. Detroit: Broadside Press, 1970.
October Journey. Detroit: Broadside Press, 1973.
This Is My Century: New and Collected Poems. Athens: University of Georgia Press, 1989.

REFERENCES

Carmichael, Jacqueline Miller. *Trumpeting a Fiery Sound. History and Folklore in Margaret Walker's Jubilee*. Athens: University of Georgia Press, 1998.
Collier, Eugenia. "Fields Watered with Blood: Myth and Ritual in the Poetry of Margaret Walker." In *Black Women Writers (1950–1980): A Critical Evaluation*. Ed. Mari Evans, New York: Anchor Books, 1984. 499–510.
Graham, Maryemma, ed. *Fields Watered with Blood*. Athens: University of Georgia Press, 2001.
Pettis, Joyce. "Margaret Walker." In *Dictionary of Literary Biography*. Vol. 76. Detroit: Gale Research, 1988. 173–81.
———. "Margaret Walker: Black Woman Writer of the South." In *Southern Women Writers: The New Generation*. Ed. Tonette Bond Inge. Tuscaloosa: University of Alabama Press, 1990. 9–19.
Traylor, Eleanor. "Music as Theme: The Blues Mode in the Works of Margaret Walker." In *Black Women Writers (1950–1980): A Critical Evaluation*. Ed. Mari Evans. New York: Anchor Books, 1984. 511–25.
Walker, Margaret. *How I Wrote Jubilee and Other Essays on Life and Literature*. New York: Feminist Press, 1990.
———. *On Being Female, Black and Free*. Nashville: University of Tennessee Press, 1997.

PHILLIS WHEATLEY

(1753–1784)

Phillis Wheatley
Credit: Atlanta University Center, Robert W. Woodruff Library

Wheatley was the first poet of African descent in the American colonies to have a book of poems published, although *Poems on Various Subjects, Religious and Moral* was published in London in 1773. Wheatley was enslaved in Boston when she prepared her manuscript, but failing to find a publisher in Boston, her owners sent her to London for finalizing publication matters and for her asthma treatment. By Wheatley's death at age thirty-one, she had lived through the Revolutionary War, seen Boston occupied by British troops, met famous people abroad, and maintained correspondence with notable persons both in Europe and on American soil. In spite of Thomas Jefferson's statement that religion had produced the woman but no poet, her poetry was known in England, in the northeastern colonies, and in Charleston, South Carolina. She had published forty-six poems but had written several more. In short, she had accomplished a noteworthy body of work given the restraints that women endured during her era and the generally poor state of her health. Possibly no predictability indices could have anticipated that Phillis Wheatley would know so much fame before she died.

Wheatley was believed born around 1753 in West Africa. She was captured and enslaved about five or six years of age, and arrived in the American colonies on a ship also named *Phillis* in 1761. John Wheatley, a well-to-do Bostonian and owner of slaves, purchased her in 1761 to be trained as a domestic worker for his wife Susannah Wheatley. John Wheatley's affluence accrued from his ownership of residential real estate, warehouses, and a wholesale business. The Wheatleys were members of the New South Congregational Church, and Mrs. Wheatley participated in the work of religious mission by accommodating ministers in their home in the center of Boston's business activities on King Street and by donating funds to their mission work. Phillis attended New South Congregational Church with the Wheatleys and accepted its teachings of traditional Christianity. However, in August 1771, Phillis became a member of the Congregationalist Old South Church, a different institution from the family's sanctuary.

Phillis, who was given her name by the Wheatleys, was of delicate shape and was ill when she was purchased. One of the Wheatleys' twin eighteen-year-old daughters, Mary, began to teach the young child literature and theology and probably English as well. Recognizing Phillis's natural intellectual gifts, the family expanded her education. She was taught to read and write English and Latin, and her school subjects increased to include geography, astrology, and the Greek and Latin classics of Virgil, Ovid, Terence, and Homer. Perhaps more important for the poetic style Phillis would later adopt, her classes also included the British writers John Milton, John Dryden, and Alexander Pope. Her education was as good as that of most Boston women of the period.

The Wheatleys' social position and their interaction with important personalities in their home seemingly provided a predominantly Christian context through which Wheatley viewed herself in relation to Boston and the world. Many of her poems and extant letters suggest her knowledge of and intellectual involvement with current events and her intimate connection with the Wheatleys.

Wheatley was given light housework or, if inclined to write on a particular day, absolved of her chores. Contact was restricted between her and the other slaves. Her writing was encouraged and supported by Susanna Wheatley, who made contacts for the young writer and provided monetary backing. This support also took the form of allowing Wheatley to have heat and light in her room.

Scholars have documented a broad outline of Wheatley's publishing and interests that motivated some of her writing through her poems, personal correspondence, and proposals for her books of poems, though only one book appeared. "On Messrs. Hussey and Coffin" was published in the Rhode Island *Newport Mercury* on December 21, 1767. Based on a survivor story on the seas, it was Phillis's first published poem at age fourteen. Her poem to the students at Harvard College in 1767, "To the University of Cambridge in New England," indicates the extent to which she valued Christian instruction. In general, the poem recognizes the mental expansion that comes with study but reminds students of the power and presence of evil and charges them to avoid it. The most intriguing lines of the poem are its opening and closing, which reference Africa. Wheatley seems unambiguously to accept the prevailing view of white colonial America that Africa was a "land of errors and Egyptian gloom" from which she had been delivered. In reminding students of avoiding sin, however, Wheatley refers to herself as an *Ethiop*, the term for Ethiopian, which in the period generally referred to Africa. The term, used objectively in the poem, thus seems contradictory to the view of Africa in the first stanza as a "dark abode." Wheatley's elegy "On the death of the Rev. Mr. George Whitefield. 1770," a major figure in the religious movement known as the Great Awakening, was a boon to her emerging reputation as the slave who wrote poetry.

In 1773, Phillis carried her manuscript for a book of poems as she traveled to England on the family-owned, three-masted schooner named *London Packet* with the Wheatley's son Nathaniel, who had bought part of the family business. They left Boston on May 8 and arrived in London on June 17. The captain of the schooner, Robert Calef, had negotiated the acceptance of Wheatley's poems for publication by a London bookseller, Archibald Bell, whose specialty was religious books. Dedicating the book to the countess of Huntingdon, for whom Reverend Whitefield had been chaplain, increased the volume's significance. The side profile of Phillis Wheatley positioned at a writing desk with an alert but thoughtful facial expression that was printed on the frontispiece of her *Poems on Various Subjects* was placed there at the request of the countess. Modern readers can be grateful for this request, since this engraving is the only available image of Wheatley.

Wheatley returned to Boston before her book was published because news of Mrs. Wheatley's severe illness reached her. Phillis was scheduled to add the countess to the list of interesting and important people she had met, but Mrs. Wheatley's condition prevented her from meeting the countess to whom her book was dedicated. Phillis sailed for Boston in July and arrived on September 13. *Poems on Various Subjects* appeared in early September, was for sale in London, and was reviewed in various publications in England and in Scotland. Phillis had to wait until January of the following year to see her book. Meanwhile, her liberation from slavery by the Wheatleys occurred during this period, sometime between her return from London and October 18, 1773.

Poems on Various Subjects (1773) included thirty-eight titles, of which fourteen were elegies, or meditations on death, some occasional poems, and several poems to important people such as George Washington. Beginning a practice that persisted in published work by black Americans, it also had at its beginning signed statements attesting to the authenticity of the work by the identified writer.

Wheatley's work is considered by scholars to be as good as any other poetry being written in the colonies during the time she was writing. It illustrates the cultural and literary dependency on British models that marked the genres of American literature in one form or another until almost the middle of the nineteenth century. The poetic language of Wheatley's work, its rhyming patterns, its appeal to the muses, and allusions to mythology mark its neoclassical spirit and its stylistic indebtedness to British poetry, especially the work of Alexander Pope. Although Wheatley is applauded for writing poetry, modern sentiment about her work has questioned her apparent failure to identify with and to write about the oppression of slavery. Some contemporary scholars have identified coded language or the potential of irony in her work and have interpreted these as evidence of a subversive identification with or statement on oppression. Wheatley's letters reveal, however, that she had the sensibilities of her era and of those with whom she was in constant contact, namely, well-to-do whites who placed heavy emphasis on Christianity. Having been enslaved at such an early age, her conditioning was religious and educational. The conditioning seems clearly revealed in her brief eight-line poem "On Being Brought from Africa to America," with its enigmatic lines from which some readers seem compelled to extrapolate ironic and satiric intent. Similar to her sentiments in the poem to Harvard College students, "To the University of Cambridge, in New England," however, Wheatley says in "On Being Brought" that mercy delivered her from a non-Christian land and taught her about a Savior who had been unknown to her. For those who disdain blackness, equating it with evil, she counters that "*Negroes*, black as *Cain*" can undergo redemption and be admitted to heaven. This position seems merely reflective of her religious grounding and nothing more.

Wheatley's identity as a Christian woman seems to have been generally known in her community. Her letters contain two references to an invitation to return to Africa as a missionary, offers that she seemed to cherish but nevertheless declined. The choice of the countess of Huntingdon, in fact, in the dedication was connected to that lady's religious and evangelical ties.

The decade of the 1770s proved as full of possibilities for Phillis Wheatley as had the 1760s. In 1773, the Wheatleys granted her freedom, but apparently Phillis remained in the Wheatley household as a free woman. Susanna Wheatley died in March 1774. Phillis, along with the Wheatleys, endured dislocation from the home during the British occupation of Boston. Her famous poem to George Washington, whom she visited in 1776 in Cambridge, was sent from Providence in October 1775. Between December 1774 and 1784, apparently Phillis did not publish. Both Mr. Wheatley and his daughter Mary died in 1778. In these early post–Revolutionary War years, extant correspondence and book proposals published in Boston journals in 1779 and 1784 establish that Phillis clearly intended to publish a second book of poems. However, no volume was forthcoming, and Phillis married John Peters on April 1, 1778.

Little information has been unearthed about John Peters, but it is known that he was a free man and that his financial existence was precarious. In the early 1780s they lived north of Boston in Wilmington, Massachusetts. Phillis's health had always been delicate, and the trials of childbirth and poverty in her marriage are thought to have contributed to her deteriorating health. Three children were born to them, the last dying quickly enough to be buried along with Phillis. The other two children also did not survive their mother. In less than seven years after marrying John Peters, Wheatley was dead. Local papers carried notice of her funeral in Boston and identified her, according to the scholar Julian Mason, as "known to the literary world by her celebrated miscellaneous poems."

POETRY

Poems on Various Subjects, Religious and Moral. London: A. Bell, Bookseller, Aldgate, 1773.

REFERENCES

Bassard, Katherine Clay. *Spiritual Interrogations: Culture, Gender, and Community in Early African American Women's Writing*. Princeton, NJ: Princeton University Press, 1999.

Mason, Julian. *The Poems of Phillis Wheatley*. Chapel Hill: University of North Carolina Press, 1989.

Reising, Russell J. *Loose Ends: Closure and Crisis in the American Social Text*. Durham, NC: Duke University Press, 1996.

Richmond, Merle A. *Bid the Vassal Soar: Interpretative Essays on the Life and Poetry of Phillis Wheatley and George Moses Horton*. Washington, DC: Howard University Press, 1974.

Robinson, William. *Critical Essays on Phillis Wheatley*. Boston: G.K. Hall, 1982.

———. Phillis Wheatley: A Bio-Bibliography. Boston: G.K. Hall, 1981.

———. Phillis Wheatley and Her Writings. New York: Garland, 1984.

JAY WRIGHT

(1935–)

Jay Wright
Credit: Louisiana State University Press
Photo credit: D. Usner

W right's detailed study of literature, anthropology and the history of African cultures provides a rich, multitextured background for his poetry. In fact, he is frequently referred to as a learned poet and regarded as one of the most original, remarkable, and powerful African American poets currently writing. In spite of such sterling attributes, Wright's is neither a household name nor a compelling choice for classroom study.

Wright was born to Leona Dailey and Mercer Murphy Wright in Albuquerque, New Mexico. His mother's home was in Virginia, and his father, a mechanic and jitney driver, had been born in Santa Rosa, New Mexico. His parents raised Wright in New Mexico, where he began school in Albuquerque. However, he completed high school in San Pedro, California.

Wright earned a B.A. degree in 1961 from the University of California at Berkeley after he had played semiprofessional baseball and served in the army. After his undergraduate degree, he relocated to New York and briefly attended Union Theological Seminary. He began work on his M.A. degree at Rutgers University and eventually completed all requirements for a Ph.D., except for writing the dissertation. During this period Wright spent time in New York in Greenwich Village where he encountered the distinctive literary traditions of the Beat Generation. Between 1971 and 1973 Wright was a Hodder Fellow at Princeton University and the Joseph Compton Creative Writing Fellow at Dundee University in Scotland. Between 1973 and 1978, he was in New Hampshire, and from 1975 to 1979 he was a professor at Yale University.

The complexity and richness of Wright's poetry is indebted in part to his fertile engagement of different poetic traditions. The work and traditions of Caribbean novelist and poet Wilson Harris, Cuban poet Nicolás Guillén, and Alejo Carpentier have influenced Wright's vision of poetry as well as Dante's *Commedia*, Benjamin Banneker's *Letters to Thomas Jefferson*, and the jazz of Albert Ayler and John Coltrane. Goethe and the Nigerian writer Wole Soyinka also figure prominently in Wright's poems because they are both models and providers of myth. Exercising his full cultural inheritance, Wright's work also shows an affinity with the mainstream modernist poets Hart Crane, T.S. Eliot, Ezra Pound, and Louis Zukofsky and African Americans Melvin Tolson, Michael Harper, and Robert Hayden. The focus of the latter two on African American history as a fecund terrain for poetry makes their work attractive to Wright. In fact, Wright's "Crispus Attucks" and "W.E.B. Du Bois at Harvard" show the influence of Robert Hayden, for whom Wright has offered superior praise.

The complexity of Wright's poetry is traceable to his near obsession with the relationship between literature, myth, and history; for him the poet is both artist and historian. His poetry crisscrosses various cultural traditions as he seeks to incorporate the tension between myth and history. In fact, as Vera Kutzinski writing on Wright has said, "[M]yth is rendered historical and the historical mythical." ("The Descent of Nommo" 106). Wright's use of Europe, Africa, and the Americas as geographical sites in his work reflects his interest in myth and history and interactions between cultures. America in Wright's work is used as a distinct geography through its interchanging cultures rather than with the imperialistic association that users imply when they substitute "America" for the "United States." The complexity of some of Wright's poetry results from his explorations of European and New World history and mythology and African religion. The poetry is informed by the cosmologies of African peoples including the Dogon, Bambara, and Akan and by Ifa divination. Wright is able to integrate the diverseness of these traditions into a complex historical vision. In language use, he can also be complicated because he uses different grammars as well.

In an interview with *Callaloo* editor Charles Rowell, Wright bristles at the statement that some readers find his work inaccessible. He suggests that the complexity of his work is merely equal to the multicultural history and experiences of its readers. That Wright's readers will need assistance identifying many of his allusions, images, and symbols, however, is apparent in the request from publishers that he provide a glossary or note page at the end of his books. In the notes to *Dimensions of History* (1976), Wright admits that nearly every line derives from a historical event or its consequences.

Wright has suggested that readers of his poetry should follow the order below rather than the publication chronology for his books appearing through 1980: *The Homecoming Singer, Soothsayers and Omens, Explications/Interpretations, Dimensions of History,* and *The Double Invention of Komo.* His request suggests his awareness of an overarching design or unity to his work. Wright's attention to concept and unity is also apparent in his meticulous attention to arranging the poems that he reads to an audience and to his arrangement of poems within a respective book.

The primary subjects of Wright's poetry are religion, myth, and history. Wright equates being labeled as a religious poet with making him African. He finds that traditional African societies are moral, spiritual, and metaphysical. Religion is distinctly a subject in "Wednesday Night

Prayer Meeting" and "Collection Time" in *Death as History*; in "Sources," section four of *Soothsayers and Omens*; and in *Dimensions of History*. History in Wright's poetry is global. He uses it as both a unifying and a thematic device. Family relationships, travel, and exile rank second in the frequency of their appearance in Wright's work. He explores his primary and secondary subjects through images, motifs, and symbols such as song, dance, birds, masks, eggs, seeds, and doubling.

Wright considers his work *Death as History* "a pamphlet of poems" rather than a book. The publication resulted from a planned tour at black southern schools, an initiative of the Woodrow Wilson National Endowment for the Arts program. The press produced a limited run of 200 copies. From a chapbook, Wright's next book, *The Homecoming Singer* (1971), was picked up by a press whose significance in the literary world has been recognized. Corinth Books, according to critic Robert Stepto, published "avant-garde" poets of the 1960s that included numerous mainstream poets, including John Ashbery, Allen Ginsberg, and Jack Kerouac, but also the African Americans LeRoi Jones (later Amiri Baraka), Al Young, and Jay Wright. The poets published by Corinth did not comprise a philosophically unified group, but in their individual ways they have helped to shape and influence important traditions in African American (and American) poetry.

The lyrical intensity of *Death as History* is followed by an increasingly complex foray into mythology and history in the subsequent volumes. *The Homecoming Singer* involves the interplay between history and mythology less forcefully than the later books. It relies on autobiographical elements, and the persona is reflective and journeying away from the familiar. Perhaps one of the most obviously autobiographical poems is "A Non-Birthday Poem for My Father," but Wright's interest in history and mythology is nevertheless apparent. The persona has his "ritualistic materials" and his life and art. The father's numbers fit "in the proper mythological pattern." Nevertheless, the father's life is too large, too capable of being unknown, to fit a poem. The father in the poem chooses a life of action rather than the quiet profession that his physical appearance might have led him to have. Seeking a different experience, however, he leaves the hills of New Mexico and anchors himself in San Pedro, California. Life remains difficult, however, as confirmed in the poem by "stuck in credit unions, doing two shifts." Perhaps anticipating his own defeat, the father anticipates that his son will achieve a dream by becoming a doctor. The son, however, looks for the father in a past that the father refuses to return to. Thus the repenting for lost history and family that might occur cannot happen.

The larger questions implied in "A Non-Birthday Poem," questions of displacement and of connecting to a little-known heritage, inform the title poem of the volume, "The Homecoming Singer." First, the word *homecoming* is doubly vested to mean a return to one's physical residence and to mean a return to one's cultural home as well. Both "A Non-Birthday Poem" and "The Homecoming Singer" suggest that the South offers a significant component of that heritage. The father in the former poem took to those "new friends [who] came up out of the south." In "Singer," the persona, arriving in Nashville, Tennessee, is welcomed home, albeit in a dream, by a singer who comes to his room and "welcomes the displaced." "An Invitation to Madison County," concerning the persona's travel to Tougaloo and Jackson, Mississippi, is focused by the same themes, inhabiting a culture that is at once familiar but also alien. Thus, psychological and physical journeys become structural metaphors on which Wright can begin to investigate overwhelming questions of history, myth, ritual, and literature.

Soothsayers and Omens and *Dimensions of History* involve individual development. The first three sections of *Soothsayers* focus on family relationships, while Part IV consists entirely of the African myth on which the later *The Double Invention of Komo* is based. Although all of Wright's poems are grounded in personal experience, the individual journey metamorphoses into a broader and inclusive journey. The design of *Soothsayers and Omens* illustrates Wright's meticulous plotting out of its parts, as his subsequent volumes will do. Interestingly, given Wright's emphasis on history and heritage, he uses the city as a focal point in several poems. "Benjamin Banneker Helps to Build a City" and "Benjamin Banneker Sends His Almanac to Thomas Jefferson," both in *Soothsayers and Omens*, are significant in Wright's work for their emphasis on the past and for illustrating America's transition from a colonial presence to autonomous nationhood. Banneker is representative of eighteenth-century black self-inventiveness not only as a self-taught astronomer but also as a planner of the city of Washington, the site that symbolically conveys both nationhood and power. The Banneker poems also convey Wright's comprehensive vision of history into an American context and advance the idea that black African Americans have striven to participate in all historical processes. Wright's history examines basic human connections across barriers of time. The central focus of *Soothsayers* seems to be the individual effort to place personal experience within a broader cultural home. The book concludes with references to the view of the Dogon in interpreting the world.

Progressively, *Dimensions of History* investigates a cultural history. Unlimited by African American cultural history, the poems also include references to Spain's forays into Mexico and numerous other geographical and historical references.

In his interview with Wright in *Callaloo*, Rowell praises Wright's poems as "living aesthetic creations that pull us to their centers." (15). The poet responds that he works to make his poems engage his reader, to draw the reader into the experience through various strategies. Wright has a clear concept of how he wants his work to reflect multiple cultural traditions and to be anchored by investigations of religion and history.

Wright's reputation rests on the complex, evocative work he has published since 1971. The publication of *Transfigurations* (2000), however, in 619 pages has the potential for affecting Wright's reputation in a grand manner. It brings together all of the poet's previously published full-length collections, in chronological order, and includes new poems. The totality of this major edition is as staggering as Wright's singly published volumes have been daunting. The sheer magnitude of the work invites comparison, Rochelle Ratner declares in *Library Journal*, to "the mythopoetic scope of [Ezra] Pound's *Cantos*, [Robert] Olson's *Maximus*, or the work of Robert Duncan" (147).

Although Wright has not been widely read, several prestigious awards recognize his work. They include a Rockefeller Brothers Theological Fellowship, a grant from the National Endowment for the Arts, an Ingram Merrill Foundation Award, a Guggenheim Fellowship, an American Academy and Institute of Arts and Letters Literary Award, an Oscar Williams and Gene Derwood Award, and a MacArthur Foundation Fellowship. In 1996 Wright was named the recipient of the 62nd Fellowship of The Academy of American Poets for distinguished poetic achievement, an award with a monetary value of $20,000.

POETRY

Death as History. Millbrook, NY: Kriya Press, 1967. (Out of Print)
The Homecoming Singer. New York: Corinth Books, 1971. (Out of Print)
Dimensions of History. Santa Cruz, CA: Kayak, 1976. (Out of Print)
Soothsayers and Omens. New York: Seven Woods Press, 1976. (Out of Print)
The Double Invention of Komo. Austin: University of Texas Press, 1980. (Out of Print)
Explications/Interpretations. Callaloo Poetry Series. Lexington: University of Kentucky Press, 1984. (Out of Print)
Elaine's Book. Charlottesville: University Press of Virginia, 1986. (Out of Print)
Selected Poems of Jay Wright. Princeton, NJ: Princeton University Press, 1987. (Out of Print)
Boleros. Princeton, NJ: Princeton University Press, 1991. (Out of Print)
Transfigurations: Collected Poems. Baton Rouge: Louisiana University Press, 2000.

REFERENCES

Barrax, Gerald. "The Early Poetry of Jay Wright." *Callaloo* 6.3 (Fall 1983): 85–102.

Kutzinski, Vera M. *Against the American Grain: Myth and History in William Carlos Williams, Jay Wright, and Nicolás Guillén.* Baltimore: Johns Hopkins University Press, 1987.

———. "The Descent of Nommo: Literacy as Method in Jay Wright's 'Benjamin Banneker Helps to Build a City.' " *Callaloo* 6.3 (Fall 1983): 103–119.

Ratner, Rochelle. "Jay Wright's *Transfigurations.*" *Library Journal*, December 20, 2000. 147.

Richard, Phillip M. "Jay Wright." *In Dictionary of Literary Biography.* Vol. 41. Ed. Trudier Harris and Thadious Davis, Detroit: Gale Research, 1985. 350–60.

Rowell, Charles H. " 'The Unraveling of the Egg': An Interview with Jay Wright." *Callaloo* 6.3 (Fall 1983): 3–15.

Stepto, Robert B. "After Modernism, After Hibernation: Michael Harper, Robert Hayden, and Jay Wright." In *Chant of Saints: A Gathering of Afro-American Literature, Arts, and Scholarship.* Ed. Michael Harper and Robert B. Stepto. Urbana: University of Illinois Press, 1979. 470–86.

———, ed. "Introduction." *Selected Poems of Jay Wright.* Princeton, NJ: Princeton University Press, 1987. ix–xv.

AL YOUNG

(1939–   )

Al Young
Credit: University of California Press

Al Young, born Albert James Young, has been establishing a significant niche for himself in African American literary arts since the 1960s, his creativity sprawling among music, professional screenwriting in Hollywood, editing, fiction, and poetry. He has written five well-received novels and four volumes of poetry. Along with fellow black novelist, poet, and essayist Ishmael Reed, in 1972 Young cofounded *Yardbird Reader*, a magazine that reflected the need for promising multicultural writers to have publication opportunities. After *Yardbird* ceased publication in 1976, Young and Reed established *Quilt*, a magazine begun with a similar mission in 1981. Young is credited with originating a hybrid genre called the musical memoir, a form where selected reminiscences sparkle against a backdrop of songs meaningful to the author. Young has written three of these. His joy in music and musicians is apparent as well in *Mingus-Mingus: Two Memoirs*, written with journalist Janet Coleman. This memoir is also structurally novel since Young and Coleman each pen their different reminiscences about the jazzman Charles Mingus. Music is indeed the flourishing presence against which Young evokes his life, and it is the muse that elicits and shapes much of his poetry.

Young was born in Ocean Springs, Mississippi, where he lived for a few years before his parents, Albert James and Mary Campbell Young, moved to Detroit, Michigan, the first of several quixotic relocations. The family moved with some frequency, settling temporarily in New Orleans, Pennsylvania, and Chicago. By age twelve, Young estimates he had attended about twelve schools. Young's father, Albert James, was an amateur musician and autoworker, but the son and father were separated at an early age.

Young grew up loving to read and to experience active characters in his head. He began writing at age six or seven and by age nine or ten was writing short science fiction. His reading was varied but included *Adventures of Huckleberry Finn* and *Adventures of Tom Sawyer*; his parents read comic strips or stories to him. As a college student at the University of Michigan between 1957 and 1961, Young was an anomaly as a Spanish major, but this academic focus merely reflected the interest he'd had in language all of his life. Young moved to San Francisco in 1961, convinced that its specific atmosphere would enhance his creativity. He received his B.A. degree from a different institution, the University of California, Berkeley, in 1969.

Young was as drawn to music as he was to literature and considered a career in music. In fact, he became a freelance musician, singing and playing guitar and flute professionally between 1957 and 1964 and also during this period working as a disc jockey at KJAZ-FM in Alameda, California. Young also turned to teaching and became a writing instructor in San Francisco in 1961. He married Arline June Belch, a freelance artist, in 1963, and the couple had a son, Michael James.

Young's wide interests are reflected throughout his writing, and his influences have been vast and various. When he frequented the home of his grandparents in Mississippi, they engaged in storytelling at night, a practice that Young loved. This early exposure fueled his interest in the black oral traditions of storytelling. Young also has cited numerous literary traditions among his many influences, for example, the T'ang dynasty Chinese poet Li Po and the prose writer Kenneth Patchen. Young also includes novelists John Steinbeck and Jack Kerouac, the dramatist William Saroyan, poet Langston Hughes, the detective novelist Chester Himes, the Cuban poet Nicolás Guillén, and the black writer from the Belgian Congo Rená Moran. The work *Studs Lonigan* (1935) by James T. Farrell provided the example in fiction that the working class and people like those whom Young knew could also be subjects in literature.

Young's poetry has been praised for its representation of colloquial language, for revealing the poet's interior emotions, and for its vivid recall of the past. African American music, particularly the blues and jazz, often functions as the metaphoric presence through which Young explores and exposes the past. His interest in music stems from his love of its creative potential, specifically its way of uniting a community by lyrically capturing its pains, joys, and spirituality. Young also envisions himself as a working-class writer whose vision reflects a blues aesthetic. Young's poetry illustrates the hand of a rigorous craftsman who labors to produce the art but keeps that labor well concealed.

Young's first published volume of poetry, *Dance* (1969), illustrates his near obsession with music and dance. The opening selection, "Dance for Militant Dilettantes," one of the poet's most admired poems, establishes dance as a structuring metaphor for the life experiences poetically detailed in the volume. Specifically, the poem softly satirizes the militant poetry of the 1960s, as is evident in the lines "they don't want no bourgeoise woogie." They want a poet who can preach racial violence and ink his poem in red bood, the speaker says. Having established in this comic poem the kind of poet that is desired in the late 1960s, Young moves swiftly in the other direction, using the metaphor of dance to identify himself with working-class people's ordinary lives. In "Dancing Day to Day," for example, the speaker lives in a multicultural neighborhood of mundane life activities like working, cutting lawns, or watching television. In "A Dance for Ma Rainey," one of the classic blues performers from the 1920s, the speaker has a blues that joins him not only with the famous singer but also with emptiness "first felt by some stolen delta nigger." The majority of poems in the volume have the word *dance* in their titles. Overall, the volume attempts to explain the state of America at the end of the decade and the poet's stance in relationship to his country.

The Song Turning Back into Itself (1971) reflects Young's belief in the cyclical theory of history and evolution. He fits music into this theory as a result of listening to 1960s black popular music and noting its relationship to folk sources. Some progressively circular movement is apparent in the seven poems, each titled "The Song Turning Back into Itself." The first one, highly imagistic, is structured by the speaker's coming into an awareness of a self who without intervention would have experienced a series of mishaps. The second poem advocates human unity through love that is graced with music. Young's memories of Ocean Springs, Mississippi, his birth community located near Biloxi, shape the third poem of the series. The poem's speaker suggests that Ocean Springs is a blues community with its train tooting "like a big ass blues man." The good memories exist alongside the bad through positive images of a small wooden house and of the speaker's mother, a woman with the sun in her voice. With music a consistent motif in the poems, "The Song Turning Back into Itself 4" offers the idea that love, music, and peace are proper responses and antidotes to diffusing hate. In poem five, the power of song can supplant old images with new ones. In poem six, the soul reaches out but is not always recognizable. The self is part of everything but, paradoxically, of nothing as well. The answer lies in communion with others. Poem seven is the poem of the soul's liberation, also graced by song.

The collection *Geography of the Near Past* (1976) introduces O.O. Gabugah, a fictional alter ego for the poet who also reappears in Young's third musical memoir, *Things Ain't What They Used to Be*. This alter ego allows the poet to produce a different and more critical voice. Additionally, the volume contains lyrical poems on Young's wife and some of his friends, but it also offers contrasting poems about loss, hope, and personal destructiveness. The volume shows the broadening growth of the poet's vision.

Young's work has been recognized by numerous awards. He won the Wallace E. Stegner fellowship in creative writing at Stanford University for 1966–1967 and a National Endowment for the Arts grants in 1968,

1969, and 1975. *Dancing* won the Joseph Henry Jackson Award of the San Francisco Foundation. For 1969–1970, he won the National Arts Council awards for poetry and editing, and in 1973, he received the California Association of Teachers of English special award. These were followed by a Guggenheim Memorial Foundation Fellowship in 1974, a Pushcart Prize in 1980, the New York Times Outstanding Book of the Year Citation also in 1980, and the Before Columbus Foundation Award in 1982.

POETRY

Dancing. New York: Corinth Books, 1969. (Out of Print)
The Song Turning Back into Itself. New York: Holt, 1971. (Out of Print)
Geography of the Near Past. New York: Holt, 1976. (Out of Print)
The Blues Don't Change: New and Selected Poems. Baton Rouge: Louisiana State
     University Press, 1982.
Heaven: Collected Poems 1958–1988. Berkeley: Creative Arts Book Company, 1989.

MUSICAL MEMOIRS

Bodies and Souls. San Francisco: Creative Arts Book Company, 1981.
Kinds of Blue. San Francisco: Creative Arts Book Company, 1984.
Drowning in the Sea of Love. Hopewell, NJ: Ecco Press, 1995.

ANTHOLOGY

(With James Hicks, James D. Houston, and Maxine Hong Kingston). *The Literature
     of California: Native American Beginnings to 1945*. Vol. 1. Berkeley: Univer-
     sity of California Press, 2000.

REFERENCES

Chirico, Miriam M. "Al Young." In *Oxford Companion to African American Liter-
     ature*. Ed. William L. Andrews, Frances Smith Foster, and Trudier Harris.
     New York: Oxford University Press, 1997. 798–99.
Draper, James P., ed. *Black Literature Criticism*. Vol. 3. Detroit: Gale Research,
     1992. 2032–47.
Mackey, Nathaniel. "Interview with Al Young." *MELUS: The Journal of Multi-
     Ethnic Literature of the United States* 5 (Winter 1978): 32–51.
O'Brien, John. *Interviews with Black Writers*. New York: Liveright, 1973.

SELECTED ANTHOLOGIES

Adoff, Arnold, ed. *Black Out Loud: An Anthology of Modern Poems by Black Americans*. New York: Macmillan, 1970.

———. *Celebrations: A New Anthology of Black American Poetry*. Chicago: Follett, 1977.

———. *The Poetry of Black America: An Anthology of the 20th Century*. New York: Harper & Row, 1973.

Barksdale, Richard, and Keneth Kinnamon, eds. *Black Writers of America*. New York: Macmillan, 1972.

Bell, Bernard, ed. *Modern and Contemporary Afro-American Poetry*. Boston: Allyn & Bacon, 1972.

Brooks, Gwendolyn, ed. *A Broadside Treasury*. Detroit: Broadside Press, 1971.

Brown, Patricia L., Don L. Lee, and Francis Ward, eds. *To Gwen with Love: An Anthology Dedicated to Gwendolyn Brooks*. Chicago: Johnson, 1971.

Chapman, Abraham, ed. *Black Voices: An Anthology of Afro-American Literature*. New York: Mentor, 1968.

Cullen, Countee, ed. *Caroling Dusk: An Anthology of Verse by Negro Poets*. New York: Harper, 1927.

Davis, Arthur P., J. Saunders Redding, and Joyce Ann Joyce, eds. *The New Cavalcade: African American Writing from 1760 to the Present*. Vol. 1. Washington, DC: Howard University Press, 1991.

Donalson, Melvin, ed. *Cornerstones: An Anthology of African American Literature*. New York: St. Martin's Press, 1996.

Gates, Henry Louis, and Nellie Y. McKay, eds. *The Norton Anthology of American Literature*. New York: W.W. Norton, 1997.

Gilbert, Derrick I.M. (a.k.a. D-Knowledge), ed. *Catch the Fire: A Cross-Generational Anthology of Contemporary African American Poetry*. New York: Riverhead Books, 1998.

Gilyard, E. Keith, ed. *Spirit and Flame: An Anthology of Contemporary African American Poetry*. New York: Syracuse University Press, 1997.

Harper, Michael, and Anthony Walton, eds. *The Vintage Book of African American Poetry*. New York: Vintage, 2000.

Honey, Maureen, ed. *Shadowed Dreams: Women's Poetry of the Harlem Renaissance*. New Brunswick, NJ: Rutgers University Press, 1989.

Jones, LeRoi, and Larry Neal, eds. *Black Fire: An Anthology of Afro-American Writing*. New York: William Morrow, 1968.

Komunyakaa, Yusef, and Sasha Feinstein, eds. *The Jazz Poetry Anthology*. Bloomington: Indiana University Press, 1991.

———. *The Second Set. The Jazz Poetry Anthology*. Vol 2. Bloomington: Indiana University Press, 1996.

Long, Richard, and Eugenia Collier, eds. *Afro-American Writing: An Anthology of Prose and Poetry*. University Park: Pennsylvania State University Press, 1985.

Major, Clarence, ed. *The Garden Thrives: Twentieth-Century African-American Poetry*. New York: HarperPerennial, 1996.

Miller, David Adam, ed. *Dice or Black Bones: Black Voices of the Seventies*. New York: Houghton Mifflin, 1970.

Miller, E. Ethelbert, ed. *In Search of Color Everywhere: A Collection of African-American Poetry*. New York: Steward, Tabori & Chang, 1994.

———. *Women Surviving Massacres and Men: Nine Women Poets, an Anthology*. Washington, DC: Anemone Press, 1977.

Mullane, Deirdre, ed. *Crossing the Danger Water: Three Hundred Years of African-American Writing*. New York: Doubleday, 1993.

Murphy, Beatrice M., ed. *Ebony Rhythm: An Anthology of Contemporary Negro Verse*. New York: Books for Libraries Press, 1968.

Pool, Rosey E., ed. *Beyond the Blues: New Poems by American Negroes*. Lympne, Kent: Hand and Flower Press, 1962.

Powell, Kevin, and Ras Baraka, eds. *In the Tradition: An Anthology of Young Black Writers*. New York: Readers, 1993.

Quashie, Kevin Everod, Joyce Lausch, and Keith Miller, eds. *New Bones: Contemporary Black Writers in America*. Upper Saddle River, NJ: Prentice Hall, 2001.

Randall, Dudley, ed. *The Black Poets. A New Anthology*. New York: Bantam Books, 1971.

Reed, Ishmael, J.J. Phillips, Gundar Strads, and Shawn Wong, eds. *The Before Columbus Foundation Poetry Anthology*. New York: W.W. Norton, 1991.

Salaam, Kalamu Ya, and Kwame Alexander, eds. *360: A Revolution of Black Poets*. Alexandria, VA: BlackWords, 1998.

Sherman, Joan R., ed. *African-American Poetry of the Nineteenth Century: An Anthology*. Urbana: University of Illinois Press, 1992.

———. *Collected Black Women's Poetry*. 4 vols. New York: Oxford University Press (The Schomburg Library of Nineteenth-Century Black Women Writers), 1988.

Stetson, Erlene, ed. *Black Sister: Poems by Black American Women, 1746–1980*. Bloomington: Indiana University Press, 1980.

Ward, Jerry, ed. *Trouble the Waters: 250 Years of African-American Poetry*. New York: Mentor, 1997.

Weatherly, Tom, and Ted Wilentz, eds. *Natural Process: An Anthology of New Black Poetry*. New York: Hill & Wang, 1970.

INDEX

Ai: awards, 3; biography 3–4; writing, 4–7; Works: *Cruelty*, 5; *Greed*, 5; *Killing Floor*, 5; *Sin*, 5

Alighieri, Dante, 21, 110

Amini, Johari, 227

Angelou, Maya: awards, 11, 13; biography, 11–13; writing, 14–17; Works: *And Still I Rise*, 15; *I Know Why the Caged Bird Sings*, 11; *Just Give Me a Cool Drink of Water 'Fore I Diiie*, 14–15; "On the Pulse of Morning," 16; *Shaker Why Don't You Sing*, 15

Atlanta University, 173

Auden, W.H., 151

Baraka, Amiri: biography, 20–23; influence on Nathaniel Mackey, 219; writing, 21; Works: "Black Art," 23; *The Dead Lecturer*, 23; *In Our Terribleness*, 24; *Preface*, 23

Bell, James Madison, 137

Black Arts Movement (also Black Aesthetics Movement), 20, 38, 51, 77, 93, 125, 152, 199, 211, 227, 272

Blues: in Cornelius Eady, 111–12; in Jayne Cortez, 69; in Mari Evans, 119; in Sonia Sanchez, 296

Bontemps, Arna, 310; awards, 31; biography, 28–29; writing, 29–31; Works: "A Black Man Talks of Reaping," 30; *Black Thunder*, 29; *God Sends Sunday*, 29; *The Old South*, 29; "The Return," 31

Borges, Jorges Luis, 205

Braithwaite, William Stanley, 76, 77, 174

Broadside Press, 38, 214; history of, 273

Brooks, Gwendolyn: awards, 35; biography, 34–35; writing, 35–39; Poems: "The Anniad," 36; "The Bean Eaters," 36; "A Bronzeville Mother Loiters in Mississippi. Meanwhile a Mississippi Mother Burns Bacon," 37; "Gay Chaps at the Bar," 36; "Kitchenette Building," 36; "The Last Quatrain of the Ballad of Emmett Till," 37; "Of De Witt Williams," 36; "The Rites for Cousin Vit," 36; Works: *Annie Allen*, 36; *The Bean Eaters*, 36; *Maude Martha*, 36; *In the Mecca: Poems*, 36; *A Street in Bronzeville*, 36

Brown, Sterling: awards, 47; biography, 43–44; writing, 44–46; Works: *Collected Poems*, 47; *The Last Ride of Wild Bill*, 46; *Southern Road*, 45–46

Burroughs, Margaret, 35

Callaloo, 2, 19, 54, 93

Campbell, James, 103

Cave Canem, 83, 109

Césaire, Aimé, 169, 317
Chicago Defender, The, 35
Civil rights movement, 51, 68
Clifton, Lucille: awards, 53; biography, 51–53; writing, 52–58; Works: *Blessing the Boats*, 55–56; *The Book of Light*, 54, 55; *Good Times: Poems* 51; *Next*, 55; *The Terrible Stories*, 55; *Two-Headed Woman*, 54, 55
Coleman, Wanda: awards, 62; biography, 62–63; writing, 63–65; Works: *Bathwater Wine*, 64; *Hand Dance*, 64–65
Colman, Ornette, 219
Coltrane, John poems about: influence on Amiri Baraka, 22; in Michael Harper's work, 145; poems about, 219, 221, 296
Cortez, Jayne: biography, 68; writing, 68–72; Works: *Festivals and Funerals*, 70; *Pissstained Stairs and the Monkey's Wares*, 70; *Poetic Magnetic*, 68; *Scarifications*, 69; *Somewhere in Advance of Nowhere*, 71
Crane, Hart, 305
Crisis, The (magazine), 29, 75, 174
Cullen, Countee, 151, 152, 174; biography, 75–76; writing, 75–79; Poems: "Heritage," 21; "Yet Do I Marvel," 77; Works: *Caroling Dust*, 77, 74; *Color*, 76; *Cooper Sun*, 77, 78; *On These I Stand*, 79

Danner, Margaret, 273
Derricotte, Toi: awards, 88; biography, 83–84; writing, 84–88; Works: *The Black Notebooks*, 88; *Captivity*, 86, 87; *The Empress of the Death House*, 84; *Natural Birth*, 85; *Tender*, 86
Dialect poetry, 103, 180
Douglass, Frederick, 102, 138
Dove, Rita: awards, 91–92, 93; biography, 91–92; writing, 93–97; Works: *Grace Notes*, 95; *Mother Love*, 96; *On the Bus with Rosa Parks*, 96; *Thomas and Beulah*, 94; *The Yellow House on the Corner*, 93
Du Bois, Nina Yolande, 78
Dunbar, Paul Laurence: biography,

101–2; grave site, 105; influence on Melvin B. Tolson, 302; writing, 102–5; Works: *Lyrics of a Lowly Life*, 104; *Majors and Minors*, 102–3; *Oak and Ivy*, 102
DuSable Museum, 35, 228

Eady, Cornelius: awards, 109, 113; biography, 109; writing, 109–13; Works: *The Autobiography of a Jukebox*, 111–12; *Brutal Imagination* 112; *Victims of the Latest Dance Craze*, 110–11; *You Don't Miss Your Water*, 109–10
Eliot, T.S., 145, 221, 305
Evans, Mari: awards, 116–17; biography, 116–17; writing, 117–19; Works: *I Am a Black Woman*, 117–18; *Nightstar*, 118

Fauset, Jessie, 174
Fisk University, 29, 34, 43, 44, 123, 124, 151, 152
Folk tradition, 44, 45
Frost, Robert, 44, 58

García Marquez, Gabriel, 205
Ginsberg, Allen, 21
Giovanni, Nikki: awards, 125–27; biography, 123–25, 128; writing, 125–29; Works: *Black Feeling, Black Talk*, 125; *Black Judgement*, 125–27; *Cotton Candy on a Rainy Day*, 127; *Re: Creation*, 127
Guillén, Nicholás , 71, 169, 347
Gurdjieff, George, Toomer's involvement with, 310

Hammon, Jupiter: biography, 131–33; Work: "An Evening Thought," 132, 133
Harlem Renaissance, 28, 75, 164, 182, 195
Harper, Frances Ellen Watkins: biography, 136–37; writing, 137–39; Works: *Moses: A Story of the Nile*, 138–39; *Poems*, 138; *Poems on Miscellaneous Subjects*, 137; *Sketches of Southern Life*, 138–39

Harper, Michael S.: awards, 143; biography, 143–44; writing, 144–47; Works: *Dear John, Dear Coltrane*, 145; *History Is Your Own Heartbeat*, 146; *Images of Kin*, 143

Hayden, Robert: awards, 152; biography, 151–52; writing, 152–55; Works: *American Journal*, 154; *Heart Shape in the Dust*, 152; *Words in the Mourning Time*, 154

Hoodoo, influence on Ishmael Reed, 280

Horton, George Moses: biography, 158–59; writing, 159–61; Works: *Hope of Liberty*, 159–60; *Naked Genius*, 160; *The Poetical Works of George Moses Horton*, 160

Houseman, A.E., 4, 44

Howard University, 44, 47, 53, 173

Howells, William Dean, 103

Hughes, Langston, 34, 43, 51, 77, 78, 145, 151–52, 174, 182, 205, 228, 347; awards, 169; biography, 164–66; writing, 167–69; Works: *Fine Clothes to the Jew*, 166; *Montage of a Dream Deferred*, 168–69; "The Negro Artist and the Racial Mountain," 75, 117; *The Weary Blues*, 166

Hurston, Zora Neale, 43, 167

Imagists, 44, 311

Jackman, Harold, 76, 310

Jazz, 145, 167, 168, 197, 219, 220; in Baraka, 22

Johnson, Charles, 76

Johnson, Georgia Douglas: biography, 173–74; writing, 174–75; Works: *An Autumn Love Cycle*, 175; *Bronze*, 175; *The Heart of a Woman*, 174

Johnson, James Weldon: biography, 179–81; writing, 181–84; Works: *Fifty Years and Other Poems*, 181; *God's Trombones*, 182; *St. Peter Relates an Incident: Selected Poems*, 183

Jordan, June: awards, 188–89; biography, 187–88; writing, 189–91; Works: *Haruko/Love Poems*, 190; *Kissing God Goodbye*, 191; *Living Room*, 191; *Passion*, 190; *Things That I Do in the Dark*, 189

Killens, John Oliver, 124

Kitchen Table Press, 213

Knight, Etheridge: awards, 199; biography, 195–96; writing, 196–99; Works: *Black Voices from Prison*, 199; *Born of a Woman: New and Selected Poems*, 199; *The Essential Etheridge Knight*, 199

Komunyakaa, Yusef: awards, 203; biography, 203–4; writing, 204–8; Works: *Copacetic*, 205; *Dien Cai Dau*, 203, 205–6; *I Apologize for the Eyes in My Head*, 207; *Magic City*, 205

Lanier, Sidney, 103

Lindsay, Vachael, 44

Locke, Alain, 174

Lorde, Audre: biography, 211–13; writing, 213–15; Works: *Between Ourselves*, 214; *The Black Unicorn*, 214; *Cables to Rage*, 214; *The Cancer Journals*, 213; *The First Cities*, 213; *From a Land Where Other People Live*, 214; *The Marvelous Arithmetics of Distance*, 214–15; *The New York Head Shop and Museum*, 214

Lowell, Amy, 44

Lowell, Robert, 145

Mackey, Nathaniel: biography, 219; writing, 219–24; Works: *Eroding Witness*, 221; *Four for Trane*, 221; *School of Udhra*, 221, 223; *Septet for the End of Time*, 221; *Whatsaid Serif*, 221, 223

Madhubuti, Haki: awards, 227; biography, 227–28; writing, 228–31; Works: *Black Pride*, 228; *Directionscore*, 230; *Don't Cry, Scream*, 228; *Heartlove*, 230–31; *Think Black*, 228

Mazeroski, Bill, 253

McElroy, Colleen J.: awards, 235; biography, 234–35; writing, 235–37; Works: *A Long Way from St. Louie*, 234; *Music from Home*, 236; *Queen of the Ebony Isles*, 235; *Travelling Music*, 237

McKay, Claude: biography, 241–42; writing, 242–46; Works: *Constab Ballads*, 242; *Harlem Shadows*, 244; *A Long Way from Home*, 245; *Songs of Jamaica*, 242; *Spring in New Hampshire*, 244

Miller, E. Ethelbert: awards, 253; biography, 249–50; writing, 250–54; Works: *First Light: New and Selected Poems*, 251; *In Search of Color Everywhere*, 254

Minstrel Shows, 104, 180

Moss, Thylias: awards, 258; biography, 257–58; writing, 258–61; Works: *Hosiery Seams on a Bowlegged Woman*, 258; *Pyramid of Bones*, 258; *Rainbow Remnants*, 258; *Tale of a Sky Blue Dress*, 257

Negritude poets, 69

Nelson, Marilyn: awards, 268; biography, 264–65; writing, 265–68; Works: *Fields of Praise: New and Selected Poems*, 266, 268; *For the Body*, 265; *The Homeplace*, 266; *Hundreds of Hens and Other Poems*, 265; *Magnificat*, 267, 268; *Mama's Promises*, 267

Neruda, Pablo, 7, 317

Oakwood College, 29

Opportunity (magazine), 29, 76, 175

Oral tradition, 44, 45, 127, 137, 145, 196; in Margaret Walker, 325

Poetry (magazine), 35

Poetry of the Negro 1746–1970, 51

Pound, Ezra, 44, 305

Praise poems, 69

A Raisin in the Sun, 168

Randall, Dudley: awards, 275; biography, 272; founder of Broadside Press, 273; writing, 272–75; Works: *Cities Burning*, 274; *A Litany of Friends*, 274; *For Malcolm: Poems on the Life and Death of Malcolm X*, 274;

More to Remember, 274; *Point, Counterpoem*, 273

Reed, Ishmael: awards, 280; biography, 279–80; writing, 280–83; Works: *The Before Columbus Foundation Fiction Anthology*, 280; *Catechism of D Neoamerican Hoodoo Church*, 280; *Conjure: Selected Poems*, 280

Riley, James Whitcomb, 102

Rilke, Rainer Maria, 91, 96

Robinson, Arlington, 44

Rodgers, Carolyn: awards, 287; biography, 286–87; cofounder, Third World Press, 287; writing, 287–89; Works: *The Heart as Ever Green*, 289; *How I Got Ovah: New and Selected Poems*, 288; *Paper Soul*, 287; *Souls of a Blackbird*, 288

Roethke, Theodore, 145

Rowell, Charles, 220, 223, 259; *Callaloo*, 2, 19, 54, 93

Sanchez, Sonia: awards, 298; biography, 293–94; writing, 294–98; Works: *A Blues Book for Blue Black Magical Women*, 294; *Does Your House Have Lions?*, 297; *Homecoming*, 294; *Homegirls and Handgrenades*, 295, 296; *I've Been a Woman: New and Selected Poems*, 295; *Love Poems*, 294; *Shake Loose My Skin*, 295; *Under a Soprano Sky*, 295; *We a BaddDDD People*, 294

Senghor, Léopold Sédar, 169

Slave narratives, 84

Slavery, 93–94

Spencer, Ann, 182

Terry, Lucy, 137

Third World Press, 38, 227

Thurman, Wallace, 29, 310

Till, Emmett, 37

Tolson, Melvin B.: awards, 306; biography, 302–3; writing, 303–6; Works: *A Gallery of Harlem Portraits*, 303; *Harlem Gallery: Book I*, 305; *Libretto for the Rendezvous with America*, 303; *Republic of Liberia*, 304–5

Toomer, Jean: biography, 308–11; writing, 311–12; Works: "The Blue Meridian," 312; *Cane*, 311–12

Tougaloo College, 213

Troupe, Quincy: awards, 316–17; biography, 316; writing, 317–21; Works: *Avalanche*, 318, 320; *Choruses*, 318, 320–21; *Snake-Back Solos: Selected Poems*, 319

Tuskegee Airmen, 267

Tuskegee Institute, 92, 104, 242

Underground railroad, 136, 137, 152

Walker, Alice, 188; on June Jordan, 191

Walker, Margaret Abigail: 43, 169, 189; awards, 325; biography, 324–25; writing, 325–28; Works: *For My People*, 325–26; *Prophets for a New Day*, 325–27; *This is My Century: New and Collected Poems*, 327–28

Washington, Booker, T., 104

Waters, Muddy, 112

Wheatley, Phillis: biography, 331–32, 334; writing, 332–35; Works: *Poems on Various Subjects*, 333

Whitfield, James, 137

Whitman, Walt, 145, 205

Whittier, John Greenleaf, 137

Williams, Mississippi Joe, 23

Williams, William Carlos, 109, 145; influence on Nathaniel Mackey, 219, 221

Wilson, Harriet E., 136

Wright, Jay: awards, 342; biography, 338; writing, 339–42; Works: *Death as History*, 340; *Dimensions of History*, 341–42; *Double Invention of Komo*, 341; *Soothsayers and Omens*, 341; *Transfigurations: Collected Poems*, 342

Young, Al: awards, 348; biography, 346–47; writing, 347–49; Works: *Dance*, 347; *Geography of the Near Past*, 348; *The Song Turning Back into Itself*, 348; *Things Ain't What they Used to Be*, 348

Yugen, 21

About the Author

JOYCE PETTIS is Professor of English at North Carolina State University, where she teaches courses in African American Literature. She is the author of numerous articles on Margaret Walker, Charles Chestnutt, and others, and of the award winning *Toward Wholeness in Paule Marshall's Fiction*.